Fighting for the Farm

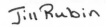

Fighting for the Farm

Rural America Transformed

Edited by
Jane Adams

PENN

University of Pennsylvania Press
Philadelphia

10   9   8   7   6   5   4   3   2   1

Published by
University of Pennsylvania Press
Philadelphia, Pennsylvania 19104-4011

Library of Congress Cataloging-in-Publication Data

Fighting for the farm : rural America transformed / edited by Jane Adams.
    p. cm.
    Includes bibliographical references and index.
    ISBN 0-8122-3695-5 (cloth : alk. paper)—ISBN 0-8122-1830-2 (pbk. : alk. paper)
    1. Agriculture—Economic aspects—North America. 2. Agriculture—Economic
aspects—United States. 3. Agriculture—Economic aspects—Canada. 4. Agriculture
and state—United States. 5. Agriculture and state—Canada. 6. Agricultural credit—
United States. 7. Agricultural credit—Canada. 8. Farms, Small—United States. 9. Farms,
Small—Canada. 10. United States—Rural conditions. 11. Canada—Rural conditions.
12. Agricultural innovations—Environmental aspects. I. Adams, Jane (Jane H.)

HD1750 .F54 2002
338.1'0973—dc21

                                                                    2002029145

Contents

Chapter 1
Introduction

Jane Adams

Idealistic

At the beginning of the twentieth century, North American agriculture
prospered. A century ago, one could imagine that agriculture and industry were, or could be, balanced and complementary. The countryside was densely populated with agriculture, timbering, and mining
supporting dynamic small towns. Farmers produced both for their own
needs and for the needs of the larger society, creating complex and
regionally specific circuits of commercial and customary exchange.
Often riven with class, racial, ethnic, religious, and gender divisions
and conflicts, rural communities provided the hearth for much of the
U.S. and Canada's political, intellectual, and cultural life.

At the beginning of the twenty-first century, a revolution in production has been virtually completed. The countryside is depopulated.
Agricultural labor has been almost completely replaced with mechani-
cal, chemical, biological, and information technologies. The few commercial farmers left provide few of their daily household or enterprise
needs from their own production. Firms offering specialized supplies
and services sell the resources that were once part of a farmer's necessary stock of knowledge and skill.

North American farms have always been part of the larger national
and world economies, but at the beginning of the twenty-first century,
their role as primary producers has been vastly overshadowed by
other elements in the agriculture-food system (Magdoff, Foster, and
Buttel 2000). In the process, small towns that once served as seats of
government, market centers, and manufactories for their rural hinter-
lands have lost their reason for existence. Those in the orbits of urban
regions have become bedroom communities. Those that do not lie
within easy reach of cities are withering and dying, populated largely
by retirees and the people who care for them.[1]

This transformation flags a sharp shift in the issues facing rural America. While farmers continue to face volatile and unpredictable weather, marketing, and labor conditions, the attention of the nation, and of some farmers, has shifted to the environment and to community quality of life. The environmental movement of the mid-twentieth century signaled this shift. It framed apocalyptic visions of a future laid waste by overpopulation and pollution. It has been the leading foe of the application of genetic engineering to agriculture, and among the strongest critics of the green revolution and its biotechnologies. At its more radical edges, but with broad sympathy from large portions of the population, it began creating visions of human-nature interrelations far different from scientific and technical models of knowledge and control. As many of the articles in this volume document, "green" politics have become an increasingly important aspect of debates regarding farming and farm policy.

The Politics of Agriculture

Throughout most of the twentieth century, agricultural and rural policy debates have been framed in technical and economic terms. Only rarely have social relationships been highlighted. And, aside from an enduring concern with conservation, the destructive consequences of radically simplifying the ecology were unforeseen. As Ferguson (1990) observed, mid-twentieth century theories of development assumed that all social problems would yield to expert-driven technical solutions.[2] For much of the century, most rural people seemed to agree that expert advice not only promised but provided unprecedented prosperity and comfort, and they accepted the downsides of declining populations and emigrating children as a necessary consequence. Governmental policies and private initiatives created enormous material abundance, signaled by the year-round availability of inexpensive fresh and processed foods in every North American supermarket. Except for a few dissenting voices, the direction of the postwar food system received virtually unquestioned support. That is no longer the case.

At the end of the century, as several of the essays in this book demonstrate, those policy decisions have led to the threat of both ecological and social death. They have eliminated most farmers, emptied out the countryside, and created production systems predicated on chemicals that contaminate surface waters, drain ancient aquifers, and often poison the farmers themselves. My own work has traced this transformation (Adams 1994b). Nostalgia and regret are not attitudes becoming of a scholar, but one cannot look at the current conditions of rural America without feeling that, as Kathryn Dudley says in this volume, "something has gone terribly wrong." And, as immigrants from Mexico, other Latin American countries, and other regions of the Third World pour into the United States and other industrial nations, it is obvious that the current wave of capitalist development, termed globalization, is restructuring the peasant agricultures that have remained in the rest of the world.

Understanding the political dynamics that brought us to this current state is, therefore, not an idle exercise. But, curiously, while social scientists have devoted considerable energies to developing and critiquing specific policies for agriculture and for rural communities, very little scholarship has analyzed the political process itself. Of that scholarship, most analyzes the state. Far less attention has been paid to the ways that people become agents, interest groups form, issues become framed and debated, and alternatives are constructed. These questions assume that the governance of society is a process of continual invention by human actors, rather than the rehearsal of an inherited script or one written by larger social forces. Sometimes, as the articles in this collection demonstrate, people do appear to act in service to some external playwright. More often, however, they tap into their received knowledge and desires to create unforeseen alternatives. A focus on political dynamics forces the analyst to come face to face with uncertainty, indeterminacy, and invention.

The aim of this volume is to collect the work of scholars from several disciplines who bring their specific disciplinary and theoretical perspectives to bear on political processes within North American agriculture.[3] It is impossible, of course, within a single collection, to present all relevant theoretical and topical issues. This volume does, however, provide the student of North American agriculture with a window into how, at the beginning of the twenty-first century, scholars are attempting to comprehend the play of power and the political process in North American agriculture.

Plan of the Book

This collection begins with an overview of the development of North American agriculture, using two specific regions as case studies based in somewhat contrasting theoretical approaches. Alan Rudy bases his analysis of the Imperial Valley on O'Connor's work on the fiscal crisis of the state and the environmental crisis; Murray Knuttila places the development of western Canadian prairie agriculture in the context of the world system and Canada's place within it. Douglas Constance, Anna Kleiner, and Sanford Rikoon take up five theories of the state in the era of globalization and test their applicability to a specific political battle over large-scale hog production in Missouri. Miriam Wells analyzes the formation of specific interest groups in the ethnically stratified strawberry fields of California within a shifting legal and political arena.

The second section takes up some of the historical roots of U.S. agricultural policies, with Stuart Shulman's analysis of the agenda-setting debates around the first farm credit legislation and Jess Gilbert's and Mary Summers's rethinking of the New Deal. These readings not only recast our understandings of the agricultural New Deal, but demonstrate the contingent and contested outcomes of one of the major policy arenas of twentieth century farm policy. Barry Barnett then presents a particularly lucid and complex account of the causes of the farm crisis of the 1980s, arguing that the intellectual and ideological framework within which agricultural economists operated made them unable to accurately analyze the crisis as it occurred.

Barnett's article forms a bridge to the third section, "The political implications of daily life." Kathryn Dudley and Laura DeLind turn from politics as direct engagement with state institutions to the "micropolitics," or cultural context, within which political action occurs or does not occur. Dudley's provocative ethnography of a Minnesota farming community's response to the 1980s farm crisis captures the paradoxical nature of these farmers' moral commitments in communities that, as she says, "reproduce the logic of market capitalism." DeLind addresses, as well, the problem of creating viable communities. She demonstrates the power of a vision of an alternative food system and social order and the pressures exerted on this vision by the daily practices required to operate within a capitalist order.

While both Dudley and DeLind focus on the practices of daily life that create or undermine durable communities, the final section examines the discursive arena, where meanings are publicly deployed and contested. Alan Hall shows how, in the play of Canadian political processes, the trope of "sustainability" has become stretched to the limits of its meaning, even as its practical usage remains contested. Ann Reisner applies formal discourse analysis to understand the ways in which various groups draw upon discursive resources and use them in political struggle. Her article demonstrates, as Constance, Kleiner, and Rikoon and Wells have already indicated, that, on occasion, social movements can create compelling formulations that allow them to prevail in the political arena, even when opposed by powerful, heavily financed interests.

Harriet Friedmann's article, with its utopian vision supported by a deep analysis of contemporary global political economy and by an attempt to shift paradigmatic assumptions through alternative tropology, completes the volume.

The remainder of this Introduction orients the reader to the major debates and issues relevant to the topics taken up in each section.

North American Agriculture in the World System

This section contains four chapters. The first two sketch more than a century of development, from European settlement in the case of Canada and from U.S. settlement in the case of the Imperial Valley of California. The second two analyze specific political struggles: over concentrated animal feeding operations (CAFOs) in Missouri and the organization of strawberry production in California. All these studies focus on the role of the state in relation to localities, drawing on different, albeit not necessarily contradictory, theories to describe the processes the authors try to understand. These chapters lay out many of the key theoretical and analytical issues facing the analysis of North American agriculture. These include problematics of historical periodization, the nature of the modern democratic state in a capitalist economy, the salience of classes and other significant social groupings, and the significance of territoriality. They begin to address the contingent nature of "actors," understood as the identities claimed by and attributed to people who appear within the play of power in public arenas.

Periodization

With the historical turn in the social sciences, the question of periodization, central to historiography but little attended to by functionalist analyses, becomes important. Rudy and Knuttila orient us to the development of farming in western North America. Striking in their accounts is the brief span of time that has elapsed since the opening of the western lands to U.S. and Canadian agriculture. Equally striking is the displacement of agriculture from the center of these regions' economies. Barely a century after their opening, potentially irreversible ecological and social degradation, respectively, of the two regions threatens their continued social viability.

Rudy's and Knuttila's accounts indicate that the development of both regions was intimately linked to larger national and global development projects. Canada formed as a nation in the 1860s, establishing the west as a "new frontier of investment" by the "various fractions of capital," ushering in the period Knuttila diagnoses as the beginning of the corporate phase of capitalist accumulation. This coincided with the consolidation of U.S. control over its western territories following the Civil War.

In both western Canada and the Imperial Valley settlers did not firmly establish themselves until the early years of the twentieth century. The processes of industrial development in North America and Europe drove demand for agricultural products, stimulating the development of new technologies and marketing systems and displacing European populations, many of whom migrated to the Americas. Both states strongly supported the development of a class of landowning agriculturists. This was a period of considerable instability and fluidity as nature was subdued, communities were formed, labor supplies were established, and governing institutions were created. It was characterized by crises: in the case of the Imperial Valley, misplaced irrigation works that diverted the Colorado River into the Salton Sink, creating the Salton Sea; in western Canada, crises attendant on marketing of wheat. In each case, the federal governments moved aggressively to resolve the crises in order to preserve the landowning farmers its policies had created.

Knuttila locates the beginning of the next period with the Great Depression; Rudy with World War II. These periodizations are based, in part, on differences in the two regions and countries: Knuttila sees the depression as the end of a period of expansion and the beginning of a period of sustained crisis and instability, contextualized by Canada's location in the continental economy and the establishment of Keynesian principles in state regulation of the economy. Rudy focuses on the institutional stability established by the New Deal with the completion of irrigation works and the federal government's postwar commitment to providing Mexican migrant agricultural labor through the bracero program. Western Canada's reliance on wheat, in contrast to the diversified agricultural products of the Imperial Valley, must also be considered as a factor in their differences, as the crises and population declines afflicting Saskatchewan also afflicted the other grain (and cotton) producing regions of the United States. Some of the issues raised here will be more fully addressed in chapters 5 through 8.

Both Rudy and Knuttila place the beginning of a new period in the 1970s, with the neoliberal economic policies often referred to as globalization. The 1970s, as Wells says in Chapter 4, mark a global economic watershed. In the wheat growing regions of Canada, state-led institutions that attempted to regularize and support wheat production and marketing were dismantled; in the Imperial Valley, globalization undermined established labor relations. More significant in California, the ecological limits of irrigation agriculture began to threaten the

continued viability of many crops with increasingly severe pest outbreaks and degradation of the general environment.

Ironically, the cases studied by Constance, Kleiner, and Rikoon in
Missouri, and Wells in California locate the 1970s as a period when
popular, subordinate groups were successful in obtaining government
regulations. In Missouri, independent farmers won exclusion of absentee corporate operations; in California, farm workers unionized
and gained protections long available to other workers. These gains
were, however, short-lived, as the forces unleashed by globalization re-
worked the terrain.

The State

The state is an obvious focus for those concerned with political processes
and the play of power. Within their territorial reach, state institutions,
with their monopoly of legitimate force, are arguably the most powerful single entity. They are, almost by definition, political in their constitution and processes—concerned with the ordering of power relations
and the attendant resources within their domains. Their forms of
authority and modes of financial support derive from non-market
mechanisms of accumulation; the modern nation-state has, in addition, enormous capacity to regulate and direct other sectors of society.
The chapters in this section and Shulman's chapter on the formation
of the Farm Credit system, in particular, document the growing capacity of the U.S. and Canadian states to affect the course of agricultural development.

The nature and role of the state has been a subject of sustained
debate in western social, political, and moral theory. All of the articles
in this volume, insofar as they theorize the state, draw their primary
influences from Marx and Weber. They are all historical, locating their
analyses within a logic formed by prior actions, what Shulman, following Skocpol, terms "path dependent." They are, as well, structural,
concerned with defining the key societal forces, metaphorically understood as structures, within which individuals and groups act.

The chapters in the first section draw, more or less explicitly, on a
tradition that problematizes the relationship between state and civil
society.[4] They vary somewhat in how they understand this relationship, and in their analyses of salient social groups: Knuttila, writing
about the development of western Canada, views the state as providing services to or acting as the agent of capital accumulation. The
Canadian state he describes appears much like the executive branch
of the capitalist class theorized in some of Marx and Engel's and Lenin's
writings. Rudy, in contrast, understands the state as semi-autonomous,

being both the agent and the product of rural and agricultural development. Drawing on O'Connor's (1973, 1988, 1998) work, he views liberal democracies as forced to resolve often conflicting and sometimes contradictory demands in order to maintain their own apparatus and operations: they must create the conditions in which the (capitalist) economy can function smoothly and promote capital accumulation, and at the same time they must legitimate the social and ecological consequences of accumulation.

Constance, Kleiner, and Rikoon's analysis of the political battles regarding corporately owned, large-scale hog operations views governing bodies in much the same way. They are a contested terrain in which government mediates class conflict derived from the needs of the state to promote economic development and, simultaneously, deal with the environmental, class, and community consequences of this development.

Throughout the twentieth century the governments of Canada and the United States have increased their capacity to effect their institutional goals. Not only have they increased overall capacity, in some quantitative sense, but their arenas of action have expanded and shifted. Knuttila focuses on the shift from promoting private infrastructure development through providing domestic and international legal structures and financial support (e.g., railroads, wheat pools) to actual administration of key aspects of the economy, as with the Canadian Wheat Board, and direct regulation of production, as with acreage allotments, crop insurance, and providing farm credit. In the Imperial Valley, as well, the U.S. and California governments shifted from providing primarily infrastructure support and land for settlement and irrigation works to creating and administering key dimensions of the economy.

Constance, Kleiner, and Rikoon directly address the issue of state capacity in their overview of theories of globalization. As they indicate, globalization appears to undermine state capacities to regulate and administer their domestic economies. Many of their prerogatives appear to be in the process of being supplanted by global bodies like the World Trade Organization (WTO), the North American Free Trade Agreement (NAFTA), the International Monetary Fund (IMF), and the International Standards Organization (ISO).[5] Constance, Kleiner, and Rikoon view the current conjuncture as a period of deregulation and reregulation, through which the nation state retains crucial, but different, functions in the new world order that has not yet congealed.

States can be viewed as the primary entities that install formal, codified order upon the rest of society. The creation, implementation, and enforcement of law is one of the key functions of centralized polities.

Wells and Constance, Kleiner, and Rikoon focus on this aspect of the state. Wells reveals the way that legal regimes, created through the contest between farmworkers organized in unions and growers, shifted the nature of the relationship between grower and worker. In this new terrain, growers found it easier to assure a stable and responsible labor supply through shifting to sharecropping. This converted farm laborers into independent contractors. A changed legal identity, based on judicial rulings, shifted the contractors back once again to wage laborers.

The contract relationship has increasingly come to characterize the relationship between many agricultural producers and other entities in the food industry. Poultry, cattle, and hogs, in particular, are now raised by farmers as contractors for transnational agribusinesses. Constance, Kleiner, and Rikoon analyze the contests of popular and corporate interests over the establishment and regulation of concentrated hog operations. They demonstrate that governing bodies (local and state, more than national) face strong limits to their regulatory capacity, since corporate interests not only have considerable power to obtain laws that override local control, but they also have the power simply to leave for less regulated territories should popular or other opposing forces prevail.

Territories

Constance, Kleiner, and Rikoon also indicate the shifting significance of territories. In Knuttila's telling, in the nineteenth century western Canada appeared to eastern capitalists as a domain from which to extract resources, and one which, as it became settled, would absorb investments and provide markets for their products. The Imperial Valley, although always dealing with the Mexican nation from which it was formed and which it abutted, began its settled history as a relatively insular region, articulating with the outside world largely through markets, investments, and agricultural labor, regulated by the federal and state governments. These territorial arrangements have shifted. No longer do states have solid control over financial flows; the regulation of labor, as Wells argues, has slipped out of the control of territorial entities; and, as Constance, Kleiner, and Rikoon demonstrate, sites of production shift according to the regulatory and other "climates" imposed by governments. Insofar as states are defined by a territorial integrity, the new regimes of globalization undermine that integrity. Yet, as Arce, Long, and others stress (Arce and Long 2000; Harvey 1989), territories remain important sites of contestation.

All the chapters in this section take class as a key analytical category. Class, as used in this volume, refers to social categories defined by relations of production. Economic relations have frequently been analyzed as key determinants of historical processes; however, all the analysts in this volume see economic relationships as important but not necessarily determinative aspects of political processes.[6]

Class position, it is often argued, shapes individual and group interests. However, as Wells notes, in many instances people act contrary to putatively objective economic interests. People involved in agricultural production, in particular, seem to act in ways that do not further their individual or collective interests, nor do they form solidarities primarily on the basis of class (Adams 1997). Mooney (1988), arguing that political consciousness arises from the economic base, diagnosed this as due to farmers' contradictory class position as both capitalist and laborer.

Rudy specifically argues with this proposition. Drawing on O'Connor's theorization of the environment, he argues that labor and capital are opposed not only because their "interests" differ, but because human labor cannot be reduced to a pure commodity; it remains a "fictive commodity" (Polanyi 1957) necessarily embedded in the lifeworlds of the human beings who work. Similarly, the communities within which people live and recreate themselves and the "natural" world cannot be reduced to, nor reproduced as, commodities.[7] Class, from this perspective, is a necessary but incomplete analytic tool.

Wells's study challenges the premise that economic position determines individual interest. Her argument lies both with (some) Marxists and with neoclassical economists and others who draw on utilitarianism to posit objectively discernable interests. While giving considerable interpretive weight to class as a structural position individuals inhabit, she imaginatively stands in the experience of those she seeks to understand, viewing their lives as including their past and anticipated future and their kin and other significant relationships. She also begins to theorize other communal identities, specifically those created by shared language, values, and national origin.

Wells, as well as Constance, Kleiner, and Rikoon, also alludes to an important dimension of what is being termed globalization, the decline in secure industrial employment and the proliferation of low-wage jobs that largely escape the regulatory view of the state. The processes involved in these transformations are complex, among other effects, undermining peasant farming where it has persisted. In the United States, the sharp rise in the number of Hispanics, and particularly Mexicans, counted in the 1990 and 2000 Census signals this process.

Simultaneously, production processes become detached from specific locales. As Constance, Kleiner, and Rikoon document in the case of Continental Grain, major transnational corporations link together localized agricultural production systems. These transnational corporations perceive the world through a lens constrained to view the factors that gain them greatest profit and those that pose a risk for economic loss. This optic leaves obscure many aspects of the world that people, communities, and ecologies require for their sustained reproduction, and in many cases undermines the communities in which they operate (Magdoff, Foster, and Buttel 2000; Heffernan 2000; Friedland et al. 1991; also Friedmann chapter 14).

The great labor struggles of the nineteenth and twentieth centuries created institutional forms through which both working people and the "captains of industry" became actors as members of social classes. The processes of globalization have fundamentally undermined these institutions, both as arenas for acting and as loci of social identities. In a manner similar to earlier forms of technological development that brought into being and then eliminated diverse kinds of labor, North American family farmers now seem to be on the cusp of virtual elimination, both as direct producers and as social actors.

Actors and Arenas

State, territories, and classes are all conceptual categories as well as social "containers" for human action. They are, in the modern era, important arenas in which people contend. Whether or not land will be operated in chunks of tens or thousands of acres, who will own that land, what rights adhere to ownership, and who will work on it under what conditions have and will remain important politically. Whether people appear as independent contractors, as salaried employees, or as temporary workers sometimes is contested through direct negotiations, sometimes through organized agencies like labor unions or labor contractors, and sometimes through the creation and institutionalization of legal standards.

In the first two chapters the highly contingent nature of the social orders that were created and repeatedly reconfigured does not come to the fore, necessarily submerged in narratives that summarize more than a century of settlement. The dynamics that occur are more visible in the account of how large-scale hog operations became a flash point in Missouri agricultural politics, shifting rural people from acting primarily as "farmers" to acting as "rural residents," concerned with odor and water quality at least as much as, if not more than, the viability of independent hog production. State entities like the Department of Natural Resources and the Environmental Protection Agency (EPA) took on regulatory powers once in the purview of the Department of Agriculture, if they existed at all. New organizations also have arisen, in this case the Family Farm Movement, born during the 1980s farm crisis as a coalition of family farmers and activists committed to environmentally and socially sustainable farming. New institutional, organizational, and individual actors have appeared on the stage.

Wells takes this as her central problematic, carefully analyzing the ways in which strawberry growers and Mexican laborers, with some degree of mutuality, despite their very different degrees of power, reconfigured their labor relationships as the legal environment shifted. "Identities" appear as contingent positions taken on by and/or attributed to people as they act in social arenas that they themselves participate in bringing into being.

The first section sets the stage for issues which will recur repeatedly throughout this volume: history, state, territory, class, actors.

Foundations of Twentieth Century U.S. Farm Policy

The four case studies in this section trace the history of twentieth century U.S. farm policy. Shulman analyzes the interests that framed the terms of debate over establishing a federal farm credit system in the first two decades of the century. Gilbert examines efforts in the "Third New Deal" to establish agricultural planning based on grassroots education and participation. Dealing with the same crucial period, Summers reads the demise of this effort at grassroots democracy through the actions of two significant players: Arthur Raper, a sociologist who studied and participated in the Farm Security Adminstration planning efforts in Georgia, and Congressman Jamie Whitten, who steadfastly opposed them. Finally, Barnett analyzes the 1980s farm crisis. These four studies open up the political arenas touched on by the historical studies of California's Imperial Valley and Saskatchewan, Canada. They bracket the 80-year period during which North American agriculture became fully modern. These four chapters, in addition to deepening the debates introduced in the first section, bring to the fore the importance of public debate over policy and the centrality of specific actors in effecting policy.

By the early years of the twentieth century, agriculture had become secondary to industrial production. Although farmers remained active politically, the great agrarian movements of the late nineteenth century had subsided. Many individuals and groups sought to modernize farming and see it operate with "sound business practices." Farmers were, however, notoriously resistant to the forms of modernization that were promoted (R. Scott 1970; J. Scott 1998), at least those that would increase agricultural productivity (Danbom 1979, 1995:163–64; Cochrane 1993:110). They did, however, become consumers, seeking the conveniences and comforts created by the expanding industrial order (Danbom 1995; Blanke 2000; Owenby 1999), largely without specific government promotion.[8]

While much of the agricultural leadership, particularly in those areas in which freeholding farmers predominated, sought to improve agriculture as one branch of business, they were divided by regionalism and by the specificity of their different cropping regimes, as well as by other, less well analyzed, ethnic and religious differences (Gjerde 1997; Salamon 1992; Wells 1996). As Shulman indicates, the National Farmers Union was specifically concerned about the effects of federal policies on the growing class of tenants and the increasing failure of the "tenure ladder" to provide rungs for their movement from tenantry to farm ownership. Other farm organizations, notably the Grange and the Farm Bureau, drew their membership primarily from propertied farmers and so were less concerned with the growing class divisions within agriculture.

Finegold and Skocpol (1995) argue that the U.S. state's capacity was greater in the arena of agriculture than in other sectors of the society. Beginning with the establishment of the Department of Agriculture (USDA) and passage of the Morrill Act establishing the land grant colleges in 1862, the federal government created powerful institutions which, while central to U.S. farming, were independent of it. Through the USDA and its counterparts in the various states, a system of higher and adult education developed which aimed at improving agriculture and farm life.

The great political struggles of the Populist era, however, focused on the private sector: farmers sought protection from and regulation of those who provided credit, markets, and transportation for farmers and the commodities they produced. In opposition to creditors and to manufacturers, they demanded easy money and low tariffs from the federal government. Farmers themselves remained served by, but not enmeshed in, those governmental agencies specific to agriculture. Canada, as Knuttila demonstrates, was similar.

By the twentieth century, federal regulatory regimes had ameliorated many of farmers' greatest complaints against the railroads and marketers, and the currency issue had been settled. But, with a now dominant non-agricultural population, the problem of food supply became important not only to farmers but (as during the U.S. Civil

War) to the nation at large. As Knuttila demonstrates, the growing war in Europe, with its strong demand for wheat, also played a decisive role in the second decade of the century.

During this period the U.S. and Canada took somewhat different courses: Canada created a state board that directly oversaw the marketing of Canadian wheat, while the U.S., as Shulman demonstrates, solved the perceived problem of insufficient and usurious agricultural credit through a federally supported private institution, the system of private land banks. But the path had been staked out: from now on the modern state would play an ever increasing role in administering the economy, throwing its resources, as well as its laws and supporting administrative apparatus, into the larger society.[9]

The outlines of the debates that have engaged those concerned with agriculture and rural life throughout the twentieth century can be discerned in the arguments that developed over the Federal Farm Loan Act, which was passed in 1916 after six years of deliberation. Shulman documents, in contrast to other interpretations, that the initiative for credit reform did not originate with the organizations that represented farmers. It came, rather, from urban agrarians and business interests who were concerned, among other things, by the failure of farmers to increase agricultural productivity. These business interests and progressive elites, Shulman argues, set the policy agenda and successfully framed the terms of the debate. Farmers, through their organizations, followed behind. When farm organizations supported the business and urban interests, their voices were heard. When, however, they brought up different concerns, as did the National Farmers Union with its concern for small farmers and farm tenants, they were unable to shape the debate. This does not appear as an issue of "he who pays the piper plays the tune," so much as the strategic ability to stake out and defend positions. The political process, Shulman posits, is as much shaped by the issues that are placed in the public arena and how they are framed as it is by the raw power of different classes. "Interests," as Wells argued, are not transparent. In Shulman's telling they are defined through the process of public debate (see also Reisner chapter 13).

The New Deal dramatically accelerated the development of state institutions that became known as the welfare state. Gilbert and Summers examine the New Deal. They seek to redeem a tradition that Gilbert names "low modernism" against the critique of statist programs that, as Summers argues, has accreted on both the left and the right since the New Deal. Gilbert does this through close analysis of a specific program that aimed to marry intellectuals, experts, and farmers in an institutionalized planning process. Gilbert argues that key administrators within the USDA strongly promoted programs that would empower people at the local level. These bureaucrats established grass roots planning out of their attachment to Dewey's theories of participatory democracy (Gilbert 2000a) and as a tactical move in their ongoing battle with a conservative coalition that sought to roll back many aspects of the New Deal. These battles took place on many levels; they were fought in the public arena, in the creation of coalitions of interest groups, and in battles behind closed doors in Washington, D.C. We will never know whether or not a truly democratic planning process could have been established had it been allowed to proceed, for by 1942 the program was eliminated through legislative action.

Here Summers takes up the story. She describes the activities of one local program in Green County, Georgia, studied by Arthur Raper (1943), as exemplary of the programs Gilbert describes through the lens of Washington, D.C. She then analyzes Jamie Whitten, who arrived in Congress in 1941 as these and other USDA programs directed at low income farmers and farm workers were under fierce attack. From his position on the Agriculture Subcommittee of the House Appropriations Committee, Whitten became a leader in these attacks. As chairman of the subcommittee and, from 1979 to 1993, chair of the full committee, he became known as the "permanent Secretary of Agriculture." In her sketch, Summers exposes Whitten's class and racial interests as well as his actions within the legislative structure to defeat his enemies. This structure, she reveals, is not only the legislative arena for hammering out national laws; it also provides a privileged platform from which to shape the public discourse. If one conceives of these battles using the analytic tools of "resource mobilization" (McAdam, McCarthy, and Zald 1996), the office of Representative can be a powerful resource indeed, particularly when combined with an organized constituency and a rhetorical tool kit that resonates widely in a large public.

Summers's chapter also demonstrates the power of a story well told, in which the author situates herself within the story without making the story revolve around her. This stance, theorized by feminist and postmodern critics of putatively objective science (Hartsock 1987), allows the scholar to signal to the reader her own location within the narrative, while respecting the autonomy of the events she analyzes.

Barnett, an agricultural economist, shifts our gaze from state institutions specifically dealing with agriculture to the state's financial regulators, telling a compelling story of the farm crisis of the 1980s. His keen analysis brings the key players and processes to the fore as farmers, now defining themselves as investors as much as agricultural producers, calibrated their investment and production decisions to the rapidly changing fiscal environment of the 1970s. The arena in which they operated was created by agents far beyond their control: The U.S. government had a strong interest in balancing U.S. foreign trade and simultaneously eliminating agricultural surpluses through pushing U.S. agricultural products onto global markets. Tax policies that stimulated production were passed at the same time that monetary policy stimulated inflation. In 1973 the oil producing nations, through OPEC, effectively drove up the price of oil, sending petrodollars sloshing through the international financial system. This created powerful inflationary pressures worldwide, even as it initially created strong markets for American agricultural products and, with it, spiraling land prices.

The Republicans who took over the reins of government from the Democrats in 1980 did not have agriculture at the center of their concerns. Rather, they sought to resolve the "stagflation" that had begun to seem endemic—high unemployment rates coupled with high inflation rates. As Barnett indicates, the tax cuts implemented as part of their supply-side efforts were no more rational than the previous administration's tax and fiscal policies. But the money managers at the Federal Reserve did, finally, manage to drive interest rates higher than the rate of inflation. It also dramatically strengthened the dollar relative to other currencies, pricing U.S. agricultural commodities out of world markets that were already feeling the pinch of debt repayment. The shift in the financial landscape sent land values plummeting. The farm crisis of the mid-1980s began in earnest.

The farmer of the 1980s was a significantly different actor from the farmer of the early twentieth century. Fundamental assumptions had shifted, no longer grounded in a production system in which the vast majority of farmers provisioned significant parts of their operations through non-market institutions. By the 1970s, almost all farmers had adopted business practices, and the largely college-educated young men and women who stepped into their parents' shoes were predisposed to seek out expert advice. These experts, Barnett shows, utterly failed to grasp the lineaments of the farm crisis of the 1980s as it unfolded.

The Political Implications of Daily Life

In the third section, Dudley picks up the story with a close ethnographic study of the farm crisis in a community in western Minnesota.

In an account congruent with O'Connor's argument, made in Chapter 2 by Rudy, Dudley exposes the way that the cultural foundations of capitalism erode and bring to crisis the community forms through which people create meaningful and supportive relationships. What, she asks, makes possible the personal, individual actions which seem, when one steps into a larger arena, an inexorable performance of an economically determined script? Her narrative probes the ways in which people create notions of self and morality that cast out those who betray that morality by their financial failure. This culture, she argues, is founded on an "entrepreneurial self" that radically individualizes even as it requires adherence to larger community norms.[10]

Kenhelm Burridge (1969), an anthropologist who sought to understand social movements created by Melanesians in the face of British colonization, posited that every society establishes modes of what he termed "redemption." The redemptive process, as he conceived it, is "indicated by the activities, moral rules, and assumptions about power which, pertinent to the moral order and taken on faith, not only enable a people to perceive the truth of things, but guarantee that they are indeed perceiving the truth of things." It has to do with "the process whereby individuals attempt to discharge their obligations in relation to the moral imperatives of the community" (Burridge 1969:6–7). This process establishes the bases on which people recognize the worth and dignity of themselves and others. As numerous historians have persuasively argued, the terms for conferring worth and dignity have continually shifted as commodity relations supplanted those mediated through reciprocity and what Mauss (2000 [1927]) termed "gifts." This replacement was not solely a shift in exchange relationships; rather, it entailed a broad set of ideas and practices associated with modernity. These ideas and practices, Arce and Long (2000:1) argue, are "appropriated and reembedded in locally situated practices, thus accelerating the fragmentation and dispersal of modernity into constantly proliferating modernities." The entrepreneurial self discerned by Dudley is characteristic of one of these specific modernities. It is neither the self of the captain of industry who manages a vast industrial and financial empire, nor the self of the farmers who, coming from a variety of regional and national backgrounds, settled the North American countryside during the nineteenth century. It is, rather, a negotiation between past and future, at a moment of crisis when a contested and always improvised moral order makes its imperatives felt.

Members of farming communities developed what Dudley calls the entrepreneurial self out of a complex negotiation between a proselytizing industrial order and a range of ethnic traditions that variously embodied the old American yeoman attachment to autonomy and independence. At the beginning of the twenty-first century, only the Amish among American farmers remain committed to maintaining a community that simultaneously requires individual initiative and subordination to a covenanted community. In the wheat growing regions of the U.S. and Canada, Hutterites have created small communities governed through theocratic gerontocracies that effectively compete with entrepreneurial farmers.[11] Elsewhere, the individualized entrepreneurial farmer predominates, and the bonds of community thin to the point of disappearing.

Dudley's account demonstrates the permeability of individual identity: the way in which the belief in an autonomous individual requires a social ordering of values through which a person and those around them recognize whether they succeed or fail. Like the economists of whom Barnett writes, few members of farming communities were able to translate system failure into a reformulation of the codes for establishing worth and value. Those who did, aligning themselves with political activists, were largely shunned, by their profession, in the case of agricultural economists, and by other members of their communities, in the case of farmers. The existing set of assumptions about the truth of things proved more powerful than the imagination of either experts or those directly affected. This, also, is political, insofar as the contradictions were sutured over and the existing system of power remained largely unchallenged. When crisis exposes large numbers of people to extraordinary personal pain and threatens the viability of important institutions, as did the farm crisis, the failure of imaginative alternatives to be effectively placed in the public arena is as significant as their success.

The failure was not total, however. Rather, it moved into other domains. Although the farm crisis spurred only minor reforms to the existing agricultural system, including agricultural policy, it fueled a growing set of alternatives. Most of these derived from the organic and sustainable farming movement, whose roots lie more in the environmental movement that emerged from the social unrest of the 1960s and 1970s than within the farming community itself. That diverse grouping of individuals and organizations lumped together as "environmentalists" came to provide the conceptual tools to expose the contingent nature of conventional agriculture. The environmentalist critique of conventional agriculture struck at its epistemological, institutional, and pragmatic assumptions. Through their sustained critique of conventional agriculture, environmentalists challenged the organization of power within the society as a whole, not simply in the domain of agricultural production.

These challenges are foundational: the radical actors within the environmental movement posit fundamentally new modes of redemption, to use Burridge's terminology. They seek not only new forms of governmental power, but new modes of regulation and governance. They seek, as Friedmann demonstrates in Chapter 14, to rearrange social life fundamentally, from the intimacies of daily life to the overarching structures of global commerce.

DeLind captures well the tension within one practical program developed within the environmental movement: Community Supported Agriculture (CSA). Community Supported Agriculture began in part as an instrumental means for low income farmers to combine capital with labor to grow needed crops for a reliable market (Whateley 1987). However, it quickly became a vehicle through which to imagine a radically reformed system of agricultural production, in which consumers and producers break down these identities and meet one another in a community based more on notions of reciprocity than commerce. All of the participants, however, live inside a world regulated through commodity exchange and virtually all rely on the institutions of the existing order to maintain daily life. As DeLind documents, the utopian vision often falters in the face of the farmer's day-to-day necessity to make farm payments, buy supplies, and get the crop out and distributed. And, on the consumers' side, work in urban jobs and complex family responsibilities do not easily give individuals the ability to include a demanding rural activity and new set of social relationships. In this case, imagination outstrips institutional and individual capacity.

DeLind uses Stevenson's (1998) notion of "warrior work" and "builder work" to distinguish between actions that directly engage the existing order through political action and those that seek to institutionalize viable alternatives in the interstices of the existing order. The CSA movement, while specifically oriented toward creating alternative relationships between producers and consumers, does have its directly political dimensions. Members of CSAs work for altered regulations; they seek governmental support for research and other support; they enlist government functionaries and agencies, such as the Cooperative Extension Service, for various kinds of services and advocacy.

The Politics of the Environment

The radical revisioning of human to nature and human to human relationships by the environmental movement has moved into other domains as well. The chapters by Hall and Reisner directly address the processes through which the imaginable becomes part of public debate. They demonstrate the power of language as a political resource. Hall analyzes the battle over the meaning of the term sustainable agriculture, while Reisner takes up the hotly contested domain of biotechnology. Both these articles assume, and simultaneously demonstrate, the power of discourse in creating larger social realities. The theoretical debates of the mid-twentieth century over whether or not people's concepts determine social forms have been largely settled. Both ethnographic demonstration and various strands of language theory have largely persuaded both Marxists and utilitarians that human beings construct their social universes through discourse. In the process, the concept of discourse has been enlarged from pointing solely to language to including other orderings of cognition, including the ordering of space and time. Questions of power have, therefore, moved to the center, since order does not appear spontaneously but is, rather, instituted and reproduced within contingent yet durable regimes. The shift from "symbol" to "cognition" as the central aspect of discourse has, simultaneously, permitted actors to reappear as central to the creation of social relations (Giddens 1979, 1987; Long and Long 1992). In this sense, the CSAs analyzed by DeLind create new discourses of knowledge and power as much by the new social relations they instantiate (or seek to instantiate) as by the purely linguistic programs and arguments they put forward.

Hall and Reisner both deal with the more restricted notion of discourse as language. Their analyses, however, point toward the ways in which battles in the political arena over the meanings of terms create effects in the political process as a whole—how resources are distributed, who gets targeted by regulations, and so forth. As Shulman demonstrates in his study of the establishment of the Farm Credit system, durable institutions are created through both setting agendas for public debate and framing the specific terms of debate.[12]

Hall takes up the discourse of "sustainable agriculture" in Canada. Symbols, as anthropologist Victor Turner (1974) observed, are multivocalic, and their varied meanings are most easily seen in what he termed social dramas. Most terms carry multiple meanings even when closely defined; their meanings become vastly, and unpredictably, extended when deployed as metaphors and other tropes (Lakoff and Johnson 1980). They therefore become resources to be deployed in strategic action (McAdam, McCarthy, and Zald 1996). Although the term "sustainable" was first established in public debate by organic and other farmers who sought alternatives to industrialized agricultural production, it contains, as Hall demonstrates, sufficient ambiguity to be vulnerable to appropriation by proponents of conventional agriculture. In this case, Hall argues, the hegemony of the existing order becomes reinstantiated specifically through a strategy to redefine "sustainable" so that it conforms to normal business practices. This process is significantly different from that analyzed by DeLind, in which the hegemony of commercial transactions became revealed in the daily practices that undermined the viability of an articulated vision. In both instances, however, the power of an institutionalized order is revealed through the attempts by mobilized actors to transform the system.

Reisner presents a somewhat different outcome. In the case of genetically modified organisms (GMOs), a coalition of groups that she characterizes as "social movement organizations" (SMOs) successfully placed the regulation of GMOs on the public agenda, and they have been able to continue to frame the debate largely in their terms. The degree to which promoters of the use of GMOs in agriculture will be successful remains undecided. To a considerable extent, it will be decided by forces outside the purview of the U.S. government. Anti-GMO rhetoric has been sufficiently persuasive, both in the U.S. and elsewhere, to alter popular consciousness and actions regarding food safety. Large fast food chains like McDonald's now screen out GMO products, fearing customer backlash; and the European Union has steadfastly rejected foodstuffs containing genetic modifications. In an economy in which consumer choice plays a large role, extra-governmental action demonstrably affects the relations of power. The food system, which has long been focused on production and mass distribution, now has to take into account consumer concerns for their health and for the ecosystem.

Reisner's study also provides a robust methodology for studying the contestation of political discourses, critical discourse analysis. This method provides some tools with which to expose the "universe of the undiscussed" (Bourdieu 1977), the commonsense, taken-for-granted foundations of understanding. Insofar as scientific methodologies attempt to push the boundaries of both sensory and cognitive perception, critical discourse analysis is such a methodology. Grounded on the assumption that discourses reproduce existing relations of domination, generally "behind the backs" of actors, it provides a tool for exposing the relations of power as they are expressed and instantiated in language.

This collection ends with Friedmann's envisioning of a new ordering of nature and culture, of geographic space, of temporality. Friedmann provides a new set of metaphors derived from ecology and the improvisational art of jazz to imagine a future unimaginable within hegemonic discourses. She envisions, in short, a fundamentally transformed ordering of knowledge and power.

Part I
North American Agriculture in the World System

Overview and Case Studies

Chapter 2
The Social Economy of Development
The State of/and the Imperial Valley

Alan P. Rudy

This chapter argues that the state is both an agent and a product of rural and agricultural development through an analysis of the development of California's Imperial Valley. The actions of state agencies, or (put another way) the state's agency, were and remain a necessary if not sufficient component of rural and agricultural development in the Imperial Valley. Depending on the era and development concern in question, different moments in the state's agency, different levels of governance, regulation, and administration have been brought to bear.

I have abstracted five eras of Imperial Valley development.[1] The first era, in which the preconditions for desert irrigation gradually emerged, runs from 1850 to 1900. The second period, from the initiation of irrigation until the establishment of reliable ecological, labor, and infrastructural conditions for agriculture, is played out from 1901 to 1941. The third epoch, from the beginning of the bracero program to the rise of the United Farm Workers and the first oil crisis, runs from 1942 to 1972. The fourth period, during which ecological crises, labor struggles, and infrastructural threats multiply, runs from 1973 to 1993. The fifth cycle, continuing through the present, represents the ongoing reconstruction of natural, social, and communal conditions, in part through a reduction in the region's economic dependence on agriculture. These stages of development, of ever-decreasing duration, point to accelerating rates of change, crisis resolution, and regional reconstruction within the valley. The state's agency is of pivotal importance in all of the periods.

James O'Connor's work on the fiscal crisis of the state in the 1970s, and on "environmental" crisis since the 1980s, provides the theoretical background for this chapter (O'Connor 1973, 1998). O'Connor theorized the state's contradictory position between the economic demands that it facilitate accumulation and its role in the democratic legitimation of the social and ecological consequences of accumulation. His central innovation, in conversation with similar points made by Habermas in *Legitimation Crisis* (1975), was to theorize the relation between macroscopic economic crisis and the state's fiscal crisis tendencies. Under conditions of economic downturn, and as the state's tax revenues fall, capital demands even less corporate and business taxation, greater state investment in the development of new science and technology, and greater social investments in new, more efficient, productive infrastructures. Simultaneously, popular social movements demand greater state support for social programs and environmental protection. These demands are often intensified in response to corporate cost cutting and cost externalization in such periods. The state, therefore, is caught between conflicting, negative-sum demands from capital and social movements for incommensurable patterns of greater social investments as less money flows into state coffers.

Should the state prioritize the deregulation of capital and increasing investments in research, development, and productive infrastructures, the social legitimation of both the state and accumulation is threatened in the eyes of social actors who seek to defend working class and environmental reproduction. The other choice, that of greater social, ecological, and infrastructural regulation and/or expenditures, reduces the state's ability to help capital recover from economic crisis and may accelerate economic decline and thereby delegitimate of the state in the eyes of capital. Attempting to satisfy both accumulation and sociopolitical legitimation exacerbates tendencies towards fiscal crisis as the state must go into debt.

This analysis of economic and fiscal crisis tendencies undergirds O'Connor's thesis on the second contradiction of capitalism (O'Connor 1988, 1998). This thesis is an effort to understand the environmental crisis tendencies under capitalism. Importantly, O'Connor defines *the environment* as the ecological, personal, and communal conditions necessary for capitalist commodity production which are not themselves (re)produced as commodities. *Conditions of production*, as he calls them, are (re)produced "outside" commodified labor relations and yet are treated as commodities "within" production. In Polanyian language, the conditions of production are "fictitious commodities" (Polanyi 1957).

Capital treats ecologies, workers, and communities as if they were commodities while externalizing costs into the social ecological realms wherein nature, persons, and communities reproduce themselves. O'Connor subsequently theorized that a central role of the state is to mediate capital's access to the environmental conditions necessary for capital accumulation (O'Connor 1973, 1998). Again, the state must execute this mediation in a manner that both facilitates accumulation and legitimates the ecological, personal, and cultural consequences of capital accumulation for civil society.

This theoretical exegesis works at a high level of abstraction—one that cannot be simply imported into an analysis of rural and agricultural development. Nevertheless, the theory suggests that studies of rural and agricultural regions need to look closely at the role of the state in the processes of rural and/or agricultural development. The theory sees the role of the state as omnipresent but by no means omnipotent. There are notably more actors, and often more potent actors, than the state and its representatives. Among these actors are the ecologies, the persons, and the communities within, through, and for which capital produces commodities and profit.

Perhaps most importantly, just as ecologies, persons, and communities change, and are changed through accumulation, mediation, and legitimation processes, so too does the state. The state's role in facilitating accumulation, maintaining legitimacy, and mediating the relation between capital and the conditions of production is never static. Nor is this relation evenly expressed over time or space. This is most clearly the case because of the uneven development of rural/agricultural ecologies (Smith 1991), the diversity of rural/agricultural labor processes (Swanson 1988), the myriad cultural and infrastructural relations in rural/agricultural areas (Salamon 1985; Mooney 1988), and the changing nature of the science, technology, and global economy in rural/agricultural areas (Kloppenburg 1988; Busch and Tanaka 1996; Goodman and Watts 1997).

This chapter reviews the essential roles of the state in the development of agro-ecological conditions and rural communities in the Imperial Valley. In the space available here, I will stress the state's role in ecological and labor mediations as the Imperial Valley developed and generally underplay issues of community (under)development in the region.

Ecological Characteristics Past and Present

The desert ecology of Imperial Valley is extreme. One hundred twenty miles north to south and eighty miles east to west, the region is hot, dry, and generally shadeless. The valley's mean annual temperature is 73° Fahrenheit and summer temperatures regularly top 100°. Temperatures over 110° are not uncommon (Tout 1931). On either side of the valley are high, hot, and dry mountains. On average, less than three inches of rain falls each year (Shenas 1989). Before irrigation, the only year-round flow into the valley was Carrizo Creek, which oozes out of the western mountains and disappears into the sand. Further-more, temporary pools left behind by Colorado River overflows were the only (periodically) available water across the center of the valley. These pools emerged a few times each century when Colorado River floods would break through the river's deltaic banks and flow north, away from the Gulf of California, temporarily filling the valley's de-pressed center until the river returned to its channel, and these fresh-water bodies of water would gradually evaporate.[2] During each flood the sediment-heavy waters would deposit their loads of rich soils along the floor of the valley. It was these soils, the slope of the terrain, and the region's 365-day-a-year growing season that attracted irrigators.

Mexico ceded the region to the United States in 1848, following the Mexican-American War. During the late nineteenth century, American promoters attempted unsuccessfully to settle the California desert. One group eventually formed the California Development Company (CDC) in 1896 to take advantage of the federal Desert Lands Act, which authorized private development of water for irrigation. Finally, in 1901, the CDC completed the first irrigation works, opening the valley to agriculture.

The Negotiation of Environmental and Working Conditions of Production, 1901–1941

The early years of the twentieth century presented engineers and pro-moters with a fortuitous historical window for developing irrigated agriculture in the desert southwest. This period has been referred to as the golden age of American agriculture as strong commodity prices followed the closing of the frontier, the expansion of industrial cities in Europe and the United States, and a new U.S. hegemony over the Western Hemisphere after its expulsion of Spain from the hemisphere in 1898.[3] Established during a period of U.S. imperial aspirations, the Imperial Valley can be understood as coevolving with U.S. market-based neoimperialism.[4] At the same time, both the U.S. and California were growing demographically and economically, and no other region had developed fruit and vegetable production for late fall, winter, and early spring markets. Given these factors, once irrigation systems were installed, the Imperial Valley was very well situated to compete on na-tional markets. The strength of agricultural production in the valley is indicated by the great profitability of its agriculture throughout the period from 1901 to 1941, despite repeated ecological disasters, labor struggles, and a global depression.

During these forty years, hegemonic control over environmental and labor conditions in the valley's agriculture was established through the successive institutional activities of the CDC, the Southern Pacific Railroad (SPRR) and the Imperial Irrigation District (IID). As with other regions of the country, local action was often enabled and periodically constrained by forms of state mediation at federal, state, and local levels. At the level of material struggles with, and negotiations over, natural conditions, land ownership had to be legalized, forms of transportation created, water had to be reliably supplied, fields had to be cleared and leveled, cropping patterns had to be tested, and pests of many kinds had to be removed and new ones defeated. State and federal governments provided both the legal and much of the institutional infrastructure necessary for these developments, including soil surveys and crop research funded by the U.S. Department of Agriculture (USDA) and the University of California's Agricultural Experiment Station.[5]

Operating under California irrigation law, the CDC built the last great private irrigation project in the United States. However, this development coincided with the evolution of the Progressive Era and the scientific management of irrigation development by the Department of Interior's Bureau of Reclamation. Populist acreage and residency limitations within the 1901 Reclamation Act led the Bureau to look unkindly on the private and speculative character of the CDC's under-capitalized project. Other problems arose. The initial cut in the banks of the Colorado had been made just above the international border in U.S. territory and a low-cost headgate had been installed to control irrigation diversions. From the headgate, water was gravitationally transported south and west across the international border and sixty miles of Mexican territory until crossing back northward into California near the present site of the twin cities of Mexicali and Calexico.

When siltation of the CDC canals caused the company's water delivery to become increasingly sporadic and uncertain during 1903 and 1904 the CDC, frustrated by its inability to sell its works to the Reclamation Bureau or efficiently contact the Mexican government to build necessary new works, made an unregulated cut in the lowland banks of the river south of the international border.[6] The cut was intended to resolve the water delivery problems and remove the potential jurisdiction of the Reclamation Bureau. The cut succeeded for only a short while. Soon after it was made, the cut was washed away by repeated floods of the Colorado River and its tributaries.

The floodwaters flowed through the lowland cut for two and a half years, during which time the whole of the Colorado River flowed into and all but filled the Salton Sink. The resulting "lake" was soon thereafter christened the Salton Sea. The New Liverpool Salt Company's

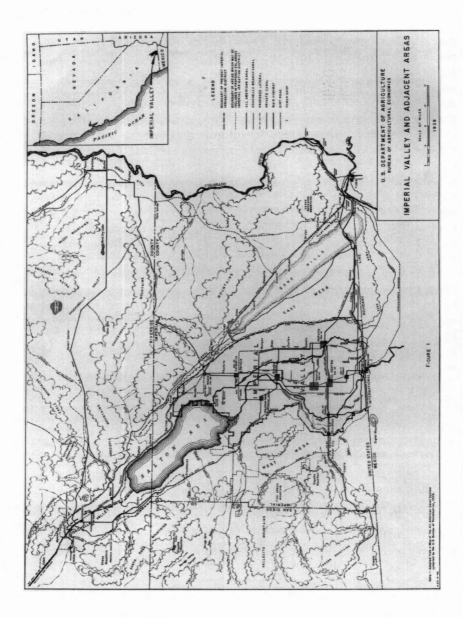

Figure 2.1. Imperial Valley and Adjacent Areas. Poli 1942.

plant, Southern Pacific rails, and many fields were washed away as the river cut back into the soil, eroding approximately three times as much dirt as was removed in the digging of the Panama Canal (Cory and Blake 1915). In the process, the flood gouged out 20 to 40 foot deep channels within which the Alamo and New "Rivers" now flow to the Salton Sea.

While at one level this was an ecological and economic disaster of almost unprecedented proportions, its consequences did not exclusively constrain the long-term productivity of agriculture in the valley. Ecologically, the great gullies were to later ease problems with perched water tables, delaying the need for massive drainage development—subsidized by state and federal agencies—for thirty years or more (Crosby 1930). Without the terrible consequences of the flood, which hit smallest producers hardest, the whole project could have failed before the Hoover Dam and All-American Canal could be constructed.[7]

The gap was finally closed and a headgate built in 1907 after six attempts to close it and the expenditure of two to three million dollars by the SPRR (Kennan 1922). State action was key to the railroad's initiative, however. The SPRR agreed to a last effort to close the gap only after obtaining a promise from President Theodore Roosevelt that repayment would be forthcoming. The cut that generated the disaster was made as a means of avoiding state intervention and the closing of the break was only made following an inquiry into, and the promise of, another form of state mediation. In the end, however, the disaster transferred power in the valley from the CDC into the hands of the SPRR as the only collateral the CDC had to pay the SPRR for its efforts was the works themselves.

Dissatisfaction with the SPRR's management style and governance from afar, among other things, immediately stimulated the valley's residents to separate themselves from San Diego County, forming Imperial County in 1907.[8] Further, residents and the new county government established a semi-public, semi-private institution, the Imperial Irrigation District (IID) in order to buy the irrigation works from the SPRR in 1909. The capacity of the new county and irrigation district to negotiate the sale of the irrigation works was unintentionally eased as Congress repeatedly refused to pay the SPRR for closing the gap.

By the mid-teens, the valley's leaders were well aware that they needed flood control works on the Colorado and/or a canal exclusively on U.S. soil. Levee construction and irrigation maintenance work across the border was costing far more than the District could afford and federal coffers and patience were limited (Dowd 1956). There was also a real, though exaggerated, fear that the multiracial growers on the Mexican side would use all of the water during the winter growing season, the season that often coincided with periods of low flows. In a complex and protracted attempt to create a secure supply of irrigation water, the Imperial Irrigation District initiated the creation of the Colorado River Compact and the Boulder Canyon Project Act of 1928. The compact and act laid the plans and appropriated the funds for the construction of Hoover Dam and the All-American Canal (see Hundley 1975; Nadeau 1974; Worster 1985). Legally, some of the region's power derives from the fact that the IID holds the first, perfect right to water from the southern Colorado and the largest right to that water because a CDC founder staked a claim along the river in the early 1890s, before the Bureau of Reclamation was legislated into existence.[9] Politically, Philip Swing, the chief counsel for IID, and eventually the Congressional Representative from the valley, was mentored by Senator Hiram Johnson when Johnson was governor of California. Swing was the sponsor in the House and Johnson the sponsor in the Senate of the Boulder Canyon Project, or Swing-Johnson, Act.

The completion of the dam in 1934 and the canal in 1941 finally produced a reliable and well-regulated flow of water for the Valley. It is worth noting at this point that these infrastructures were completed at the cost of the canal only, since electricity generated by the dam was sold to pay for the dam's construction. Further, the IID was granted control over the canal's electrical generating capacity, and used those proceeds to pay off the canal's construction costs. Importantly, despite the federal construction of the dam and the canal, neither the 160-acre limitation on subsidized water deliveries nor the residency requirements written into the Reclamation Act of 1901 have ever been enforced by the bureau in the valley. Legal and bureaucratic arguments concerning the legitimacy of this situation continued until Congress rewrote reclamation law in the late 1970s.

Taming the natural environment was not the only aspect of the valley that required governmental intervention. Given the emerging industrial form of agriculture and the often seasonal residency patterns of valley producers, issues associated with the supply and docility of labor were as important as ecological rationalization. In this arena, indigenous Cocopah and Yuma men recruited from the area made the largest contribution to the initial canal construction and land leveling. Subsequently, almost all of the dangerous work done by the SPRR in closing the gap in the river's bank was also done by indigenous men. Even before the floodwaters had settled, field labor patterns in the Imperial Valley created prototypes for the racial and class divisions of labor that have been widely studied throughout California.[10] By the time of the federal immigration restrictions of the 1920s and the associated exclusion of Mexican immigrants from federal immigration quotas Mexican field workers were more prevalent in the Imperial Valley than anywhere else in California agriculture, setting the pattern of agricultural labor relations in the southwest for the next seventy years (Wolf 1964).

Equally important, virtually all the land was owned and managed by white settlers from the midwest. The situation was radically different on the Mexican side of the border. Outside of Mexicali, the Chandler Syndicate (with ties to the *Los Angeles Times*) leased and sold land to farmers of all races (see Gottlieb and Fitzsimmons 1991; Barnett 1978). This situation fed incipient nationalism and racism in the Imperial Valley. Among other things, during low-flow periods the farmers of many races on the Mexican side had first access to irrigation waters, before the white farmers on the American side—farmers who believed the project had been initiated for them and that only the vagaries of landscape and gravity left them at the mercy of those in Mexico.

Between 1928 and 1934, as the Congressional negotiations for the construction of the dam and canal were being completed, agricultural labor struggles in the valley set the stage for the extraordinary violence that characterized California's croplands during the depression era. The first and the last of the major farm worker strikes in California occurred in the valley in 1928 and 1934 respectively. While most studies of agricultural labor struggles in California during the 1930s focus on the events around the 1933 Central Valley cotton strike, the Imperial Valley cantaloupe pickers strike in 1928 established the precedent for Mexican consulate involvement in field worker struggles, usually in a fashion that encouraged company-style unions (Rudy 1994a).[11] The 1928 strike, as much against the labor contracting system as it was against the growers, also points to the radicalization of moderate workers that occurred during the period (Wollenberg 1973).

Two years later, the 1930 Imperial Valley lettuce strike represents the first moment in the involvement of the Communist Trade Union Unity League (TUUL) in California agricultural labor struggles. The 1933–34 lettuce, pea, and cantaloupe strikes in Imperial Valley represent the end of TUUL activity in this arena. This strike was rife with the most serious civil rights violations associated with the movement (Gray 1977). The last two strikes generated two sets of convictions under California's 1919 Criminal Syndicalism Law, which was eventually struck down as unconstitutional by the U.S. Supreme Court in 1968. This law, as well as other legislation, clearly mediated business's relationship with workers in a manner that served business interests.

In the struggles of the period, California growers generally and

Imperial Valley growers in particular wielded virtually unchecked power. The state and federal governments did nothing other than study the strikes and, during the struggles of 1933–34, send an un-directed and powerless mediator.[12] This power, rooted in the highly capitalized, vertically structured, lease-based, concentrated, and large-scale agriculture practiced in areas such as Imperial Valley, coincided with and foreshadowed developments throughout the rest of California and across the nation (Poli 1942; Poli and Nielsen 1942). In rela-tion to the agricultural sector, the state largely acquiesced to grower interests during this period, acting primarily to support the large-scale growers. In addition to providing irrigation water, the state actively intervened to provide a consistent, docile labor force. The people who migrated to the California fields from the dust bowl received virtually no state assistance and, when they left the fields in the mobilization for World War II, the federal government negotiated with Mexico for what would become the bracero program.[13]

The key point is that, during this period, growers were involved in a number of struggles simultaneously. These included struggles with la-borers; struggles with federal legislative bodies and bureaucracies over water supply, drainage subsidies, and farm loans; and struggles with nature over water quality, soil moisture, and crop reliability. They sought government support for their needs, while simultaneously seeking freedom from state regulation. Among other things, the Im-perial Irrigation District and growers throughout the Valley were deeply concerned that the construction of the Hoover Dam and All-American Canal would finally and effectively subordinate them to fed-eral reclamation law, including the 160-acre limitation and residency requirements. They also appear to have been gravely concerned that the growers and institutions of the valley would not survive to see the completion of the All-American Canal. The depression had con-strained markets, the Federal Land Bank had suspended loans to the area given water delivery and soil drainage problems constraining productivity in the mid-to-late 1930s, the IID was almost bankrupt (Leeds et al. 1943; Quinton, Code, and Hill 1937), and drainage prob-lems had begun to force thousands of acres out of production, directly threatening their economic survival.[14] Perhaps as a result of their sense of embattlement, the growers and county officials were among the most violent in their reactions to laborers' attempts to organize. However, they also acted in ways that limited their flexibility in the face of economic crisis. Here, the most important issue was their al-most universal opposition to cooperative marketing and production schemes (Crosby 1930).

The social hegemony of large growers and investors, augmented by the get-in-make-money-and-get-out intentions of most of the smaller growers, meant that almost as soon as the dam and canal were completed most growers moved off the land, in many cases out of the valley. This would have been impossible had residency requirements been enforced and would likely have been less economically feasible had acreage limitations been enforced. These concerns with the state's regulation of agricultural development were certainly as deep as growers' concerns with the quality and quantity of nature and labor. Nevertheless, by 1941, as a result of local struggle, state and federal support for irrigation water, drainage, labor stability, and credit, and, in relation to grower regulation, state and federal inaction, all of the conditions for reliable, low-risk, accumulation were established. To this day, a visit to the Imperial Valley Museum, run by local historians and the Pioneer Association, shows that the end of the 1930s is treated as the end of "history" in Imperial Valley.

Normalcy, Displacement, and Profitability, 1942–1972

After the completion of the federally constructed water works and the signing of an agreement with Mexico for an "emergency" supply of field laborers during World War II, the stage was set for thirty years of superabundant, often record-setting, accumulation in Imperial Valley. The previous section addressed the means and trajectories by which growers established hegemonic control over regional conditions of production within a market context such that effectively all crops and livestock produced in the Valley would sell. This section looks at the "normal" development of agriculture between 1942 and 1972.

Growers in the Imperial Valley produced a staggeringly wide array of crops, all of which experienced strong postwar markets. Between 1942 and 1972 gross agricultural income in Imperial Valley increased by more than 600 percent.[15] Despite the valley's fame as a producer of vegetables and melons, field crops and cattle actually provided a larger share of the valley income. Every national agricultural census from 1940 to 1974 ranked Imperial County first in the volume of alfalfa hay harvested. Over time, sugar beets became increasingly important, as did cotton. Cattle feedlots expanded, particularly after 1960. In contrast vegetables, primarily lettuce, cantaloupes, carrots, and tomatoes, increased their contribution to the Valley's gross income very slowly until 1965 after which time gross vegetable income more than doubled.[16] Income from vegetables largely stagnated during the 1940s and 1950s due to the short, seasonal domination of national markets for these goods by valley growers. Able to market vegetables and melons later in the fall and earlier in the spring than other regions of the country, and yet refusing to cooperatively plant or market their produce, Valley growers would regularly saturate markets for these perishables during their window of market opportunity. Over time, growers adapted planting schedules on their extensive acreages to generate serial ripening rather than work together.[17]

Throughout this period, the development of the valley was predicated on cheap water provided by federally constructed water regulation and delivery infrastructures; the federally sponsored and state-regulated agreement with Mexico for bracero labor—at wages that did not increase during the 1950s (Wolf 1964); the federal and state support of research and development into the chemicalization and mechanization of agriculture; hundreds of thousands of Soil Conservation Service dollars each year to support the installation of drainage tile and drainage canals throughout the Imperial Irrigation District; and the lack of administrative and juridical enforcement of the 160-acre limitation and the residency requirements associated with federally funded reclamation and water projects (Taylor 1973).[18] Outside of agriculture there was a failure, at both the state and federal levels, to respond to the flooding of extensive tracts of newly developed retirement communities and recreational facilities as irrigation runoff raised the level of the Salton Sea (U.S. Department of Interor 1974). There was also an administrative inability on the part of local government officials and resident business to effectively respond to the ongoing emigration of educated and capable young people to areas with more jobs and a higher quality of life.[19] In short, the conditions for agricultural profitability were well established while the generation of a more diversified economy, more stable communities, and a more dynamic labor force was largely forestalled. This period of "normalcy" and expanded intensive production represents an extraordinary example of political economic cooperation that lowered the costs of agricultural production while simultaneously displacing ecological crises and labor struggles into other places and into the future.

The period after 1964 most clearly illustrates the ability of Imperial Valley growers and their representatives to externalize costs through the exercise of political power and the adoption of new forms of production relations. In 1964, the growers faced a combined assault on their power in three crucial areas: labor, ecology, and access to irrigation water. That year Congress voted to terminate the bracero program, a solicitor for the Department of Interior ruled that acreage limitations ought to be applied within the valley, and state and federal investigations into the flooding of Salton Sea, were initiated. In the end, however, the growers were able to accommodate the loss of bracero labor and successfully to turn back the threat of government regulation.

Despite repeated, loud, and dire predictions from growers throughout California and the West, the termination of the bracero program in 1965 did not deleteriously affect vegetable production and had no effect on already mechanized field crop production. In the Imperial Valley, after the region sought and received short-term extensions of bracero-like programs during 1966 and 1967, income from vegetables, as a percentage of gross county agricultural income, *increased*. While some of this can be attributed to inflation, growing markets, and mechanization, no one has argued that the growth would have been greater had braceros continued to be contracted.[20]

At the same time the Secretary of Interior, Morris Udall, elected to negotiate with the Imperial Irrigation District over the pace of the enforcement of the 160-acre limitation, rather than impose it. He was stonewalled. Growers in the valley organized Imperial Resources Associates (IRA), led by the two largest producers in the county. The IID and IRA hired "southern California's most prestigious law firm, O'Melveny and Myers," to fight the limitations (Fradkin 1981: 284). An attorney for O'Melveny and Myers, Warren Christopher (later deputy attorney general during the presidency of Lyndon Johnson, deputy secretary of state under President Carter, and foreign secretary under President Clinton) wrote a long opinion opposing the limitations. Other supporters of the IID/IRA positions included Richard Nixon, who had campaigned against the limitation as early as his campaign against Helen Gahagan Douglas in the 1940s and continued to oppose them as vice president and president. Ronald Reagan, both as governor and as president, Senators George Murphy and John V. Tunney, Governor Jerry Brown, Senators Alan Cranston and S. I. Hayakawa, and editorial writers for the *Los Angeles Times* and *San Francisco Chronicle* all opposed the imposition of the limitations.[21]

With such powerful forces, both Democratic and Republican, arrayed against enforcement of the 160-acre rule, the Udall-IID negotiations failed. The Department of Interior finally resorted, in 1967, to bringing suit against the IID to force the District to enforce the acreage limitations. The IRA intervened on the side of the District. With Nixon's election to the presidency in 1968, the Department of Interior dropped its suit. In 1969, Ben Yellen, a local doctor, and 121 Imperial Valley farmworkers sued Walter J. Hickel, Nixon's Secretary of Interior, seeking enforcement of the residency and acreage limitation provisions (Fradkin 1981). Enforcement of the acreage limitation would have transformed ownership relations to the land in the Imperial

Valley, while enforcing the residency requirements would have revolutionized productive and ownership relations and would likely have generated extensive community development in the region, since by this point virtually all landowners lived outside the county.

In January 1971, in Federal District Court in San Diego, Judge Howard B. Turrentine, appointed by Nixon on the recommendation of California Senator Murphy, ruled in favor of the IID, rejecting the application of acreage limitations. Turrentine also found that Yellen did not have standing to intervene as a friend of the government. Turrentine's arguments almost perfectly replicated those made by the IID, IRA, and O'Melveny and Myers. The IID hoped strongly that the case would not to be appealed, thus terminating the controversy. The IID's manager, Robert F. Carter, along with valley landowners including IRA President Steven Elmore, met with their congressman, Victor V. Veysey, Interior Secretary Rogers Morton, Deputy Attorney General Richard Kleindienst, and Attorney General George Mitchell, among others, to encourage the Department of Interior not to appeal. The bureau acquiesced in March 1971 (Fradkin 1981:285–86).

However, Yellen appealed the decision, arguing that Turrentine's investments in nearby Borrego Springs represented a conflict of interest.[22] Six months later, visiting Judge W. D. Murray from Wyoming, sitting in the same San Diego Federal District Court, decided in favor of Yellen's appeal, arguing for the enforcement of residency requirements. Confusion reigned as the same court had handed down two contradictory decisions. As we will see below, this issue took another decade to reach the Supreme Court, and it was settled in the IID's favor by the court and subsequent Congressional action. In any event, the administrative decision made in the early 1960s, based in large part on internal documents prepared in the 1930s when the initial studies of the issue were made within the Bureau of Reclamation, was not resolved for almost twenty years.

Stepping away from water and land issues, the application of pesticides in the Imperial Valley exploded after World War II. Despite warning from entomologists at the University of California at Berkeley (Van den Bosch 1989), it took a quarter century before the ecological consequences of chemical intensification became clear, first with massive problems with pink bollworm in the 1970s, and even worse problems with the silver leaf whitefly in the 1990s. In the five years between 1949 and 1954, 35,716,593 pounds of pesticides were dropped on the 400,000 acres of irrigated agricultural land in the valley—almost 90 pounds per acre and 18 pounds per acre per year. From 1951 to 1954, 19,074,344 gallons of sprays were placed on the same agricultural acreage, 12 gallons per acre per year. Also, from 1952 to 1954, almost 400 tons of flake bran and chlordane, to control grasshoppers and crickets, were dropped on agricultural land at 10 pounds per acre.[23] Imperial County ranked fourth, in 1969, and third, in 1972, in non-fertilizer chemical expenditures in the U.S. (*U.S. Census of Agriculture* 1945, 1969), indicating that these tendencies did not change over the ensuing years. If 1976 usage resembled 1972, somewhere around 1,500,000 pounds of restricted pesticides were sprayed by the end of the period in question (California Division of Pest Management 1978). Both federal and state legislatures and regulatory bureaucracies refused, or failed, to respond to the ecological consequences of chemical applications such as these despite warnings by Rachel Carson (1994 [1962]) and others including many in the Environmental Protection Agency (EPA), established in 1968. The safety of working conditions around these chemicals was also bracketed.

During the period from 1942 to 1972 the growers and various levels of government agencies turned the valley into a rural area unlike any other in the United States. Throughout most of rural America, the economy stagnated and the number of small farms fell sharply. In the Imperial Valley, by contrast, the agricultural economy prospered under a regime of large-scale irrigation agriculture. Leading the trend in the rest of the country, those small farmers who had established themselves in the interstices of the Valley's large-scale enterprises failed. Accelerating this trend was a desire among many farmers to sell and move off of land whose value had soared following the construction of the Hoover Dam and All American Canal. The number of farms reported to the Agricultural Census peaked in 1945 at 2,932, only to fall to one quarter that many, 771, in 1974. Over that same period, the average operating size rose from 181 acres to 666. In 1945, 36 percent of farms in the valley fell into the top two Agricultural Census income categories. In 1974, that percentage had risen to 70 percent. In 1945, 20 percent of farms were larger than 200 acres. In 1974, 20 percent of farms were larger than 1000 acres.

The large growers in the region, augmented by growers and allies beyond the Valley, enjoyed and defended their access to—and some might say abuse of—the ecological and personal conditions necessary for what they saw as normal profitability. For the first half of this period, state actions legitimated and promoted extraordinary forms of capitalist agricultural production relations and the development of more intensive productive forces. In the second half of the period the state found itself effectively powerless to re-mediate relations between growers, nature, and labor despite rising national commitments to more environmentally and socially sustainable practices. This was in part because the state contributed to the transformation and disappearance of the social and ecological conditions, extant in 1942, upon which more sustainable forms of agricultural and rural production might have been built.

Despite extreme ecological conditions and a much more highly industrialized form of production, agricultural production and rural life in Imperial Valley greatly resembled that of other regions producing intensive agricultural commodities. Communities experienced notable out-migration, ecologies presented occasional problems, and labor struggles blossomed to a minor extent in 1951 and 1961. During this period the growers and their representatives were able to forestall all significant threats to their continued profitability. Neither markets nor conditions of production generated situations that could be described as crises. By 1972, however, all of that was about to change.

Renewed Negotiations and Crises: 1973–1993

The early to mid-1970s represent a period widely viewed as a turning point in the national and international economy. The period also marks the beginning of fiscal crises and new forms of regulatory administration in the U.S. Further, the agricultural economy was radically transformed as a result of the U.S.-Soviet grain deal and détente with China, new programs from the USDA, and rapid inflation throughout the economy (see Adams 1994b; Buttel 1989; Barnett chapter 8). Finally, directly associated with the unique combination of inflation during a stagnant economy, the oil shocks of the middle 1970s greatly affected the costs of agricultural production, raising the price of all petrochemical inputs to agriculture. In the Imperial Valley, these changes occurred simultaneously with renewed struggles over, and with, the ecological and personal conditions of production. These struggles threatened to seriously destabilize agricultural production and profitability in the region.

Ecological conditions, from the state of the Salton Sea to renewed pest problems, had reached a point where they were widely regarded as degraded and worsening. Mechanization continued apace after the bracero program ended. As a partial result of mechanization, low pay, no benefits, and the health consequences of pesticide application practices, Mexican American farm laborers organized within the increasingly militant United Farm Workers (UFW) at the same time that new forms of specialty services and labor contracting evolved (see Wells 1996 and chapter 5). The changing structure of valley agriculture included forms of corporatization that drew the profits from agricultural production and processing to headquarters outside the region.

Under these conditions, many of the towns historically dependent on agriculture underwent a major decline, and eventual diversification, in their economic base. With their vitality undermined by a decline in tax revenues from agriculture, advocates of community development grounded in retail opportunities for the residents of Mexicali, the construction of two new state prisons, and the opening of a new border crossing to facilitate trade under NAFTA moved into dominant positions in local politics. At this same time, federal and state environmental and labor regulation exacerbated agriculture's already tight "cost-price" squeeze, effectively constraining the ability of grower-shippers with huge capital investments to respond to new national and international competition within changing consumer markets.

In 1980, the IID and Imperial Valley landowners won the Supreme Court case exempting the region from the acreage and residency limitations under federal reclamation law.[24] Soon thereafter, Congressional revisions of reclamation law dramatically increased minimum acreages for water subsidies and rejected residency requirements altogether (Worster 1985). Remarkably, these juridical and political victories made little difference in the valley since many growers had by that time begun to move elsewhere as a result of pressures unrelated to reclamation law. As land was concentrated after World War II, the larger growers had added shipping and processing to their enterprises. In the late 1970s and early 1980s, many of these enterprises divested themselves of their landholdings and machinery and focused on processing and shipping (California Employment Development Department 1992). Fifty years of litigation, administrative negotiations, and legislative struggles resolved questions about the applicability of federal reclamation law to lands within the Imperial Valley at just the moment when large, nonresident landowners and corporations were selling their land in smaller units—though often to other nonresidents.

One reason for the sell-off was related to the threatened ecology of the region. As the bracero program was eliminated, the Mexican government was compensated with federal programs that encouraged the development of industrial production and assembly within the border industrialization, or maquiladora, program along the Mexico-U.S. border. The population of Mexicali grew as Mexican citizens migrated to the city for day labor across the border and to find work in maquiladora factories. This population growth dramatically increased the volume of untreated industrial pollution and domestic sewage entering the valley, particularly through the New River channel (Lewis, Kaltofen, and Ormsby 1991; Setmire et al. 1990). Further, the increasing salinity and fluctuating levels of the Salton Sea led to close federal and state studies, a new U.S.-Mexican border water quality Minute (superseded in 1993 by NAFTA side agreements), and a lawsuit forcing a water-for-conservation-infrastructure payments deal between the Metropolitan Water District of Los Angeles (MWD) and the IID (National Research Council 1992; Reisner and Bates 1990).

Struggles over water conservation and the possibility of future water deals for the IID and its landowner clients have recently been complicated by complaints from Mexican growers and the Mexican government claiming rights-in-use to water that has historically seeped into the sand from the unlined All-American Canal. Further, the elaboration of water delivery and irrigation infrastructures along the lower Colorado related to the completion of the Central Arizona Project and the ongoing development of Las Vegas hint at impending struggles over the distribution of oversubscribed Colorado River water. Agriculture in the Imperial Valley is particularly threatened by these developments since the IID has long taken more than its share of Colorado River water. All concerned with these potential issues now also aver that the river carries less water than the amount divided by the states under the Colorado Compact during the 1920s.[25]

Most recently, increased salinization of the Salton Sea, along with high levels of selenium and other poisons, have caused steep declines in fish and bird populations. Political agitation by the Audubon Society and investors in recreation and retirement developments along northern reaches of the sea's shoreline, added to the historical research and planning by the U.S. Department of Interior concerning the sea's degradation, led to the creation of a California joint-powers agency, the Salton Sea Authority, in 1993. This group, comprised of representatives from Imperial and Riverside Counties, the Imperial Irrigation District, and the Coachella Valley Water District, held a conference in January 1994 to explore technical solutions to the ecological problems of the sea. Federal, state, and local agencies concerned with the sea's ecological and economic future participated and the public was welcome.[26] However, all of the solutions proposed cost upwards of $500,000,000 (in 1994 dollars) to construct and, as has been the case in all previous proposals of this sort, progress over the last eight years has been quite limited.[27] In 2000, a series of pilot projects and test systems was initiated. However, at this writing, the Authority has done effectively nothing to arrest or reverse the processes degrading the sea's ecology, nor to respond to the anticipated accelerated degradation of the sea due to water conservation programs under the MWD-IID agreement. It was widely predicted in 1994 that by the turn of the century no game fish would live in the sea and that declines in wildfowl and resident bird populations due to selenium poisoning and avian diseases would accelerate. While fish populations remain relative stable, if threatened, tens of thousands of birds regularly die at the sea.

Massive pest outbreaks in the 1970s, most dramatically associated with cotton, were followed by whitefly infestations in the early 1980s, and the extraordinary devastation associated with the new silver leaf whitefly in the 1990s. These outbreaks raised questions concerning the sustainability of conventional intensive agriculture in the valley. Agricultural advisors in the Meloland Cooperative Extension office made significant strides against silver leaf whitefly populations in the early 1990s. However, their efforts to change cultivation, rotation, and irrigation patterns over the long run have been fought by growers who express beliefs that the threat of massive reinfestation has disappeared. Many returned within two years to the patterns of agricultural production that generated the silver leaf whitefly infestation in the first place.[28] The EPA and USDA eventually legalized a new pesticide regime to control the silver leaf whitefly in the mid-1990s. While this has kept the lid on the economic damage the pest has done, the whitefly has been moving north and east over the last seven years, threatening crop production in Arizona and California's Central Valley.

In terms of agricultural employees, social reformers and the UFW have abundantly documented the unhealthful dietary, residential, and educational life of Mexican field workers during the labor struggles in the late 1970s (Martin, Vaupel, and Egan 1988; Mooney and Majka 1995; Moreno 1987). The struggles between growers, the UFW, and the Teamsters Union in the valley ran deep and culminated in a massive lettuce strike in 1979. While some contracts were won by the UFW, many were not, and almost none of those won were renewed five years later. The combination of increased federal and state regulation of agricultural chemicals and workers and the 1979 lettuce strike led many growers to move to newer production areas with lower labor and ecological costs. Most headed to Yuma, Arizona, while others expanded production in the Mexicali Valley. The movement of large grower-shippers out of the valley, including the sale of farmlands and closing of processing sheds, has led remaining growers to rely on poorly regulated labor contractors. Also, increased mechanization and field packing has changed the gender and age division of labor in the fields as more Mexican women and older men are hired, effectively displacing younger men previously relied upon for heavy work in the fields and sheds (Marin 1989). The expanded use of custom services, including labor contractors, revolutionized the local conditions for organizing fieldworkers as their number declined and their immediate relations with owners and managers became increasingly impersonal and tenuous. These changing labor relations were due to a convergence of factors, including internal divisions within the UFW and its consequent loss of momentum, the election of state and federal governments that were unsupportive of labor organization and protection, and the larger shifts in political alignments attendant on globalization (see Wells chapter 5; Constance, Kleiner, and Rikoon chapter 4).

In the 1990s, there was some expansion of employment in the valley (California Employment Development Department 1992a). This new employment was associated with national chain stores (retail and warehouse), fast food restaurants, the growth of geothermal energy development, and the construction of two new prisons in the valley (Imperial County Community Economic Development Department 1993). The vast majority of the new jobs paid poorly and local towns extended large tax breaks and zoning variances to the new businesses. The shifting economy affected farm laborers most sharply. At the same time that agricultural land has been transformed into strip malls and new residential tracts, the employment opportunities in construction and retail service industries generally have not been made available to men and women who once were employed in field labor.

The geothermal industries are generally tied to international energy firms and bring their own employees from outside the region. The two new state prisons have generated new construction and retail sales; however, the prisons also employ guards and administrators primarily from outside the valley, increasing the number of jobs but doing little for unemployed residents of both the Imperial and Mexicali Valleys. Whereas the region's economy was organized primarily around nonresident grower-shippers, the new economy has intensified agricultural extraction while introducing new forms of equally extractive consumer and service goods. As most of the new chain stores depend on the augmentation of purchases made by residents of the Imperial Valley by the expanding middle income and high income groups in the Mexicali Valley, any downturn in Mexican purchasing power, like the 1982 devaluation of the peso, will have great consequences for the non-agricultural redevelopment of the Imperial Valley.

The Imperial Valley faces a number of immediate problems. The extraordinary internationalization of the agricultural economy is transforming the market conditions for Imperial Valley vegetable and field crop producers. The instability of markets for Imperial Valley agricultural commodities, the ongoing decline in market control in the hands of Imperial Valley producers, and the calls upon the Colorado River water by other powerful interests, means that the historical basis of the region's economy can be expected to remain in flux as the people and representatives of the valley attempt to renegotiate the basis of their future economy and environmental conditions. Lastly, unresolved environmental issues associated with water supplies and quality, water conservation, and the healthy reproduction of the Salton Sea, and the consequences of the valley's ongoing commitment to pest control strategies associated with the pesticide treadmill (Van den Bosch 1989) remain central to the region's future development.

If present struggles resemble historical circumstances, the documentation of what is going on within and between nature, people, communities, political institutions, and economic actors in the region will not be available to scholars for some time. Nevertheless, the globalization of agricultural production and markets and the associated changes in national regulatory structures and processes will clearly have an impact on the conditions of production and life in the Imperial Valley. For now, and despite the diversification in the region's economic basis, it appears that historical patterns of ecological, social, and community crisis displacement are more likely to be reproduced in the future than these tendencies are likely to be addressed head-on in a participatory and democratic fashion.

Conclusion

In order to understand how to respond to the many forms of ecological, social, and infrastructural crisis in places like the Imperial Valley, we must develop the means to understand them in spatio-temporally situated fashion. As O'Connor's theoretical work argues, states act in ways to mediate both fiscal and legitimation crises. These crises are generated not only by contradictions within the production process itself, but also in the ways that these processes affect the natural environment and human communities. Such mediations are inevitably contingent, grounded in specific conjunctions of actors and processes. This chapter has used the history of the Imperial Valley and its present condition to concretize these theoretical claims through examination of a particular case.

Perhaps most importantly, historical and contemporary struggles over ecological, personal, and communal conditions in the Imperial Valley are remarkable in their temporal and spatial coincidence. Equally important is that all of these struggles, whether associated with the establishment of reliable conditions for agricultural profitability, the intensification and defensive displacement of changes related to the state of production relations, or the attempts to restructure social ecological relations and conditions in sustainable directions, are centrally mediated by many levels of state activity. These mediations are imbued with powerful contests over the state's promotion of accumulation and its legitimatory responsiveness to social movements seeking to defend and improve the state of ecological, personal, and communal reproduction. The state is not, however, a monolithic actor, and must be seen as fragmented and contradictory in its own right. Not only do different levels of government—local, state, and federal—perceive and respond differently to local problems, but different actors are able to influence governments depending on particular conjunctures of local and extra-local interests.

The greatest efforts to renegotiate political and infrastructural relations over water and soils, to renegotiate labor relations, practices, and law, and to redevelop the communities of the Imperial Valley occurred simultaneously in the late 1920s and 1930s, and again in the late 1970s and 1980s. Other more environmentally and economically diverse regions are likely to express less coordination in the comprehensive and broad character of such renegotiations than occurred in the Imperial valley. The clarity of the valley's environmental and political economic history shows the interrelatedness of struggles over conditions of production that are most often treated as distinct and discrete. Political-economic analyses and historical regional studies in environmental sociology provide theoretical tools and the empirical scope for building complex analyses of the many layers of global-local negotiations involved in specific historical processes. The theoretical and methodological lines suggested here stress the importance of local specificities but only as situated within wider contexts. Such perspectives are necessary as we learn to develop democratic and multidimensional policies for a sustainable future.

Chapter 3
From the National Policy to Continentalism and Globalization
The Shifting Context of Canadian Agricultural Policies

K. Murray Knuttila

Rural Saskatchewan is experiencing a continuing process of social, economic, and political transformation. The fact that the transformation involves declining numbers of farms, increasing farm size, struggling and disappearing communities, the loss of many rural services, and high levels of personal stress means that it is a crisis as well as a transformation. In the past such crises have often resulted in producers being able to convince the national government to undertake relief and emergency assistance programs; however, government responses to the current crisis are more and more characterized by inaction. Indeed, there is a common refrain coming from federal governments, that might be summarized in the following manner: "We are part of a global economy and need to restructure in order make ourselves more efficient and better able to compete."

In order to understand recent government responses it is necessary to place the ongoing transformation of Western Canadian prairie agriculture in its larger context. In one of his two classic studies of the development of Western Canada, Vernon Fowke suggests that the best way to understand the development and fate of agriculture in an industrial society is to place it within the larger economic context. He wrote:

In this study the hypothesis is advanced that agricultural policy can best be explained by an historical consideration of agricultural functions. Essential to an understanding of governmental treatment of the agricultural community, it is argued, is an historical knowledge of the uses to which agriculture has been put from time to time and from place to place. If we can learn why agricultural development was wanted at a particular time and place there arises the possibility of knowing why agriculture was encouraged or neglected, what groups were interested in its development, and the political pressures under which agricultural assistance was extended. (Fowke 1947:vii)

If we are to understand the nature of the current crisis in Western Canada it is useful to follow Fowke's advice and attempt to understand the relationship of prairie agriculture to the larger patterns of economic development in Canada. The initial section of this chapter provides an overview of recent stages in the development of capitalism as a world system. This will provide a context for understanding the role that agriculture has played vis-à-vis industry in the Canadian economy. The second section describes the basic patterns of economic development in Canada since Confederation in the context of the overall development of the capitalist world system. The final section suggests an approach to periodizing the development of agricultural policy in Canada in order to provide an understanding of the nature of the current crisis and the response of the state.

Canada, the World System, and the National Policy

In order to understand Canada we must place its essential patterns of economic development from before Confederation to the present within the context of the world capitalist system. The accumulation of capital is the core activity that literally drives this system. The conservative Canadian nationalist, George Grant, is among the diverse thinkers who have recognized this fact. Grant (1965) summarized the essence of the capitalist system in the following manner: "Capitalism is, after all, a way of life based on the principle that the most important activity is profit making" (47). In a recent essay, "The Drive for Capital," Robert Heilbroner (1992) uses the phrase "the rage for accumulation" (32) to describe the inner logic of the system that drives the continual changes that characterize capitalism:

Capital thus differs from wealth in its intrinsically dynamic character, continually changing its form from commodity into money and then back again in an endless metamorphosis that already makes clear its integral connection with the changeful nature of capitalism itself. (30)

The core activities that provide the basis for the accumulation of capital have changed radically since the emergence of the capitalist system in the early sixteenth century. Scholars such as E. K. Hunt (1990), Broadus Mitchell (1967), Paul Baran and Paul Sweezy (1966), S. B. Clough and C. W. Cole (1967), and Robert Heilbroner (1968) argue that capitalism has passed though a series of distinct phases or stages, each marked by different regimes of accumulation characterized by different levels of technical development and different social relations of production. Although there are variations among the schemas employed by these writers, the following represents a synthesis of the major epochs the system has passed through:

1500s–1770s   Mercantilism or merchant capitalism
1770s–1860s   Industrial capitalism
1860s–1930s   Corporate capitalism
1930s–1970s   Keynesian state/corporate capitalism
1970s–present Neoliberal global capitalism

[handwritten annotation: supply-side economics]

As noted, different modes of capital accumulation characterize each of these phases or periods. These differences include roles that various geographical regions and nation states have played in fostering capital accumulation in different periods. For this necessarily brief account, and following Fowke's thesis that the development of prairie agriculture has been fundamentally conditioned by the nature of the industrialization process in Canada, I will use the beginning of the process of industrialization in Canada as a convenient starting point.

Canada's history as a British colony meant that its industrial development was initially conditioned by a colonial relationship with Britain. As the work of Harold Innis (1930, 1940, 1950) demonstrated, the industrialization process in Britain offered opportunities for British investors and merchants to develop staples production regimes in the colonies. In the case of Canada, after the beginning of the nineteenth century the fishery and fur trade were supplanted by the production of timber and agricultural products in the region of the St. Lawrence. The new staples and the settlement they fostered stimulated a continual stream of immigrants out of Britain. New villages and towns complete with small craft producers, millers, brewers, and a range of artisans and others providing different services accompanied the growth of exports, population, and settlement. An expanding transportation system was developed to handle the exports and the imports that British manufactures were eager to sell abroad.

Along with these developments and changes, the first two decades of the nineteenth century witnessed the emergence of a number of new classes, including the germ of what was to become an indigenous class of industrial entrepreneurs. The established mercantile interests and colonial administrators held power in an undemocratic state structure. This produced the Rebellions of 1837/38, which in turn led to the Durham Report and the union of the two St. Lawrence colonies into the colony of Canada in 1840.

Two decades of economic growth followed the creation of a united colony on the St. Lawrence as the British and colonial government poured money into enhancing the canal and railroad systems. As Stanley Ryerson (1973) argued, the 1840s and 1850s were crucial in terms of the subsequent development of the Canadian economic and class structures because during these decades the initial stages of industrial development were established.

By the 1860s a series of crises produced a proposal to restructure the existing colonies of British North America into the new nation of Canada. Both the merchants and industrialists understood that expanding the boundaries of the colony of Canada was a prerequisite to economic development by incorporating western Canada, a region that was viewed as a potential market for industrial goods and a source of export cash crops.

A unique feature of Canada is that its formal creation was planned as part of a larger economic development strategy. Confederation was only the first step in a series of actions in order to facilitate economic development in Canada. Vernon Fowke explained the situation in these terms:

A number of important steps were necessary to the creation of a second national, economic, and political unit in British North American territory. The first of these was the creation of a national constitution. The main outlines as well as a good deal of the detail of such a constitution were provided for in the British North America Act of 1867. Development and integration were the indispensable and inseparable economic requirements. Both rested heavily on the possibility of facilitating trade among the existing colonies or provinces. Confederation removed the tariff barriers which had previously existed between the separate units, and the British North American Act provided for the completion of an intercolonial railroad by the national government. Further development, however, would require the exploitation of some vast new areas of resources, the establishment of a new frontier of investment. Attention was thus directed even before Confederation to the prospects in Rupert's Land and the Pacific colonies. (1947:7–8)

"National Policy," when used in lower case, refers to a triad of federal government policies and actions designed to facilitate industrialization between Confederation and the Great Depression (Fowke 1947:17; Mackirdy, Moir, and Zoltvany 1971:227). These policies were the establishment of a protective tariff, the settlement of the west through land incentives and various forms of agricultural assistance, and the building of a transcontinental Canadian railroad. When used in upper case it typically only refers to the protective tariffs of 1878–79. The policies promoting industrialization and agricultural development in the west were, historian Donald Creighton argues (1955:120),

"two closely related national policies," with the building of the transcontinental railway providing "the physical link between the two."

The nature of the development that was envisioned has been subject to a number of interpretations. It is generally agreed that at the
time of Confederation the major capitalist activity in Canada was confined to commercial and merchant activities. A segment of the capitalist class was of the opinion that this was the kind of activity that should
be expanded. There were, however, other interests in this class who
proposed alternate forms of development for the new nation. This
group wished to see the new nation become involved in industrial
production rather than confining their activities to circulation. According to Stanley Ryerson, "The new ruling class of colonial capitalists comprised a sort of patchwork of variegated interests" (1973:276).
He identifies its main components as remnants of the mercantile
bourgeoisie, aspiring industrialists, financiers, transportation entrepreneurs, and representatives of the Church (Ryerson 1973:167–77).

The balance of power among these various interests was not worked
out until after the formal establishment of the new nation. It was clear
to all members of the dominant social group that the initial task was
the establishment of a formally independent nation. The relative positions of commerce and industry would be worked out later. The formal establishment of the new nation in 1867 with the passing of
the British North America Act by the British Parliament provided the
framework within which the various fractions of capital would develop
their subsequent activities.

During the immediate post-Confederation period MacDonald headed
a coalition government. The expansionary thrust of the new state was
evident in actions such as the acquisition of Rupert's Land by the federal government and the creation of the new provinces of Manitoba
and British Columbia in 1870–71. These actions provided the basis
for securing the western regions of Canada by the Dominion government. Through military and diplomatic action the government then
began to alienate the aboriginal population from the land, thus preparing the area for settlement. The government provided the legal basis
for western settlement in 1872 with the passing of the Dominion Lands
Act. Under the terms of this act settlers could secure title to a quarter
section of land by beginning cultivation within a specified time, with
the only cash outlay for the land being a nominal registration fee. The
free land was designed to attract settlers to the area who would produce cash crops that the eastern commercial interests would handle.
Industries and manufacturers in central Canada would also fill the
needs of the settlers for industrial goods. A Cabinet member, Charles

Tupper, speaking in the House of Commons, explained the essential role of the west in the national policy:

No person can look abroad over the Dominion without feeling that the Great NorthWest Territory is the district to which we must look for our strength and development. . . . not only may we look for strength by reason of an additional Customs Revenue from the increased population of that Territory, but we must look upon that western country as a field for the manufacturing industries of the older and more settled parts of Canada. Every person acquainted with this country knows we have exhausted to some extent its breadgrowing power, but under the National Policy that Canada has adopted, we must look forward not only to building up thriving centres of industries and enterprise all over this portion of the country, but to obtaining a market for those industries after they have been established; and I say where is there a greater market than that magnificent granary of the North-West, which, filled up with a thriving and prosperous population, will make its demands upon Ontario, Quebec, Nova Scotia, and New Brunswick for these manufacturing products that we, for many years, will be so well able to supply. (House of Commons Debates July 15, 1880)

Other politicians were to repeat the theme, as the following statement by Clifford Sifton, Minister of the Interior, in 1904 indicates:

I do have to say a word as to what we expect western Canada will do for itself. But it will not be enough that it shall do only for itself. It is a portion of Canada. Canada is a national entity. Canada is an organism, and you cannot develop a single part of an organism satisfactorily. Each and all parts must contribute to the vitality of the whole. What then will western Canada do for the Canadian organism? Sir, it will give a vast and profitable traffic to its railways and steamship lines. It will give remunerative employment to tens of thousands of men, to keep the permanent way in order, to man the trains and ships, and to engage in the multitude of occupations which gather around the great system of transportation. It will do more. It will build up our Canadian seaports. It will create volume of ocean traffic which shall place Canada in short time in its proper position as a maritime nation. It will furnish a steady and remunerative business to the manufacturers of eastern Canada, giving assured prosperity where uncertainty now exists. These are things which the west will do for the east. In a word, I may say it will send a flood of new blood from one end of this great country to the other, through every artery of commerce. (Quoted in Bliss 1966:202–3)

A year later Sir Willfred Laurier spoke to the Canadian Manufacturers Association in similar terms:

They [the settlers filling up the prairie west] will require clothes, they will require furniture, they will require implements, they will require shoes—and I hope you can furnish them to them . . . they will require everything that man has to be supplied with. It is your ambition, it is my ambition also, that this scientific tariff of ours will make possible that every shoe that has to be worn in those prairies shall be a Canadian shoe; that every yard of cloth that can be marketed there shall be a yard of cloth produced in Canada; and so on and so on. (Mackirdy, Moir, and Zoltvany 1971:135)

The settlement of western Canada with an agricultural population was an intentional and deliberate process designed to integrate the west into a burgeoning national economy. The national policy of tariff protection was important for both the commercial and merchant interests of the east as well as for those desiring to establish an industrial economy provided the necessary conditions for its acceptance by both of the major parties. As the century ended and the Liberal government replaced the Conservatives for a time, the main features of the plan remained the same. J. M. S. Careless (1986:312) confirms: "It spelt success at long last for the National Policy, which the Liberals now took over as their own. The National Policy of protection was firmly fixed on Canada from then on since both major parties accepted it." The decades following the turn of the century finally brought about the successful completion of the national policy of industrial development. The transportation link had been in place since 1885, the protective tariff since 1878–79, and now the third component, western settlement, was added. Easterbrook and Aitken summarize the major factors responsible for these developments:

The salient features of the great decade 1901–11 are easily distinguished. After thirty years of waiting and frustrated hopes it was at last Canada's turn to be drawn into the world network of trade and investment. Not only was there stimulus provided by such developments as the rapidly growing demand of the industrial countries for primary products, the zeal of British investors for capital exports to other areas than the United States, and the end of the land frontier of the American west; in addition and as important as any of these was the spectacular rate of technological advance in the United States economy of the late nineteenth and early twentieth centuries, a consequence in part of the huge inflow of cheap labour from southeastern Europe and a remarkably high level of domestic investment in new technologies of production and distribution. Canada's ability to borrow her neighbour's innovations easily and freely contributed greatly to progress in both agriculture and industry. (1956:483)

The success of the national policy in terms of the settlement of the west can best be illustrated by examining population figures. In 1901, four years before the province of Saskatchewan was created, the estimated population of the area was just over 91,000, representing just over 1.5 percent of the total Canadian population. By 1931 the population of Saskatchewan reached 922,000, or 8.9 percent of all Canadians.

The majority of these new arrivals were involved in farming. Between 1901 and 1931 the number of farms jumped from about 13,500 to 136,500. The total acreage under cultivation rose from about 3.8 million acres to nearly 56 million.

Within the development of Canada as a whole, the western regions fulfilled a number of explicit roles. James McCrorie summarizes these functions:

> The decision to settle the west was part of an overall plan to develop a national industrial economy. The National Policy treated agricultural development in the West as functional, yet subordinate to this goal. The tariff policy was designed to foster industrial growth in the East; the railway policy was designed to integrate the Atlantic with the Pacific and provide transportation of goods and services across Canada. The immigration program was designed to create new markets for Canadian products in the west and to provide a new investment frontier for the East; agriculture was developed to serve an emerging industrial complex. (1964:19)

By the end of the nineteenth century, the national government, through its policies, had populated western Canada with a class of agricultural producers, an agrarian petite bourgeoisie, tightly linked to eastern interests. These producers served as an essential market for the industrial goods produced in central Canada. The agrarian community in the west also provided agricultural products that were handled, processed, and exported by different interests within the domestic business elite. The settlement of the west provided a tremendous demand for credit and financing, a demand that benefited the banking and financial sector.

The Evolution of Canadian Agricultural Policy

Let us now focus our attention more on agricultural policy and the current crisis in Saskatchewan. The material above is intended to provide a backdrop against which we can begin to understand the present crisis and the responses of federal governments. In what follows I examine the development and evolution of federal agricultural policy in order to explain the responses of federal governments to the present crisis. For analytical purposes I divide Canadian agricultural policy into three overall phases or stages that somewhat match the epochs outlined above. During the first phase, lasting from Confederation to the Great Depression, federal governments adopted a series of policies and undertook a number of measures to facilitate the establishment and expansion of agricultural production in western Canada. Simply put, the focus of agricultural policy between 1867 and 1930 was on the establishment, enlargement, and maintenance of an agricultural population on the prairies. The second phase of agricultural policy encompasses the eras of the Great Depression, World War II, and the postwar boom. During this period the orientation of federal agricultural policies was toward managing crises and maintaining the structures and institutions that had been established in the formative period of the national policy. Assisted by the significant benefits of hindsight, we can now see that the late 1960s marked the beginning of the third period of agricultural policy. The economic difficulties that many producers were beginning to experience during that decade prompted the establishment of the now famous Task Force on Agriculture in April 1967. The 1970 report of the Task Force, *Canadian Agriculture in the Seventies,* was a watershed document, pointing to a new understanding of the role of agriculture in the Canadian economy and the third era in agricultural policy.

Phase One: The National Policy Realized, Establishment, and Expansion

During the initial period of agricultural development in the west, federal governments demonstrated a consistent willingness to facilitate western agricultural settlement. As we have seen, in the first order land was made virtually free under the provisions of the Dominion Lands Act. In addition, the government assisted farming and farmers through the establishment of a series of experimental farms to produce new varieties of cereal grains more suited to the prairie climate and growing season. The government established low statutory freight rates for grain through the Crow's Nest Pass Agreement (for some differing perspectives on the issue see B. Wilson 1981:173–85; Gallagher 1983; and Darling 1980). In addition, as we shall see below, the government was more than willing to regulate and oversee the operation of the grain handling system in response to agrarian demands. Indeed, perhaps there is no stronger indicator of the importance of prairie agriculture to the federal government and its industrialization strategy than the extent to which the various agrarian protest movements were able to have the federal government intervene in the handling, storage, and sale of their cereal grain crops. As settlement proceeded a significant agrarian protest movement arose. This movement has been extensively studied from a variety of perspectives (Lipset 1971; Macpherson 1953; Wood 1975; Morton 1950; McCormack 1977; Laycock 1990; Conway 1994; Sharp 1997; Smillie 1991). For the purposes of this chapter we will demonstrate that during Phase one, when farmers demanded action in regulating and even replacing the private grain trade, they truly had the government's ear. Let us review some key developments in the grain marketing system during this period.

One of the major events of this era was the collapse of the international wheat marketing system with the onslaught of the First World War. In Canada the initial problem caused by the war was oversupply as the Canadian government sought to dispose of the 1915 crop in a world market made considerably smaller by trade restrictions that applied to a number of major European markets. During 1915 the situation changed, however, and it soon became apparent that rather than facing the problem of disposing of existing stocks it was a matter of coming up with sufficient quantities of wheat to meet the orders coming in from the Allies. The federal government moved quickly to solve the initial problem by commandeering all available wheat stocks at Port Arthur, Fort William, and points east. As the war situation continued to develop the problem of providing sufficient foodstuffs for the Allied powers continued to grow more serious. Many European nations moved away from open market purchasing to centralized state controlled purchasing. In Canada the open market continued to operate until the purchaser for the British Royal Commission literally cornered the wheat market and the federal government was forced to actively intervene with the establishment of the Board of Grain Supervisors.

While direct government involvement in the marketing and handling of wheat was action forced on the Canadian government by the world market situation, the western producers generally supported the move. After realizing that the Board actually tended to stabilize prices many in the agrarian community generally approved of situation. There was little agrarian agitation on the issue until 1919 when the open market was reestablished in Canada. Although some agrarian producers were opposed to the reestablishment of the open market, the government went ahead with the decision. Following the reestablishment of the open market, including futures trading, the price of wheat increased rapidly. In the United States and most parts of Europe open market trading had not yet resumed and in the face of the rapid price increases in Canada the federal government moved to curtail the operation of the open market. On July 30, 1919, the federal government created the Canadian Wheat Board as the sole marketing and purchasing agent (C. F. Wilson 1979:92).

The first wheat board was only a temporary measure scheduled to have jurisdiction for one year. As the year passed the question of the board's future began to loom large. Among the agricultural producers substantial splits emerged with one faction arguing for a continued government presence in the grain handling system through the wheat board, while another faction sought a return to the prewar system. The federal government soon made it apparent that it would not reappoint the board. The segment of the agrarian petite bourgeoisie that was convinced that the wheat board was the solution to many of their problems greeted the news with protest. The debate that ensued was important in terms of the larger development of the movement because it clearly indicated the emergence of important divisions among the producers. As the debate raged on the government announced its decision to return to the open market, an event that occurred on August 18, 1920. The reopening of full operations on the Winnipeg Grain Exchange was followed by a precipitous drop in wheat prices due to the British withdrawl from the market and the imposition of a tariff on imports by the U.S. (C. F. Wilson 1978:171–72). Not surprisingly there were calls for the board's reestablishment.

While some producers sought to have the wheat board reestablished others began to develop an alternate strategy: the producer pool. It was argued that the essential benefits which the board had brought to the producers could be provided by some form of a voluntary producer-operated and controlled pool. The issue was debated within the movement, in the House of Commons, and in special hearings of the Standing Committee on Agriculture and Colonization. In 1922 the federal government did present a bill to reestablish a form of the wheat board, although the government's interpretation of its constitutional powers resulted in a board that differed in important ways from the initial board. By the middle of the 1920s Canadian wheat was primarily marketed through the open market on the Winnipeg Grain Exchange. At the local level farmers sold their grain through producer managed pools, through cooperatives, or through or the private grain trade.

In summary then, the period from the turn of the century to the Great Depression marks one of the most rapid periods of economic development in Canadian history. In essence the national policy "worked to a tee" as the farmers filling the prairies served as a tariff protected expanding market for Canadian industry while producing export cash crops and making profitable demands on the Canadian banking industry. In addition, by the twenties a new sector of the Canadian economy was opening up as the exploitation of new Canadian resources such as pulp and paper, minerals, and hydroelectric power began. Though a significant proportion of the investment that was occurring was in fact undertaken by emerging U.S.-based multinationals, little concern was expressed because investment from any source yielded growth and development and the national policy was about growth and development.

The discussion above highlights the central role that the west, and its predominately agricultural population, was designated to play in the Canadian industrial development strategy known as the "national policy." As I noted above, the national policy is best understood as a series of policies and measures designed to facilitate industrial development via a tariff protected domestic industry and the creation of an expanding market by way of the settlement of the west with a population of independent agrarian commodity producers, or, if you prefer, an agrarian petite bourgeoisie. The agrarian petite bourgeoisie was to serve a dual role as consumers of Canadian manufactured products and producers of export cash crops. All fractions of capital benefited from western settlement. Those engaged in manufacturing had an expanding market, while those with capital invested in the transportation, financial, and export trade sectors also prospered.

We have seen that, in addition to the triad of actual policies which made up MacDonald's national policy (tariffs, western settlement, and the construction of a transcontinental railroad), successive federal governments enacted other measures to facilitate the establishment of the wheat economy. As was noted, these actions included the establishment of a system of experimental farms to facilitate research into new varieties of cereal grains and systematic and ongoing investigations and regulation of the activities and operation of the grain trade. Federal governments were also willing to support various cooperative ventures, provide government owned terminal elevators, and, when needed, intervene in the marketing of wheat. It is clear that key decision makers in the state throughout the entire period subscribed to the viewpoint of the Minister of Agriculture who stated in 1886: "There is no industry in which we are all so deeply interested as that of agriculture, and we feel that everything which can be done for the farmers should be done by the Parliament" (House of Commons Debates April 30, 1886:962). As we shall see, the end of the 1920s brought the completion of the national policy, but before the potential benefits of the new economic reality could be fully appreciated a series of catastrophic events forced federal governments to begin to focus on maintenance and stability, not building.

Phase Two: Depression, War, and Continentalism: Crisis Management and Maintenance

The thirty year period of significant, albeit with minor interruptions, expansion came to an abrupt halt with the onset of the Great Depression. The extent of the crisis is illustrated by the fact that some provinces were so close to total bankruptcy that in 1937 the federal government undertook a full-scale review of the political structures of the nation. As a result a Royal Commission on Dominion Provincial Relations was established. One of the important documents to come out of the process was *The Rowell/Sirois Report* (Smiley 1964), an historical review of Canadian Confederation. The study concluded that the depression era ushered in a change in the Canadian political economy and the role of the state in building a unique Canadian federalism. Up until the depression Dominion governments had pursued, subject to minor hesitations and variations, a number of national policies that brought about an economic integration of the country and helped make political unity a fact. The Great Depression destroyed markets for many Canadian products while the catastrophic drought in the West literally drove farmers to the brink of starvation. Social discontent and the threat it posed to the system spurred governments to take several different types of actions in an effort to stimulate the economy.

Like many western governments the federal government instituted Keynesian style make-work projects in an effort to increase aggregate demand. Canadian governments also attempted to increase exports of staple products through the negotiation of international trade agreements. At first Canada increased tariffs, but the newly elected Liberal government soon realized they could not go toe-to-toe with the major industrial powers so they began to discuss tariff reductions, at first with Commonwealth partners and then with the United States. While the impact of these alterations to Canadian tariffs may have been minor, the significance of this change in policy was enormous. For the first time since the MacDonald Conservatives established their policies, a Canadian government announced its willingness to begin an alternate economic development strategy. It was in essence the beginning of the end for the historic national policy (Norrie and Owram 1991:503–5).

One problem which demanded almost immediate action was the potential collapse of the wheat pools caused by the dramatic drop in the price of the wheat which they had previously purchased and had in storage awaiting resale. This required federal action if only to avoid a potential disaster for the entire banking system. The intervention of the federal government ultimately involved the recreation of the Canadian Wheat Board. In 1935 legislation was passed creating the wheat board and giving it broad powers. The bill was eventually passed; however the situation was further complicated by the Bennett government's defeat in the 1935 election.

As the debates and controversies surrounding the wheat board continued, the new federal government once more appointed a Royal Commission to investigate the situation. Appointed under terms of reference set out in June 1936, the Turgeon Grain Commission was to investigate a number of issues, by far the most important being the basic structure of the Canadian grain marketing system. The merits of compulsory vs. voluntary pooling and compulsory vs. voluntary wheat boards were the most vital issues to be addressed. After extensive national hearings the Turgeon Commission issued its report in May 1938. The long report addressed numerous aspects of the grain trade both nationally and internationally. In terms of the central questions of the role of the wheat board, the private grain trade, and the wheat pools, the report recommended the resumption of the full operation of the Winnipeg Grain Exchange. In addition to the recommendation that the open market system be reinstated the report further demonstrated its private sector orientation in suggesting that the wheat pools conduct their business in accordance with the practices established by the private grain trade:

Those who buy our wheat are shrewd businessmen interested in getting a good product at a price measured in relation to their necessities and to the value of competing products. They do their buying quietly and on considerations which they have reduced to a science. It seems to me that selling also should be conducted without undue publicity, on business principles, by men who keep themselves free to shape and reshape their policy from day to day, if necessary, to meet shifting conditions. There is no reason why a pool should not be operated on such lines. (Royal Inquiry Commission 1938:93)

Many of the issues addressed by the Turgeon Commission were again discussed at a major conference on grain marketing held in Winnipeg in December 1938. Attended by some 200 representatives of the grain trade, government, and agriculture, the conference pointed out the continued disagreements concerning the basic contours of future grain trade policy (C. F. Wilson 1978:518). When Parliament resumed on January 12, 1939 the Throne Speech noted that the government would take action regarding the issue: "Bills will be introduced to regulate the grain exchange along the lines laid down in the report of the royal commission on grain marketing, to revise the Canada Grain Act, and to assist further in the marketing of farm products" (House of Commons Debates, January 12, 1939:4).

The announcement in the Throne Speech was followed by legislative action. In May 1939 the Board of Grain Commissioners passed the Grain Futures Act, providing for closer supervision and regulation of the operations of the Winnipeg Grain Exchange. The same year saw the enactment of the Wheat Co-operative Marketing Act, which was essentially designed to facilitate the establishment of producer pools via government guarantees of a minimum price for wheat marketed through such pools (MacGibbon 1952:26). A related piece of legislation, the Agricultural Products Co-operative Marketing Act, extended these provisions to products other than wheat (C. F. Wilson 1978:606).

The actions we have been describing were necessitated by crises associated with the Great Depression, but soon there was another problem with quite a different root cause: agricultural overproduction. The return of more normal climatic conditions resulted in the second largest crop to that date being harvested in 1939. As producers expanded production in anticipation of an increased wartime demand in the 1940 crop year, the government was faced with a mushrooming surplus of wheat. Now the problem, which was both economic and political, was how to reduce production. In April 1940 the government took the first action in this direction through an Order-in-Council measure to pay compensation to producers for reduced acreage. That measure was followed by the Wheat Acreage Reduction Act of 1942 (MacGibbon 1952:55).

The massive unsold supplies of various cereal grains led to another action, this time by the Canadian Wheat Board. In an effort to regulate deliveries at various delivery points so as to provide more equal access to the market for all producers, a policy of utilizing permit books was created for wheat, oats, and barley. Producers were required to present their permit books that contained a stated authorized acreage for the producer. This was the basis for determining the amount of grain the producer was allowed to deliver. The permit books were designed to prevent any given producer from selling more than their allotted quota. This method of controlling deliveries was again used in the 1943–44 crop year when producers were only allowed to deliver 14 bushels per authorized acre of production.

As the year 1943 passed, the Canadian and indeed the world cereal grain picture changed again in a rather dramatic fashion. Partial crop failures in the United States and eastern Canada combined with increased wartime demands began to deplete both the American and Canadian reserves. As a result the price of wheat began to increase, moving from below 90 cents a bushel in March to over $1.23 by November. The Canadian government was now faced with a new problem. The war had forced Britain to adopt a centralized purchasing agent for its cereal grains. The agent, the Cereal Import Committee, sought to do business with the Canadian Wheat Board on an agency to agency basis. This system required substantial stocks in the hands of the wheat board: With the price of wheat rising, however, producers had the choice of accepting the wheat board's low initial price and a later final payment, or going to the open market for a now high payment upon delivery. Producers were choosing the latter. In addition, the federal government was concerned that a rapid rise in the price of wheat would undermine its efforts to control the general domestic price structure and hamper its commitments to use wheat as part of mutual aid agreements. The prospect of rising prices for wheat was thus not attractive and the federal government moved to make the wheat board the sole marketing agent for wheat. MacGibbon (1952:64) has noted the irony of the reestablishment of the board at this time: "The earlier theory had been that compulsory marketing would bring higher prices, but when compulsory marketing was actually established it was to keep prices under control."

After the war, in 1947, legislation to amend the Canadian Wheat Board Act was passed by the government. The amending legislation actually increased the powers of the board and codified in legislation many actions and regulations passed by Orders-in-Council during the war. The amendments were debated in four days and passed by a vote of 172 to 7, an indication of the overall political support for the continuation of orderly marketing. The explicit reasons given at this time for the retention and even extension of the board was its importance in carrying through the Canadian supply end of a Canadian British Wheat Agreement.

The British Wheat Agreement was the outcome of a series of international bilateral and multilateral negotiations after the war which sought to prevent international grain market instabilities in the postwar period. A series of International Wheat Conferences dating back to 1931 had been held; these, however, came to naught. The agreement signed between Canada and Britain was, to that date, the single largest bilateral wheat agreement in history. The agreement provided for the sale of specified amounts of wheat in each of the first three years at a specified price with a price to be negotiated for the amounts delivered in the last two years. While there was considerable subsequent debate concerning the merits of the measure, it was clear that the government was keenly interested in any measures which would provide some basis of stability in the wheat economy.

The wheat board was initially established under powers assumed by the federal government under the War Measures Act and thus there were no challenges to the federal government's right to intervene. After the war the powers of the board were retained and extended to July 31, 1950 under the provisions of the National Emergency Transitional Powers Act. The federal government, under pressure from a variety of interests, extended the mandate of the wheat board, but made the extension dependent on the provinces passing permitting legislation. Producer support for the concept of orderly marketing resulted in immediate action. Thus by 1949–50 the board was the sole agent for marketing of wheat, oats, and barley. Opponents of what was to become called "orderly marketing" challenged the constitutionality of the board in court in a case that reached the Supreme Court of Canada. The power of the federal government to enact such legislation was upheld (Schwartz 1959:60–62).

Continental Drift: The Canadian Economy in Transition

In terms of the larger national economy, it is clear that as important as the government spending on domestic infrastructure projects and tariff reductions were, it was the state spending that accompanied the preparation for and conduct of the war that ended the depression in Canada. The war effort spurred the government to greatly enlarge its role in the Canadian economy. The war effort also promoted coordination and cooperative ventures involving American and Canadian capital in industrial production. By the end of the war many Canadian companies had learned that such arrangements were advantageous, and in the aftermath of the war many Canadian companies sought to retain the benefits of continental integration.

The development of a continental economic philosophy need not surprise us because it is fully in keeping with the central logic of capitalism, the drive to accumulate on an expanded basis. George Grant summarized the point both theoretically and historically in the following manner:

[A]fter 1940 it was not in the interests of the economically powerful to be nationalists. Most of them made more money by being representatives of American capitalism and setting up branch plants. No class in Canada more welcomed the American managers than the established wealthy of Montreal and Toronto, who had once seen themselves the pillars of Canada. Nor should this be surprising. Capitalism is, after all, a way of life based on the principle that the most important activity is profit making. That activity led the wealthy in the direction of continentalism. (1965:47)

The shift that Grant refers to must be understood in the context of the significant changes that occurred in the structure of the Canadian ruling class in the postdepression and postwar period. The precise composition of the capitalist class in Canada has been a matter of contention for some time. Robert Brym (1993) presents an excellent summary of the debates that emerged around the issue of whether Canada was dominated by a mercantile/financial elite who deliberately eschewed efforts to industrialize. I find Brym's conclusion that both sides in the debate tended to overstate their arguments compelling and agree with his claim that "the Canadian capitalist class cannot at present be characterized either as purely continentalist and dependent or as purely independent of foreign interests" (37). While there was significant debate among academics as to whether the national policy was *intended* to attract foreign investment, the fact is that this tended to happen. Perhaps of more importance is the fact that, by its very nature, capital knows no boundaries, and it flows into areas where profit is to be made. As a result, during the three decades of prosperity that ushered in the twentieth century Canada was the recipient of considerable American direct investment. This process was exacerbated during the Second World War as the Allies coordinated their war effort, and it continued unabated during the postwar boom. The net impact of consistent high patterns of direct foreign investment was a capitalist class with some unique features. In his analysis of the Canadian class structure Henry Veltmeyer notes:

The extensive foreign ownership of Canadian firms has created three distinctive categories of Canadian capitalists: (1) indigenous capitalists who are involved in Canadian-controlled corporations; (2) foreign capitalists who serve in Canada as representatives or delegates of the international (usually American) capitalist class in corporations under its control: and (3) Canadian capitalists who are involved in foreign-controlled corporations. (1986:39)

As a result of the existence of a ruling class that contains powerful and important domestic, foreign, and foreign-associated interests, Canada occupies a somewhat unique position in the world economic and political arena. William Carroll (1985:45) refers to Canada as "the example of a middle-range imperialist power in an increasingly internationalized economy." Whereas the founders and early proponents of the national policy did envision the possibility of a Canadian domestic industrial economy with an adequate domestic market, the depression, the economic integration brought on by the war effort and the cumulative impact of continuing investment from the U.S. changed the nature of the Canadian ruling class and its economic outlook. Jorge Niosi (1981) uses the phrase "continental nationalism" to describe the economic philosophy of the postwar capitalist class in Canada. By this he means an approach that accepted a significant but specialized role for Canada in a North American continental economy. In an important analysis that explains some basic dimensions of Canada to Americans, Joseph Roberts (1998) refers to Canada as a "rich dependency" with a ruling class that represents both domestic and international interests.

In short, Grant is saying that Canadian nationalism was no longer a philosophical orientation that made sense to the major business elites. Whether we can attribute the postwar boom in Canada to the decision of the Canadian ruling class to adopt an increasingly continentalist economic strategy is not clear, but it is clear that Canada did experience a postwar boom while its rulers embraced continentalism. As we shall see, however, the significant period of economic and population growth that marked the decades of the 1950s and 1960s was in Canada, as in many other jurisdictions, characterized by growing government deficits and debts.

Returning to the agricultural sector, during and after World War II Canadian cereal grain farmers once more experienced a period of growth. Rapid mechanization of many farms accelerated the process of concentration and centralization of capital in agriculture. Many farmers who were unable to afford the new technologies left the land, migrating most often to other provinces. The number of farmers in Saskatchewan fell from 139,000 in 1941 to 93,925 in 1961 (Statistics Canada 1941, 1961). Some of the remaining farms became larger and more capital intensive. A process of differentiation within the farming community was beginning to produce an agrarian class structure with clearer divisions between various fractions.

Even a cursory review of the literature on the precise class position occupied by farmers within the context of an industrial capitalist economy is beyond the purview of this chapter. I view class as essentially defined in terms of structural position or relationship to society's productive capacities, market relations, and the productive assets brought to market. When we examine the economic structures of Canada and focus on agricultural production, we immediately become aware of the existence of individuals who hold formal possession of agricultural land and equipment and who largely operate these productive resources without purchasing labor power. These individuals derive income from the sale of the commodities they and their families (or others providing unpaid labor) produce. There is, of course, a major debate involved here; however, for want of a better term we will refer to this class of individuals as independent commodity producers (See Friedmann 1978, 1986, 1993b; Hedley 1985; Ghorayshi 1986).

If we examine independent commodity producers in Canada, it quickly becomes apparent that this class is not a homogeneous class. Independent commodity producers are differentiated in economic terms on the basis of numerous factors including the commodities they produce, the region they live in, the size of their units, the structures that influence how they market their commodities, their degree of mechanization, their income level, and their family and household organization. Conway and Stirling (1988) have examined some of the dimensions of these divisions in Saskatchewan. Their work makes clear that the process of the development of internal class divisions, class fractions, has been underway for some time in Saskatchewan. Though we still lack a completely adequate mode of understanding these divisions in both theoretical and empirical terms, we can tentatively identify three major divisions among cereal grain based farmers in Saskatchewan

There seems to be a fraction of large scale producers employing the most recent technological developments in a form of agricultural production that is highly mechanized and dependent on the use of chemicals, fertilizers, the newest strains of crops, and so on. These producers are also increasingly the employers of wage labor. There is also a middle fraction of producers operating what might be termed the "traditional family farm." It must be noted that this fraction itself is highly diverse and heterogeneous, utilizing a number of different strategies and household structures in their efforts to survive the crisis (Hansen and Muszynski 1990; Diaz and Gingrich 1992). This fraction tends not to employ wage labor and is not as financially capable of adopting all the newest innovations in terms of technology and mechanization. The third major fraction represents those producers whose farm-based incomes are not sufficient to make them viable. Often labeled part-time farmers, these producers are most often the smallest in terms of farm size and more reliant on the income generated by off-farm activities for day to day survival.

While this description lacks empirical and theoretical rigor it does, I would argue, represent a sketch of the broad parameters of the changing class structure in cereal grain production. There is substantial evidence that a similar process is occurring in other countries (Lawrence 1987). The central point which has been made by Lawrence as well as Stirling and Conway draws the political implications of these developing splits. There was a time when cereal grain producers were a relatively homogeneous fraction and thus more or less shared common problems, concerns, values, and political positions. That time, however, has passed and it is increasingly apparent that the possibility of concerted political action on behalf of a broad cross section of cereal grain producers is only a remote possibility. This fact obviously has important implications for how producers do and are able to respond to crises.

The federal government, whether by intent of not, encouraged the process through measures such as the crop insurance program of 1959 and the establishment of the Farm Credit Corporation the same year. In spite of the apparent prosperity, all was not well. By the end of the 1960s the dynamics of the market generated a cost/price squeeze that spelled difficult times for some cereal grain producers. The input side of cereal grain production, for example the production of machinery, fertilizers, and chemicals, is dominated by a relatively small number of corporations, most of them multinationals. Smaller equipment and service providers exist; however their role in the overall picture is minor. Heilbroner (1968) and Baran and Sweezy (1966) argue that large multinational corporations tend not to engage in systematic price cutting behaviour. In an era of oligopoly, price setting and price leading tends to be the rule. As a result the costs farmers face for their inputs have been on a quite steady upward trajectory at least since World War II.

On the output side the picture is different. Despite the development of class fractions amid the loss of thousands of farms, producers of cereal grain did not disappear. Because of their numbers and the isolated nature of their production, these producers are not able, individually or collectively, to impact the price they receive for the product they sell on the market. As a result commodity prices have experienced cyclical patterns. In recent years the subsidy policies of the United States and the European Community have further destabilized commodity process driving cereal grain prices down to levels not seen since the Great Depression. The cereal grain producers in Saskatchewan were thus squeezed between escalating costs and unstable prices, facing periods during which their profit margins expand and others during which they lose money. Instability and a steadily declining number of producers was the result.

Reduced to brutally simple terms it means that the producer is squeezed on the input side by costs that tend to always escalate while on the output side there is fierce competition with fluctuating and variable prices. As a result there are times when input costs rise faster than output prices. Needless to say, during these times farmers lose money. In response to growing farmer discontent the federal government investigated Canadian agriculture and a task force report issued in 1969 recommended a radical restructuring of Canadian agriculture that would include the elimination of about two-thirds of the producers. This was quite a change from the era of the national policy when western agriculture was considered to be an essential element of a prosperous national economy!

In summary then, the period from about 1930 through the two decades following the Second World War witnessed a new orientation to Canadian agricultural policy. Rather than seeing agriculture as an essential building block in a domestic industrialization scheme, successive governments struggled to maintain and stabilize the overall system. As a result we have significant government efforts to stabilize the grain marketing problems caused by the depression and the war. In addition, the major drought that ravaged the west brought on further government interventions in the form of the Prairie Farm Rehabilitation Act (1935) and the Prairie Farm Assistance Act (1939). Even after the end of the depression and the war which facilitated the end of the depression, federal governments continued to attempt to stabilize and maintain agricultural production and prices through a series of legislative initiatives including amendments to the wheat board, negotiations regarding international wheat agreements, and measures such as the Farm Improvements Loan Act of 1944, the 1959 Crop Insurance Act, and the establishment of the Farm Credit Corporation and the Agricultural Rehabilitation and Development Act. We thus see the establishment of the Turgeon Grain Inquiry Commission, the creation of a permanent wheat board, the 1939 Grain Futures Act, and the regulation of the activities of the Winnipeg Grain Exchange by the Board of Grain Commissioners as illustrative of ongoing government efforts to build a consensus, stabilize incomes, retain farmers, all in a valiant effort to save the entire system from collapse.

In spite of the fact that agricultural policy in the postwar era was geared to maintaining the status quo, the dynamics of the world capitalist system, the evolution of the Canadian economy, and the social organization of western Canadian agriculture itself were all changing and transforming the external and internal context of the region and its producers. In terms of agricultural policy, the severity of the crisis and the overall threat that it represented to the entire social, economic, and political system forced the federal government into some immediate actions.

If we want to understand these changes we need to return to the more macroeconomic level, where it could be argued that the logic of the era we are calling Keynesian corporate/state capitalism contained the seeds of its own transformation. By the end of the 1960s the success of the Marshall Plan began to create problems in the international market as western European and Japanese corporations challenged the traditional markets of American based multinationals. Added to this were the problems associated with growing government debts, debts to be sure which had in large part been incurred as a result of spending in areas that directly benefited the corporate sectors. Other international events such as the emergence of OPEC accentuated the instability of the international system until by the 1970s another crisis loomed.

Phase Three: The Restructuring of Prairie Agriculture in the Global Era

By the decade of the 1970s the growing international competition which accompanied the fiscal crisis of the state in many western nations gave rise to a sustained and well articulated critique of Keynesian economics and the state practices that have sustained the system since the Great Depression. The popularization of supply side and monetarist economics and governments committed to state cutbacks under the banner of so-called neoconservative (correctly neoliberal) philosophies ushered in a new era of capitalist development.

The rhetoric of deregulation, fiscal responsibility, and freeing the market from the fetters and burdens of government intervention and interference informed the actions and policies of more and more governments. As the market is given a freer hand, its inherent logic will, of course, come to dominate. This will mean a still greater concentration and centralization of capital. To the extent that government regulations since the turn of the century have prevented the emergence of monopolies, it seems safe to assume that the removal of those regulations will lead to the emergence of larger and more powerful blocks of capital in many sectors of the economy.

In current vogue, the terms "restructuring" and "globalization" are illustrative of the kinds of processes we might expect capitalist development to bring. The limitations imposed on nation-states by the terms and conditions of international agreements such as the General Agreement on Tariffs and Trade, as well as the ongoing authority and power of agencies such as the International Monetary Fund all point toward a global economy in which the power of internationalized capital is supreme. Nation-states, national economies, and even capital with a regional or national base seem to pale in the face of global capital supported by transnational "international" accords. The accumulation strategies and plans of giant multinational corporations are increasingly based on calculations concerning inputs, labor supplies, and markets that are truly global in scope.

In terms of the direction and objectives of federal agricultural policy, it is now clear that the 1960s were the beginning of a transitional era. The 1970 *Report of the Task Force on Agriculture* (Task Force on Agriculture 1970) suggested that the problems that agriculture was facing were the result of a series of national and international processes, and that the eventual result would inevitably be a radical restructuring of Canadian agriculture. Indeed the key recommendations all pointed to a new era in agriculture and agricultural policy in which there would be fewer producers and in which governments would play a diminishing role while market forces played a greater role.

The political reactions to the *Task Force Report* were immediate and varied, with some lauding it for being a progressive and foreword looking blueprint for a rational restructuring of Canadian and prairie agriculture, while others argued that the recommendations were a prescription for decimating Canadian federal agricultural policy.

We must keep in mind the fact that western Canadian agriculture has always been intimately connected to the world economy. As a result conditions in international grain markets tend to have an immediate impact on the region. It follows that the structure and operation of what Friedmann (1993b) refers to as the postwar food regime had a significant impact on western farmers. For example, there was a relative measure of economic security in western rural communities when prices were rising and stable during the 1960s and 1970s. As we have seen, on the domestic front, the spinoff effects of the baby boom, significant immigration, and high levels of government spending provided the basis for a couple of decades of significant prosperity and economic growth. As I argue above, significant structural changes occurred during the postwar boom, especially in the areas of state finances and the internationalization of capital. The massive influx of transnational capital that entered Canada during the period of the war and the boom that followed changed the nature of the Canadian economy. The virtually uncontested rise of U.S.-based multinationals to positions of economic supremacy was part of a change in the nature of the world economy that influenced the development of many national economies.

In the early 1970s it became increasingly apparent that the postwar boom was indeed over. The world capitalist system and the nations that compose it faced persistent inflation, growing government debts, currency instabilities, intracapitalist competition (as the economies of Western Europe and Japan prospered), and instabilities in the prices of many basic commodities including foodstuffs. On the agricultural front, prices and demand remained high in part as a result of the U.S. policy of using food as foreign aid under the Marshall Plan and the huge U.S.-Soviet wheat deal of the early 1970s. As wheat markets and prices began to fall in the face of increasing international competition, the fear of shortages was replaced by growing cereal grain stocks in North America, Europe, and Australia.

Larger economic changes included the continuing concentration and centralization of capital on a global scale, and continual mergers, bankruptcies, takeovers, and buyouts that produced ever larger and more explicitly international blocs of capital. The terms globalization and world economy gradually became part of the standard language of those in charge of the economy and the state. The widespread recognition that capitalism is indeed a global system was accompanied by shifts on the ideological front. In many Western nations including Canada, the emphasis on the role and importance of international competition was accompanied by increasingly shrill calls for nation-states to make themselves more competitive, trim, and fit to fight the good fight. At the national level this typically meant the adoption of neoliberal, anti-Keynesian, economic policies that called for less and less government spending, less regulation, and less government involvement in the economy. Deregulation and government cutbacks became the order of the day. Since decades of spending, deficits, and growing debts brought most Western governments to the brink of a fiscal crisis, politicians and the media were able to convince beleaguered taxpayers that the new international order demanded changes. The 1980s may well be remembered as the decade of state retrenchment, deregulation, cuts to certain areas of spending, and a massive ideological campaign to convince the citizenry of the necessity of various sorts of "tough medicine." It should also be remembered as the decade of declining incomes, expectations, and futures.

In terms of agricultural policies and governmental attitudes toward agriculture, the decade appears to be somewhat contradictory. On the one hand, the massive American-European subsidy war drove the international price of wheat down to levels that had not been seen since the Great Depression, while on the other these subsidies contributed to state spending at a time of apparent fiscal restraint. As a result of these developments the agricultural sectors, particularly the cereal grain industries, in nations such as Canada have been driven into crisis. Although the Canadian governments developed subsidy programs of their own, they simply lacked the fiscal means, not to mention the ideological and political will, to make them really effective.

Since World War II nation-states have experienced an increasing loss of economic sovereignty as organizations associated with, and responsible to, the General Agreement on Tariffs and Trade, the World Trade Organization, the World Bank, the International Monetary Fund, and various regional trade agreements such as NAFTA have enforced new rules and regulations concerning tariffs and trade policies, economic strategies, and agricultural policy. In the area of agricultural policy, it seems apparent that as the twentieth century has progressed, the room to maneuver once available to nation-states and blocks of national capital are simply no longer there. During earlier historical periods, such as the era from Confederation through the Great Depression, it was in the interests of Canadian industrial, commercial, and financial capital to establish and maintain an agricultural population on the prairies. However, with the continued concentration and centralization of capital which has characterized the twentieth century and the emergence of huge blocks of multinational capital seeking accumulation strategies on the world scale, the role of the agricultural sector in Canada changed. Since multinational capital, by definition, seeks inputs and markets outputs on the international market, the central role that agricultural producers once played in capital accumulation in Canada changed. As George Grant (1965) argued, manufacturers and financiers, once interested in capital accumulation in Canada, increasingly became part of international circuits of production, distribution, and capital accumulation. If we assume that capital has an overwhelming capacity to influence state policy, as I have set forth elsewhere (Knuttila and Kubik 2001), then we should expect that this "new reality" will bring new agricultural policies.

The past two decades represent a virtual revolution in Canadian agricultural policy. Various Canadian governments, under the ideological umbrella of free market economics and a more laissez faire approach to politics, have demonstrated a propensity to move away from supporting and encouraging agricultural production. In terms of western Canada, the decline in government support for income support programs, agricultural research, the ending of the historic Crow Rate benefit, transportation deregulation, the massive abandonment of thousands of kilometers of rail lines, and the ongoing diminishment of the power of the Canadian Wheat Board are indicative of the new era. When coupled with various proposals and policies regarding "rural adjustment" (read the elimination and relocation of rural residents) and diversification, the new policies are clearly designed to allow the logic of the market to restructure prairie agriculture. If this means the elimination of thousands of producers and their communities, then it is to be understood as the price of progress and what is necessary if we are to compete in the new economic reality of the global marketplace.

Global Capitalism and the Rural Crisis

If the arguments presented above have validity, then an understanding of the evolution of capitalism as a world system will help understand why governments have reacted differently to agricultural crises at different moments in history. The maturation of capitalism has accentuated the tendencies towards the concentration, centralization, and internationalization of capital, and resulted in differing roles, opportunities, and possibilities for capital accumulation in different parts of the world. From around the middle to the end of the nineteenth century there was room for indigenous economic development in nations such as Canada. Although chronic shortages of capital, small markets, and less than state of the art technology prevented it from overtaking or equaling the United States or Britain, Canada achieved significant levels of economic and industrial development. While much of that development occurred as a result of foreign investment, much of it occurred under the auspices of indigenous capital. There were key historical moments during which national industrial capital (along with nationally based international capital) sought to use the national state to develop industrial development strategies involving tariff protection and an expanding agrarian market. Ultimately the presence and power of transnational corporate capital swamped these efforts. The adoption of a continentalist economic strategy spelled the end of the national policy in Canada.

As far as agricultural producers are concerned, they too operate and must be understood in the context of national economies which are part of a world system. At various times the Canadian government undertook systematic efforts to develop or facilitate domestic industrialization based on expanding internal markets and the use of tariff protected import substitution. Agricultural producers, especially cereal grain producers, figured prominently in these plans because they were deemed to be an essential part of the domestic market. There is evidence that agricultural producers fared better when they were central to domestic capital accumulation strategies. It follows that when agricultural producers were important to industrial development because they represented the core, or at least an important part, of an expanding domestic market, governments undertook efforts to maintain their position and keep them on the land. However, when the industrial capital becomes organized on an international scale and the market becomes global, the role and significance of particular national markets, such as western Canada, diminishes. Once the corporations producing inputs into agricultural production no longer rely on any particular domestic or national market, the loss of several thousand producers in Saskatchewan is no longer of any consequence to them. For some the declining number of producers is not a problem in terms of the role that agriculture in Canada plays as a contributor to export earnings because new technologies and scales of production allow fewer producers to produce even more commodities.

I am suggesting that the current calls for a restructuring of agriculture must be placed in the context of the role of agriculture in the "new international order." If we are to fully understand the transformations that are occurring on the Canadian prairies we need to spell out in more detail the precise nature of the changing role of agriculture in Canada, and the role and changing nature of state policy. Such an understanding is essential in order to engage in an analysis of the actions and reactions of the state. A clear understanding of the logic and direction of state policy is essential if agricultural producers and residents of rural communities are to be successful in resisting the destruction of their communities and way of life that the "new reality" threatens to unleash. The fact that prairie agriculture, with its fractured internal class structures, is firmly integrated into international circuits of capital accumulation, along with the fact that national governments have tended to view the social and economic transformation of the region as inevitable, might generate a sense of political pessimism when it comes to popular resistance to the restructuring. While political realism must always guide the efforts of community leaders and activists, we must never assume that social and economic changes are inevitable or that social and economic processes are subject to some law of nature. If the population determines that a radical restructuring of its social and economic institutions are not in the interests of the majority, then it must seek ways and means of resisting that change and revitalizing its existence. Given what we know about the nature of the contemporary international market this may mean that it is necessary to work internationally with like-minded people in other nations who understand the value of rural communities.

Chapter 4
The Contested Terrain of Swine Production
Deregulation and Reregulation
of Corporate Farming Laws in Missouri

Douglas H. Constance, Anna M. Kleiner, and J. Sanford Rikoon

The U.S. hog industry is being transformed from an agricultural to an industrial model (Ikerd 1998; Rhodes 1995; Welsh 1996; Zering 1998), while at the same time becoming integrated into the global economy (DiPietre and Watson 1994; USDA FAS 1998; Plain 1997). This process is characterized by the decline of a production system based on family farms and the emergence of a system based on corporate controlled concentrated animal feeding operations (CAFOs) growing thousands of hogs in a small geographic area (Marbery 1994b; Rhodes 1995; Stout 1996; Welsh 1996). From Minnesota to Texas and North Carolina to Utah, states across the U.S. are embroiled in the industrialization of the pork industry (Cecelski and Kerr 1992; McMahon et al. 1998; Thompson 1998). CAFOs have become so controversial that as part of the Clean Water Action Plan the USDA and EPA launched a national strategy to regulate the negative impacts (USDA/U.S. EPA 1999).

The number of hog farms in the U.S. peaked in 1940 at almost 4 million, dropping to 2 million in 1964, 330,000 in 1982, and 110,000 in 1997 (U.S. Census of Agriculture 1997a). Since the 1950s the number of hog farms with fewer than 1,000 hogs per year of production has decreased. At the same time, those producing over 1,000 head per year have steadily increased (Rhodes 1995). The fastest growth is coming from the "super" hog farms (50,000–500,000 hogs/yr) and the "mega" hog farms (greater than 500,000 hogs/yr). Rhodes (1995) also reports a steady increase in hogs produced under vertical integration. In Missouri, over the period 1964 to 1997, the number of hog farms declined from 62,000 to 5,400, while the number of hogs sold increased from about 6.2 million to 8.5 million (U.S. Census of Agriculture 1969, 1987, 1997b).

For some people in rural areas, large scale hog production is seen as a desirable form of socioeconomic development that complements the historical agricultural activities of the area and provides needed jobs. For others, hog CAFOs are an illegitimate model of development in which the negative impacts outweigh the benefits (see Heffernan 1999b; Schiffman 1998; Thu 1996b). The negative impacts include corporate vs. family farm ownership, odor problems, water quality and health concerns, depressed property values, and community disruption. Rural communities across the U.S. are struggling with these issues as a new part of the global food system comes to their areas.

DeLind (1995) was the first to document the socioeconomic impacts and controversies related to hog CAFOs in her study of Parma, Michigan. Since then other researchers have reported similar scenarios in Iowa (Durrenberger and Thu 1996; Holtcamp et al. 1994; Padgett et al. 1998; Thu 1996a), Missouri (Hendrickson and Pigg 1998; Kleiner and Constance 1998a; Seipel et al. 1998), Nebraska (Allen et al. 1998), North Carolina (McMillan and Schulman 1998; Thu and Durrenberger 1994; Wing and Wolf 1999), Texas (Bonanno and Constance 2000; Constance and Bonanno 1999a); and Utah (Kleiner and Constance 1998a). The hog CAFO issue is so contentious that corporate farming laws have been changed in several states to deal with the public uproar (Dummermuth 1997; McMahon et al. 1998). In 1998 alone, legislation to further regulate CAFOs was enacted in Colorado, Indiana, Iowa, Kansas, Kentucky, Maryland, Minnesota, Mississippi, Nebraska, New York, Oklahoma, South Dakota, Virginia, and Pennsylvania (National Conference of State Legislatures 1999). The CAFO-based hog industry has migrated west from North Carolina and nearby areas to the midwest and Great Plains and brought the controversy with it. The cover of the June 1998 *National Hog Farmer* magazine declared, "An Industry Swirling in Controversy" superimposed over the picture of a CAFO (National Hog Farmer 1998).

This contest between advocates of CAFOs as a rural development strategy and their opponents is largely carried out within the arena of the state. It is the state that balances the needs of capital accumulation with societal legitimation (Bonanno and Constance 1996; Friedland 1991b; O'Connor 1974). For our analysis, we focus on the local state, Missouri, and on its counties and townships as loci of struggle. We use the concept "contested terrain" to examine the creation and implementation of laws aimed to restrict corporate farming that accompanied the introduction of hog CAFOs into Missouri. This analysis sheds light on processes involved in the increasing globalization of the agrifood sector of the economy, particularly the contestation that occurs as food and agricultural production become globalized. In our case, powerful political and economic actors—hog corporations and their political supporters—and coalitions of subordinate groups—populists and environmentalists—use the state's legal apparatus to advance their agendas.

We begin our chapter with a general overview of the literature on the globalization of the agri-food system, including a presentation of the contested terrain framework. We then document the emergence of corporate farming laws in Missouri. We discern three periods, regulation, deregulation, and reregulation, in the introduction of and resistance to swine CAFOS. In the next section we analyze the case within the contested terrain framework by focusing on the use of the state by both pro-CAFO and anti-CAFO groups. Finally, we offer suggestions of how this research might inform the ongoing discussions on the characteristics of the globalization project.

The Globalization of Agriculture and Food

The globalization of the agri-food sector is a central topic of discussion in the literature on the sociology of agriculture and food (Arce 1997; Bonanno 1992, 1993, 1994; Bonanno et al. 1994; Bonanno, Constance, and Lorenz 2000; Bonanno and Constance 1996, 1998b, 2000; Constance and Bonanno 1999b, 2000; Constance and Heffernan 1991; Friedland 1984, 1991a, 1994b; Friedmann 1992, 1993b; Friedmann and McMichael 1989; Goodman and Watts 1994, 1997; Gouveia 1994; Heffernan 1999b; Heffernan and Constance 1994; McMichael 1994, 1996a; Raynolds and Murray 1998). Much of this discussion is couched in the debated transition from a Fordist to a post-Fordist system of societal organization (see Aglietta 1979; Bonanno and Constance 1996; Harvey 1989; Lipietz 1987, 1992a). The Fordist period began in the early part of the twentieth century and fell into decline in the early 1970s. Fordism was characterized by national systems of mass production matched to mass consumption through the actions of an interventionist nation-state. This corporatist arrangement between labor, capital, and government provided a stable era of socioeconomic development after World War II. During the 1960s this arrangement entered into several crises brought about by enhanced power on the part of labor, environmentalist, and Third World (especially OPEC) social movements, rising global competition from Europe and Japan, and declining profits for U.S. corporations. The ensuing crisis of capital accumulation pushed U.S. corporations towards capital flight and business expansion overseas to avoid the rigid business relations in the U.S. and thereby revive accumulation.

The globalization of production was carried out through three related

decentralization *unregulated labor* *global sourcing*

strategies. First, firms decentralized production away from single large production plants near cities and toward several smaller plants in different geographic localities to minimize the rigidities associated with environmental regulations and labor union power over the production process. Second, through the strategy of the informalization of labor, firms were able to lower labor costs by avoiding full-time, union jobs with benefits, often dominated by white males, and replacing this system with a labor force characterized by higher percentages of women and minorities, part-time work, and decreased benefits. Lastly, firms employed the concept of "global sourcing" whereby the factors of production were obtained globally at the lowest costs possible. In effect, to revive business profits, global corporations abandoned their historical production base in highly regulated First World economies and sourced the world for the most lucrative factors of production. By doing so, the rigid Fordist system based on mass production was replaced by a much more flexible post-Fordist system that could respond to the increasing pace of changing consumer demands and still generate capital accumulation.

The debate concerning the globalization of the agri-food sector and the accompanying transition from Fordism to post-Fordism is informed by at least five positions in the agriculture and food sector literature. For McMichael and his associates (Friedmann and McMichael 1989; McMichael 1996a, 1996b; McMichael and Myhre 1991), the primary factor in the collapse of Fordism was the failure of the "development project" and its replacement by the "globalization project" characterized by the emergence of transnational finance capital (TFC) and powerful transnational corporations (TNCs) utilizing global sourcing to obtain the most profitable factors of production. As developing countries found themselves unable to pay back the industrialization loans provided by global banks in the 1970s as part of the "development project," they experienced a debt crisis and ensuing structural adjustment programs administered by the International Monetary Fund (IMF) and World Bank. This process of neoliberal restructuring, termed the "globalization project," was orchestrated by a global elite of financial managers, global bureaucrats, and corporate leaders. One of the results was the increased power of global corporations as the privatization of national assets and the opening of domestic markets reduced wages and weakened the powers of nation-states while at the same time enhancing the power of global statelike entities such as the IMF and the recently (1995) created World Trade Organization (WTO). McMichael concludes that post-Fordism is the most recent attempt to stabilize capitalism.

Friedland (1994a, 1994b, 1995) argues that the crisis of Fordism did not result in the creation of post-Fordism but rather a more advanced Fordist period he terms Sloanism characterized by a sophisticated mass production system based on small, independent units but controlled by TNCs. The creation of niche markets allows TNCs to respond to the crisis of Fordism's "overstandardized" mass markets and cater to the diversified demands of global consumers via a Sloanist approach of expanded options (as Alfred Sloan did for General Motors as compared to Henry Ford at Ford Motor Company). Fordism was modified into Sloanism. Sloanism is a mass production system, controlled by large corporations, that offers a differentiation of products and therefore provides the impression of the end of mass production and its replacement with craft production. Under this system the nation-state is hampered in its ability to coordinate its national economies due to the enhanced power of global corporations.

Goodman and Watts (1994, 1997) stress that globalization has supported the emergence of TNCs as the major agents involved in agri-food restructuring through the deregulation of production and distribution in the public arena and their reregulation on private grounds (see also Marsden 1994 on reregulation). They question the utility of the Fordism/post-Fordism schema to analyze the agri-food system because it is based on an industrial analytical system that does not consider the intrinsic characteristics of land-based agriculture. For them, agri-food production processes entail significant local components which make the local-global relationship much more complex than that assumed by analyses that make the local residual to the global. Rather, globalization is a very complex process whose analysis should privilege the role of human agency. While they agree that globalization has expanded the role of transnational forms of the state, they stress that the nation-state continues to play a crucial role in the negotiation of competitive global arrangements. They call for a focus on the simultaneous processes of territorialization—processes based on place-specific social relations and practices—and deterritorialization—the elimination of place-specific practice and social relations—to better understand agrarian production structures in the global era.

Arce and his associates (Arce 1997; Arce and Fisher 1997) also criticize the Fordism/post-Fordism dichotomy when it is used to explain local events through reference to a global determinant. They agree that new global forms of economic activity are emerging, but they assert that local actors interpret and translate global phenomena into local practices. Employing an actor-oriented approach (see, e.g., Long and Long 1992), Arce and his associates contend that because global processes are fragmented and reinterpreted at the local level, individuals and communities can experience further emancipation by taking advantage of conditions emerging globally. Because global phenomena are mediated by local actors, it is important to undertake a close-up analysis that captures the intricacies of emerging global-local linkages.

Bonanno and Constance (Bonanno and Constance 1996, 1998a, 1998b, 2000; Bonanno et al. 2000; Constance and Bonanno 1999a, 1999b, 2000) portray the transition from Fordism to post-Fordism as a contested terrain in which groups operate both locally and globally. Fordism collapsed when the legitimized rule of dominant classes was countered by the demands of subordinate groups. This confrontation required dominant groups to devise new strategies to enhance capital accumulation and social legitimation. Post-Fordism emerged as a result of these attempts. The contested terrain framework sees the globalization project as an open-ended process in which corporate actors pursue strategies to revive business profits (accumulation) but are systematically challenged by subordinate groups (legitimation crises).

While Bonanno and Constance agree that the end of Fordism signified the possibility of enhanced freedom (e.g., Giddens 1994; Lash and Urry 1994), they argue that the opening of these "free spaces" has been successfully countered by TNCs' actions which diminish the political power of subordinate groups. They link the declining political power of subordinate groups to the crisis of the nation-state and its inability to control the flows of resources and actions within its territory. They argue that despite their strength TNCs are still vulnerable due to new concerns related to the protection of the environment. These environmental, rather than labor or other class or communally based concerns, now inform anti-corporate actions. TNCs have been able to profit from this situation by pitting labor against environmental groups. In the end, Bonanno and Constance conclude that this situation problematizes the struggle for democracy as emancipatory groups find themselves divided and, at times, at odds with each other.

These five views generate valuable insights into the mechanisms and effects of globalization in general and the changing nature of state/firm relationships in particular. They all assert that we are witnessing a significant shift from national to transnational forms of economic organization. While some authors are more likely than others to see this shift as an evolution rather than a fracture between eras, they all stress the important qualitative differences between older and current forms of globalization. Friedland and McMichael are similar in their more structuralist views on the emergence of powerful TNCs that eclipse the sovereignty of individual nation-states. Arce highlights the mediated aspects of globalization as the local actors negotiate their own roles and realities with economic and state actors. While Goodman and Watts also highlight the growing power of TNCs, they incorporate Arce's "empowered local" dimension and also see the nation-state as still maintaining an important role in negotiating the terms of global investments within its territory. With their "contested terrain" framework, Bonnano and Constance are similar to Goodman and Watts on this topic but differ in that they see globalization as significantly weakening both the local (subordinate) groups and the nation-state. On this point, Bonanno and Constance are more similar to Friedland and McMichael.

The changing role of the nation-state in relation to the globalization of the agri-food sector is a central theme in these discussions. All perspectives (except Arce and his associates who don't deal with this topic) contend that the nation-state's traditional powers have been redefined in ways that reflect its new role in a globalized agri-food sector. They argue that the nation-state still plays a vital role in the global socioeconomic system, but this new role tends to be centered increasingly on facilitating neoliberal restructuring policies in order to attract transnational finance capital for socioeconomic development to the detriment of social and environmental policies. Again, McMichael and Friedland are the most pessimistic in their interpretations of this process, with Goodman and Watts the most optimistic regarding the ability of the nation-state to preserve substantial portions of its sovereignty.

These analysts generally agree that the nation-state has traditionally and still performs important roles which provide stability to the socioeconomic system (Bonanno 1991, 1993, 1994; Bonanno and Constance 1996; Constance and Bonanno 2000; Friedland 1991b; see also O'Connor 1974). First, the state must maintain a stable business climate that attracts capital investment and supports economic accumulation—the "accumulation" function. Second, while the state must provide avenues for accumulation, it must also ensure that the socioeconomic system is accepted as legitimate by the citizens—the "legitimation" function. Finally, the state plays the role of mediator of class conflicts—the "mediation" function. These functions of the state provide analytical tools to interpret the case.

CAFOs and Corporate Farming Law

In the mid-1970s, at the beginning of rapid globalization marked by the OPEC-induced oil crisis, farmers in Missouri lobbied for and obtained an anti-corporate farming law. Missouri's Corporate Farming Statute was enacted September 28, 1975 in response to increasing concerns for the family farmer in the face of corporate competition. Specifically, legislation was spurred by plans for a large hog farm in northeast Missouri (Ganey 1994). The statute was designed to serve as

a public policy tool favoring the preservation of the family farm. It prohibited non-family corporations from entering into farming or from
buying agricultural land (Revised Statutes of Missouri section 350.015;
Stout 1996). The law defines a family farm corporation as one in which
at least half of the voting stock and half the stockholders are members
of a related family. At least one stockholder must actively manage the
farm. Two-thirds of the corporation's earnings must come from farming (Revised Statutes of Missouri section 350.010(5), 350.010(2)).

In 1982, Missouri enacted a statute intended to protect the nature
and heritage of family-owned and -run farms. Commonly known as a
right-to-farm statute, it provided that a farm was not a nuisance as
long as it has been in operation for more than a year and so long as it
was not a nuisance when it commenced operations. The catalyst for
this type of statute, which by 1983 existed in forty-seven states, was an
effort to protect America's shrinking agricultural base and to respond
to conflicts in land use due to urban encroachment (Joplin 1998).

Missouri's Right to Farm Act states that there must be a "changed
condition in the locality" in order for a farm to be deemed a public or
private nuisance (Revised Statutes of Missouri section 537.295). This
does not provide protection from actions by neighbors and residents
who already live there as only new residents are barred from action
(Joplin 1998). There is no statutory protection for negligent or improper operation of a farm, such as water pollution. In 1990, the
Right to Farm Act was amended to allow agricultural expansion "in
terms of acres and animal units without losing its protected status so
long as all county, state, and federal environmental codes, laws, or
regulations are met by the agricultural operation" (Revised Statutes of
Missouri section 537.295).[1] Livestock operations were required to
maintain waste handling capabilities meeting or exceeding standards
established by the University of Missouri Extension Service. There
were only three reported decisions involving hog farm nuisance cases
based on odor prior to the 1994 case *Premium Standard Farms, Inc. v.
Lincoln Township of Putnam County* (Joplin 1998).

Exemptions and Loopholes: The CAFOs Come to Missouri

The insurgence of hog corporations into the state through statutory
exceptions meant to benefit family farmers reveals that the statute
does not satisfy its intended purpose of preserving the integrity of the
family farm (Stout 1996).[2] This failure is demonstrated through the
entry of three major hog corporations: Premium Standard Farms
(PSF), an authorized farm corporation, and both Murphy Family

Farms and Continental Grain, family-farm corporations (Stout 1996). The entry of these hog corporations into northern Missouri is based on the nearby packing plants in Iowa combined with the high quality clay for lagoon construction and the relatively sparse population (Joplin 1998).

In 1988, Dennis Harms and Tad Gordon started PSF near Princeton, Missouri. They quickly expanded their sow numbers to about 80,000 over the three counties of Mercer, Putnam, and Sullivan. PSF had tried to locate in Iowa but was denied permits for its waste lagoons due to violation of the state's wastewater laws and proximity to a park (Kilman 1994; Mihalopoulos 1995). Harms stated that the "State of Missouri's aggressive business climate attracted PSF to start its project in Mercer County. Support from Missouri Governor John Ashcroft, the Missouri Department of Agriculture, the Missouri Department of Economic Development, and a very industrious Industrial Development Board made Mercer County 'impossible to pass up'" (*Princeton Post-Telegraph* 1989b). The local State Senator and State Representative cut red tape to facilitate PSF's decision to locate in Mercer County. U.S. Senator Jack Danforth also welcomed PSF to Missouri, stating that this "is an excellent opportunity to strengthen the economy of north Missouri, which has been hit hard in recent years" (*Princeton Post-Telegraph* 1989a).

PSF was a vertically integrated company created through venture capital "junk bonds" by Morgan Stanley Group, Inc. "and its merchant-banking fund partners" (Jereski and Smith 1996:c8). It raised its own hogs in company owned facilities, provided them feeds from its own mills, slaughtered the animals at its processing plant, and marketed the finished product. It located the farrow/nursery and finishing operations on 37,000 acres of company-owned land. Following industry norms, sows farrow twice a year and wean an average of eleven pigs per litter. Piglets are weaned at about 14 pounds and remain in a nursery until they weigh about 40 pounds. At that time they are moved to finishing barns that hold 1,100 hogs each, usually in rows of eight barns. Slaughter weight is reached at 255 pounds within approximately 15–16 weeks.

In 1993 PSF began operation of a new pork processing facility in Milan, Missouri, in Sullivan County. With both shifts operating, the plant employed about 900 workers, mostly Hispanics recruited from Texas and Mexico (Bell 2000b). In June 1994 PSF also purchased an 18,000-sow operation on 14,000 acres in the Panhandle of Texas that increased its capacity to about 2.1 million market hogs per year (McMahon 1996). By 1996 PSF was the fifth largest producer of hogs in the U.S. (Successful Farming 1997). It was the first U.S. pork company certified to export fresh pork to the European Union (Grossfield 1998) and it exports an increasing amount of its production to Japan and other parts of Asia (Marbery 1994c).

Murphy Family Farms established its sow facilities and feedmill in Vernon County in Southwest Missouri starting in 1992. Murphy started with 3,500 sows and expanded to about 44,000 by 1997. The fourteen sow farms in the area typically have 3,600 sows per site. About thirty-five nursery sites are contracted with local farmers. The feeder pigs are shipped to Iowa and South Dakota to be finished (Johnson 1997). At the time of its entry into Missouri, Murphy Family Farms was the largest producer of hogs in the U.S. with over 275,000 sows on 125 sow farms and over 500 contract farmers in North Carolina, Missouri, Iowa, Oklahoma, Kansas, and Illinois (Forbes 1998; Successful Farming 1997). In 1999 Murphy Family Farms was bought by Smithfield Foods, the largest vertically integrated pork producer in the U.S., with 675,000 sows (Successful Farming 1999). Smithfield Foods is the largest hog producer and pork processor in the world. It produces and/or processes pork in the U.S., France, Canada, Mexico, and Brazil and exports pork products to numerous sites around the world (Miller 2000; Smithfield 2000).

Continental Grain erected its first swine production and finishing facilities in Missouri during 1994 in Daviess and Gentry Counties. In 1996 Continental Grain had 144,000 hogs in the region (Connor 1996). By 1997 Continental Grain was the twelfth largest producer of hogs in the U.S. (Successful Farming 1997). As part of the Conti-Group, Continental Grain has extensive agricultural related activities globally, including the largest animal feed and poultry company in China; substantial animal feed, poultry, and flour milling operations in Ecuador, the Caribbean, Paraguay, Venezuela, Peru, and Haiti; and substantial feed and poultry investments in Europe (ContiGroup 1998a). In 1998 Continental was the world's largest cattle feeder, third largest fully integrated hog producer, sixth largest integrated poultry company, and an important player in the global animal feed and nutrition business (ContiGroup 1998b).

In May 1996 PSF defaulted on $412 million in junk bond debt (Jereski and Smith 1996). In July it declared Chapter 11 bankruptcy and after restructuring emerged with Putnam Investments and Morgan Stanley its largest shareholders (Faircloth 1996; McMahon 1996; Stroud 1998). In 1998 Continental Grain bought majority interest in PSF. At that time their combined operations in Missouri included about 105,000 sows on eighteen farms in six counties and produced over 2 million market hogs per year (Stroud 1998).

By 1998 PSF/Continental was the third largest hog producer in the U.S. (Bryant 1999) and by 1999 it had risen to second with 162,000 sows (Successful Farming 1999). By 1999, then, the first and second largest hog producing firms, PSF/Continental and Smithfield Foods, had major operations in Missouri. Two of the other major global food corporations operated in the state: Tyson, the largest poultry producer and processor in the world, and Cargill, ranked fifth and sixth nationally in pork production, making Missouri a "Pork Powerhouse" (Successful Farming 1999, 2000). Due to the entry of PSF, Continental Grain, and Murphy Family Farms, the number of hogs within the CAFO counties increased dramatically from 1987 to 1996, from about 134,000 per year in 1986 to over 1,400,000 in 1997 (MASS 1987, 1998)(see Figure 4.1).

Deregulation

The 1993 Omnibus Legislation

In 1993, as it sought to build a pork processing plant, PSF found it difficult to obtain financing because, although it conformed to Missouri's anti-corporate farming law, should PSF default on a loan secured by the farm the financier would be left with property it could not operate (Stout 1996).[3] To facilitate PSF's plans to build a processing plant and to encourage a lender to finance the project, the Missouri legislature created an exemption in 1993 exclusive to swine and related products for the three counties in which PSF operated. This exemption allayed lenders' fears and enabled PSF to acquire the capital to build the plant. It also enabled PSF to structure its corporate status in any fashion it desired or to sell to any farm corporation (Stout 1996).

The legislation was attached as an eleven-line provision to an unrelated 182–page economic development bill in the "waning hours of the session" by representatives from the PSF and Continental Grain areas. State Representative Phil Tate (D-Gallatin) sponsored the amendment in the Missouri House and State Senator Steve Danner (D-Chillicothe) provided sponsorship in the Missouri Senate. There were no public hearings and no notice to farm groups. Estil Fretwell, lobbyist for the Missouri Farm Bureau Federation, said, "The amendment was adopted before opposition could be mounted. . . . If there had been more of an open discussion of what the amendment was doing, the opposition would have been overwhelming" (Ganey 1994:4).

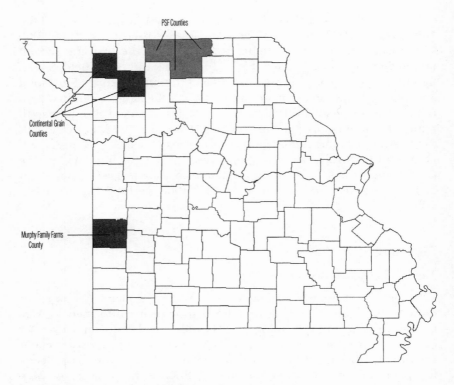

Figure 4.1: Missouri CAFO Counties and Changes in Number of Hogs, 1986–1997

County	1986	1997
Mercer (PSF)	12,900	*
Putnam (PSF)	8,400	*
Sullivan (PSF)	13,400	*
Gentry (Continental)	44,600	145,000
Daviess (Continental)	32,200	114,000
Vernon (Murphy)	22,700	165,000

*Data not provided by county due to disclosure restrictions; total hogs for the three counties was 985,000.
Sources: MASS 1987, 1998.

Failed Attempts to Repeal the Anti-Corporate Farming Act of 1975

This introduction of corporate farm entities prompted a movement by corporate farming advocates to repeal Missouri's anti-corporate farm act. When the exemption for PSF was passed in 1993, there was a minor movement for repeal; however, this met with strong opposition (Wolfe 1994). In 1994 another bill was introduced to repeal the act and allow the free introduction of farm corporations into the state. The Legislature soundly rejected the bill, with legislators referring to opposition by residents and a lack of information. Some suggested that PSF be viewed as a pilot project on the issue. The Farm Bureau, a major opponent of repeal, stated that it wanted a waiting period to follow the 1993 three-county exemption to assure the bureau that independent producers could compete (Wolfe 1994).

Reregulation

Fish Kills and Stricter Environmental Regulations

In the fall and winter of 1995 there were nine hog waste spills killing over 250,000 fish in northern Missouri. The Missouri Department of Natural Resources (MDNR) fined Continental Grain $268,495 for two spills and PSF $241,083 for seven spills (Walsh 1996). PSF announced that it would spend $508 million on preventive measures in 1996 and an average of $51,000 per year for the following four years (Patrico 1998).

In response to the hog waste spills and growing public complaints from individual citizens as well as the Missouri Rural Crisis Center and the Sierra Club about the odor problems presented by CAFOs, in May 1996 the Missouri General Assembly passed H.B. 1207 to "significantly upgrade" existing CAFO regulations (Organ and Perry 1997). Most of the specific mandates in the bill applied to Class IA CAFOs, which are those facilities with 7,000 or more animal units, or 17,500 swine over 55 pounds on one site. Under the law, signed by Governor Mel Carnahan on June 25, 1996 with a five year sunset, the Class IA facilities located in sensitive watershed areas were required to submit a spill prevention plan to the MDNR. All large facilities were required to inspect their lagoons twice daily, have automatic shut-off capabilities, have a failsafe retainment structure for unauthorized discharge, keep detailed records, and report regularly to MDNR. They were not eligible for tax credits or other state assistance, and they were required to establish an indemnity fund. The law further required a buffer distance between confinement buildings and lagoons built after the law's enactment and public buildings and occupied residences. It also gave primacy to local controls, if they were more stringent.

Other County and Township Level Regulatory Efforts

Numerous other local efforts were initiated to control hog CAFOs relative to setbacks of structures and lagoons. In 1989, the Missouri Legislature had granted townships special zoning and/or planning power in the event that the county had no such regulations. Although townships were precluded from regulating farm structures and farm buildings, ambiguous language in the law allowed activists to argue that they could regulate the waste lagoons (Joplin 1998).

In April 1994 PSF bought over 3,000 acres of land located in Lincoln Township in Putnam County and began to erect hog production facilities. In anticipation of these activities, in June 1994 Lincoln Township voters passed regulations pertaining to CAFOs requiring lagoons to be set back from dwellings at a distance determined by the aggregate capacity of all the lagoons on the site—the larger the lagoon the greater the setback (Barrette 1996). As PSF was constructing its hog production facilities and lagoons in early July, a Lincoln Township zoning officer inspected PSF's facilities and determined that it had violated several of the CAFO regulations. In late July, PSF sued Lincoln Township, alleging that it lacked the statutory authority to enact the zoning regulations. Lincoln Township counterclaimed, arguing that PSF's operation constituted a public nuisance and sought enforcement of its zoning regulations. PSF then filed three summary judgment motions. The case was appealed to the Missouri Supreme Court, which found that Lincoln Township did not have the authority to regulate PSF's operations, ruling that lagoons were "farm structures" and that the state constitution prohibited a township from regulating farm buildings or structures. The Court also rejected the argument that PSF was not a farm (Joplin 1998; Thompson 1998).

The case became a major focus of the national Save the Family Farm movement, which had developed during the farm crisis of the 1980s. Local activists formed a coalition of farmers, environmentalists, religious and labor leaders, and animal welfare groups in an organization named the Campaign for Family Farms and the Environment. They kicked off their campaign with a Farm Aid concert, hosted by country singer Willie Nelson, in Lincoln Township in April 1995, reportedly attended by about 3,000 people (Allison 1995). Following the rally, PSF dropped the monetary damages attached to its lawsuit with Lincoln Township, which activists attributed to the national attention focused on the issue by the rally (Allison 1995). Later that year USDA Secretary Dan Glickman met with representatives of the Campaign for Family Farms and the Environment in Lincoln Township to discuss their concerns regarding hog CAFOs (Joplin 1998).

Aware of Lincoln Township's failure to control CAFOs within its jurisdiction, Pettis County tried a different strategy. In 1996 it enacted a health ordinance targeting CAFOs exclusively, under the authority of a state statute that allows counties to pass regulations intended to enhance the public health and prevent the entrance of infectious, contagious, communicable, or dangerous diseases into such counties (Joplin 1998). The ordinance requires Class IA CAFOs to be set back three-fourths of a mile from an occupied dwelling not owned by the CAFO, with an additional quarter-mile for each 500 animal units in excess of 2,000, and a two-mile setback between a Class IA CAFO and a populated area, with a quarter-mile increase for each 500 animal units in excess of 2,000. Pettis County also requires buffer areas and slope regulations for the application of manure. Class IA CAFOs could not exist within a mile of each other; smaller class CAFOs had shorter spacing requirements (Barrette 1996).

Other Missouri counties followed Pettis County's lead and established ordinances regulating CAFOs, including Linn, Livingston, Caldwell, Camden, and Henry. Several incorporated CAFO regulations into countywide health ordinances (Marbery 1998). In February 1998, in the first court challenge to home rule by a pork producer, a local family sued the Linn County Commission for restricting their proposed 2,750-sow farrow-to-finish operation planned on 1,120 acres. Enacted in August 1997, Linn County's health ordinance required a 4.5-mile setback to homes and 5.5 miles to towns. Waste storage bonding based on facility size was also required. In this case, the plaintiff was required to provide $350,000 in bonding and contended that the Linn County ordinance was illegal, due to it being more restrictive than Missouri's 1996 CAFO regulations (Marbery 1998).

The county health ordinance was upheld in court and again in the Missouri Court of Appeals (Bell 1998) due to the documented health hazards associated with hog CAFOs (*Columbia Daily Tribune* 1996:B6). This case was considered to be a landmark Missouri health ordinance case with possible far-reaching impacts on the ability of other Missouri counties to regulate CAFOs. The plaintiffs in this case were backed by commodity groups such as the Missouri Farm Bureau and the Missouri Pork Producers Association that have opposed efforts at local control, believing that it would hurt small producers more than pork companies. Proponents of the health zoning maintained that these fears were designed to intimidate opponents of corporate farming and argued that family farmers typically do not build 2,700-sow operations (Marbery 1998). The initial regulations, aimed at a form of business organization, yielded to regulation in another domain, that of community health. As Scott Dye, the agricultural coordinator of the Missouri Sierra Club, observed, because Missouri farms are largely exempt from zoning regulations, "health ordinances are the next best regulatory alternatives for those who oppose giant hog farms" (Bell 1998). Continued attempts at economic regulation by the Campaign failed, when a 1998 bill they promoted to redefine CAFOs (class 1A and 1B) as industrial facilities died in committee (Missouri House of Representatives 1998).

Aside from efforts to change state and local laws, resistance to the hog CAFOs has also resulted in a number of lawsuits against the corporations. In February 1994 Neighbors Against Large Swine Operations (NALSO) sought an injunction with the Missouri Attorney General to keep Continental Grain from building swine facilities. The group contended that allowing Continental Grain to locate in Daviess County was in violation of the anti-corporate farming laws. Corporations such as this, like PSF, could only locate in Mercer, Putnam, and Sullivan Counties. They contended that Continental Grain was illegally registered as a family farm corporation. NALSO also believed that the state statutes require that an operation must be incorporated for the purpose of farming (Freese 1994). Continental Grain claimed that under Missouri law it qualified as a family-farm business and could therefore own and operate a hog facility in the state. It noted that it meets the family farm definition, because at least one-half of the stockholders are related, and at least one stockholder resides on or is actively involved in the Missouri operation. The plaintiff's issue was that the 1975 corporate farming law was enacted to protect family farmers against unfair competition (Marbery 1994a). The Attorney General did not pursue the lawsuit so NALSO adopted a new strategy.

In 1996, 108 people associated with NALSO sued Continental Grain over hog odors, fly infestations, water pollution, and related problems that they said made their lives miserable and reduced their ability to use their properties. In May 1999, 52 of the 108 plaintiffs were awarded $100,000 each for punitive damages by the St. Louis Circuit Court. The jury did not award the requested compensatory damages (Bryant 1999).

In 1997 a group of sixty families from Mercer, Putnam, and Sullivan Counties in northern Missouri, named the Citizens Legal Environmental Action Network (CLEAN), filed suit against PSF and the EPA, alleging violations of the Clean Water Act and the Clean Air Act, by allowing pollutants into waterways through spills and from runoff where excessive manure was spread on the land. The suit also alleged that PSF's waste lagoons had never been properly tested for leaks and that its operations allow illegal amounts of particulate chlorine, methane, and hydrogen sulfide into the air. Furthermore, the suit charged the EPA with lax enforcement of environmental laws (Walsh 1997) and charged PSF with illegal spraying of waste and illegal disposal pits for dead hogs (Grossfield 1998). The lawsuit did not seek financial damages, but compliance with existing laws. In July 1999 the EPA joined the lawsuit citing repeat violations of the Clean Water Act (Bell 1999a). In early 2000, the EPA expanded its claims against PSF alleging that the company had violated the Clean Air Act by emitting hundreds of tons of particulate matter into the air (Bell 2000a). At the beginning of 2002 the lawsuit was still pending.

The EPA lawsuit indicates that the 1996 state law regulating CAFOs yielded inadequate results. In 1998, Missouri Attorney General Jay Nixon petitioned the Missouri Air Conservation Commission to repeal the 1996 regulation exempting hog factories from odor control because, as he said, "it adversely affects the quality of life of neighbors and generally threatens the public health, safety, and welfare of the people of Missouri" (Williams 1998:32). After years of threatening to sue PSF if it did not clean up its operations, in January 1999 Nixon sued PSF for numerous environmental violations at its meatpacking plant and hog operations. He stated that the packing plant had unlawfully discharged raw sewage and had exceeded effluent limitations. The hog operations were charged with improper construction of effluent piping and placing manure where it could discharge directly to surface watercourses that lead to the Missouri River, or it could seep or leach into groundwater (Thompson 1998). Nixon also sued under the Clean Water Act regarding hydrogen sulfide and ammonia emission standards. In July 1999 the lawsuit was settled when PSF agreed to invest $25 million to improve its manure handling system as well as pay a $650,000 fine immediately, plus another $350,000 fine if the company did not comply with the ruling (Bell 1999b, 1999c, 2000a).

Discussion

> Hog odor is the most divisive issue ever in agriculture, damaging the fabric of rural society and disenfranchising pork producers from their communities. . . .
>
> —R. Douglas Hurt, Director of the Center for Agricultural History and Rural Studies at Iowa State University [Smith 1998:1]

The discussion centers around three themes. The first theme focuses on the aspects of the case that provide evidence that the emergence of the CAFO system of pork production in Missouri is an example of global sourcing, a central process of globalization. Global sourcing is the post-Fordist strategy developed by firms to obtain the optimal factors of production globally; factors including labor, raw materials, transportation, government regulations, and access to consumer markets (Constance and Heffernan 1991; Constance et al. 1995; Friedmann and McMichael 1989; Heffernan and Constance 1994; Sanderson 1985). PSF originated as a junk bond venture capital operation that was "ran out" of Iowa because of environmental and community concerns. It was welcomed in Missouri as a model of rural economic development. Midwestern corn, water, and supporting regulations were sourced in Missouri while Hispanic labor was recruited from Texas and Central America to provide high value pork to demanding worldwide consumers. The PSF/Continental expansion into northern Texas also decentralizes the production system and again sources a more conducive business climate with less stringent regulations (Bonanno and Constance 2000; Constance and Bonanno 1999b) as Missouri re-regulated to a less corporate friendly stance. In both cases, global sourcing is combined with capital flight, the decentralization of production, and the informalization of labor—all aspects of post-Fordist restructuring organized by TNCs under the globalization project. PSF provides the ContiGroup a state of the art vertically integrated pork production model, via the packing plant, to add to its portfolio of other global operations. Similarly Smithfield, the largest pork producer and processor in the world, as well as Cargill and Tyson, source Missouri for pork products. Through its subsidiary, EXCEL, Cargill also operates a pork processing plant in Marshall, Missouri.

The second theme focuses on the state of Missouri's attempt to balance capital accumulation and societal legitimation through a contested process of regulation, deregulation, and reregulation. Bonanno and Constance (1996) discuss the concepts of deregulation and reregulation as characteristics of globalization. This concept centers on the idea that as part of the ongoing globalization project, the state's ability to regulate the activity of TNCs has been diminished. More specifically, the state's ability to continue to advance and protect the interests of subordinate groups is limited in the face of capital flight and efforts to promote accumulation. Accordingly, the state "deregulates" and/or "reregulates" policies that previously limited accumulation. At the same time, the withdrawal of the state from these spheres of influence opens opportunities for groups that have not previously participated in policy development to advance their agendas.

In 1975 due to the efforts of populists and their allies in Missouri government, corporate farming laws were passed that regulated and protected the interests of family farmers from corporate encroachment. After the farm/debt crisis of the 1980s, state representatives aligned with economic development interests argued that these corporate farming laws limited the development of the hog industry in their regions and across the State of Missouri. PSF was welcomed to the state and the State Legislature passed special legislation that deregulated specific counties to allow PSF to build its packing plant and expand operations by attracting outside investors. After PSF successfully gained a stronghold in Missouri, Continental Grain and Murphy Family Farms soon followed.

Proponents of deregulation of the corporate farming laws for the three counties in which PSF operates argued in terms of the enhanced economic development opportunities in this depressed region. It should be noted that a disproportionate number of farms in northern and western Missouri had failed during the farm crisis of the 1980s, which was one of the first domestic effects of the global economic restructuring we term "globalization"(see Barnett chapter 9). This strategy to advance accumulation met with a legitimation crisis. Populist dissent regarding the demise of the family farm and the negative impact on land values and property rights, combined with environmental degradation due to several incidences of hog effluent spills and subsequent fish kills, brought about a push for reregulation centered on the management of waste produced by CAFOs. A coalition of populists and environmentalists, The Campaign for Family Farms and the Environment, successfully worked to bring about new laws to reregulate the previously welcomed and deregulated CAFO TNCs. Additionally, several counties and a township enacted local health ordinances as attempts to reregulate CAFOs.

Confronted by a PSF lawsuit and rebuffed by the state Supreme Court, Lincoln Township's attempted regulation via zoning laws was not successful. County level reregulation via health ordinances was more successful. Again, the economic development welcomed by the State of Missouri met with legitimation crises in various counties and other political units, creating a series of attempts to reregulate the hog industry due to health concerns. These are some of the several examples of how the state must mediate conflicts between various class fractions.

The third theme centers on the possibilities for local resistance in the face of globalization. The events of the case provide support for the thesis that the globalization of the agri-food system is a contested process whereby corporate efforts at global sourcing are challenged by subordinate groups. In this case the Campaign for Family Farms and the Environment and the other groups in the different counties used various forms of regulation to try to control the advance and impacts of hog CAFOs. Indeed, the hog corporations and their political allies do have substantial powers to shape their political economic environments. These powers, however, are not absolute; new coalitions also have opportunities to use the state to advance their agendas regarding environmental protection and agrarian philosophies.

Conclusion

The increase in large-scale swine facilities is one of the most critical and contentious issues at the intersections of agriculture, environment, and community. We argue that our case provides valuable evidence showing that the globalization of the hog industry in Missouri is a contested process in which subordinate groups do have opportunities to prevail against corporate interests. The anti-CAFO challenge included many aspects and interests: agrarian populist, environmental, property values/rights, quality of life, and those concerned with community disruption, and it operated at many levels: state, county, and township. The coalescence of this broad spectrum of interests into a unified challenge exemplifies the fact that the globalization of the agri-food system does meet with resistance; the globalization project is best conceptualized as a contested process whereby the strategies of global, regional, and national economic actors to foster accumulation are countered within the state apparatus by subordinate groups who declare these strategies illegitimate.

As we try to understand the globalization of agriculture and food, the contested terrain is where the global meets the local. It is where Arce's self-identified producers and consumers attempt to negotiate with and/or counter the plans of McMichael's and Friedland's TNCs sourcing the planet for profits. The evidence from Missouri's broad, diverse, and creative anti-CAFO movement illustrates that the more dialectical positions advanced by Bonanno and Constance and Goodman and Watts better describe the contested nature of the globalization of the agri-food system than either the more structuralist accounts of McMichael or Friedland or the more postmodern accounts of Arce and associates.

By 2002, in Missouri, the pork TNCs were more regulated and the great expansion of the early 1990s had slowed to a trickle. Continental, now including PSF, was not expanding in Missouri but was shifting its focus to operations in the panhandle of Texas. Murphy Farms, now owned by the largest pork producer and processor in the world, Smithfield, also slowed expansion in Missouri and has set up new operations in Texas and Oklahoma. Expansion continued in other areas of the country like the panhandles of Texas and Oklahoma (Bonanno and Constance 2000; Constance and Bonanno 1999a) and Utah (Kleiner and Constance 1998a). In conversations, representatives of PSF indicated that if they had to do it all over again, they would have never gone to Missouri, but only to Texas where they are welcome (Arnot 1996). Some victories were won in Missouri and other places that made these regions less attractive for global sourcing. As a result, the firms moved on to more fertile grounds, and the battles over hog CAFOs moved along with them.

Chapter 5
The Contingent Creation of Rural Interest Groups

Miriam J. Wells

Late twentieth century changes in U.S. agriculture have reconfigured the interests of rural people. The intensity of public debate and the range of policy claims surrounding them are unparalleled. Concerns range from the use of land, public water, and hazardous chemicals, and the relations between the U.S. and its trading partners, to protections for farm laborers and the physical environment. In all of these controversies, the processes through which individuals and groups come to be formed as social actors—and how these processes influence the problems that are addressed, the ways that issues are defined, and how production systems further change—are of crucial import.

Policy analysts and social movements scholars often take the interests of social groups as given or constant, leaving the process of interest group formation outside the realm of critical inquiry.[1] This exclusion makes policy formation appear to be relatively straightforward—a simple reflection of the balance of interests that exist. It leads, moreover, to a vision of policy formation and political-economic change that is relatively static, in that it omits crucial sources of indeterminacy and transformation. This chapter explores the processes of interest identification and interest group formation generated by the restructuring of U.S. agriculture. It argues that patterns of rural politics are highly unpredictable and have become more so over the course of recent decades. The analysis deals with a certain set of rural actors and period of time: harvest workers in California's central coast strawberry industry in the late twentieth century. It aims to identify some of the difficulties inherent in predicting the character of rural interest groups and to specify some of the key determinants and consequences of their formation.

The data on which this chapter is based are drawn from a long-term study of California's central coast strawberry industry (Wells 1996),[2] an industry that underwent significant swings in economic structure in the last several decades of the twentieth century. Most important for the present analysis, after the mid-1960s and persisting into the mid-1980s the industry shifted from an employment structure in which direct-hire employees brought in the harvest, to one in which over half of harvest workers were sharecroppers, defined as independent contractors under the law. This economic restructuring altered the relationship of harvest workers to the production process and to the law. It also heightened ambiguity as to where workers' interests lay and created new consequences for alternative representations. In this context, social intermediaries—here public interest lawyers, nonprofit organizations, and union leaders and organizers—played key roles in shaping group interests and forming interest groups.

The following analysis will (1) identify three key influences on contemporary interest group formation which make its processes and outcomes especially fluid and indeterminate; (2) show how the restructuring of the California strawberry industry increased the complexity and ambiguity of harvest workers' interests and introduced new constraints on their group formation; and (3) examine two episodes of interest identification and group mobilization, to illustrate the contingent character of rural interest group formation.

The Determination of Interests and Interest Groups

Any discussion of interest groups must begin by acknowledging the distinction that sociological patriarchs Max Weber and Karl Marx found so important: that between *objective* interests—the way circumstances actually impact an individual or group, the things that an objective observer would say are "in their interest"—and *subjective* interests—the interests that are explicitly affirmed by that individual or group, the things that participants are actually "interested in." The former notion of interests identifies a set of people in a similar objective plight. The latter notion identifies a set of people who perceive themselves to be part of a collective "we" and may choose to act on this perception.

On the face of it, the process of interest identification and interest group formation could be one of an individual's simply recognizing "what is" and joining with others in comparable objective situations. In fact, however, the process is neither as straightforward nor as individual as this characterization implies. Three factors introduce particular volatility and indeterminacy into contemporary interest group formation: the increasingly diverse pulls of socioeconomic status, the changing constraints of institutional structure, and the intervention of social intermediaries.

The Multiple and Ambiguous Pulls of Socioeconomic Status

An individual or group's position in society is often taken to be the primary source of its perceived interests. Economic position is considered especially influential. Thus for Marx and for power elite/power structure theorists of political power holding more generally, a group's position in the production process is thought central to establishing its objective interests (Domhoff 1990; Marx 1977; Mills 1956). Moreover, making subordinate economic actors aware of these interests is considered the key to mobilizing them to change an unrewarding status quo.

Socioeconomic status is not as straightforward as often thought, however, and it constitutes an uncertain guide to interests. This is in part because individuals may hold more than one economic position, either simultaneously or sequentially. Such situations have become increasingly common in recent decades, as the proportion of secure, full-time industrial jobs in the U.S. has shrunk since the mid-1970s and the proportion of low-wage service sector jobs has ballooned. As a result, more and more individuals have several different sets of economic experience and investment, so that identification of their interests is a matter of interpreting and prioritizing the elements of a complex objective reality.

Second, in advanced capitalist societies generally (Wright 1976) and in U.S. agriculture as well (Wells 1984), certain economic actors occupy "contradictory locations within class relations," in that their jobs endow them with objectively conflicting economic interests, making their affiliation with one class or another problematic. Such positions have proliferated in the U.S. since the global economic watershed of the mid-1970s, as employers have replaced direct-hire employees with a variety of distanced economic agents, both in order to lower costs and increase flexibility and profits in the increasingly volatile and competitive global market (Harrison 1994; Piore and Sabel 1984), and to free themselves from costly political constraints (Portes 1983; Wells 1996). Such workers—often called "contingent" to emphasize the unprotected and impermanent nature of their employment—include contractors and subcontractors; at-home workers; temporary, part-time, and leased workers; the self-employed; and firms too small to be covered by protective legislation. Studies indicate that such positions comprise the most rapidly growing sector of the U.S. economy, accounting for about 25 to 30 percent of the civilian labor force (Berch 1985; Callaghan and Hartman 1992; Castro 1993; Villarejo and Runsten 1993).

The social dimensions of status constitute a third source of indeterminacy. As Max Weber cautioned and as became especially evident after the U.S. civil rights movement of the 1950s and 1960s, economic position is neither the sole nor necessarily the primary status defining individual or group interests. After African Americans effectively argued in the public forum that their persisting socioeconomic subordination violated American principles of equal opportunity and merited special public dispensation, a variety of other ethnic and social minorities followed suit (see, e.g., Piven and Cloward 1975). The result has been a politicization of non-economic statuses, in which the common bonds established by shared language, values, social practices, and/or places of origin, as well as the common burdens incurred by comparable subordination within U.S. society, have come to constitute important additional bases for group cohesion. Such affiliations and resultant political claims bridge the divisions of economic position, making the formation of interest groups even less predictable.

The Constraints of Institutional Structure

The legal apparatuses of the state are an important and often overlooked influence on the construction of social interests and the formation of interest groups. In the U.S. as in other advanced capitalist societies, laws and legal institutions limit and regulate the relations among economic actors to ensure social stability. As a result, economic positions are circumscribed by bodies of law and institutional practice that accord prerogatives to, and impose obligations upon, particular sorts of actors. Because they are a source of power, such legal constraints foster contestation (Lazarus-Black and Hirsch 1994). They draw economic contests out of the fields and factory halls and into the courts. In the process, they engage new intermediaries and encounter new procedural protocols. The resolution of such contests is highly unpredictable, in part because of the indeterminacy inherent in the law. That is, under the Anglo-American common law tradition, the basis for law is a fabric of cases that interpret and determine the meaning of legislative statutes. This foundation by definition admits considerable controversy, because cases are set in specific and varying circumstances, so that the applicability of a precedent is often ambiguous and the requirement to follow it is not absolute (Bodenheimer, Oakley, and Love 1980).

The Intervention of Social Intermediaries

The indeterminacy conferred by socioeconomic status and legal-institutional constraints permits—even encourages—the involvement of intermediaries. Included among them are labor unions, ethnic movements, and community and nonprofit organizations, as well as lawyers and their various assistants. Such agents often have their own agendas, as the representatives of organizations with certain values and priorities, and/or as individuals committed to certain visions of social justice.

These intermediaries attempt to influence the perception of individuals' lived experience and to effect a prioritization and reframing of their multiple interests. They draw on their professional knowledge of the law and on the conveyed experience and context of their clients to characterize exactly what interests are involved in a particular context and what recourses are available. They may also urge a certain interpretation of the law and use their positions, knowledge, and influence to skew the outcome of economic contests in the direction they find most desirable. Because intermediaries operate in particular historical contexts, the outcomes of their representations and efforts to mobilize groups are highly variable. All in all, their intervention interjects a high degree of contingency into the formulation of group interests and the coalescence of interest groups.

The Case of the California Strawberry Industry

California's central coast strawberry industry provides a fruitful context within which to examine the contingent creation of rural interest groups. Its economic changes and social dynamics in the late twentieth century show how the fluidity and complexity of socioeconomic status, the changing constraints of legal structures, and the transformative roles of social intermediaries make it hard to predict the course and character of rural politics. To develop these points, let us first specify the causes and character of the industry's economic restructuring.

California's central coast region, including Santa Cruz and Monterey Counties with their urban centers of Watsonville and Salinas respectively, is arguably the world's premier strawberry-producing locale. California has regularly produced three-fourths of the nation's strawberries since the mid-1950s. Within the state, the central coast is especially privileged. Situated about 160 miles south of the San Francisco Bay, the region's fertile, ocean-cooled Pajaro and Salinas Valleys consistently yield longer and heavier harvests than almost any other

berry-producing district (Wells 1996:19–54). While the regional industry's profitability has much to do with its climate, which keeps the
plants producing from March through November in a good year, it
also has much to do with growers' careful management of labor. Strawberries are one of the most expensive and labor-intensive crops to produce. Labor is the largest single cost, comprising almost half of total
production expenses. Its timing and steady availability are imperative,
because straying from the optimal timetable depresses yields and because the high value, volume, and perishability of the crop make harvest interruptions costly. In addition, because the fruit is so delicate
and production practices so refined, and because the plants require
constant tending, the care, skill, and judgment with which workers
harvest the fruit is, according to University of California researchers,
the single greatest determinant of market price.

From World War II until the mid-1960s, central coast berry growers
were able to secure conscientious, careful, and reliable workers through
wage labor contracts. At that point, however, the constellation of circumstances supporting the profitability of this employment structure shifted.
Growers responded by moving to a "contingent" workforce: to sharecroppers and their unpaid family members and hired workers. By the
mid-1970s, as much as half of the berry acreage and growers in the two-
county region were involved in sharecropping. The causes of this economic restructuring were not the shifts in global market structure and
competition so often touted as causes of distanced employment relationships in U.S. industry. Rather, they were shifts in political constraints on
the regional context of production. Three developments were most influential: a change in border policy, the extension of protective legislation to agricultural workers, and the rise of agricultural unionism.

First, the wage workers that brought in the berry crop from 1942
through 1964 were Mexican nationals recruited and managed by the
U.S. government through a contract agreement with Mexico commonly known as the bracero program. These workers, called *braceros*
(individuals who work with their arms), received a contract wage insu-
lated from citizen employment, and were required to return to Mexico
immediately after their contracted job was over. The federal government shouldered the burden of labor recruitment, and workers who
were difficult or otherwise unsatisfactory were promptly decertified
and deported. Needless to say, local growers praised *braceros* as their
most tractable and diligent workers ever; however, labor unions decried
their undercutting of domestic wages and union organizing (Jenkins
1985; Majka and Majka 1982). In December 1964, after years of pressure, an alliance of urban labor unions, the United Farm Workers

union (UFW), and national civil rights activists was able to force the program's termination.

The end of the bracero program created a labor supply crisis in the central coast strawberry industry. Labor shortages and delays became endemic. Sharecropping was in part a solution to this policy shift, in that it helped growers reinstate a stable labor supply. Through it, growers displaced the difficulties and risks of labor recruitment, training, and management onto sharecroppers, capturing the social capital of their unpaid family labor and their networks of personal acquaintance.

Second, during the mid-1960s, a second aspect of the political context of production began to shift as well. Although farm laborers had been explicitly excluded from most prior labor protections on the grounds that such protections were unfair and unneeded in agriculture, after the early 1960s the state and federal governments began to limit the treatment and specify the rights of agricultural workers (Morris 1966). In 1963 California instituted a minimum wage for farm workers; in 1966 they were brought under the federal Fair Labor Standards Act (FLSA). In 1974 the FLSA set a minimum working age of 12 for farm laborers, and in 1975 California enacted the California Agricultural Labor Relations Act (CALRA) which gave agricultural workers protections for organizing and collective bargaining comparable to those granted nonagricultural workers during the New Deal. In 1976 state unemployment and workers' compensation insurance were extended to farm laborers and overtime pay requirements were instituted for adult males working in agriculture. The UFW and the civil rights movement played important roles in motivating all of these developments.

Collectively, this legislation enhanced workers' leverage and ability to organize. It also increased the cost of engaging employees and reduced growers' discretion in managing them. Sharecropping buffered growers from these impacts, in that it altered employment contracts to exclude labor suppliers from coverage. Following the reasoning of New Deal legislative pioneers, agricultural protective laws applied to "employees"—individuals who were considered particularly at risk in the unbridled operation of the market (Marshall 1965:71–134). Independent contractors, supervisors, and sharecroppers, by contrast, were excluded from coverage under most circumstances because they were seen as more economically secure, and as independent entrepreneurs or management agents. Although in theory the laws covered sharecroppers' employees, in practice, agricultural contractors' practices were notoriously underpoliced, and ignorance and social ties limited their employees' complaints (California Employment Development Department 1992b; Vaupel and Martin 1986).

A third political development clinched the shift to sharecropping: the rise of the UFW and its focus on the central coast. In August 1970, with contracts covering about 20,000 workers in California's inland table grape industry, the UFW launched a major organizing drive against large central coast vegetable growers, who had just signed sweetheart contracts with the Western Conference of Teamsters in order to forestall a feared UFW victory. On August 24, about ten thousand workers walked off their jobs in what was the largest strike in California's agricultural history (Majka and Majka 1982:203–5; Wells 1996:74–90). Although lettuce growers were the strike's intended targets, strawberry growers were swept up in the battle as well. For three weeks, shipments from central coast farms virtually stopped; berry growers lost an estimated $2.2 million (Federal-State 1972:2, 30). This strike demonstrated incontrovertibly to central coast berry growers that they were vulnerable in a climate of regional labor mobilization. Although only one strawberry contract emerged from the strike, and though its momentum subsided with the end of the harvest, the central coast remained the center of union militancy to the end of the decade, pushing wages in the region to the highest in the state. The UFW also drew government attention to labor law violators, sometimes increased border patrol apprehensions (Amplia Huelga 1979), and supported workers' claims under the CALRA.

In short, UFW activity increased production costs, constraints, and uncertainty, and enhanced the impacts of the other political constraints on production. In this context, sharecropping importantly diminished berry growers' exposure to union pressure. Because sharecroppers were labor supervisors and employers, they were not legally eligible for union membership because their interests were potentially at odds with those of employees. Nor, on the face of it, did the CALRA protect their right to organize and bargain collectively. Moreover, because their workers were often friends or family members, they tolerated less favorable wages and working conditions and were unlikely to join the union. For their parts, UFW organizers regularly ignored sharecropping ranches because sharecroppers were their ethnic compatriots and were admired as successful ethnic entrepreneurs.

In practice, strawberry sharecropping was adopted primarily by larger growers with from 60 to 300 acres each, for whom the costs and burdens of labor recruitment and protective labor laws, and the exposure to union pressure, were especially great. Sharecroppers were chosen from the cadre of experienced berry pickers—usually men with large families or networks of acquaintance.[3] Almost all were born in Mexico, had little formal education, occupational training, or capital, and were illiterate in both Spanish and English. The majority were already documented, or they quickly obtained their documents by virtue of their sharecropping contracts. Most received written contracts that specified the terms of their engagement; they were required to sign these as a condition of employment. Although contracts formally lasted for a year, growers could terminate or refuse to renew them virtually at will.

The contracts stated explicitly that sharecroppers were independent contractors, and they laid out the rights and obligations of the participants in production. Farm owners supplied all inputs requiring capital or expensive technology. They prepared and provided the land and they supplied plants, machinery, irrigation equipment, fertilizer, pesticides, and herbicides. Although the contracts specified that owners had no right to oversee or control the growing of the crop, in fact sharecroppers were supervised, though less intensively than wage workers. Sharecroppers were each allotted a parcel of land, generally from 2.5 to 3.5 acres. These they planted as part of their contracts or were paid separately to do so. Sharecroppers were responsible for maintaining the plots, harvesting and packing the fruit, and hiring, managing, and paying any labor required to carry out these tasks. They were to deliver the packed crates of berries to the owner to be transported to market and sold. Each received a share, typically 50 to 55 percent, of the proceeds from the sale of their berries. From this share, owners deducted half or all of the cost of crates and boxes, half of the cost of precooling, loading, hauling, handling, and marketing, a per-crate assessment levied on all growers by the California Strawberry Advisory Board to pay for promotion and research, and in some cases a plant patent fee.

Interviews revealed that sharecroppers valued this arrangement because it gave them the opportunity to reduce periods of unemployment and maximize family income in a surplus labor market, to bring all family members from Mexico and live together without migrating, to give their children uninterrupted schooling, and to "become (their) own boss." Sharecroppers working for a high-resource grower could make considerably more than a farm laborer—an average of $18,600 as individuals in 1985, as opposed to an average of $6,300 for individual wage workers. However, their incomes were also much more variable, ranging from a low of $4,000 to a high of $45,000. Sharecroppers working for a low-resource grower could actually lose money in a bad year. Some survived such periods with the help of family members' off-farm income; others abandoned their parcels midseason and returned to wage labor or Mexico.

The Contingent Formation of Sharecropper Interest Groups

This economic restructuring, then, altered the relationship of strawberry workers to the process of production and the law. It created two categories of workers, "independent contractors" and "employees," with differing production responsibilities and prerogatives and apparently differing legal protections. Overarching these differences, sharecroppers and wage workers shared language, culture, and Mexican national origin, as well as social connections, position in the regional opportunity structure, and the experience of wage labor in the industry. As a result, economic restructuring heightened the ambiguity as to where workers' interests lay, and it created new consequences for alternative representations. In this context, social intermediaries—here public interest lawyers, nonprofit organization staff, and union leaders and organizers—played key roles in shaping group interests and forming interest groups. An examination of two instances in which sharecroppers joined to assert common concerns and press for particular outcomes demonstrates the contingent character of their group formation and the influential roles of intermediaries.

The first instance arose during the 1970 general strike. As employers, sharecroppers could have been expected to oppose the union. Legally they were not entitled to join it because they themselves employed workers. Yet they did not directly experience union pressure because, as noted, the union avoided their ranches. Moreover, many had belonged to the union in the past and expected to belong in the future, should they lose or abandon their fragile positions as sharecroppers. Most had friends and relatives who were union members; some, who were union organizers. As prior and possible future wage workers, and also as precariously placed independent contractors, sharecroppers had experienced the economic dependency that the UFW decried. Perhaps most important, in the opinion of involved sharecroppers, they resonated to the UFW's message of ethnic power. Interviews revealed that regional farm workers had followed the union's victories in the grape industry closely and eagerly watched and discussed news broadcasts of its rallies, speeches, and marches. They appreciated UFW President Cesar Chavez's evident "Mexicanness": his small stature, dark skin, humble bearing, and Mexican-Catholic religiosity. The vision, purveyed by union leaders in the news and by union organizers in the fields, of a social movement of Mexican farm workers standing up to Anglo and Japanese growers felt as if it represented them. Sharecroppers' excitement at the magnitude of the 1970 strike matched that of wage laborers.

In this setting, many sharecroppers participated in UFW gatherings and marches. When Chavez urged local workers to form groups and formalize their grievances against farm owners, a group of central coast sharecroppers working for the Driscoll corporation gathered to discuss their concerns. Their chief complaint was the small size of their share, despite the magnitude of their risk and labor contribution. After discussion, they decided to approach Cesar Chavez, whose own family had been sharecroppers and who had publicly decried their exploitation. In their meeting with the union leader, the group characterized sharecropping as one of the historical injustices against Mexicans which the union was committed to eradicate. They asked him to form a special bargaining unit of sharecroppers to represent their interests to growers. Although sympathetic to the spirit of their request, Chavez could not let them join the union because they were employers. In compromise, he assigned UFW spokeswoman Dolores Huerta to bargain on their behalf with Driscoll growers. As a result of these negotiations, the market shares of Driscoll sharecroppers were increased from 50 to 55 percent. Interestingly enough, and demonstrating the role of contingency in assigning a weight to the variables determining interest group formation, in that context of intense labor mobilization growers did not challenge the legal propriety of a UFW leader's representing sharecroppers. Rather they chose to compromise, in the interest of restoring peace to the fields.

The second incident directly engaged the law. Five years after the general strike, when labor relations in the industry had stabilized, fifteen sharecroppers working for Driscoll Berry Farms (DBF) initiated a suit jointly against this company and its marketing association, Driscoll Strawberry Associates (DSA), on behalf of the approximately 200 sharecroppers that DSA engaged statewide (*Real v. Driscoll* 1975). These sharecroppers were incensed by DBF's repeated refusal to provide detailed market information or allow them to sell their crop through other channels, and by its supervisor's repeated instructions as to how to care for the crop. Their ire was raised particularly by the discrepancy between their contracts' representation that they were independent and the actuality of their dependency.

Interviews with the sharecroppers involved in this episode revealed that the dream of achieving greater independence was paramount to their choosing to sharecrop.[4] Although the possibility of higher family income was an important motivator, its realization was by no means assured. Given this uncertainty, these sharecroppers chose share farming because it made them more "like growers." As sharecroppers, they saw themselves as the *dueños* (owners) of their own small businesses, the *agricultores* (farmers) who directed production tasks, and the *patrones* (patrons) of their workers, with authority and a right to deference. Unlike wage workers, they thought, "no-one could boss (them) around." The wording of the DSA contract reinforced this understanding, through its assertion that neither the farm owner nor DSA "has assumed under this agreement any rights of supervision and control over the growing of the said strawberry crop" and the sharecropper "shall be under the control of [the owner] only as to the result of the work assigned to be performed by him and not as to the means by which the results are to be accomplished." This assertion conflicted sharply with farm supervisors' careful specifications as to how and what varieties of plants to plant, with their guidance as to when and how much to fertilize, irrigate, or apply pesticides, and with their pointed reminders that pickers arrived late to the fields or picked too rarely or carelessly, or that more harvest workers were needed, or that the plants needed pruning or weeding.[5]

Lacking a context of regional labor militancy which could have connected them to the union and increased growers' receptivity to the union's mediation, this group of sharecroppers approached a local nonprofit organization dedicated to minority business development. The staff person with whom they spoke, himself a prior UFW organizer, agreed that their rights as independent contractors were being violated, and he directed them to a Salinas law firm. Their initial suit (*Real v. Driscoll* 1975), adopted their legal contracts' vision of their economic status and entitlements. It claimed that DSA and DBF were monopoly firms violating sharecroppers' rights as small, independent entrepreneurs. It charged the companies with antitrust violations, fraud, misrepresentation, and breach of contract. After this suit was filed, however, and as the sharecroppers' attorney gathered data as to their actual working relationships, he formed a different understanding of the case. In his view, these sharecroppers did not meet the criteria developed over the years by the courts to establish an economic agent as a true independent contractor: subjection to minimal outside control, substantial investment in the business, significant opportunity for profit and loss, exercise of skill beyond that required for an employee, and performance of work that is a separable, temporary part of the business (*U.S. v. Silk* 1947:716). He saw them as inadequately protected and remunerated employees, rather than illegitimately constrained independent contractors.

The attorney presented this perspective to his clients, proposing that they redirect their case to seek damages as employees. Unwilling to give up their dreams of independence, some opposed his proposal vigorously. Others, however, pointed to the economic realities of their working relationships—to their actual minimal contribution to and control over production. In the end, the sharecroppers agreed to let their attorney file an additional cause of action seeking unspecified damages for violations of the Fair Labor Standards Act, and charging that their contracts were a "sham" intentionally intended to mislead sharecroppers "into not understanding their true status as employees" (*Real v. Driscoll* 1975:3).

In the end, this interpretation of the case prevailed. Although the initial court summarily dismissed the case on the grounds of insufficient evidence, the sharecroppers' attorney appealed on the FLSA charges alone. The appellate court then reversed the summary judgment, ruling that there was sufficient evidence to believe that sharecroppers could be employees. At that point, the defendants offered to settle out of court and the plaintiffs accepted. However, the court had sent a clear message with its ruling: that contractual representations notwithstanding, strawberry sharecroppers were probably the sorts of economic actors that protective labor laws intended to cover.

This ruling eliminated some of the important benefits conferred by share farming and warned of its likely future costs. Following it, regional growers hired a labor relations expert who affirmed that they could be liable for large fines and back payments for FLSA and child labor law violations, should they continue to engage sharecroppers. Meanwhile, local workers' compensation insurance companies began to informally require growers to cover their sharecroppers, as if they were employees. UFW activity in the region subsided after the late 1970s, as the union shifted its attention to political lobbying and consumer boycotts. At the same time, the election of a conservative state political leadership in the early 1980s undercut the California Agricultural Labor Board's pursuit of unfair labor practice violators and its support for workers' rights to organize and bargain collectively (Wells and West 1989). In this context, central coast growers began to shift back to wage labor. By the late 1980s only about 10 percent of the regional berry acreage was sharecropped; at present the proportion is considerably less.

Conclusion

The foregoing analysis demonstrates that patterns of rural politics are highly unpredictable, and became more so over the course of the twentieth century. It shows that the interests of rural Americans are neither set nor foregone. Rather, they are relatively fluid, volatile, and emergent, because they are based in the multiple, ambiguous, and often conflicting socioeconomic statuses that individuals occupy, and because social intermediaries and the changing constraints of government institutions can influence the salience of one over another. Moreover, interest identification and interest group formation take place in particular historical contexts, in which contingent circumstances may press in one direction or another. As a result, an individual's claiming of a certain set of interests and interest cohorts, and his or her backing of a particular grievance or policy claim, are matters to be explained, rather than assumed.

This study shows that interest group formation is the process of an individual's converting certain *parts* of his or her objective reality into subjective reality, and allying with others in similar perceived circumstances. The research presented here confirms the difficulty of predicting group interests and affiliation from socioeconomic status alone. Economic restructuring and the growth of ethnic movements have exacerbated this problem. The increased incidence of multiple job holding and the proliferation of economic agents who occupy contradictory locations in class relations make it impossible to assert a simple connection between economic involvement and group affiliation. Moreover, the common bonds and burdens of shared ethnicity can bridge the divides of economic position, making group formation even less predictable. In the case examined here, strawberry sharecroppers were linked to wage workers through their ethnic status, but divergently pulled by their economic positions. Because sharecroppers enjoyed some of the prerogatives of growers, but suffered some of the dependency and vulnerability of farm workers, their identification or affiliation with either one was problematic. In addition, most had been, and expected again to be, wage workers, so they bore both sets of concerns and experiences.

This case demonstrates that the legal apparatuses of the state can importantly influence the character and outcomes of rural politics. Not only do laws and legal institutions foster and focus economic disputes, they also, as we have seen, shape actors' interpretations of their roles in production and the kinds of claims they are willing and able to make. In some contexts, as this study reveals, legal status can be more influential than economic status in establishing a group's perceptions of its identity and interests. Finally, because the law is so closely implicated in economic relationships, challenges to those relationships can escalate into challenges to the law, and in the process both can change. Such changes reconfigure once again the constraints on rural interest group formation.

The analysis presented here confirms the important roles that social intermediaries play in shaping and prioritizing individuals' and groups' felt interests. It shows that intermediaries—here lawyers and ethnic leaders—can actually transform actors' perceptions of class interest and alliance, as well as their claims for public and private redress. The result can be a shaping of rural politics and rural policy in ways not predictable from a simple knowledge of claimants' economic or socio-cultural statuses alone. This study also shows that the intermediaries that claimants seek out as well as the claims they are able to make, are affected by the contingent character of political conflict within the sur-rounding region. In the context of economic disruption and vigorous la-bor mobilization, the fine points of legal status and entitlement can be swept aside, whereas in more stable periods of orderly production, legal distinctions can provide the basis for economic transformation.

Part II
Foundations of Twentieth Century U.S. Policy

Rural Sociolog
O Reading
p. 113-115
or
p. 127-128

Chapter 6
The Origin of the Federal Farm Loan Act

Issue Emergence and Agenda-Setting in the Progressive Era Print Press

Stuart W. Shulman

The passage of the Federal Farm Loan Act of 1916 (FFLA) opened a new era of federal regulation of agriculture in the United States. It was the first extension of federal responsibility for farm credit and laid a foundation for New Deal farm programs. Close examination of the history of the creation and promotion of this landmark legislation reveals that it passed in spite of widespread agrarian opposition or indifference. This chapter will trace the way in which key non-farm interests set an agenda for agricultural financing, thereby establishing a path for agriculture's future that few farmers would have chosen.

As Finegold and Skocpol (1995) suggest, agricultural history is path dependent. For example, policy choices during the 1910s about who should receive subsidized credit and on what terms contributed to the rise of mass production agriculture. Lawrence Goodwyn (1978) asserts that the historic commitment of United States policy during the twentieth century has been primarily to meet the credit needs of an affluent class of commercial farmers and prosperous agricultural landowners. Defeated along the way were alternate paths of agricultural development, such as those featuring large numbers of diversified, small to mid-size ecological farms, regional economies, and progressive forms of rural cooperation (Strange 1988).

Scholarship in the field of historical new institutionalism identifies the political regulation of credit in capitalist systems as one of the most important factors in state and economic development. Skocpol (1985) argues that the financial resources of the government are a crucial measure of state capacity. The ability to channel credit to particular sectors or enterprises is fundamental to any state-sponsored effort at industrial reorganization. According to this view, a state's financial resources determine its capacity to create or strengthen organizations, employ personnel, co-opt political support, and subsidize economic development. Similarly, Berk (1994) asserts that state allocations of credit are made in contingent and political struggles over distributional rights. Credit which targets a particular form of production (e.g., mass production) determines whether a sector moves toward economies of scale or scope.

With the passage of the Federal Farm Loan Act of 1916, a portion of the agricultural capital markets in the United States initiated a new system of federal subsidy and regulation (Tootell 1967; Putnam 1916). The FFLA was the first extension of federal responsibility for farm credit, and it came to characterize the political and economic development of agriculture, particularly after the New Deal (Kenney et al. 1991; Berlan 1989).

Some of the more complex origins of this landmark agrarian financial legislation remain largely unexamined. Descriptions of the law as the result of electoral manipulations by party politicians (Link 1964), an expression of the Rural Life Movement (Bogue 1976; Sunbury 1990; Danbom 1979), or as a triumph of a populist "agrarian-statist agenda," ushered in by politically influential dirt farmers (Sanders 1999), not only contradict one another, but lack compelling empirical support.[1] Left unexamined are questions about the way latent political ideas about rural credit became accessible to large numbers of individuals or their representative interest groups as they emerged publicly in the shape of competing policy proposals.

Agenda-Setting Theory

This chapter presents an alternative analytical framework for understanding the origins of the FFLA. Historical agenda-setting theory augments interpretations focused on parties, electoral concerns of the President, voter alignments, and the United States Congress. Agenda-setting theory highlights empirical evidence derived from the print press of the period being studied. It functions in two ways. First, agenda-setting theory guides the gathering and analysis of the primary historical data. The data for this study consists of news reports and editorials from three Progressive Era print press categories: the farm, farm organization, and urban agrarian press.[2] Second, the trope agenda-setting aptly describes the role of elite journalists and other important contributors to the press who described themselves as manufacturers, conduits, and editors of public information about major policy initiatives during the Progressive Era.

Agenda-setting hypotheses look for evidence that through the institutions of mass communication, the press agenda becomes the basis for the public agenda, which in turn affects the policy agenda (Wanta and Hu 1994; Protess and McCombs 1991; McCombs and Shaw 1977; Sparrow 1997). An agenda-setting framework forces us to theorize about press autonomy and capacity in state building the same way that others in the subfield of American political development focus on state autonomy and capacity, party politics, class mobilization, and techno-logical or social change (e.g., Finegold and Skocpol 1995; James 1995).

Dearing and Rogers suggest that the agenda-setting process is about "competition among issue proponents to gain the attention of media professionals, the public, and policy elites" (1996:1–2). McCombs and Shaw (1972:184) argue that voters come to share "the media's *composite* definition of what is important." In public discourse, an issue is only considered an issue when the media turns public attention to a latent or emerging problem. Agenda-setting is, therefore, inherently a political process. Once an issue gets on the media agenda, its apparent significance, or salience, becomes the decisive factor. The task in agenda-setting research is to identify changes in salience in the media and public and policy agendas, and then to develop some means to assess causality. These causal links, as Page (1994:28) suggests, can be inferred through the use of historical methods.

Baumgartner and Jones (1993) find agenda-setting to be character-ized by bursts of media attention that can propel an issue from obscu-rity to prominence. Assuming that "repetition sets the public agenda" (Dearing and Rogers 1996:36), content analyses, both of article topics and of the content of these articles, allow the discovery of the emer-gence and relative salience of issues in public awareness. It may also indicate "how people understood their individual preferences and when these preferences were defined as politically salient" (Clemens 1997:11). Such an approach suggests beginning a study at the early stages of issue emergence, when the range of legitimate alternatives takes shape in the various concerned media.

Issue Emergence: The Rural Credit Reform Movement

Three major types of press focused on agricultural issues. Much of the urban agrarian press overlapped with major business publications (Ta-ble 6.1). Numerous independent agricultural newspapers and journals, often published by large farmer-businessmen, promoted "progressive" business farming to their readers (Table 6.2). Finally, all the major farm organizations published house organs that reflected the policies adopted by their members (Table 6.3).

Rural credit emerged as a prominent issue during the 1910s. The need for agricultural credit reform was widely accepted; however,

TABLE 6.1. Urban Agrarian Periodical Survey

Title	Dates of Publication
The Banker-Farmer	December 1913–July 1916
Business America	July 1913–June 1914
Commercial and Financial Chronicle	1911–16
Moody's Magazine	September 1911–December 1914
The Nation's Business	September 1912–March 1915
The Independent	December 1906–January 1914
The World's Work	June 1907–July 1914

TABLE 6.2. Farm Periodical Survey

Title (Headquarters)	Dates of Publication
American Agriculturist (Mass.)	January 1913–July 1916
California Cultivator (Calif.)	August 1912–December 1916
Farm Journal (Pa.)	February 1912–September 1916
Farm Life (Ind.)	January 1915–November 1916
National Stockman and Farmer (Pa.)	January 1912–July 1916
Orange Judd Weekly Farmer (Mass.)	July 1915–July 1916
The Prairie Farmer (Ill.)	January 1912–July 1916
The Progressive Farmer (N.C.)	January 1912–July 1916
Successful Farming (Iowa)	January 1914–December 1916
Wallaces' Farmer (Iowa)	January 1913–July 1916
Western Farm Life (Colo.)	January 1915–December 1916
The Wisconsin Agriculturist (Wis.)	January 1914–June 1916

TABLE 6.3. Farm Organization Periodical Survey

Title	Dates of Publication
National Grange Official Organ	October 1907–April 1908
National Grange Monthly	January 1912–October 1916
National Grange Proceedings	1909–16
Pacific Farmers' Union	January 1909–July 1916
Wisconsin Equity News	February 1910–March 1916

whether credit should be provided publicly or privately was hotly contested. In 1909, the Country Life Commission (CLC) published a report that highlighted European cooperative methods for providing agricultural credit (Bailey et al. 1909). The CLC, appointed by President Theodore Roosevelt and charged with developing policies to improve the quality of rural life and agricultural production, was made up of urban agrarians and some farm business editors and leaders of farm organizations. Commissioners included Henry Wallace, the prominent publisher of *Wallaces' Farmer*, Walter Hines Page, publisher of *The World's Work*, and Kenyon Butterfield, a founder of the discipline of rural sociology, lifetime member of the Grange, and the editor-in-chief of a rural affairs department for the magazine *Business America* (Danbom 1979; Scott 1970). The report modeled its recommendations for augmented rural credit on European forms of rural cooperatives. Roosevelt presented the report to Congress in 1909 with a hearty endorsement. Business-dominated public investigations during this period, such as the American and United States Commissions, were almost unanimous in praising European cooperative methods (U.S. Congress 1913a, 1913b, 1914). At the same time, in contrast to most European farm credit policies, they rejected all forms of federal subsidy for a new rural credit system.

Although the two major farm organizations were initially buoyed by non-farm interest in reforming rural credit, they quickly came to view the CLC report and subsequent business-sponsored reports, commissions, and press coverage as hostile outside threats to farmers' interests. The European model of rural cooperation was belatedly debated within farm organizations, with farm-organization leaders ultimately opposed to a plan based on principles developed in Europe on the grounds that American farmers were not comparable to European peasants. The farm press concurred with the urban agrarian press in opposing federal subsidies for rural financial institutions.

The Urban Agrarian Press

Business held an enormous financial stake in the future development of agriculture. The price for food in the cities influenced wage demands across all sectors of the economy. Similarly, businesses, large and small, centrally located and in the hinterland, sought farmers as a consumer market. However, farmers did not meet the increasing demand for food, fueled by rapid urban industrial expansion, with increased production. Throughout the first two decades of the twentieth century, agricultural prices rose (Cochrane 1993). Danbom (1979), who coined the phrase "urban agrarian," observes that they explicitly linked the problems of urban labor unrest and poor living conditions to the failure of farmers to increase productivity.

The prominent agrarian Seaman A. Knapp contributed to the farm credit debate in 1910 with an article in *The World's Work*. Knapp was known for his work in the cotton belt promoting demonstration farms where farmers were taught to diversify their crops in order to fight pests and maintain soil fertility. He was one of the first reformers to link the availability of reasonably priced credit to requirements for better farming practices. Knapp argued that to improve Southern agricultural practices, tenant farmers should be enabled to become farm owners. This, he observed, would require large sums of money. Foreshadowing the main point of conflict in the years to follow, Knapp suggested that the sources of much needed rural finance would be private, in the form of "some reliable body of men, backed by ample capital," rather than public "charity" (Knapp 1910:12888).

Also in 1910, the banker, lawyer, and diplomat Myron T. Herrick began a personal crusade to publicize, and then solve, the American rural credit problem. He proposed the establishment of privately financed, cooperative credit associations based on the best of the European models. Herrick had experience in state and national politics, supplemented by private organizational and public investigations of European rural finance (Sherman 1949). More than any other figure, he was reported on and published in each type of print press covered in the three surveys (e.g., Herrick 1912, 1913). As the former governor of Ohio, the former president of the American Bankers' Association (ABA), and an influential player at the highest levels of the national Republican Party, Herrick became the most widely recognized authority on the subject of keeping government money out of the proposed European-style rural credit system.[3]

In 1910, Herrick gave a speech about German land credit at a meeting of the Ohio Bankers' Association. Subsequently, he contributed to a resolution adopted at the 1911 meeting of the American Bankers' Association, organizing a Committee on Agricultural and Financial Development within the ABA. This committee was premised, in part, on the idea that much could be learned from rural finance in Europe. In early 1912, Herrick obtained President Taft's agreement to appoint him Ambassador to France, with the stipulation that he would receive a specific commission from Secretary of State Knox to investigate European rural credit. With the aid of embassies in five countries, Herrick prepared an important report on the adaptability of European models to American conditions (Mott 1929; U.S. Congress 1912).

At the 1912 ABA meeting, chairman Joseph Chapman of the Agricultural and Finance Development Committee reported that Herrick and his assistant Edwin Chamberlain had "spent considerable time in Europe, at their own expense, studying the Great Land Banks in Germany, France, and other countries, with the idea of informing this Association, and, through them, the people of this country, of the benefits derived by the people of those countries from a scientific system of farm financing" (Chapman 1912:144). Other bankers in the ABA, attributing their own work to Herrick's influence, mobilized for this project as well. Charles A. Conant (1912:120) told the 1912 ABA meeting that the lack of credit facilities for farmers represented "a grave economic crisis;" thus, there was urgent cause for reforming farm finance along European lines. In the same year, the financier, innovator, and reformer George Woodruff wrote for an audience of investors about his "pioneer" institution, the Woodruff Trust Company of Joliet, Illinois. He claimed his institution was popularizing lending practices known to have worked for 140 years in Europe. Particular attention was given to the practice of including "a clause providing for proper cultivation of the soil" (Woodruff 1912:127).

There were several early indications in this particular press that the issue of rural credit reform was driven by a number of business-backed efforts. In late 1911 and during the spring of 1912, news about the reform movement and comparable examples in Europe appeared regularly in the urban agrarian press. As the ABA was mobilizing its resources to send a private commission to Europe to study cooperative methods in more depth, the Southern Commercial Congress (SCC) was preparing to bring a national audience together to study the ideas of the audacious merchant-turned-reformer David Lubin (Hobson 1931). At an April 1912 conference, the SCC adopted Lubin's plan for a large traveling commission that would sail to Europe during 1913 for a three-month "jury of inquiry" investigation. Lubin's efforts garnered press attention in all three of the press groups surveyed and represented a significant contribution to the efforts of banking interests to set the agenda on agricultural credit (Brooks 1912; Cooperative Banks and American Farmers 1912).

The Farm Organization Press

Mary Cronin's study of the Nonpartisan League newspapers (1997:128) points out that all agrarian insurgency movements during and prior to this period relied heavily on publications to "promote and defend their cause—returning government to the hands of the people." Given the logistical problems posed by rural isolation, newspapers were "the simplest means of spreading information about agrarian reform movements." Historians, wrote Cronin, have made limited use of farm-organization papers, fearing their bias or poorly developed journalistic skills. "Yet every agrarian reform movement since the Grangers in the 1870s has relied heavily on media to state its case, rally the faithful, and seek new converts." The findings presented here reinforce Cronin's assertion that the print press was considered an all-important medium for securing organizational unity and increasing efficacy in matters of policy.

It was during the 1910s, Elisabeth Clemens suggests, that a new form of political organization refined techniques of pressure-group influence that would come to characterize twentieth-century American politics. "The new currency of political influence included procedural mastery, technical expertise, and the ability to mobilize public opinion" (1997:1). One of the roles for an institutional historian, according to Clemens, is to present "an archaeology of schema, a reconstruction of the scripts available within particular societies at particular times. This approach . . . asks how 'self-interest' is constructed and under what conditions it becomes the dominant script guiding political action" (9). For farm organizations, the most reliable and efficient means of defining self-interest—and influencing legislation—available during this period were the elaborate agenda-setting efforts found in the pages of the print press. As agricultural historian Roy V. Scott (1970:37) has noted, "agrarian organizations induced their members to read and to think, to consider questions intelligently, and to reject traditionalism, emotionalism, and apathy so deeply implanted in their nature."

Where exactly did the Grange and the other major farm organization, the National Farmers' Union (NFU), stand on farm credit prior to and during this period when various business initiatives were launched on behalf of agriculture? Through the years 1909–11, the National Grange *Journal of Proceedings*, the official source of Grange policy, contained no positive program for creating a new rural credit system. As late as June 1912, the most influential Grange policymaker of that time, T. C. Atkeson, announced the four "Grange" measures before Congress: the objectionable oleomargarine revisions, long-delayed parcels post, vocational education, and direct election of United States Senators. Despite the emergence of rural credit reform as an issue for bankers and businessmen, Atkeson made no mention of rural credit whatsoever (About National Legislation 1912).

The business-sponsored, rural credit reform movement did not appear as an issue in the official paper of the National Grange until April 1912, when a *National Grange Monthly* editorial announced that the farmer was "coming into his own," because "[p]ress, pulpit, platform and people look to him as never before." The proof was "furnished in the step taken by the bankers at their last annual session, when they entered upon a project for creating a system of farm finance for the benefit of ambitious and enterprising tillers of the United States soil. Their movement, from a farmer's point of view," concluded the paper, was "the most significant that has been undertaken in this country in centuries" (Coming to His Own 1912). The same argument appeared in the *Wisconsin Equity News*, a leading branch of the farm organization known as the American Society of Equity. It reported on "farmer" finance demands by reprinting a banker's speech, one clearly indicating it was the country bankers initiating the rural credit reform movement on behalf of farmers (Better Banking System 1911).

National Grange priorities up to this point lay elsewhere, as did those of the NFU, the only other farm organization with enough membership to be considered a national interest group. The president of the NFU, Charles S. Barrett, had served on the CLC, and during this period acquired the reputation as the most prominent farm leader, particularly when it came to dealing with Washington. Barrett wrote in his 1909 book that "the credit system and farm mortgage usages throughout the country is one of the baneful curses of farm life. . . . The farmer and his family live in mortal terror of this advance merchant, and are his slaves and must do his bidding" (Barrett 1909:98–99). The NFU, he continued, was set on changing this. Barrett cited figures showing that where the Farmers' Union was well established, organizers started to see decreased mortgages, as if to argue that farm debt was itself only a product of poor farmer organization. This, in part, may explain why the March 1911 report of the NFU's National Legislative Committee contained no demands for rural credit investigations or legislation. Their efforts were instead "centralized" on regulation of cotton and grain exchanges, parcels post, immigration restrictions, and direct elections of Senators (Callicotte 1911).

In the spring of the election year 1912, NFU president Barrett published clip-and-mail petitions for farmers to mail to Congress on these four issues. Despite the national publicity given to European rural finance the previous winter and spring, the NFU was not ready to take a formal position on an issue that it had not brought to the agrarian agenda. In the months to follow, Ambassador Herrick's investigation of European methods of providing agricultural credit for the U.S. government was presented in the NFU press as "one of the most important undertakings in Dollar Diplomacy." Noting Herrick's official work as Taft's "right-hand man," the paper concluded that the "backers of the scheme feel confident that plenty of American money at cheap rates can be found for investment in American farmland mortgages if this system is introduced here and the link is provided for the farmer to get his offer before the general investor of this country" (National Field 1912:1). By the end of the year, the Master of the National Grange declared foreign methods "worthy of investigation," but this tolerance for the business-sponsored efforts would prove to be short-lived (O. Wilson 1912:16).

During the period of issue emergence, between the CLC Report in 1909 that first introduced European credit cooperatives to a U.S. public and the introduction of formal legislation in 1912, the backers of rural credit reform were not the major farm organizations. They were, as the farm organization press confirms, led by business, primarily banking, interests.

The Farm Press

The nation's farm press occupied a unique, influential, and often neglected ideological space on the journalistic spectrum. The farm press
consisted of trade journals, precariously positioned between the two,
soon-to-be divided camps represented by the business and farm organization press. The farm press was composed of journalists who were
fiercely proud of their role as rural public opinion molders. Effective
agenda-setting for the farmer, whether in terms of agricultural, business, or policy matters, was the distinguishing mark of the sophisticated and financially successful farm paper (Shulman 1999). Farm
papers reached roughly two out of every three farm households, according to one 1913 USDA survey, and advertisers estimated a weekly
circulation of farm papers and magazines at 10 to 15 million as early
as 1908 (Smith and Atwood 1913).

When the issue of rural credit emerged, the farm papers had much
to comment on (Brooks 1912; Germany's Success 1912). Farm press
journalists regularly observed that farmers were at an economic disadvantage versus other business sectors when credit was at issue. Reports
of usury were not uncommon and farm papers decried additional exploitation, which persisted through the imposition of costly terms requiring frequent renegotiation (Interest Bug 1914; High Interest
Rates 1915; Cruel Facts 1915). These deficiencies in rural finance
were denounced in the farm press as problems which placed an inor-
dinate burden on farmers, particularly the poorest tenants, those least
organized and least able to organize. Many farm papers also made the
point that those with a "shiftless" or otherwise less than businesslike
character probably ought to be denied credit, if not for their own
good, then for the well-being of the sector (French 1913; Johnson
1914).

Many farm papers noted that credit rates and terms were the worst
in the West and South, but they countered sectional divisions by arguing that poor credit machinery everywhere was a threat to rural economic development (Jeffrey 1912; Our Credit Facilities 1913). The
farm press encouraged progressive farmers to conscientiously apply
affordable credit, where it could be found, to the problems of production and distribution. Sound mortgage credit, farm papers argued,
would be a major improvement in farm finance (Farmers' Problems
1914; Milliken 1914).

While every farm paper reported the emergence of a new, non-
farm-based movement to develop a more adequate rural credit system,
speculation about its viability, even its necessity, was wide ranging. For

example, some papers reported favorably on rural cooperative credit, whereas others looked askance at the possibility that too much of the wrong kind of rural credit publicity might ignite a demand for the farmer to be given special financial privileges. The farm press expressed a variety of viewpoints regarding the importance of rural credit and the forms it should take. The editorial policies of the papers I surveyed converged, however, on the key issue of government subsidies. On this point they established an early alliance with the business press. Some even questioned the ability of farm organizations to contribute to finance policymaking, because of the lingering dislike among the business classes of populist "soft" money schemes.

By the end of 1912, rural credit reform had emerged in the three types of print press as a likely reform issue at the national level. The business press, pushed by outspoken propagandists such as Herrick and Lubin, looked forward to the prospect of capitalizing agriculture with the aid of European models, but without the taint of government subsidy. Farm-organization papers expressed cautious optimism at the potential for using new and powerful allies in business and banking to initiate reforms that would help make farming a viable business. Within a year, however, the leaders of the farm organizations staked out their own policy preferences for a system of federal subsidies through direct government lending. The farm press viewed rural credit as an important issue in the development of progressive agriculture, but shared with the business press an antipathy to government subsidies.

The Culmination of the Rural Credit Reform Movement

When the issue of a new farm credit system emerged around 1910, the most important debate was between proponents of government financial aid (represented favorably in the farm-organization press), and the diverse champions of plans for legislated self-help (represented favorably in the urban agrarian and farm press). The agenda-setting stage was steadily giving way to a battle over these different visions for rural credit reform, and the issues to be resolved had been parsed in the pages of the print press.

In 1914 the issue moved into the legislative arena. President Woodrow Wilson, during his inaugural address on March 4, 1913, had awkwardly endorsed the issue. He placed rural credit high on the list of "things that ought to be altered" (Wilson 1978:150). Wilson soon insisted, however, that no bill would pass his desk that provided "special privileges" to farmers or any other group (Wilson 1913). Until he modified his position in early 1916, partly as an election year appeal to midwestern farmers (Link 1964:345), President Wilson represented the major barrier for those who sought to include provisions for federal money to underwrite the new system. If Wilson did shift his position for political advantage, it was probably due to the linkage all the business, farm, and farm-organization press had established between farm credit and larger agrarian issues. The press had placed a "much delayed" rural credit reform before a public that included, but was far greater than, midwestern farmers.

The proximate origin of the Federal Farm Loan Act of 1916 can be found in an agenda-setting effort in the business and subsequently the farm press. This forward-looking effort sought to adapt European models of rural cooperative credit to fit American conditions and eliminate the need for federal financial aid. This final section examines the culmination of the movement for federal intervention. It was a protracted congressional struggle that stretched over two years in which more than one hundred bills were introduced. During that period, the agenda set by urban agrarians came under attack by the two major farm organizations. Two leading candidates for passage, the Moss-Fletcher and Bathrick bills, emerged by the time of the spring 1914 Joint Hearings before the Subcommittee of the Committees on Banking and Currency. Business-sponsored commissions backed the Moss-Fletcher bill, which relied on cooperative organization and private funding. Farm organizations supported the Bathrick bill, which called for direct, low-interest loans from the federal government to the farmer.

The various committees working on rural credit failed to report a bill because of this disagreement. As a result, the committee chairs came up with a compromise measure, known as the Hollis-Bulkley bill, which ultimately was the basis for the FFLA. Much of the design of the new measure reflected the work of the business-sponsored American Commission to Europe embodied in the language of the Moss-Fletcher bill. A provision was inserted in the Hollis-Bulkley bill calling for purchase of $50 million per year of land bank bonds by the U.S. Treasury, as a gesture to subdue critics of the Moss-Fletcher bill (Putnam 1916). The Wilson administration, meanwhile, made it known that any rural credit law with a provision of this sort would be vetoed. Preoccupied with other business, the Joint House and Senate Committee tabled rural credit reform and created a new joint committee in March 1915. This committee was given a deadline of January 3, 1916, to issue a report and propose legislation for a new system of land mortgage loans (Putnam 1916).

The committee's legislative report was submitted on that day. It presented the final Hollis-Bulkley compromise bill with a provision for limited government financial subvention conditioned on eventual repayment by the new system to the U.S. Treasury. The chief author of the bill, Senator Henry Hollis (D-New Hampshire), wrote that the "successful farmer becomes more of a business man each year. . . . He must have ready cash." Current conditions, noted Hollis, provide that if a farmer could get a loan, it was on short terms with high rates, putting farmers under the "power of some hard-headed banker," whose job it was to be hardheaded. "In many parts of the country, the farmer is charged extortionate and inexcusable rates, regardless of usury laws and decent regards for human necessities" (Hollis 1916:5–6).

The solution proposed in the final Hollis-Bulkley bill envisioned a supply of private, long-term investment money seeking safe harbors for investment. The Hollis report described the aggregate sum as "enormous," and laid out a new role for the federal government in channeling capital to farmers:

We may picture the owners of this vast wealth grouped on one side of a river, the farmers desiring loans on the other side. . . . We are asked to furnish the bridge which shall bring them in touch, or rather to grant a franchise to those who would build a bridge if we will construct the approaches. Such we conceive to be a proper function of the Government. (7)

Reactions to the final bill, which was a compromise between the two major competing agendas, appeared mixed in the press surveyed for the year 1916. Farm organizations generally were not impressed by the final shape of the law, despite their success in obtaining government support. The criticism was most intense at the *Wisconsin Equity News*: "The bill meets no need of the farmers. It is overburdened with new administrative machinery. It smothers any benefits that might accrue by excessive expense." The American Society of Equity resolution on the Hollis bill reflected the organization's deep suspicion. "Like every other financial bill passed by the United States Congress, this bill has the ear-marks of the money speculator." The resolutions of the ASE were included on a clip and mail form, which stated the bill "will in no sense improve the present financial condition of our farmers, but on the contrary will retard the growth of Agriculture by providing another system of private, profit-sharing, dividend-paying, surplus-creating banks." It asked Senators and Congressmen to vote against the much-delayed rural credit legislation (Rural Credit Legislation 1916).

Soon after enactment of the FFLA into law, the president of the National Farmers Union, C. S. Barrett, noted that the rural credit bill might do some good for certain classes, those who already owned land that could be offered as security, or those who had money in the bank.

"But instead of helping the tenant to acquire land and home, it will have a tendency to increase his number." He reasoned that under the FFLA, the landlord would get the cheap money and buy more land to rent out at high prices. "Conditions are thus being created which make it more and more difficult for the homeless man to acquire any land at all." If the government would not act soon to arrest this trend, argued Barrett, America was "doomed to growing tenancy, ultimately, to agricultural pauperism" (Barrett 1916:2–3).

At the National Grange, editors noted that farmers turned a cold shoulder to the new rural credit law. "This indifference is clearly revealed, and ridicule and criticism arising from farmers is more than a local expression. That such a law was not needed and that it will bring no benefits to American farmers are comments coming from many quarters" (Give It a Chance 1916). While the paper counseled greater tolerance for the new system, it made a stunning admission during the fall of 1916: "The Grange, and in fact all farm organizations, did not have any large influence in the rural credit legislation for the reason that they were not agreed among themselves and could not come forward with any concrete plan that could be labeled what the farmer himself wanted" (Summary of a Year's Work 1916). The Master of the National Grange, however, framed the legislative outcome in a slightly more favorable manner at the 1916 annual meeting:

It is our pleasure to state that the Grange won another victory in the enactment of the Rural Credit Law—not that it is all the Grange has asked or contended for, but the principle for which we stood has been recognized. Thus, having secured a victory, the farmers should give it a fair trial and if it is cumbersome or too complicated it must be perfected by amendments. Let it be given a fair trial before we condemn. (O. Wilson 1916:12)

The farm press also reflected mixed opinion in its appraisal of the final Hollis bill. Supporters at the *Farm Journal* noted that, after much delay, the "bill has been drawn with great care in order to avoid all mistakes and provide for the greatest good to the greatest number" (Farmers' Problems 1916). One *Farm Life* editor wrote that if the bill passes as the sponsors hope, it "may well prove to be one of the most important laws ever passed in the United States. . . . It is not a partisan measure, and if the farmers O.K. the bill and take an intelligent interest in it, there should be no difficulty in obtaining its early passage" (Weymouth 1916). Long-time farm finance reform advocates at *The Orange Judd Weekly Farmer* were thrilled as the bill was about to become law. "If the new system is perfected as to prove its usefulness," stated one editorial, "the federal farm loan law of 1916 will be one of the noblest enactments in American history. That all political parties joined in its support gives it a nonpartisan character" (Farm Mortgage Reform is Here 1916). Another *Orange Judd* editorial confidently predicted that the "magnitude of the victory secured in this new act is too big to be realized at sight" (Farmers' Victory in Loan Law 1916).

However, there also was considerable skepticism in some parts of the farm press. At *The National Stockman and Farmer*, the tone of the editorial remained aloof in response to the final Hollis bill.

Evidently the committee has labored to create a rural credit system which shall not bear the taint of class legislation, but it has not quite succeeded . . . there will be few protests from farmers because the plan favors them. In fact in this region there seems to be mighty little interest in the whole matter. (New Credit System 1916:1)

As was the case in earlier stages of the rural credit reform movement, editors at *Wallaces' Farmer* could not "work up any enthusiasm over a law which is likely to do little more than inflate prices of farm lands, and make it more difficult for actual farmers to acquire homes of their own" (Farm Credit Bill 1916).

Conclusion

At the July 17, 1916, signing ceremony for the Federal Farm Loan Act, the long-time opponent of government aid going to farmers, President Woodrow Wilson, seemed to be convinced that the farmers had, as he stated,

occupied, hitherto, a singular position of disadvantage. They have not had the same freedom to get credit on their real estate as others have had who were in manufacturing and commercial enterprises. . . . [T]his bill . . . puts them on equality with all others who have genuine assets, and makes the great credit of the country available to them. . . . (quoted in Hoag 1976:214)

The compromise bill, signed by a President long opposed to its key provision for government aid, went into effect as the country's first farm finance law. It established a first-of-its-kind quasi-governmental enterprise for farm mortgage finance. This outcome was not what the original business and farm press agenda-setters sought in terms of rural credit reform. The legislative process had produced a hybrid of two competing agendas, and in doing so alienated some of the movement's key original supporters through the inclusion of a provision for government financial aid. None were more vocal in their opposition to the law than Myron T. Herrick, who stated that the movement had been corrupted by, among other things, provisions in the FFLA that made the new land banks into depositories for government funds.

"The result is the Federal Farm Loan Act, which has started the Government off on a use of public cash and public credit for private individuals on a scale never attempted in any other country" (Herrick 1916:837).

In the final analysis, the FFLA did represent a transition to a new era of government intervention in the agricultural economy. The most prolific farm press editor of the period, Herbert Myrick, wrote "the new statute may prove to be epochal in its economic and social benefits" and that the "act is the Magna Carta of American farm finance." To its credit, he argued, the FFLA was not "a scheme of visionary enthusiasts to reform the world" (Myrick 1917:5, 20). Instead, it was an attractive new means for solvent farmers with equity to enjoy amortization, long terms, easy payments, a top interest rate of 6 percent, refinancing as rates dropped, limited expenses, profit sharing, limited liability, farmer control, tax-free mortgages and shares in the system, transferability, cooperation, and a national system with supervision.

This case demonstrates that powerful interests, in this case urban agrarians and bankers, may be able to establish a public agenda that is spurned by those directly affected, in this case, farmers. However, it also demonstrates that, once the agenda has been established, the policy outcome remains indeterminate. The new agenda creates an arena in which people coalesce into interest groups that contest proposed legislation. The urban agrarians, and particularly Herrick and the American Bankers' Association, succeeded in placing farm credit on the public agenda. However, despite farmers' apparent indifference to credit reform, particularly as agriculture became increasing remunerative, they fought vigorously, and ultimately successfully, for government subsidy of any credit reform program. The final outcome, a compromise between two theories of governmental intervention, satisfied neither. It did, however, establish an institutional foundation that, during the New Deal, would reconfigure the relationship of state and society.

Chapter 7
Low Modernism and the Agrarian New Deal
A Different Kind of State
Jess Gilbert

> Democracy is about the utilization of knowledge. A democratic so-
> ciety is one in which all members are able to develop and express
> their capacities to the full in the running of that society. One of
> the tasks of a democratic state is to create the conditions for this.
> —Wainwright 1993:120

Modernisms and New Deals

In *Seeing Like a State*, agrarian scholar James C. Scott explains "how
certain schemes to improve the human condition have failed" (the
subtitle). "High modernism" is his term for the ideology behind such
human disasters as Soviet collectivization and peasant villagization as
well as lesser fiascos like the city of Brasilia, rural resettlements, and
agricultural modernization. He defines high-modernist ideology as

a supreme self-confidence about continued linear progress, the development
of scientific and technical knowledge, the expansion of production, the rational design of social order, the growing satisfaction of human needs, and, not
least, an increasing control over nature (including human nature) commensu-
rate with the scientific understanding of natural laws. *High* modernism is thus
a particularly sweeping vision of how the benefits of technical and scientific
progress might be applied—usually through the state—in every field of human activity. (1998:89–90)

High modernists are also extremely and "unscientifically optimistic
about the possibilities for the comprehensive planning of human
settlement and production" (1998:4). Scott argues that this ideology,
when joined with an administrative, authoritarian state and a weak

civil society, led to the large-scale development failures of the twentieth century. He notes that the liberal democracies have tended to resist authoritarian high modernism. Yet he names three U.S. political figures—David Lilienthal, Robert Moses, and Robert McNamara—along with Saint-Simon, Lenin, Nyerere, and the Shah of Iran, to high modernism's hall of fame (1998:88–90, 101–2).[1]

Statist social engineering, Scott further claims, is "inherently authoritarian" (1998:93). He criticizes high modernism also for its "radical authority" based on scientific rationality and its disallowance of other bases for judgment. For instance, it denigrates folk knowledge and local cultures. It breaks with history and tradition; the "past is an impediment" to be overcome (1998:95). Myth, religion, and other irrational superstitions are to be transcended. Authoritarianism follows from this stance, Scott asserts: Only the knowledgeable elite—scientific experts separated from the people—ought to rule society, and the ignorant or recalcitrant re-educated. Thus, high modernists usually devalue or banish politics, and they like to create new public authorities for giant development projects (e.g., the Tennessee Valley Authority). It is not surprising that the ideology appeals especially to bureaucratic intelligentsia, technicians, and planners (1998:93–96).

The agrarian New Deal would seem to be a classic case in point: It engaged in typically modernist state actions such as long-range planning of economy and society, the administration of huge public programs, policy education for the masses, and applied scientific research. Planned and led, in significant part, by expert social scientists (particularly economists) steeped in a Progressive state-building tradition, the New Deal assumed that a larger, administrative state was necessary to manage the modern economy. It used a massive public bureaucracy to plan, implement, and enforce the reduction of farm output in the hope of raising commodity prices; millions of farmers thereby received "benefit payments" if they signed legal contracts with the federal government (the Agricultural Adjustment Administration). The New Deal placed technical experts in every rural county to advise and assist farmers in preventing soil erosion (the Soil Conservation Service). Moreover, the government acquired millions of acres of settled but "submarginal land" (scientifically determined), then uprooted and resettled thousands of the poor farm families elsewhere, usually into new houses of a strikingly modernist design, and occasionally into entirely new rural communities (the Resettlement Administration). Late in the New Deal, political and technical elites at the federal and state levels established land-use planning as a priority. Local farmer committees, together with scientists and administrators, were to coordinate these and other new federal programs. This mechanism, in theory, would create a national plan for agriculture (the Bureau of Agricultural Economics' land-use planning program).

This all smacks of "social engineering" deep within the New Deal Department of Agriculture (USDA). Such considerations lead Scott to conclude that the intellectual leaders of USDA were high modernists. Indeed, Henry A. Wallace and M. L. Wilson, the top New Deal agrarians, are portrayed explicitly as such in *Seeing Like a State* (1998:199–201). Deborah Fitzgerald (2001) has also recently made a similar argument, particularly about Wilson.[2]

Yet, in contrast to Scott and Fitzgerald, I maintain that Wallace, Wilson, and other agrarian New Dealers were not high modernists but rather "low modernists." On the one hand, they did believe in many modernist institutions and activities (e.g., science, planning, administrative states, progressive reform). However, they interpreted these terms differently from most of their contemporary elites. And on the other hand, they rejected, both ideologically and in practice, those crucial aspects of high modernism that, according to Scott, make it authoritarian: the dismissal of local knowledge, history, tradition, and other "illegible" activities like family farming. Nor did they exhibit blind faith in science, states, the progressive future, or industrial farming (which epitomizes high modernism in agriculture). Above all, they were participatory democrats. For these reasons, I suggest that the better term to capture their moderate brand of state-led reform is "low modernism."[3]

In this chapter, I argue that the leaders of the New Deal in agriculture were statists all right, but with a twist: They believed in and pursued modernization via citizen participation. In particular, they tried to narrow the high-modernist gap between scientists/administrators and farmers. The agrarian intellectuals undertook this feat in several interrelated ways: adult education, citizen discussion groups, participatory planning and policy-making, local farmer administration of federal programs, and action research by technicians in partnership with rural communities. Through these means of civic engagement in public policy, the distance between expert and citizen could be bridged and progressive reforms advanced. Overall, this program of state-led democratization was not high-modernist but exemplified low modernism in action. Below I present the agrarian intellectuals' attempts—through adult education, planning (along with administration), and research—to narrow the gap between government experts and citizen-farmers, especially in the late New Deal. First, however, it will be useful to summarize the agricultural New Deal, which can be understood in three phases.

The Three New Deals in Agriculture

In 1933, in the depths of the Great Depression when Franklin D. Roosevelt became President, farmers nationwide were demanding that the federal government do something to provide economic relief. The first New Deal established the Agricultural Adjustment Administration (AAA) within the USDA. The AAA made "benefit payments" to farmers who planted fewer acres of certain crops; this production control plan succeeded somewhat in raising farm prices. Economist M. L. Wilson proposed that an elected committee of farmers, with a public agricultural official, administer the crop reductions in every rural county. Secretary of Agriculture Henry A. Wallace agreed, and they gained the aid of the decentralized Extension Service, based in each state land grant college. Led by Extension's county agents, farmer committees signed up millions of farmers in the new AAA programs. It was an impressive political and administrative feat, but one with certain victims and limitations as well (Badger 1989:147–89; Saloutos 1982).

The AAA was aimed at the commercially successful farmers who benefited most from higher crop prices. In places like Wallace's Iowa and Wilson's Montana, and generally where family farms prevailed, the first New Deal helped most farmers. But in class-based systems such as capitalist farms in California and plantations in the South, the AAA worked for larger farmers and against farm workers, sharecroppers, and tenants. Particularly in the Mississippi Delta, the AAA's cotton reduction program displaced many landless farmers. The USDA's policy did not assist, and often harmed, the "lower third" in rural America (Baldwin 1968:47–58, 76–84; Gilbert and Howe 1991:212–13). Could the New Deal treat persistent poverty on the farm?

President Roosevelt responded with the agrarian part of the second New Deal in 1935: the Resettlement Administration. One of the most radical federal agencies, it tried to reform both poor land and poor people. In 1937, Secretary Henry Wallace and Undersecretary M. L. Wilson reorganized the agency into the Farm Security Administration (FSA). The FSA continued the controversial second New Deal in agriculture with small-farmer "rehabilitation" loans and a "tenant purchase" program as its main activities. For the next five years, the FSA and the AAA were the USDA's largest action agencies, with quite different (and frequently antagonistic) leadership, field staffs, constituents, and ideologies (Baldwin 1968:85–192; Gilbert and Howe 1991:214–15).

By 1938, the USDA offered many new programs that often worked at cross purposes (e.g., AAA's crop reductions and FSA's loans to increase production). Enter the third New Deal, which undertook to coordinate the first two. The "third New Deal" denotes the reform agenda of President Roosevelt's second term (1937–40). It combined the interests of the first two New Deals in sectoral self-government (e.g., "grass-roots" administration) and social reform (Resettlement/ Farm Security). The third New Deal differed from its predecessors, however, by emphasizing overall coordination and administrative management as well as economic planning. Its best-known measures were Roosevelt's first Executive Reorganization Act, which called for a national planning board; more regional planning authorities ("Seven Little TVA's"); judiciary reform; and FDR's 1938 attempt to defeat some conservative Southern Democrats in Congressional elections. The defining characteristic of the third New Deal was its failure. None of these initiatives succeeded (Graham 1985:285–91; Karl 1983:155–81; Vaudagna 1989).

Only in agriculture did the third New Deal get off the ground. In 1938, the USDA started building a federal system of local institutions that joined farmers and government officials together to plan public policy. The leaders of this third New Deal—Wallace, Wilson, and many like-minded bureaucrats—saw participatory planning as the best way to democratize agricultural policy and to counter growing opposition from a powerful conservative coalition. Their chosen mechanism was the county land-use planning program, established jointly by the USDA and the land grant colleges. To the USDA planners, this program meant more power to implement their long-term vision of progressive reform and participatory modernization. Specifically, they undertook to coordinate citizen participation with technical expertise for purposes of public policy. Here was the last, best chance to narrow the gap between scientists/administrators and farmers (Gilbert 1996; Kirkendall 1982; Parks 1947).

By mid-1942, the planning program had failed—or rather was destroyed. Powerful groups of larger, wealthier farmers, notably the American Farm Bureau Federation, saw it as an organizational and ideological threat to their own control over agricultural policy. Led by an anti-New Deal coalition of midwestern Republicans and southern Democrats, and abetted by the more conservative agencies in USDA (particularly the AAA), Congress denied funding to the planning program (Hardin 1946; Kirkendall 1982:195–217). The next year the same coalition effectively killed the Farm Security Administration. In 1942–43, then, both the second and the third agrarian New Deals ended, and with them the planning/reform vision of Wallace and Wilson.

In contrast, the AAA survived World War II and became, under various rubrics, the core of American farm policy to this day. Thus, the main legacy of the New Deal in agriculture was the "farm commodity programs," established as stopgap emergency measures in 1933. This was contrary to the intent of the agrarian intellectuals. They left another, better legacy, and it should be reclaimed. In particular, their third New Deal emphasized democratizing education, participatory planning, and action research with local communities. I turn now to these low-modernist programs.

Adult Education and Policy Discussion for Farmers and Experts

One way that the agrarian intellectuals tried to close the gap between public experts and private citizens was through an innovative program of continuing education for farmers, technicians, and administrators themselves. The USDA leaders of the late 1930s had a very broad view of education, which included the fostering of democratic citizenship and the fomenting of social change. Like radical philosopher and educator John Dewey, Undersecretary M. L. Wilson believed that democracy required continuous learning, personal growth, cultural adjustment, and civic discussion. Wilson and his colleagues knew that it also demanded an informed citizenry. Secretary Henry Wallace (1937:340) thought, with Thomas Jefferson, that democracy "could not work unless there was popular education among the people." In a speech to USDA employees, Wilson (1936b:6) said that the department's role was "that of drawing forth the best qualities and the greatest potentialities of the nation's rural people and of helping in the process of utilizing these qualities in forming and shaping policy. . . . I am a great believer in the ability of the average man to find his way if he is given light." By the late thirties, the USDA leaders saw themselves as part of a "great democratic movement in this country," a movement that counted adult education as its core (Wilson 1939a:1; see also Wilson 1936b and Tolley 1943:8, 108–10).

Wilson later recalled that he and Wallace had often discussed the heightened need for adult education in the New Deal. They regretted that the agricultural colleges taught little "history, philosophy, social science and that kind of thing that are related to social change. . . . Henry saw the possibilities of [adult education], and he told me once that I should give it a good deal of attention and that I could kind of put this number one on my agenda of interests and objectives" (Wilson 1973:2065, 2091). They asked how the Extension Service could "get a greater interest in and understanding of . . . the democratic process?" (Wilson 1973:2090). As leaders of the USDA, Wallace and Wilson were in a position of power to answer their own question. In 1935, they established a Program Study and Discussion Section in

AAA's Program Planning Division. The audience was farmers as well as Extension workers. To lead this educational effort, Wilson hired his former philosophy professor at the University of Chicago, Carl F. Taeusch, who had since moved on to teach ethics in the Harvard Business School. Program Study and Discussion, which was elevated to a division of the Bureau of Agricultural Economics in 1939, had two main programs: Group Discussion for farmers and Schools of Philosophy for Extension workers and other rural leaders (Kirkendall 1982:140–43, 170, 187–90; McDean 1969:414–25, 484–88; Lachman 1991).

The Group Discussion project emphasized broad social issues of agriculture and public policy. Through the state Extension Services and their county agents, the Program Study and Discussion unit engaged local farm men and women in winter (off-season) discussions of such topics as:

"Should farm benefit payments be abolished?"
"Do farmers want the federal government to deal with farm problems?"
"What kind of industrial policy is best for agriculture?"
"What part should farmers in your county take in making national agricultural policy?"
"Is the farm laborer getting a square deal?"
"Farm security: How can tenants find it?"
"Is it in the interest of the nation to have more or fewer people living on the land?"
"Is increased efficiency in farming always a good thing?"

Over forty such subjects were covered between 1935 and 1945, and they exposed the heart of the New Deal. For instance, the first topic above (on benefit payments) asked whether FDR's key farm program should be abolished. The last two questions (on farm numbers and efficiency) also suggest wide-ranging consideration of rural policy issues by local citizens. The USDA's Program Study and Discussion unit prepared and distributed millions of copies of discussion guides, which offered diverse points of view. It also trained tens of thousands of local discussion leaders. Three million rural people took part in the discussion groups (Taeusch 1940, 1952; Lachman 1991).

Perhaps more remarkable were the Schools of Philosophy, originally for Extension workers, later including other local leaders. These four- or five-day state-wide conferences provided, as M. L. Wilson said, an "orientation or background to the phenomena of democracy in rural society" (1973:2091). The general aim of these schools was captured in an early proposal: "The point of view of philosophy is not that of solutions but attitudes of individuals and groups toward the more fundamental problems in human and national life. It is necessary to consider these [agricultural] policies in terms of the philosophical aspects of western civilization and to secure therefrom philosophical aspects of economic democracy in agriculture" (National Project, Schools n.d.). At the schools, national luminaries in the humanities and social science lectured each morning and, with USDA personnel, led small-group discussions in the afternoons.

The most frequent theme was, "What is a desirable national agricultural program?" Presumably the USDA did not claim to have all the answers. The five days of instruction were typically arranged as shown in Table 7.1. Another School of Philosophy (in Ames, Iowa, March 1939) featured lectures by Harvard economist John Kenneth Galbraith, Wisconsin political scientist John M. Gaus, Texas philosopher and economist Clarence E. Ayres, and USDA Land Use Coordinator Milton S. Eisenhower. A Program Study and Discussion staff member concluded this conference with a lecture on "How Can Education in a Democracy Be Furthered by Group Discussion?" In the schools generally, speakers and participants were encouraged to question and criticize New Deal policies; well-known critics often were among the lecturers. One hundred and twenty such schools were held, attended by more than 50,000 Extension workers and rural leaders (Taeusch 1940, 1952; Lachman 1991; USDA 1939c).

The intention behind discussion groups and Schools of Philosophy was to expand the views of local and state leaders in both government and society at large. Wallace, Wilson, and other USDA leaders thought that exposure to new ideas could help democratize as well as modernize agricultural policy and rural society. Discussion and philosophy alone, of course, would not reform the countryside, but, with Jefferson and Dewey, they believed that education led to positive social change. They wanted to plant the seed.

Not just farmers and Extension specialists needed re-education for democracy, Wallace and Wilson knew. The experts in Washington (themselves included) could use it too. Undersecretary Wilson was especially interested in enlightening USDA scientists and administrators. In the spring of 1938, for instance, he held a department-wide series of lectures on the theme of democracy. About a thousand USDA employees attended each lecture, after which the speaker and Wilson led a follow-up discussion with seventy-five departmental leaders. The kickoff speaker was the leading American historian of the time, Charles A. Beard, who addressed "The Rise of American Civilization" (the title of his and Mary R. Beard's classic text). Beard also wrote a glowing preface to the subsequent book of the proceedings. This citizen-scholar—known to be a critic of the New Deal—was followed by other public

Table 7.1 USDA School of Philosophy Agenda, Pullman, Washington, January 1936

Day and Theme		Lecture One	Lecture Two	Lecture Three
Day One	Background and Development of the Present Situation	What Can Philosophy Contribute to a Better Understanding of the Present?	General Social and Economic Background in the U.S.	Immediate Backgrounds of Present Agricultural Policies and Programs
Day Two	The Place of Government in Modern Society	Individualism, Democracy, and Social Control	The Relation of Government to Social and Economic Affairs	The Problem of Continuing a Program of Agricultural Adjustment
Day Three	Regionalism, Nationalism, and Internationalism	Unity and Diversity in Society	Political and Social Problems Involved in Nationalism and Internationalism	A Desirable Foreign Trade Policy for American Agriculture
Day Four	"Scarcity Economy" and "Economy of Abundance"	"Progress" and the Philosophy of History	A Critique of Our Present Economy	Production, Price, and Income Problems of Agriculture
Day Five	Values, Social and Human	Human Values	Living Standards in American Life	Improving American Farm Life

intellectuals, including anthropologist Ruth Benedict, who extended her influential *Patterns of Culture* (1934) to discuss "The American Cultural Pattern"; Yale law professor Thurman Arnold, who spoke from his latest book, *The Folklore of Capitalism* (1937); and George H. Gallup, who was working on *The Pulse of Democracy* (1940), about the potential of public opinion polling. M. L. Wilson entitled the published version of the lectures and discussions *Democracy Has Roots*, to emphasize the point of using the nation's agrarian past in guiding current developments (Wilson 1939b; see also Beard 1939; Gilbert 1997).

Another monument to the USDA's educational effort was the extraordinary Yearbook of Agriculture for 1940, *Farmers in a Changing World*. For Henry Wallace's eighth and last yearbook (he became vice-president in 1941), his friends created a social-science showcase. The first 300 pages of the volume are a still-useful history of American agriculture by the department's professional historians. In another chapter, Bureau of Agricultural Economics (BAE) division head Rensis Likert developed a social psychological profile of "the democratic personality"—ten years before the acclaimed work by Theodor W. Adorno and others on *The Authoritarian Personality*. Six chapters focused on rural poverty. University of Chicago social scientists Robert Redfield and W. Lloyd Warner contributed "Cultural Anthropology and American Agriculture." Harvard philosopher William Ernest Hocking wrote on freedom and capitalism. The USDA Yearbook Committee (M. L. Wilson, Howard R. Tolley, and an editor) was trying to expand the democratic mindset of scientists and administrators as well as farmers. They engaged some of the best humanists and social thinkers of the day to promote greater critical understanding in Washington, D.C., and throughout rural America—hardly a high-modernist aim.

Policy Planning by Experts and Citizens in the Third New Deal

In 1940, M. L. Wilson (then USDA's Director of Extension Work) spoke to the American Political Science Association on "A Theory of Agricultural Democracy." He specified how planning fit into the larger vision of the department:

Land use planning is based upon the definite recognition of the planning process in the formulation of agricultural policy. It is placed between the educational process with its discussion technique and the administrative process which takes place after broad policies have been formulated. (Wilson 1941:9)

County land-use planning connected the general educational pro-

gram, discussed above, to the grassroots administration of federal action agencies. Back in 1933, Wilson had built farmer committees into
the AAA to administer the federal production control program locally.
This decentralized administration had been adopted subsequently by
the Soil Conservation Service, the Farm Security Administration, and
other USDA agencies.

By the late thirties, it had become evident that this explosion of "action programs" in rural America needed some overall coordination.
This was the promise of the county land-use planning program of the
third New Deal. It got under way in mid-1938, established by the Mt.
Weather Agreement between the USDA and the land grant colleges.
Planning was to become as central as research and education were to
the federal department, the colleges, and the Extension Service. In
other words, Mt. Weather added a major new function—planning—to
the public agricultural institutions of the U.S. But *who* would do the
planning, and *what* would they plan?

In October 1938, Secretary Henry Wallace reorganized the huge
USDA to implement the federal part of the Mt. Weather Agreement.
He first summarized the agreement as "establishing democratic and
cooperative procedures and institutions that would give farm people an effective voice in formulating, correlating, and localizing public agricultural programs" (Wallace 1940:468). He also addressed
the relationship between expert knowledge and farmer participation:
"Farmers need the help that specialists can provide, and specialists
must draw on the experience and judgment of farmers. The need,
therefore, is to provide for integrating and unifying the planning of
both groups as a guide to all public agricultural programs" (Wallace
1940:469). The reorganization of USDA elevated the BAE to be the
central planning agency for the entire department. The BAE then established several new divisions, including the Program Study and Discussion Division (previously an AAA section) to expand both Group
Discussions for farmers and Schools of Philosophy for Extension workers and farmer-planners. Most important was the Division of State and
Local Planning, which directed the new federal-county planning program. This division housed BAE representatives (land-use planning
specialists) in every land grant college to work with state-level officials.
The BAE soon grew to include 768 social scientists—probably the
largest single group of applied researchers anywhere in the world (Tolley 1939:1–3; Kirkendall 1982:166).

The Mt. Weather Agreement and its subsequent implementation set
up committees of farmers in two-thirds (nearly 2,200) of the counties
in the U.S. At the neighborhood and community levels, these were

farmer-only committees. The county committees consisted of a majority of farmers (usually 10 to 15) and the local Extension agent, plus the county administrators of federal agricultural programs (AAA, Farm Security Administration, Soil Conservation Service, etc.) and land grant college specialists. The land-use planning committees, then, comprised state scientists, public administrators, and private citizens who aimed to reform public policy—the first such effort in American history. By 1941, 40,000 farm people (32,000 men, 8,000 women) served on the county committees. Another 20,000 were government workers. Over 82,000 rural people were on the community-level committees, which hosted 280,000 farm men and women at local meetings in 1941 (Gilbert 1996:239–41).

To elucidate the low-modernist vision behind this effort, I shall examine the first major documents produced by the county planning program, with attention to the relationship between scientists and citizens. In January 1939, the USDA issued the main guide for county land-use planning, "Work Outline Number 1." Addressed to Extension and research personnel, it detailed the land-use mapping and classification work that would be done over the next three years. The project's dual purpose was agency coordination and farmer participation—what might be identified as modernizing and democratizing functions. They found common ground in the immediate aim of localizing federal programs. Here, citizen participation offered what the government could use: "needed information on the location and characteristics of areas unsuited for farming" (USDA 1939a:2). Federal action agencies, as well as states and counties, employed such local knowledge as a guide to public services and rural development. The local committees, then, contributed to a more efficient administration of public programs.

Moreover, the committees could give public agencies some citizens' views of long-term goals for each local area. Farmers also would benefit from the improved effectiveness of programs and from their own increased knowledge of farm practices and land-use in their area. "Work Outline Number 1" concluded with a warning against committee domination by government technicians, and restated the objective of the program: "What is desired most in county agricultural planning is the carefully formulated opinions of the people themselves" (USDA 1939a:33). It is worthwhile recalling that this document was intended for the field staff who implemented the planning work, so such statements opposing expert domination should carry some weight. While it was not followed in all states (e.g., New York and Delaware used expert-only maps), it did provide the foundation for county land-use planning over the next few years.

The next month, February 1939, the heads of all the major agencies of USDA proposed developing a coordinated agricultural program for one county in each state. This experiment, approved immediately and enthusiastically by Secretary Wallace, tried to integrate the federal programs for land use, soil conservation, agricultural adjustment, and farmer rehabilitation into a single "unified county program." Local farmers and professional workers together directed this policy synthesis at the county level. The short-run administrative point was to test this unified procedure against the separate existing programs. The department's long-term goal was to encourage participatory planning. Again, USDA leaders thought, in their low-modernist manner, that scientific administration and citizen participation were not incompatible ends. Indeed, they believed that the one would benefit from the other, and both contribute to what they liked to call "democratic planning" (USDA 1939b).

Participatory Research and Community Action

Another way that the agrarian third New Deal tried to narrow the gap between scientist and citizen, which Scott (1998) views as central to high-modernist statecraft, was through participatory or "action" research—involving local people in research projects aimed at social change. Here, social scientists used and transferred their expertise to advance county land-use planning. Two major research divisions of the BAE led this public involvement effort, which Howard Tolley (1943:258–64) presented under the heading, "The Farmer Does a Social Science Chore." Rural sociologists typically helped a county early, in the organizational phase of the planning process; land economists later, in the actual land-use mapping work itself. Both types of social scientists assisted hundreds of county, and thousands of community-level, planning committees in the early forties.

The main non-economist unit of the BAE was the Division of Farm Population and Rural Welfare, led by prominent sociologist Carl C. Taylor. With a still-unsurpassed peak of fifty-seven professional social scientists on staff during the third New Deal, the division helped the counties organize for planning through a research process called "community delineation." One of the first steps in county planning was to determine the county's neighborhood and community boundaries. Then the people of these "natural," actually existing areas could select their representatives to the various level committees. Between 1939 and late 1941, the division, with local citizens, worked in nearly 1,800 communities and 11,000 neighborhoods in 163 counties across 32 states. They delineated almost all the neighborhoods and communities in Virginia, Alabama, Mississippi, Arkansas, North Carolina, Kentucky, and Missouri (Taylor 1939; Loomis, Ensminger, and Woolley 1941).[4]

The purpose of community delineation was to increase "real representation and active participation" in the local committees (Bureau 1940b:1). Rural sociologists believed that this was best done by people working together in local social groups that they already felt attached to—their serviceable definition of "community." Citizens, that is, were more likely to take part in public meetings if their neighbors did. Meetings, therefore, were to be held among people who interacted with each other on a daily basis, in already existing neighborhoods and communities. Sociologists had earlier done numerous empirical studies of patterns of social interaction, which allowed them to differentiate active communities geographically. The research techniques were easily simplified, and BAE technicians taught them to local citizens throughout rural America (Bureau 1940b, 1941a:7–10).

The delineation procedure was to divide a county into "natural communities" of social interaction, based on schools, churches, roads, ethnicity, trade areas, and so forth. These communities, usually eight to twelve per county, subdivided into neighborhoods, each with twenty to forty families. Every neighborhood would select a representative to the community planning committee, which in turn would select a representative to the county committee. Not only was this an effective way to insure the grassroots basis of planning—citizen participation and equal representation—but it also encouraged follow-up action by the local groups. Since they were involved in the process of determining the "natural meeting places of communities," farm people were more inclined to act effectively to solve public problems (Tolley 1943:260). Rural sociologists claimed that such local committees "bridge the gap between the 'grass roots' and the 'Great Society' " (Loomis, Ensminger, and Woolley 1941:339). These local bodies encouraged the two-way flow of information and opinions between farmers and the county committees—a major aim of the planning program (Bureau 1940b, 1941a; Ensminger 1940; Loomis and Ensminger 1942).

Community delineation research was a formalization of local knowledge. Sociologists determined community boundaries, that is, by asking people about their patterns of social interaction (associations, interests, trade, churches, schools, etc.). The technicians themselves stressed that community delineations could be done either by a trained sociologist or by a group of local citizens. The BAE received many more requests for assistance with this work than it could meet. It developed simplified techniques that specialists could teach to local people so that they could determine the boundaries of their own communities. Participatory research served both to save administrative costs and to involve citizens more in their own communities (Ensminger 1940; Bureau 1941a; Tolley 1940:32–33).

Most of the community delineation work occurred in the South, where subcounty units of government were often larger than in most other regions. In the view of a contemporary political scientist who studied the program, this large size discouraged what the social scientists sought—"a new community consciousness as a part of the planning process" (Lewis 1941:241). Along with many county agents and the BAE, this researcher believed that local communities had to be discovered "where none seemed to exist" (Lewis 1941:244). The work of the Division of Farm Population and Rural Welfare increased the participation of excluded community groups in county planning. Rather than being mainly administrative or technically oriented, the BAE research was a way to "create new units for democratic discussion and policy planning" and to "elevate social units, which may be unconscious or only half-conscious of their own unity, into active semipolitical units with a broad general advisory competence" (Lewis 1941:244). In other words, here was a social-scientific means of revitalizing local citizen organizations. The BAE rural sociologists agreed with the political scientist that their community research was engendering more citizen participation in public affairs. By leading to more adequate representation on the committees, social science was doing a bit to help democratize the rural South (Lewis 1941:241–44; Bureau 1941b:27).

After the communities were delineated and the county organized, what did the planning committees do? They mapped the land-use patterns of the county and decided what adjustments needed to be made. This phase, too, involved participatory research, combining the expertise of technicians with the local knowledge of citizens. In fact, the land-use classification done by the planning committees was the kind of work that previously had been conducted only by government employees. The BAE's Division of Land Economics had produced similar land-use maps and reports, though of higher technical caliber and also with less utility to the counties. In the county planning program, the state-level BAE representatives taught some basic land-use planning skills to the two groups most likely to use the results: local administrators of the federal action agencies and the farmers themselves. These, of course, were the three groups that constituted the county committees in the first place (Bureau 1940a:10–11).

In addition, the county committees had a significant advantage over the scientist-only work: The farmers possessed "detailed and intimate knowledge of local conditions," unlike the land grant and BAE specialists. This citizen contribution saved much research on the experts' part and led to better use of the maps "at only a fraction of the costs of the former technical surveys" (Bureau 1940a:10). Hence, much more work was completed in less time. By 1941, 789 county committees had finished their land-use maps and reports, and 440 others were under-way, compared to the handful that had been done by the scientists working alone. According to the BAE economist in charge of the county land-use planning program, the resulting maps were of a sur-prisingly high quality. The "pooling of knowledge" was working as planned (Bureau 1940a:11; Gilbert 1996).

In his 1941 annual report of the Bureau of Agricultural Economics (entitled "A Democracy Uses its Experts in a Time of Crisis"), BAE Chief Howard Tolley discussed the applied work of his land econo-mists and rural sociologists in local communities:

A valuable result of this increased participation of farmers in the planning ac-tivities of the Department has been a much needed closer integration of the various activities of all Federal agencies and State Land-Grant Colleges with the needs and wishes of actual farming communities. . . . There is thus set up a channel for the two-way flow of ideas and experience between farmers and researchers. . . . [The USDA and state agricultural experiment stations] have already adjusted their activities to effect a closer tie-up between research and actual community needs. (1941:39–40)

Evidently participatory action research was narrowing the gap be-tween expert and citizen.

Conclusion: A Different Kind of State

In 1943, Howard Tolley, a long-time USDA bureaucrat, published a remarkable book, *The Farmer-Citizen at War*. He highlighted two major problems of modern society: how to manage a complex economy without overcentralizing political power, and how to decrease the dis-tance between government experts and private citizens. Since 1933, he argued, American agriculture had gone much farther than any other sector in answering these questions. The agrarian New Deal so-lutions involved the participation of farmers in public policies. Tolley wrote: "In these first steps toward making the vast governmental structure of today as real and vital to the citizen as the New England town meeting used to be, in fighting for what Henry A. Wallace calls economic democracy, the right of all men to share in the making of the decisions that affect their economic welfare, *the farmer himself has been deliberately drawn into the process*" (1943:29, emphasis added). Democracy, to Tolley, meant far more than periodically voting for rep-resentatives who would enact laws. Rather, the democratic process demanded widespread citizen participation in policy making and program administration. Tolley knew that he had something to talk about: the New Deal agrarian experiments should "be more widely known, studied, and used" (Tolley 1943:30, 68–103, 207–8).

This is the positive view of the New Deal that Scott and Fitzgerald reject. They believe that the USDA leaders were high modernists. In contrast, I have argued that most of the New Deal in agriculture was "a different kind of state," to use Leo Panitch's apt phrase. He elaborates: "A dynamic democracy is . . . a process of collective development and education through participation" (Panitch 1993:15). The agrarian intellectuals of the third New Deal advanced a type of participatory modernization both within and beyond the state. They were concerned about technical efficiency (most were economists, after all), and saw that farmers could help manage the emerging New Deal state. However, efficiency was not their highest goal. Rather, an interest in democracy motivated their low-modernist ideals and programs.

The USDA of the late 1930s needed an intelligent citizenry to assist in administering the new federal programs at the local level—one rationale for the educational effort. The Program Study and Discussion unit of the department shared some technical as well as humanistic knowledge with the farmers who served as volunteer planners and administrators. With this kind of education, moreover, the USDA leaders were trying, in a sense, to recreate American farmers in their own image: tolerant and civic-minded students of society oriented toward reform—or, in a phrase, good New Dealers. The discussion groups and the Schools of Philosophy were not narrowly propagandistic, yet they were ideologically slanted. The farmers and Extension agents who attended the Schools should have earned certificates in institutional economics and pragmatic philosophy! Henry Wallace and Co. (not to mention FDR) would have been delighted to "produce" millions of political progressives in rural America. Equally important to the agrarian intellectuals were the career bureaucrats who ran the USDA and the land grant colleges, most of whom were unencumbered by training in philosophy, history, or social science. M. L. Wilson in particular proceeded to enlighten these scientists and administrators. As with Program Study and Discussion, the objective was two-fold: democratic education and participatory modernization.

The Mt. Weather Agreement of 1938 was probably the best example of this dual intent. The resulting federal-county land-use planning program combined administrative tasks (e.g., agency coordination) with significant citizen involvement. Unlike many theorists then and now, the USDA leaders saw no necessary contradiction in the concepts of either "democratic administration" or "efficient democracy." Local farmer-citizens were a crucial part of this experiment in national agricultural planning. The mere composition of the county committees (farmers, scientists, and local administrators of federal programs), as well as their activities, suggested that the agrarians' view of the state was low-modernist. The federal-county planning program merged their deep interests in both modern administration and citizen participation.

Participatory or "action" research was a major activity of the county and community-level planning committees. Here, too, the agrarian intellectuals departed from high modernism. The rural sociologists' research on community delineation *was* a formalization or "scientization" of local knowledge, but it was directed toward democratic ends: to advance equality of representation on the committees. Social science was here employed to increase citizen involvement—not a likely use of technical knowledge in a high-modernist state. Instead, this was, in Hillary Wainwright's (1993) words, "a new kind of knowledge for a new kind of state." Those applied rural sociologists were behind the times: They didn't know enough contemporary academic theory not to try to "improve the human condition"—or at least the rural communities that they knew so intimately.

M. L. Wilson (1973:323) believed that one "didn't have to be afraid of the 'state' if it was a democratic state." The USDA intellectuals advocated modernization with a difference. Wallace, Wilson, Tolley, Taylor, and the others envisioned—and began to institutionalize—citizen participation in all aspects of public policy. To them, even as late as the 1940s, a democratizing state was possible, if not easy to achieve. More than possible: They went a long way toward creating such a "low-modernist" state in the third New Deal.

Chapter 8
The New Deal Farm Programs
Looking for Reconstruction in American Agriculture

Mary Summers

> The people speak of being "on the government" and "off the government." They speak of "government farms," "government chickens," "government men." They say: "We belong to the government"; "The government never turns us down." The phrase "before the government came" is as definite a way of speaking about time as "back in slavery times," and "before the boll weevil." People feel they are in a new era.
>   And some do not like it.
>   —Arthur Raper, *Tenants of the Almighty* (1943:322)

For the last several decades conservative and liberal scholars alike have promoted a view of the New Deal Department of Agriculture as having set the precedents and developed the constituencies for farm programs that benefit large commercial farmers and agribusiness at the expense of consumers, the environment, the rural poor, and the public treasury (Daniel 1985; Galston 1985; Paarlberg and Paarlberg 2000). This essay argues that it was not New Dealers but their opponents who institutionalized the narrowly framed, conservative, class-based politics that have so often defined the nation's farm programs in the postwar period.[1]

A brief review of the careers of two individuals will explore this proposition. The work of one suggests that some men and women went to work for the New Deal agriculture department in part because they cared deeply about such issues as economic and racial inequality. The achievements of the other explain much of why we have forgotten the work of the New Deal reformers today.

First, however, Jess Gilbert's (2000a) article, "Eastern Urban Liberals and Midwestern Agrarian Intellectuals," provides an excellent introduction to much that is now missing in our public historical memory of the New Deal Department of Agriculture. Why is it that the personalities and programs Gilbert discusses seem so new—so difficult to put together with what we think we know about the New Deal? Why have we not learned more both from New Dealers themselves and from some of the excellent scholarship of the last several decades? Richard Kirkendall's *Social Scientists and Farm Politics in the Age of Roosevelt* (1982 [1966]), for example, first published more than thirty years ago, describes passionate debates over government policy in which some readers may sympathize with *both* positions: the Tugwellians' argument for the "big democracy" necessary to override the power of local elites on the one hand; M. L. Wilson and Henry Wallace's commitment to "grassroots democracy" and wide ranging debate and discussion at every level of government on the other. According to Kirkendall's account, some of the arguments within the New Deal Department of Agriculture sound at least as interesting as the federalist-versus-antifederalist and liberalism-versus-republicanism debates that frame so many classes in American history and politics. Today, however, Kirkendall's book is seldom assigned reading in surveys of American political history. Instead, figures such as Grant McConnell (1963, 1968) and Theodore Lowi (1979; see also Summers 1996) and their theories of interest group politics have long dominated what discussion there is of the New Deal farm programs.

As a graduate student in political science, I was troubled by the prevailing accounts of the agricultural New Deal in part because it was the family farm movement of the 1980s that had first interested me in agricultural politics. I knew that many of its leaders, such as then Texas Agriculture Commissioner Jim Hightower, held up the New Deal as a time when farm programs had actually helped the nation's farmers (Summers 2001). On a more personal level, however, I also noted that the prevailing paradigms did not have a place for the stories my mother had told me about her work with the USDA in the early 1940s. In the summers of 1941 and 1942, the Rosenwald Fund paid my mother, then U. T. Miller, to work as a research assistant to the southern sociologist Arthur Raper in Greene County, Georgia on a study of its Unified Farm Program. This was a national USDA demonstration project to establish county planning committees to coordinate the work of all government programs.[2]

The stories from my mother's work with Raper that stuck with me over the years were not about policy debates, but about talking to women who lived in shacks: women who spent hours in Georgia summers over wood stoves, using the "precious cookers" and glass jars bought with their Farm Security Administration (FSA) loans in order to meet the FSA's requirements that clients grow home gardens and can 80 quarts of food a year for every member of their family. Margaret Mead, my mother remembers, was full of enthusiasm about the way this program transformed the diets of people who had lived for years on fatback, but my mother herself speaks with a more rueful, ambivalent awe about how hard the women she interviewed worked. She shakes her head in the same bemused fashion over the kudzu so eagerly planted to control soil erosion, and people's frustration with the brooder-raised "government chickens," which had no mother to teach them to how to scratch and followed you around waiting to be fed.[3] She mentions the tensions between the Extension Service and the Farm Security Administration, but says both programs preached about much the same things: contour plowing, fertilizer, fenced gardens, canning.

My mother also talks about the tensions of living and working in the context of Greene County's Jim Crow race relations. With some friends from Raper's office, she stood on the bed of a truck one Saturday afternoon to see Georgia's Governor Eugene Talmadge speak to the crowd on a Greensboro street corner. Talmadge called on anyone in the audience who believed "that white children should go to school with nigger children to raise your hand." She remembers the deep shame she felt—and Arthur Raper's relief—when she told him that she had held down one hand with the other to keep from raising it (Summers 1986).

Raper himself was called before Greene County's grand jury in July of 1941 to respond to rumors that he had used "the titles of Mr. and Mrs. and Miss" in speaking to black people. He not only admitted to the charge, but argued that this was a common practice among southern whites associated with such civic groups as the Atlanta Christian Council and the Community Chest, as well as at colleges and universities. However, the Greene County jury would not be swayed from their position that such practices were dangerous. "Out of deference to their feelings," Raper finally agreed "to refrain from the further use of polite titles for Negroes while he was in Greene County," while resolving "in his own mind to refrain from the use of polite titles for any one," white or black (Raper and Raper 1977:58–59).

In her own extraordinary meditations on the lives of their neighbors in Greene County, Raper's wife, Martha, imagined that someday, "if the lid is taken off suddenly there will be hell to pay, and a just debt it will be, too. . . . I hope I can prepare the children for it, so they won't be bitter, whatever happens; and whichever ones survive can help rebuild a better world after the air clears" (Raper and Raper 1977:119). Even on less apocalyptic days, Martha felt "tired and blue" over how little difference her husband's research and her own "hard polishing off of his sentences" would make to the people of Greene County. Thinking about the farm women "who hardly ever read anything more than the county's weekly paper," she came up with the idea of publishing Raper's study in weekly installments in the Greene County *Herald-Journal*.

My mother remembers that the people at the Rosenwald Fund were appalled by the idea. The last thing they wanted was to attract more attention to such subjects as race relations and government programs in the South, where they thought of Negroes as without power and whites as the opposition. Like his wife, Arthur himself, however, had little faith that writing for an audience of northern liberals would ever make much difference in the South. He believed in talking directly to his fellow southerners about the legacy of plantation agriculture and Jim Crow in grinding poverty and exhausted soil, and the absolute necessity of government programs to address that legacy. Martha's proposal also received the support of both T. B. Rice, the county historian to whom Raper's book was dedicated, and Carey Williams, the editor of the paper, who decided to "offer a special subscription rate to club subscribers. . . . [O]ver 300 FSA borrowers began to take the paper. . . . 'Now, our job,' Raper said to his wife, 'is to tell the whole truth in an acceptable manner' " (Raper and Raper 1977:67–68).[4]

The title of Raper's study of Greene County was taken from a poem by Louisiana Dunn Thomas, a local "Negro farm tenant mother":

We are tenants of the Almighty
Entrusted with a portion of His earth
To dress and keep
And pass on to the next generation.

For readers who "like [their] story short," the report began with seventy-nine photographic plates from Farm Security Administration photographer Jack Delano, illustrating the county's history and the impact of the Unified Farm Program. Raper then offered up "the whole story," culled from county documents and hundreds of interviews that reflected Greene County residents' different views of slavery, the Civil War, Reconstruction, the Populists, the boll weevil, the Great Depression, and the New Deal.

The sixty-four weekly installments of *Tenants of the Almighty* that began publication in the county paper on January 9, 1942 appeared under the title "Greene's Going Great," a phrase taken from the paper's late editor, "Uncle Jim" Wilson. Raper reminded his readers that Wilson had been a strong opponent of one-crop farming, an advocate of pines for gullied hillsides, cows, hogs, hens, and extension programs, and "one of three editors in Georgia who stood steadfastly against the Klan during the heyday of its power." Raper also noted, however, that "side by side with Uncle Jim's attacks on . . . mob violence, and capital punishment, came orthodox black-belt defense of the poll tax, the White Primary, and the use of the lash in the convict camps of the state" (Raper 1943:176–80). Raper characteristically used the figure of Uncle Jim not only to make connections between the aspirations of Greene County's citizens, past and present, and the goals of the New Deal farm programs, but also to spell out the racial orthodoxies that the county's white progressives had reinforced.

Raper reported the racial and economic facts—and conflicting opinions—about every government program he studied: exactly how many white people and how many blacks in the county participated and the average benefits that the members of each race received. Under a picture of Arthur Buntling and his wife, an elderly white couple, for example, the caption read: "Old-Age Assistance checks are making life more pleasant and hopeful for 218 white people and 202 Negroes. The Whites average $9.00 a month, the Negroes $7.00" (Raper 1943, plate 45). An effort that was clearly intended in part to reassure, or as my mother says "bring along," whites, nonetheless, went on to discuss such issues as the opposition among "most of the sawmill operators, and all of the farmers" to "the wage and hour law because they felt that $2.00 or $2.80 a day was simply too much money for a Negro man to have" (Raper 1943:285–93). Raper also reported on the white community's suspicion that outsiders from the black CCC camp or some of the few black supervisors from the United Farm Program had initiated the walkout from the balcony of Greensboro's new movie theater after one of the speakers on opening night started to tell a story about an "old nigger." The walkout and subsequent boycott remained, Raper concluded, "an Exodus without a Moses . . . so far as the white public could learn" (Raper 1943:323–39).

Screens, cows, canning, chickens, fly-proof privies, wagons, the distribution of surplus commodities, public health clinics, immunization programs, new supervision of black midwives, hundreds of men, white and black, voting in the cotton allotment elections with "tenant farmers . . . sometimes warned by landlords to vote for the program if they wanted to farm the next year," new loans and debts that could sometimes never be repaid, mostly because they had been spent on the most basic necessities: there were tensions and contradictions in many of the programs that *Tenants of the Almighty* described. Raper repeatedly relayed to his readers the views of conservative critics *and* those of clients who "know how the members of each economic and racial group are expected to behave toward the other. The FSA program came, and they soon sensed what was new in it and what was old, and whether the new or the old was the more powerful." In the FSA's efforts to help clients cross "the gulf between a sharecropper and a self-sufficient farmer," Raper observed that much depended on how clients thought of themselves and their supervisors. Were they sharecroppers following orders from overseers on a "government plantation," or were they expected to be thoughtful and exercise their own judgement? (Raper 1943:287–89).

Despite his acknowledgement of many tensions and failures in the New Deal farm programs, Raper ended *Tenants of the Almighty* by arguing hard with the family-size farmer who says that "the gov'ment has . . . helped folks like us precious little." The benefits of the New Deal were "spread thinnest among small independent farmers," he declared, because government experts saw them as a model for how to survive on the land. Diversified, live-at-home farm operations did not require the exploitation of cheap labor that was the source of so much of the South's poverty and racial injustice. Raper urged Greene County's farmers to see "the FSA dwellings and red barns, chicken houses, fenced pastures and gardens" as tangible symbols of Washington's willingness to learn from their example and an ongoing commitment to their way of life. "There are good reasons," Raper urged his readers, "why the federal government should continue to cooperate in Greene's Unified Farm Program. The people here are citizens of the United States, and are entitled to the normal opportunities afforded the people of the nation" (Raper 1943:331–32, 358).

As a confirmation of some of Jess Gilbert's distinctions between the early and the later "intended" New Deal in agriculture, Raper's endorsement of the later New Deal farm programs in *Tenants of the Almighty* stands in sharp contrast to his critiques of the early New Deal in his first book on Greene County, *Preface to Peasantry* (1936). The research for this publication had been inspired and funded in large part by Will Alexander, a Methodist minister and director of the Commission on Interracial Cooperation in Atlanta. At Alexander's suggestion, Raper had first gone to Greene County as a graduate student at Chapel Hill in 1927 to compare Greene with neighboring Macon County and explain Greene's much greater out-migration of both blacks and whites. Raper's dissertation, "Two Rural Black Belt Counties," submitted in 1931, concluded that the only significant difference between the two counties was that Greene had been much harder hit by the boll weevil and falling land values: an implicit challenge to those who urged programs of social, cultural, and educational uplift, rather than economic intervention, as the key to reversing the Great Migration (Raper 1936:v–vii, 201–10).

In 1934 with funding from the Rockefeller Foundation, Alexander organized a Committee on Negroes in the Economic Recovery made up of himself, Charles Johnson, a black sociologist at Fisk University, and Edwin Embree of the Rosenwald Fund. These three men published *The Collapse of Cotton Tenancy* in 1935, which concluded that the early New Deal's cotton programs had actually served only to protect landlords and planters, while offering tenants nothing but relief— after they had been driven off the land (Johnson 1935).[5] Alexander, Johnson, and Embree also sent Raper back to Greene County to document more specifically the effects of the early New Deal in a representative black-belt county. Like *The Collapse of Cotton Tenancy*, Raper's research in *Preface to Peasantry* described the early New Deal's cotton restriction loans and relief expenditures as reinforcing the race and power relationships of plantation agriculture. Programs that served only to enable landless farmers to "pay their rents and settle their accounts," Raper wrote, served primarily to enhance the power and prosperity of planters and merchants (Raper 1936:6–7, 237–72). It was the documentation provided by scholars like Alexander, Johnson, Embree, and Raper of the effect of the cotton programs on tenants and sharecroppers, as well as the agitation of the Southern Tenant Farmers Union and the NAACP, that inspired Jerome Frank and the legal staff of the Agricultural Adjustment Administration to look for ways to stop participating planters from evicting their tenants.

How then do we explain the fact that both Will Alexander and Arthur Raper went to work for the New Deal *after* Jerome Frank and his associates had been fired for their efforts to protect sharecroppers and tenants in 1935? Part of the answer lies in the fact that, as Kirkendall and Gilbert have demonstrated, the "purge of the urban liberals" was *not* the defining story of the New Deal Department of Agriculture that so many contemporary critics and subsequent scholars have made it. Will Alexander, first as deputy administrator of the Resettlement Administration under Rexford Tugwell, and then as administrator of the Farm Security Administration, and Arthur Raper, as a researcher for the Division of Farm Population and Rural Welfare of the Bureau of Agricultural Economics, were two of many men and women who played important roles both inside and outside the New Deal administration in *ongoing* battles to define the agriculture department's goals and constituencies.[6]

Although clearly opposed to state intervention to maintain the power of the planters, Alexander and Raper became New Dealers because they were equally appalled by the results of the collapse of plantation agriculture without state intervention. The "preface to peasantry" that Raper (1936:406) saw in Greene County did not represent an agrarian ideal, but a "dependent and fatalistic people, exhausted soil, and crippled institutions." Raper's call in the book's last paragraph for "a reclamation" of the cotton South represents a virtual blueprint for many of the programs of the Farm Security Administration and the Bureau of Agricultural Economics in the later New Deal. What the South needed, Raper declared, was "a constructive land policy":

a use of the land which . . . enables the poorest farmers to build up the soil, to own livestock, to raise vegetables and fruits for their own tables, to cooperate with their fellows making their purchases and in producing and marketing crops. . . . Comfortable homes, better schools, and wholesome human relations can be maintained only through such basic economic advances. These are not simple matters, and their accomplishment will require the investment of large sums of public money and an administrative personnel with scientific training and a bold faith in the common man. (1936:406–7)

Just as much as Rexford Tugwell or Henry Wallace, Raper believed that state intervention, experts, science, education, organization, and money could benefit the countryside.

Walter Goldschmidt's *As You Sow: Three Studies in the Social Consequences of Agribusiness* (1978 [1947]), also first written as a research project for the Bureau of Agricultural Economics, provides another striking example of how some New Deal critics of agriculture department programs actually embraced the New Deal commitments to interest group politics, government programs, and expertise that many scholars today find so problematic. Goldschmidt's devastating account of the ways that government policies benefited large California growers at the expense of farmworkers and rural communities was fundamentally a call for strong farm workers' organizations. Goldschmidt did not urge an end to parity price legislation, but a guarantee that as prices rose, the minimum wage would also increase. He repeatedly cited the Extension Service as a model for a government-sponsored adult education program for farmworkers. He hoped that state action and workers' organizations would result in the "professionalization of farm labor." Like some of the populist organizers of the nineteenth century, Goldschmidt embraced the idea that organizing efforts and government institutions could bring the *benefits* of industrialization to everyone who works the land. Like Rexford Tugwell, he argued that such institutions would help *create* the values of social equity, community, and personal independence: values which agrarian romantics associated with forms of production that were, in fact, all too often rooted in inequality and exploitation.

The differences between Goldschmidt's proposals for farm workers and Raper's for tenants and sharecroppers remind us of the ongoing importance of place in agricultural political thought. Goldschmidt in California and Raper in the cotton belt, both stood somewhat outside the mainstream of the essentially midwestern New Deal Department of Agriculture. But the midwestern leaders of the department, men like Henry Wallace, Undersecretary M. L. Wilson, Howard Tolley, who directed the Bureau of Agricultural Economics (BAE), and Carl Taylor, who headed the Division of Farm Population and Rural Welfare that employed Raper and Goldschmidt, clearly wanted to make the BAE the cornerstone of a system of grassroots economic and land-use planning programs directed towards the goals of soil conservation, a full employment economy, and healthy diets for all Americans. They encouraged the efforts of the Farm Security Administration to provide to tenants, sharecroppers, and farmworkers some of the educational, technical, scientific, financial, legal, and planning services that the department had developed for commercial farmers. It was the commitment of these leaders of the agricultural New Deal to expanding the USDA's work to broader goals and constituencies that brought to a head many of the tensions of race and class that had been ignored or overridden in earlier drives for "equality for agriculture" (Lord 1947:363–66, 382–93, 409–30; Kirkendall 1982:15–17, 77–81, 136–39; Gilbert 1996).

Because of my mother's connections with him, I somewhat idiosyncratically chose the figure of Arthur Raper to represent the reformers and agrarian liberals in the New Deal Department of Agriculture. My decision to focus on the figure of Jamie Whitten to explain why we have become so skeptical about agriculture department programs in the postwar period is, however, far less arbitrary.

Whitten, a rising young southern politician, was first elected to Congress from Mississsippi's northern First District in 1941. As a freshman congressman, he watched Farm Bureau president and Alabama cotton planter Ed O'Neal and Oscar Johnston, the manager of the largest cotton plantation in Mississippi and the president of the newly forged Cotton Council, testify relentlessly against the Farm Security Administration on Capitol Hill. O'Neal, who had hired six investigators to seek out evidence of wrongdoing, came up with an Alabama probate judge, who declared that the FSA had been paying its clients' poll taxes. Johnston argued that CIO President Phillip Murray's efforts to rally political support for the embattled FSA represented proof that the two organizations were linked in a left-wing plot to destroy the plantation system (Baldwin 1968:350–51; Holley 1975:265).

Another great furor was created in late 1945 when enemies of the BAE released to Mississippi's congressional delegation an initial report on Coahoma County written by southern sociologist Frank Alexander for a survey, headed by Raper, of rural counties representative of different types of farming. Alexander described Coahoma's "schools, churches, families, law enforcement, public welfare, earning a living" as all carried on "under the domination of the plantation economy, . . . white supremacy and racial segregation." The county's African Americans, he reported, were turning increasingly to the federal government for assistance, and a number subscribed to newspapers written by the "militant Negro leadership in urban centers in the North" (Kirkendall 1982:235).

Many Southern Congressmen saw the Coahoma County report, together with the BAE's release of its postwar conversion plans for the cotton South in 1944, as acts of war. In the 1946 agricultural appropriations hearings, Jamie Whitten helped to lead the counterattack, accusing the BAE of abandoning the department's agrarian roots for new friendships with the CIO, the NAACP, urban consumers, and the internationalists at the State Department. The BAE, declared Whitten, was trying to rework "the social set-up of my section of the Nation or the rest of it with racial intermingling." By the end of these hearings the Truman administration had agreed to the congressional committee's demands that the BAE's work be confined to statistical and fact-finding research aimed only at improving the accuracy of crop and livestock reports (Kirkendall 1982:239–51).

It was also in 1946, the same year that the Republicans took control of the House, that the CIO's political action committee successfully targeted M. L. Tarver, the twenty-year Congressman who was the Chairman of the agricultural subcommittee of the House Appropriations Committee for defeat in his Georgia Seventh District Democratic primary (Key 1946:657; Flamming 1992:246, 251–53, 391 n. 57). When the Democrats regained control of the House in 1949, it was, then, Jamie Whitten who assumed the chairmanship of the agricultural subcommittee of the House Appropriations Committee.

Whitten remained in this position until 1994. For more than forty years, according to *The Almanac of American Politics*, he used the power of the purse to function as a kind of "permanent Secretary of Agriculture" (Barone and Ujifusa 1987:652). Faced by unrelenting attacks on their budgets and motives, many of the most liberal agriculture department personnel left the government's service for the academy or work with the United Nations and third-world rural development programs (Kirkendall 1982:252–53).[7] Efforts to promote mass consumption and expand international trade—programs that the leaders of the BAE had regarded as a *means* of guaranteeing a full employment economy and a better, more stable living on the land—became ends in themselves, divorced from any commitments to meeting the needs of farmers or workers, much less the rural and urban poor (Brinkley 1995).[8]

Under Whitten's leadership, cotton—one of the most environmentally costly crops—remained the most financially expensive of all federal agricultural subsidy programs. After Rachel Carson published *Silent Spring* (1994 [1962]), Whitten published *That We May Live* (1966), a book that his *New York Times* obituary described as "conceived and subsidized by pesticide industry officials," defending DDT as "an absolute necessity to our way of life" (Binder 1995).

After the Congressional Democratic caucus began electing leadership positions by secret ballot in 1974, Whitten began to lead fights against cutbacks in food stamps (Barone and Ujifusa 1987:652–53). He also called himself a New Dealer because he favored price support and soil conservation programs that protected commercial farmers from drops in commodity prices and catastrophic crop failures. Whitten's methods of operating, however, reinforced scholars' increasingly cynical views of all such programs as pawns in a log-rolling game designed chiefly to preserve government handouts to agribusiness.

It was, in short, Jamie Whitten and his allies who inspired scholars like Grant McConnell and Theodore Lowi to develop their paradigms of interest group politics. As time went on, conservative scholars increasingly embraced these liberals' critiques as a means of attacking *any* efforts to intervene in the economy. Policy makers were left with little but abstract notions of market efficiency as the sole principle on which to construct any conception of the public welfare.

The success of the Whitten-led assaults on the BAE's efforts to link the goals of a more secure agricultural economy, expanded trade, and full employment also meant, however, that it became increasingly difficult for progressive farm organizers to conceive of an American state capable of guaranteeing farmers a fair return for their labor by any means other than maintaining commodity prices. We saw the results of these trajectories in the politics of the farm crisis of the 1980s: a sharp division between farm experts, who called for abandoning commodity programs and moving toward a free-market, globalized agriculture, and the family farm movement, with its call for a farm program similar to that of the early New Deal with price supports, supply management programs, and incentives for a more environmentally sound agriculture (Summers 2001). Few scholars even seemed to recognize that it was the policy prescriptions of economists under Roosevelt that had become a cry from the grassroots under Reagan and Bush.[9]

USDA historian Wayne Rasmussen (Jones and Rasmussen 1992: 19–21) has recounted the story of Whitten's flipping through an advance copy of *A Century of Service*, the 1963 history of the department, and becoming enraged when he saw that there was "quite a bit of mention of a man named Henry Wallace. . . . He was a Communist," Whitten declared, "He ran for president for the Communist Party. I don't believe a sound history of the department would more than barely mention his name. Here is a story about Tolley. I had to see that man was fired. A good history, a history that I would think favorably of, wouldn't even have his name in the book."

Whitten did not succeed in deleting Wallace's and Tolley's names from *Century of Service*, but Whitten's image, his allies, commitments, and values have in the postwar period overshadowed all those tendencies in Wallace's department that Whitten once found so objectionable.

Jamie Whitten seems then to have won both his wars and the telling of them. The final argument of this essay is, however, that there are some parallels between the agricultural New Deal and Reconstruction; and that if these parallels hold for the historiography of these periods, the agricultural New Deal may yet be more fully reexamined. The key claim here is that, like the War on Poverty and initiatives on civil rights and affirmative action, the agricultural New Deal belongs with Reconstruction in a relatively noble pantheon of government reform efforts. Large-scale attempts to use the state to address vast social problems have always been the subject of passionate critiques. These efforts frequently demonstrated the race, class, and gender prejudices of many reformers and involved significant compromises with powerful forces of opposition. Criticism of these reform efforts' failures to do enough, however, have also all too often been co-opted into arguments that they should never have been undertaken in the first place.

Men who personally benefited from—and had a great ideological stake in—the subordination of black labor eventually succeeded in obliterating so many of the accomplishments of Reconstruction that it seemed for decades to have little relevance to anyone interested in the mainstream of American history. It was then not only racists and reactionaries who ignored or dismissed the reformers' aspirations and achievements, but scholars whose focus was on highlighting and explaining the period's most obvious outcome: the increasing power of industrial capitalism.

As part of an ongoing struggle to restore black political rights, W. E. B. Du Bois determined to wrest the history of Reconstruction from such interpretations in the early 1930s. Decades of scholarship and a civil rights movement later, few scholars today now view what was won and what was lost in the Reconstruction era only in terms of the ultimate triumph of corporate capitalism (Lewis 1992; Du Bois 1992 [1935]; Foner 1988).

It may yet be that as a result of movements both in the United States and around the world which seek to resist the impact of economic globalization, more scholars will begin to study the agricultural New Deal as something other than a catalyst for the worst features of contemporary agriculture. The New Dealers made many mistakes, but they encountered far more ferocious opposition for what they did right. Blaming the New Deal Department of Agriculture for the flourishing of agribusiness comes close to blaming the authors of Reconstruction for the imposition of Jim Crow. It leaves us without the tools and understanding that would give us some political and historical grounds on which to address the consequences of the reformers' defeat.

Chapter 9
The U.S. Farm Financial Crisis of the 1980s

Barry J. Barnett

The years 1981 through 1986 were a defining period for agriculture in the United States. During this time the farm sector experienced its worst financial crisis since the Great Depression of the 1930s. The resulting turmoil cost many farm families their vocations, lifestyles, and accumulated wealth. While farm families were the hardest hit, impacts were felt throughout rural communities. Also affected were those economic sectors that support production agriculture, such as manufacturing and marketing of agricultural inputs, and most notably, agricultural finance.[1]

The seeds of the 1980s farm crisis were sown principally during the 1970s. During the early 1970s, institutional change and socioeconomic influences created a boom atmosphere in agriculture that speculative activity fueled further. By the late 1970s, the boom began to show signs of vulnerability. In 1979, the Federal Reserve adopted monetary policy changes that had tremendous and largely unforseen ramifications for all sectors of the nation's economy. The impact on agriculture was particularly severe.

This chapter examines the boom and bust cycle of American agriculture in the 1970s and 1980s. A principal theme is the integration of the U.S. agricultural sector into larger national and global economic systems and this sector's subsequent vulnerability to outside economic and political influences. Subthemes focus on the status of contemporary economic theory and why, at the time of this crisis, so few agricultural economists recognized the sector's vulnerability.

Depression era reforms in the U.S. banking sector and the establishment of fixed exchange rate regimes following World War II caused monetary policy to be an issue of little concern for most professional economists. British economist John Maynard Keynes had taught, and the experience of the 1930s had demonstrated, that expansionary fiscal policy (increases in government spending or decreases in taxes) could be used to stimulate the economy. Keynes had also shown that when interest rates are very low, expansionary monetary policy (increasing the growth rate of the money supply) may not increase output. Economists increasingly treated monetary policy as an exogenous factor and focused their attention on fiscal policy as a means of fine-tuning the economy.

During the early 1970s, in the aftermath of the first U.S. trade deficit since World War II, the dollar was generally thought to be overvalued relative to the currencies of major trading partners. This exchange rate disequilibrium made U.S. exports relatively expensive in the world market and imports relatively inexpensive to U.S. consumers. Consequently, the Nixon administration devalued the dollar, meaning that less foreign currency would be required to purchase a dollar. By 1973, devaluation was determined to be insufficient to stem mounting U.S. trade deficits. The U.S. moved to a flexible exchange rate system: the forces of supply and demand determined the value of the dollar, although the Federal Reserve intervened on occasion to maintain the exchange rate at perceived long-run equilibrium levels. As a result, the dollar depreciated further and the balance of trade improved largely on the basis of massive increases in agricultural exports.

Also during this time, the Vietnam War and burgeoning entitlement programs not only increased overall federal spending but made it less discretionary than ever before. Policy makers were so concerned with the "high" rate of inflation (around 5 percent) that the Nixon administration imposed wage and price controls. In 1973, increasing oil prices shocked the U.S. economy as the Organization of Petroleum Exporting Countries (OPEC) began severely restricting supply on the world market. Along with the continued rising inflation came high levels of unemployment. Economists were bewildered. Conventional wisdom held that, with appropriate Keynesian policies, inflation and unemployment would tradeoff; when one was relatively high, the other would be relatively low. The job of economic policy makers was to manage this relationship for the economy's overall good. Yet in 1974, the unemployment rate had climbed to 5.6 percent while the inflation rate was at the unprecedented level of 11 percent. In 1975, the inflation rate fell slightly to 9.1 percent, but the unemployment rate climbed dramatically to 8.5 percent. A rather ugly word—stagflation—was coined to describe such a period of high inflation along with high unemployment.[2]

that's an overstatement

Economists did not fully realize that fiscal policy, though theoretically symmetrical, is politically asymmetrical (Galbraith 1987). Expansionary fiscal policy is politically acceptable during times of recession, but contractionary fiscal policy is not politically acceptable at any time: a policy of higher taxes or less provision of government services has no political constituency. Though it would likely have reduced inflation, no one dared suggest that what the economy really needed was higher taxes or less government spending. Thus, as a matter of necessity, attention was turned toward monetary policy as a method for fighting inflation. As an autonomous body, the Federal Reserve was considered somewhat beyond the pull of political expediency. But the move to flexible exchange rates had introduced complications into the process of managing the economy with monetary policy. The impacts of money-supply changes would now be reflected immediately in the value of the dollar. The tremendous expansion of international flows in both goods and capital had increasingly integrated the U.S. economy with the economies of major trading partners. Monetary policy changes would now have direct implications for the domestic economy and also indirect implications through the influence of exchange rates on trade flows.

During the years 1973 to 1981, the U.S. tax code contained enormous incentives for investment. Among these incentives were investment tax credits and accelerated depreciation schemes. For example, only 40 percent of any capital gain was treated as taxable income. A person who purchased an asset that doubled in value and was then sold would not pay income taxes on the full 100 percent appreciation in the value of the asset but only on 40 percent. However, the most important incentive for investment was the income tax deduction for interest expenses. To illustrate, assume a nominal interest rate of 10 percent and a marginal income tax bracket of 50 percent. Interest expenses of a given amount will shield from taxation that same amount of income. Therefore, as long as interest expenses are used to reduce taxable income, the "effective" nominal interest rate is only 5 percent [10%−(10% x 50%)]. Also, note that in a progressive income tax system (marginal tax brackets that increase with income), the relative benefit of interest deductibility is greater for those with larger incomes. Returning to the earlier example, if an individual is in a 70 percent marginal tax bracket (the highest tax bracket during this period) the effective interest rate drops to 3 percent.

While government tax policies encouraged investment in general, government agricultural policies encouraged agricultural investment in particular. Various price support and supply control programs were used to stabilize and maintain the price of selected agricultural commodities at artificially high levels. The potential for relatively high and stable returns attracted investment to agriculture. Also during this time, the federal government was making loans to agricultural producers at below-market interest rates through what was then the Farmers Home Administration, now the Farm Service Agency. These loans were primarily for land purchases.

Government tax policies and agricultural policies encouraged investment in agriculture at a time when the inflationary economic environment promoted investment overall. During periods of inflation, the relative purchasing power of money decreases with time. For this reason people chose not to hold on to their money, but rather to invest in assets that appreciated in value along with the general inflationary climate.

Further, during times of inflation, borrowers pay back their debts with dollars that have depreciated in purchasing power throughout the loan period. Therefore, the real cost of borrowing money, what economists call the real interest rate, is the nominal interest rate minus the rate of inflation. During the 1970s nominal interest rates and the rate of inflation were high. But the difference between these two—the real rate of interest—was exceptionally low throughout much of this period, actually being negative at times. In real (inflation adjusted) terms, debt financing for investment purposes was unbelievably inexpensive.

While government tax policy, government agricultural policy, and the general U.S. economic environment all encouraged investment in agriculture, world markets for U.S. agricultural exports were also expanding rapidly. In 1972, President Nixon visited China, signaling a fundamental shift in the United States' relations with the world's most populous nation. The opening of the Chinese market had potential for tremendous increases in U.S. exports of agricultural commodities. Because of extensive crop failures, the Soviet Union purchased heavily in world wheat markets in 1973. Analysts predicted that the Soviets would continue purchasing large quantities of wheat in the future. Also around this time, drought in many developing countries reduced world grain reserves and triggered concern for the future. Conferences on world food needs were held in the United States and around the world. In 1974 Lester Brown wrote, "Over the past two decades, nations have devised numerous means for managing commercial *abundance*—including special farm-subsidy programs and the withholding of cropland from production. It has now become essential to develop the policies and institutions, both national and international, for managing *scarcity*" (1974:15, emphasis in original).

The world's leading financial institutions, intent on recycling massive deposits of petroleum dollars, helped turn the potential demand for agricultural exports into effective demand. The relatively low value of the dollar and U.S. government programs that encouraged production helped insure that the United States would be the bargain supplier in world export markets. Thus, with extensive incentives for investment and demand seemingly assured, U.S. agriculture geared up to "feed the world."

Strong demand for U.S. exports generated a boom atmosphere in American agriculture and producers demonstrated an exceptional capacity to increase production. Between 1970 and 1973 U.S. exports of feed grains and feed grain products grew from 20 million metric tons to 42 million metric tons. During this same period, exports of wheat and wheat products increased from 19 million metric tons to 38 million metric tons. Due to the phenomenal increase in export volume, agricultural income reached levels unrealized since the 1940s (USDA 1988:5). Between 1970 and 1973, net farm income (measured in constant 1982 dollars) doubled, growing from $34 billion to $69 billion (Johnson 1990).

Such high returns from agricultural production, along with the incentives for investment discussed earlier, led to massive investment in agricultural assets. American agricultural producers invested heavily in both land and equipment. Between 1969 and 1978, the value of farmland and buildings in the U.S. (measured in constant 1982 dollars) increased 73 percent, from $519 billion to $900 billion (U. S. Department of Commerce 1982–83:656). Many factors contributed to the rapid rise in land values. Obviously, increased returns from agricultural production stimulated increased demand for agricultural land. In addition, the overall inflationary environment strongly affected land values. Many viewed agricultural land as the perfect hedge against inflation. This was particularly true for agricultural producers. During the 1970s some individuals were fortunate to have income streams that were indexed to the rate of inflation—Social Security benefits and some labor union contracts, for example. Of course, this was not the case for many, including agricultural producers. Those who were not able to index their income streams to inflation hoped to at least "index" their wealth to inflation by purchasing land as a store of wealth. This hedging activity further intensified the overall demand for agricultural land.

The most striking aspect of this period in American agricultural history is that debt capital largely financed the massive investment in agricultural assets. In 1950, 42 percent of all agricultural real estate transactions occurred without the use of outside debt capital. By 1978, this figure had dropped to only 11 percent. Of those transactions where debt was incurred, in 1950 the amount of debt was on average only 57 percent of the overall purchase price. By 1978, the debt incurred averaged 76 percent of the purchase price (Lins and Duncan 1980:1051). Between 1970 and 1980, the amount of farm mortgage debt outstanding in the U.S. grew from $71.4 billion to $113.2 billion in constant 1982 dollars, an increase of 59 percent (U. S. Department of Commerce 1990). One analyst indicated that debt had not played such a large role in capital formation in agriculture since the period 1915–19 (Melichar 1977:970). Farmers and other landowners understood both how low real interest rates had fallen as well as the tax advantages associated with debt financing.

As the decade wore on, there seemed to be no limit to how high land prices could go. Those who had purchased early in the 1970s or who were ready to retire and sell the farm realized huge capital gains. As described earlier, these capital gains received preferential tax treatment. Speculators, both farmers and nonfarmers, entered the market in search of capital gains from rising land values. One farmer told a *New York Times* reporter that he had borrowed so much money to buy so much land that was going up in value so fast, that every morning he "woke up $8,000 richer" (Strange 1988:20). The existing incentive structure insured that most of this speculative activity would be debt financed.

The increased demand of the early part of the decade was met by phenomenal increases in production, both in the U.S. and abroad. By the mid to late 1970s, prices of agricultural commodities and net farm income had both leveled off. Average net farm income for 1975–79 was around 25 percent below the average for 1970–74 in real terms (Johnson 1990).[3] Land prices were so high that in many cases producers could no longer pay for agricultural land with the returns from agricultural production on that land. However, the equity that agricultural producers had tied up in land continued to grow rapidly, along with the rate of inflation. In other words, many agricultural producers who owned land found that their wealth was increasing dramatically, while at the same time they were experiencing cash-flow difficulties. This problem was overcome by refinancing with lenders on a periodic basis, perhaps annually, to reflect the increased value of the land that was being used to collateralize the loan. Though the loan might not be paid off with agricultural income, most lenders were secure in the knowledge that their collateral was continuing to rise in value. Even those lenders who were not comfortable with such refinancing arrangements were forced to go along or else risk losing a significant part of their market share. Investors in land were confident that someday they could sell the land, pay off the mortgage, and realize a substantial capital gain on their investment. Under these circumstances debt-financed land could be appropriately compared to a Wall Street growth stock purchased on margin (Melichar 1979:1091).

Economists have long argued that agricultural producers are rational economic decision makers who respond quickly and correctly to changes in the existing incentive structure. This was certainly the case during the 1970s. Agricultural producers and outside investors recognized the market signals, evaluated the existing incentive structure, and reacted accordingly. As reward for their rational behavior, the individuals received initially higher levels of net farm income and continued growth in net worth. In addition, widespread food scarcity was averted. And standing on the sidelines, simultaneously playing the roles of coach, cheerleader, and fan, were a whole host of agricultural experts. These experts had encouraged the nation's agricultural producers to gear up to meet the increased demand of the 1970s. Producers were challenged to strive for maximum efficiency. This rallying cry was used to both prompt and rationalize a massive infusion of capital into the agricultural production sector. Many producers were told essentially to "get big," ("efficient" or "capital intensive") "or get out." With the halcyon days of the 1970s coming to a close, very few recognized the vulnerability of the agricultural sector. Fewer still wished to express their concerns and risk being labeled pessimistic or nonprogressive.

In fact, there were signs of trouble on the horizon. As commodity prices fell in the late 1970s due to the tremendous increases in production, some highly leveraged producers experienced financial trouble. In 1977, and again in 1978, a populist farm organization known as the American Agriculture Movement (AAM) came to Washington, D.C. to protest low commodity prices and demand government price supports at parity levels.

Inflation peaked in 1974 at 11 percent. Between 1975 and 1978, it ranged between annual averages of 5.8 and 9.1 percent. By 1979, inflation had climbed back to 11.3 percent. On October 6, 1979 the Federal Reserve decided to restrict the money supply's growth rate (contractionary monetary policy) in order to fight the upward trend in inflation. The desired impact did not occur immediately. The inflation rate for 1980 was 13.5 percent, but by 1983, inflation had fallen to 3.2 percent and by 1986, it was 1.9 percent.

The Federal Reserve administrators were well aware that constraining the money supply's growth would lead to higher interest rates and slower economic growth, yet they were unsure as to the magnitude of these impacts. The relationship between the money supply and interest rates is not stable or easy to predict. Given the historical emphasis on fiscal policy for fine-tuning the economy, understanding the impacts of money supply changes had not been a high priority for economists. The prime rate in 1978 averaged 9 percent. Inflation was 7.6 percent, so the real rate of interest was 1.4 percent. By 1981 the prime rate was 18.9 percent. Inflation was 10.3 percent so the real rate of interest was 8.6 percent—an increase of more than fivefold in three years.

The Reagan presidency entered this environment in 1980. With the new administration came a rather intriguing notion called supply-side economics by its proponents and far less benign names by its detractors. The basic premise of supply-side economics was that by decreasing tax rates, the government could stimulate the economy to such a degree that overall tax revenue would actually increase. In other words, though tax rates would fall, taxable income would rise to the extent that tax revenue would increase.

Supply-side economics got its first trial run with the 1981 Economic Recovery Tax Act (ERTA). This law made wholesale changes in depreciation rules that effectively decreased tax rates, most significantly by dramatically increasing the speed with which various assets could be depreciated. Interestingly, Congress passed the legislation, though no evidence exists that the majority of members subscribed to supply-side ideology. In fact, the Congressional Joint Committee on taxation estimated that the new legislation would cut $872 billion in federal revenue through fiscal year 1986. As a result of the ERTA, the nation was now experiencing the rather bizarre combination of Congress and the administration practicing expansionary fiscal policy at the same time as the Federal Reserve was practicing contractionary monetary policy; it was as though one foot was on the accelerator while the other was on the brake. Once again, the asymmetry of fiscal policy because of political constraints was revealed (Harl 1990:12).

As federal budget deficits mounted throughout the 1980s, supply-side ideology went out of vogue leaving in its wake a mountain of debt. The tremendous increases in government borrowing put further upward pressure on interest rates. The demand for dollars rose as foreign investors bought dollar-denominated financial assets to take advantage of high U.S. interest rates. Between 1981 and February 1985, the dollar appreciated more than 70 percent against other major trading currencies (Harl 1990:15).

Both nominal and real high interest rates hit hard in an agricultural sector that had become highly leveraged during the 1970s. The rising value of the dollar slowed agricultural exports as American commodities became relatively more expensive on international markets. Land values peaked and began to fall as the Federal Reserve was successful at reducing inflation.

American agricultural exports peaked in 1981 at $46 billion. By 1986, the value of agricultural exports had fallen by 50 percent in real terms (USDA 1988:4). The loss of export markets caused prices to plummet. From 1980 to 1986, corn and soybean prices fell 64 percent and 52 percent in real terms, respectively. The real price of wheat planted in 1986 was 51 percent lower than that planted in 1980 (USDA 1991:40, 1990a:27, 1990b:43). Low prices and drought conditions in 1980 and 1983 took a heavy toll on farm income. Average net farm income in real terms for the five-year period 1980–84 was 35 percent less than for the period 1975–79, and over 50 percent less than for the period 1970–74. Due to extensive drought, net farm income for 1983 was only $12.2 billion (in constant 1982 dollars), the lowest figure on record since the USDA began collecting farm income data in 1910 (Johnson 1990:5).

The combination of low net farm income and high interest rates sent asset values plummeting. Nationally, the value of farm assets in nominal terms declined about $300 billion or 30 percent between 1981 and 1987 (Shaffer 1989:68). In some areas it was worse. Land values in the corn belt and lake states fell by approximately 50 percent in nominal terms. Between 1984 and 1985 alone, each state in the corn belt reported a drop of at least 20 percent in nominal land values. This is approximately equal to the annual drop in U.S. agricultural land values between 1932 and 1933 (Reimund and Brooks 1990:11; Reed and Skees 1987:2, 17). Falling land values eroded the accumulated wealth of farm owners. Between 1980 and 1986, national farm owner equity dropped 26 percent in nominal terms (Reimund and Brooks 1990:9, 12, 13). By 1986, the USDA had classified 10.5 percent of U.S. farms as "vulnerable" and another 11.1 percent as marginally solvent.[4]

Having low net farm income many producers experienced debt distress. Because asset values were now falling, lenders would no longer refinance loans when borrowers were unable to make payments. The aggressive leveraging activity that took place during the 1970s now came back to haunt both lenders and borrowers. The Farm Credit System lost $2.7 billion in 1985, the largest one-year loss of any financial institution in U.S. history. This was followed by a loss of $1.9 billion in 1986. In 1981, only one agricultural bank failed. Sixty-eight agricultural banks failed in both 1985 and 1986, and fifty-eight more failed in 1987 (Harl 1990:25).

The situation got so bad that a 1986 CBS News Poll reported that a majority of Americans—quite erroneously—believed that the farm financial crisis would drive more than half of all farmers out of business (Bonnen and Browne 1989:12). Young beginning farmers were particularly vulnerable because they typically had little equity capital. Many borrowed heavily to purchase land and other assets during the boom time of the 1970s. In some cases, parents or grandparents expanded their farm operations in order to bring a child into the business. The tragedy of seeing young people lose their investment was often compounded by the accompanying loss of a parent's or grandparent's accumulated equity capital (Harl 1990:21–25).

But the impact did not stop at the farm gate. The November 29 and December 2, 1985 editions of *The Washington Post* contained articles by James Dickenson describing conditions in Odebolt, Iowa, and the surrounding county. Dickenson described how the county had endured three bank failures, forty farm bankruptcies, declines in school and church enrollments and the loss of two major farm equipment dealerships (quoted in Harl 1990:266). While this may have been an extreme case, it was certainly not atypical of conditions throughout much of the midwest and great plains.

The farm crisis of the 1980s did not end abruptly. Instead, it slowly faded away due to changes in Federal Reserve monetary policy and massive increases in direct government payments to farmers. Inflation fell steadily throughout the early 1980s. Convinced that inflation had finally been brought under control, the Federal Reserve began increasing the growth rate of the money supply. By 1986, the prime interest rate, which had been almost 19 percent in 1981, was at 8.3 percent. Inflation had been reduced to 1.9 percent.

Average annual real net farm income for the period 1985–88 was 55 percent higher than for 1980–84. This was largely the result of the Food Security Act of 1985 initiating tremendous increases in direct government payments to farmers. For the period 1985–88 the federal government paid more than $50 billion directly to farmers. During this period, government payments were responsible for 31 percent of net farm income. While government payments and lower interest rates moderated the effects of the farm crisis, improvements in exports, commodity prices, and farm asset values would lag several years behind (Johnson 1990:4, 5).

The farm crisis of the 1980s was different from prior farm crises in some respects. The U.S. adoption of flexible exchange rates in 1973 meant that contractionary monetary policy would now simultaneously impact inflation, interest rates, *and* exchange rates in ways that were harmful to agriculture. The impact of exchange rate movements was exaggerated by agriculture's increasing reliance on export markets.

Throughout much of the 1970s, increased exports brought about higher commodity prices and farm incomes. Exports also made the agricultural sector vulnerable to currency exchange rate fluctuations and economic distress abroad. Each of these factors emphasizes the integration of the domestic U.S. farm economy into larger economic systems.

Yet in some ways the farm crisis of the 1980s was not unique. U.S. agriculture has always been susceptible to periods of reduced inflation or even deflation. The populist movement of the late 1890s was largely a reaction against a sustained period of declining prices. William Jennings Bryan's famous "cross of gold" speech was a response to the deflationary impact of holding the national currency to a gold standard. Many in the populist movement clearly understood that inflation allowed farmers to repay their debts in depreciated dollars, while deflation had the opposite effect (Greider 1987:246, 253, 254).

Even so, many seemed surprised by the crisis of the 1980s. The *Chronicle of Higher Education* reported that

> The farm crisis caught most university researchers—along with nearly everyone else—by surprise. Few agricultural economists foresaw just how quickly or how drastically the agricultural bull market of the 1970s would change in the 1980s. Nor did they predict the severe debt burden that today besets as much as a third of American farmers. (Quoted in Harl 1990:259)

A search through issues of the *American Journal of Agricultural Economics* for the mid-1970s to early 1980s revealed only one article that expressed concern about the vulnerability of the farm sector (Melichar 1977). That article was based on a historical analysis of past boom and bust periods in American agriculture.

Why did agricultural economists not anticipate the farm financial crisis of the 1980s? First, they almost exclusively relied on mathematical modeling to explain economic phenomena. As is true with all models, the mathematical models abstracted from reality. Unable to work in controlled laboratory environments, economists are forced to identify relevant variables to include in their models and assume all others are held constant. In practice, variables are often excluded, not because they are of minor relevance but rather because they are difficult to quantify. In other words, mathematical modeling causes economists to ignore relevant but nonquantifiable variables. While mathematics introduces an important logical rigor to economic analysis, it often does so at the cost of realism.

By the late 1970s inflation had become a thorn in the flesh for the American economy. Though landowners and holders of other assets did not mind high inflation, consumers found it frustrating. Even economists discussed the transactions costs imposed by high inflation because of the frequent need to renegotiate contracts. Given that contractionary fiscal policy was politically unacceptable and that the WIN (whip inflation now) buttons of the Ford administration were even less successful at fighting inflation than the wage and price controls of the Nixon administration, it should have been clear that whenever decision makers decided inflation had to be controlled, contractionary monetary policy would be the only tool available. Yet it appears that this seemingly obvious point was lost on many contemporary economists.

Another important reason economists failed to anticipate the events leading to the 1980s farm financial crisis was that they ignored the political constraints under which decision makers operate. Many economists have simply become accustomed to excluding political and other social factors from their economic thinking (a problem that is likely intensified by the academic specialization and separation of the academy). Economists falsely assumed these hard-to-quantify factors to be constant.

For similar reasons, history's role has largely been lost in contemporary economics training. Economics and agricultural economics students at most major universities are not required to take a course in either economic history or the history of economic thought. With the exception of certain specialized journals, historical analysis is rarely found in published accounts of economics research. Evidently, issues of historical context are also considered unimportant.

Finally, research in agricultural economics tends to focus on microeconomic issues such as commodity market analysis or optimal decision making by farm businesses. Macroeconomic phenomena, such as inflation, interest rates, or currency exchange rates are often treated as exogenous factors that are important but outside the specialized purview of most agricultural economists. Even those with extensive macroeconomic interests have tended to focus primarily on Keynesian fiscal policy prescriptions. Agricultural economists were ill-prepared to understand the implications of the monetary policy changes initiated in 1979.

The farm crisis of the 1980s revealed much about the increased integration of U.S. agriculture into global financial and commodity markets. While providing unique opportunities, this integration also makes the sector vulnerable to outside economic and political influences. Interestingly, the crisis also revealed limitations within the contemporary practice of agricultural economics. Failure to anticipate the crisis was likely due, in part, to a traditional microeconomic orientation and an emphasis on analysis that is largely divorced from political and historical contexts.

Part III
The Political Implications
of Daily Life

Chapter 10
The Entrepreneurial Self
Identity and Morality in a Midwestern Farming Community

Kathryn Marie Dudley

> Everything revolves around one little thing going awry and forc-
> ing us to move in a different direction than we ever went before:
> we've become fragile. I don't know what way we're gonna go, and
> I don't know what's gonna change it. But we're so fragile in this
> world today that we can't have specific things that we've grown up
> with all these years. We live in a fragile community. The people
> are fragile; they're falling apart. They're stress-full. We're not
> tough any longer. If another country ever attacks us, I'm sure
> they'll beat the pants off us! We're not what we were before.
> —68-year-old farmer

Something has gone awry in America. From the deserted shops of
Main Street to the abandoned farms of the countryside, a puzzling
state of affairs looms large in the heartland. For here in the midwest,
one of the most fertile agricultural regions in the world, small towns
are dying and families who have worked the land for generations are
losing their farms.[1] As residents of rural areas struggle to make sense
of what is happening to their families and communities, they compare
the present to the past and find it wanting. They are haunted by a
sense that something of incalculable value has been lost, not just in
material terms, but in spiritual terms as well. They fear that the moral
fabric of the country has been weakened and feel at the mercy of
forces beyond their control.

Industrial restructuring is a culturally mediated process. When economic dislocation erodes the institutional infrastructure that organizes
a particular way of life, a cultural system can be stretched to the limits

Main point →

of coherence and its underlying contradictions revealed.[2] In this chapter, I argue that the traumatic loss of family farms during the 1980s exposed a basic paradox of liberal democratic culture: our commitment to the value of economic growth (and the progress it is said to represent) is always shot through with ambivalence about the precarious social forms that unlimited growth produces.[3] Drawing on ethnographic interviews with residents of Star Prairie, a farm-based county in western Minnesota, I show how the transformation of the rural economy is translated, at the local level, into a problem of community—that is, into questions about identity and moral responsibility in the context of radically individualizing forces.[4] I suggest that a cultural commitment to economic growth has instantiated a system of morality which requires a distinctive conception of the self: one that is held personally accountable for the consequences of economic risk-taking. This *entrepreneurial self*, I propose, is the conceptual linchpin of capitalist culture. It facilitates a moral order that allows Americans to endow their lives with meaning, even as it undercuts collective resistance to the conditions that have made traditional ways of life increasingly hard to sustain.

In the argument that follows, I sketch out a way of thinking about the experience of economic dislocation which puts the problem of community into anthropological perspective. In particular, I want to complicate the commonplace notion that "community" expresses and fulfills enduring human needs for mutuality, reciprocity, and solidarity—in short, that it is a pattern of social interactions which is at variance with, if not in opposition to, the instrumental, market-oriented relationships that characterize a capitalist society.[5] To be sure, certain communities do constitute themselves as subcultural alternatives to a putative "mainstream," and are, in this sense, anti-normative. However, to focus exclusively on forms of community which operate according to principles that deviate from the prevailing cultural logic, as is now common practice, only serves to canonize that logic and shield it from scrutiny. Few scholars in the "community studies" tradition have bothered to ask if there are, in fact, forms of community that reproduce the logic of market capitalism. Yet that, I argue, is what a farming community is all about.

The Anthropology of Disorder

The anthropological study of economic disorder has demonstrated that the effects of industrial restructuring are not uniform across different communities and occupational groups. Whether job loss is experienced as a personal failing, a capricious event, or political oppression will greatly depend on the kind of cultural resources that members of a given social group bring to bear on their situation. Educational credentials, networks of association, and geographical proximity to employment opportunities all shape the way people interpret and respond to economic dislocation (see diLeonardo 1985; Nash 1989; Newman 1985, 1988). Although most ethnographic studies of industrial disorder have focused on the problem of *deindustrialization*—the systematic dismantling of basic manufacturing industries—it is possible to view the problem of agricultural *industrialization*—the consolidation and vertical integration of food and fiber production—through much the same lens. The restructuring of agriculture and dispossession of established farmers may be viewed as a manifestation of the same economic process that has created profound occupational insecurity and financial instability in the lives of the urban poor, blue-collar workers, and white-collar business managers over the past thirty years. Whether we refer to this systematic transformation as deindustrialization or the globalization of industry, the problem for anthropologists remains the same. Our task, as anthropologist Katherine Newman suggests, is to investigate "the survival strategies of different communities locked in crisis" and "to understand what this powerful, disorganizing force means in the everyday lives of the communities we study" (Newman 1995).

For the most part, anthropological work on farming communities in the United States has focused on the problem of farm persistence—that is, on determining which types of farmers are surviving the changing structure of American agriculture.[6] By paying attention to such variables as family goals and farm management styles, these studies, and others conducted by rural sociologists and historians, have consistently found a basic tension between cautious and ambitious management strategies, with a tendency for more ambitious managers to be at greater risk of farm failure. In general, this tension is thought to emanate from an underlying cultural difference in the way particular groups of farmers define success, and hence, from the more or less effective business strategies they employ to achieve it. In the typology proposed by recent studies of the farm crisis, *cautious managers* are those who define success in terms of family continuity. They value keeping the farm in the family and therefore minimize financial risk by avoiding debt, even if this means settling for a modest standard of living and sacrificing other economic opportunities. *Ambitious managers*, in contrast, are those who define success as maximizing financial profit. They value personal achievement for themselves and upward mobility for their children, and therefore do not hesitate to expand their operation through debt financing, even if this means they run the risk of losing their farm in an economic downturn.[7] Some studies link these divergent management styles to ethnic identity, suggesting that a national culture or ethnic heritage (typically German) inculcates family values that are antithetical to the individualistic values of a market-oriented society (Neils Conzen 1985; Flora and Stitz 1985; Salamon 1992). Other studies point to the erosion of a native agrarian ideology brought about by persistent poverty, out-migration, and the historical mixture of ethnic groups (Barlett 1993). Regardless of how the distinction between cautious and ambitious cultural orientations is figured—as agrarian versus industrial or yeoman versus entrepreneur—the ethnographic research is agreed on one point: whereas the entrepreneurial style was strongly encouraged during the relatively prosperous 1970s, in retrospect, farmers who survived the crisis of the 1980s were those who carried relatively little debt.

Although I, too, found that residents of Star Prairie made a distinction between farmers who leveraged capital to expand and those who resisted the pressure to borrow, I am not convinced that the differential survival rate of family farms reflects a basic difference in the cultural values of farm operators. For although farmers who survived the 1980s were quick to attribute *someone else's* loss of a farm to "bad" farm management and the "go-go" mentality of the 1970s, farmers who lost their farms during the same period saw *themselves* as victims of circumstances beyond their control. Unless we are prepared to denounce these farmers' accounts as disingenuous face-saving, then it is a serious mistake to assume, as much of the existing literature does, that the relentless decline in farm numbers—and, specifically, the economic practices which put farms at risk in the 1980s—is evidence of the encroachment of "industrial" or "capitalist" values and the erosion of an otherwise stable, "republican" or "agrarian" cultural system.

The family farm system of agriculture, as it developed in this country, has long existed on the horns of a very American dilemma: it embodies the individualistic interests and values of independent producers, but that vaunted independence comes at the cost of social solidarity and the ability to pursue a common cause with others (see Bellah et al. 1996 [1985]). Farmers participate, like it or not, in a market system which rewards entrepreneurial risk-taking and competitive individualism. The difference between those who fail and those who succeed is, in this sense, less a matter of cultural values than it is one of luck. For the truth is that a majority of American farmers happily took advantage of the economic opportunities presented to them during the 1970s. Had inflationary conditions continued in the 1980s—had the Federal Reserve not caused interest rates to hit the ceiling virtually overnight, and had export demand and commodity prices remained high—the tables would now be turned: those who took the experts' advice would be laughing up *their* sleeves at the short-sighted management practices of their frugal neighbors.

If, as I argue, Star Prairie's community norms are rooted in the logic of market capitalism, the critical task for an anthropology of disorder is not to delineate opposing "cultural orientations," one cautious and the other ambitious, but rather to analyze these management strategies as aspects of the *same* cultural system. If the goal of family farm continuity were incompatible with the goal of individual achievement and profit maximization, then it might be plausible to posit the existence of divergent value systems. In this bicultural model, we would expect that the strategy of financial leveraging would *only* be used by ambitious managers in pursuit of a higher standard of living with no concern for future generations, and *not* by cautious managers who desire to bankroll their children's start in farming. Moreover, if we assume that yeoman culture has the greatest staying power, then we would expect that long-time residents who seek to pass their farm down to their children would *not* employ risky management strategies. As it happens, however, none of these expectations are substantiated by the existing research.

Quite the contrary. There is evidence, for example, even in studies that develop a bicultural model, that so-called yeoman farmers did take on considerable debt in the 1970s, thereby putting their farms at risk, in order to bring children into larger, more capital intensive operations. Anthropologists Sonya Salamon and Karen Davis-Brown explain this phenomenon as follows:

[S]ome yeomen have failed; these strayed from their yeoman values into more entrepreneurial behavior. . . . Certainly, the social context of the 1970s caused more than one yeoman to ignore family-traditional wisdom that continuity should be attained without placing the farm at risk. When these yeomen failed they ultimately betrayed both values. (Salamon and Davis-Brown 1986)

It may be that farmers who lose a farm under such circumstances feel that they have done something "wrong" or that a different course of action might have spared them some grief. But it is not clear how one "strays" from the value of family continuity by trying to make it possible for one's children to farm. Most of the families I interviewed who went into debt to expand during the 1970s put their farm at risk *in order to* bring sons or daughters into the operation. Expansion and debt financing were perceived to be the only way of passing a family legacy on to the next generation. Some lost their farms as a result, and some did not. To focus on the fact of farm loss—and then to attribute that loss to a betrayal of the values that farmers hold dear—only serves to blame the victims of dispossession for causing their own misfortune.

An anthropology of economic disorder must be able to account for the feeling shared by all of Star Prairie's farm losers: that they had no choice *but* to act as they did. To have risked nothing, they argue, would have been the biggest risk of all. Under such circumstances, the instability of American culture reveals itself *not* as a tension between two divergent value systems, but in the deepening insecurity and precarious identity of people who share the *same* cultural orientation. In other words, we are looking at a form of community that *endorses* the very actions that give rise to the disorder its members experience.

The Entrepreneurial Self

When residents of Star Prairie assess the transformation of rural society, they lament the loss of what they call the "entrepreneurial spirit." Farmers today, they believe, are increasingly at the mercy of government bureaucrats, big city banks, insurance companies, and commodity brokers. There is no longer the reward there once was in efficient, productive small-scale farming. With commodity prices so low that they consistently fail to cover the cost of production, farmers say, whatever profit you used to make is now gone before the seeds are even planted. To survive under these conditions, you have one of two choices: you can tighten your belt, get by with used machinery, and supplement your income with off-farm employment, or you can join the rat race, take the risk of going into debt, and hope that stepping up your productivity will generate greater returns. Neither option, however, is considered ideal, and both represent growing constraints on farmers' freedom and independence. Everyone—from urban politicians and bankers to environmentalists and animal-rights activists—is allowed to have a say, farmers feel, in what they can or cannot do with their property. The qualities of character that made America great— the drive to push beyond what has already been done—is the entrepreneurial spirit, as originally embodied in the pioneer. And this, farmers believe, is precisely the cultural sensibility that is lost as more and more farmers are forced out of farming. As one middle-age farmer put it:

The individuals who took off from the East Coast, they were looking for something. They walked out here because they *wanted* to. When they got to the Mississippi River they thought the end of the world was there, but they kept on going, you know? And that's part of the thing that is still in the rural communities and still in the farmer. Because he actually is closest to the land and the land supports us all. He still has most of that left in him. He hears it more often from his parents and it happens amongst us more than it does in the metropolitan areas. There's more of that in us. [More of what? I ask.] More of the feeling that you *have* to do it. You *have* to go out there. You *have* to see what's on the other side. Well, if we got 125 bushels of corn an acre last year, this year we're gonna get 140. Because we can do it, and the challenge is there. You go to work for somebody else and if you put out X number of units during a day, the pay is so much, and you keep on doing that for six months and you get a little bit more, but that's all you get, so that's all you do. That's what fueled the independent business man, [the realization that] if I go down to my gas station in town here and open an hour earlier, maybe I'll get some extra trucks. The farmer has to go out there because there are so many things that can change for him. He buys these steers and he finishes them out, but he doesn't know what he's gonna get paid for 'em until he sells 'em. If he doesn't get enough to pay for his lifestyle, he's gotta figure out something else. So you try a little harder. There isn't that much security offered by [working for] somebody else. The security is in yourself and what you do yourself.

In many respects, this individual is exactly the sort of farmer that ethnographers have in mind when they refer to the "yeoman farmer" or cautious manager. Like almost half of the farmers in Star Prairie, this man is of Norwegian descent (the other half of the farm population is German), and like many, he operates a farm established by some of the county's earliest settlers. When he explains how he and his brother survived the farm crisis, he emphasizes their conservative management style, yet attributes the failure of other farmers—as well as the smaller number of young people going into farming—to their *lack* of entrepreneurial spirit:

We're very, very conservative. If somebody tells you that you need a 150 horsepower tractor, go and buy a 75 horsepower tractor. If somebody wants you to have a new piece of equipment, make use of the old and do for yourself. Farming is like owning any other business and too many people treat it like a job. When somebody tells you what to do, and you go do it, you get paid and everything is fine. But if *you've* got to figure out what to do, and then go do it, it gets complicated. *Management.* Management is the basis of the whole situation. Our schools are not producing entrepreneurs. The entrepreneurial spirit has disappeared.

Star Prairie's farmers share a worldview in which a conservative management style and an entrepreneurial ethos are not incompatible. The independence and self-reliance of the self-made entrepreneur *is* the moral legacy of their pioneer forebears, and they keep these values alive by working the land and driving beyond the limits of what seemed possible in the past. They see themselves as not just "free" to compete against one another and their own production records, they believe they *have* to do so. Competitive production is a moral obligation in this community, and individuals base their identity on how well they measure up to the managerial standards and definition of success established by the community. Farmers keep meticulous records of their production histories not solely for the purpose of managing a business, but also to know where they stand in the community and in comparison with their ancestors. They share a powerful feeling that they *owe* it to the generations who farmed the land before them to surpass past production records in order to demonstrate that they are worthy of their inheritance. Family continuity, far from being antithetical to the value of competitive individualism, actually depends upon it.

This is not to say that *any* form of competitive economic behavior is positively sanctioned in Star Prairie. Simply put, a farmer is judged to be a "bad manager" if he appears to value conspicuous consumption and leisure pursuits over and above the nitty gritty business of farming. Bad management is not "ambitious" management, but *irresponsible* management. Farmers fail, my informants believe, because they lack the ability to be their own boss. Farming is no business for people who cannot think for themselves, take responsibility for their actions, and most importantly, "pay themselves last"—that is, draw money for living expenses only after all other bills have been paid. If you want a regular paycheck and can't sacrifice personal pleasures when economic conditions demand it, they contend, you have no business being a farmer. Thus, as one elderly farmer observed of those who got caught in the credit crunch:

A farmer who lost his farm is a lousy manager. Where in the world can you be a lousy manager and keep your job? A gas station, a store, no matter what it is, you've got to be able to say, I will work as hard as I can to manage this thing with some logic. And if you can't, you're gonna hafta work for somebody else that's gonna do all the managing for you. You'll just get paid your daily wage, and that's all there is to it.

Entrepreneurs are people who manage their own business, risks and all. And farming is a risky business, I was repeatedly told. The person who knows how to manage risk—for risk is impossible to avoid completely—is the person who will be a successful farmer. Thus, it is not indebtedness per se that draws the scorn of Star Prairie's established residents, but debt incurred to support a life lived high off the hog. Consumer practices that are perceived as showy displays or arrogant one-up-manship mark a farmer as irresponsible and, in an important sense, dangerous. For competitive individualism, when taken to its logical limits, *is* antithetical to social solidarity. Only with strong sanctions against the ostentatious display of status inequalities can members of a community counteract the centrifugal force of occupational identities based on market competition. Given the capital intensive structure of modern agriculture, farming as a form of work is a highly individualizing occupation. An entrepreneurial conception of the self serves to explain why people act as they do, while also justifying those actions with the belief that this is how people, at bottom, naturally are. Listen, for example, to the way this farmer describes the kind of person farmers are:

Farmers are competitive. We've got a better barn; we got better cows; we got better horses; we got better everything. They're competitive and sometimes they don't even like each other very well. They're jealous. They may drain their water off on their neighbor's land and inundate his crops and so on. The only time we're real is when our neighbor is hurt, then all of a sudden everything is forgotten. I can't understand how we can do this. There's something wrong in our theology. But I don't think it's any different than neighbors anywhere else. Competition, greed, a whole series of things seem to ball up together and provide us with a nasty attitude towards the guy next to us, who had, by sheer luck, gained something that we didn't gain and so we're jealous of him. Rains on his land and it doesn't rain on yours kind of thing. I don't know what it's all about. It's a lot deeper than I could ever think. But it's there.

As much as Star Prairie's farmers may lament this state of affairs, virtually all would agree that competitive individualism, despite its nasty underside, is an innate characteristic of human beings. Thus, when I asked another farmer what caused the farm crisis, he had this to say:

Greed and fear. Greed: I don't want any more than my neighbor, but I want everything that he's got. And the fear comes in, the fear of the unknown: well, what's gonna happen? Is it gonna keep on raining like this? Are we gonna get a crop? How do I protect myself? How do you cover yourself so that you can live as well next year as you do this year? That's the two most leading factors of the human animal. That's all there is to it, greed and fear. In the 70s there was an awful lot of greed. Terrible much. And the bankers and everybody else, they were happy about it because it was very profitable for them. And the lawyers fueled their own furnace by doing bankruptcies for the farmers, and it was a chance for them to make themselves wealthy at somebody else's expense. It all goes back to that. We're a predatory group, the human animal. That's a fact'a nature.

In a market-oriented society, people cannot be blamed for consumerist behavior, since the cultural logic which celebrates the creation of wealth by self-reliant individuals must also encourage an unlimited demand for consumer goods (Douglas 1992). Therefore, in a culture that naturalizes competitive individualism, the problem of community becomes one of articulating a vision of moral order which sets certain limits on a person's freedom to consume. Community norms can act to regulate private consumption practices by establishing a vision of the collective good, over and above the interests of the individual. Such a vision must necessarily suppress marked disparities of wealth and constrain the amount of goods each person consumes. In Star Prairie, powerful sanctions in the form of gossip, invitations to social functions, membership in community organizations, and the like, served to enforce an ethic of moderation in farm expansion and debt financing. Yet no matter how well a community acts to buffer competitive individualism, the danger of unrestrained consumption is omnipresent. For the same cultural tension that drives economists to tout the virtues of economic growth also impels the consumer to pursue the elusive promise of personal advancement.

The American dream of upward mobility—the notion that each generation can and should do better than the previous one—glosses a fundamental paradox of the culture of liberalism: only by enhancing the *productivity of labor* (increasing the volume produced per unit of work) can the economy "grow," yet rising productivity consistently results in the *redundancy of labor* (decreasing the number of workers needed). As the U. S. Department of Agriculture recently declared, what is true for individual farmers is true for farming communities:

The decline in the number of farming-dependent counties is, in part, a consequence of agricultural success. Increases in farm productivity—through advances in production technology, crop science, and management—have led to decreases in farm employment. Simply put: fewer people are needed to produce an increasing amount of goods. (USDA 1995:12)

The paradox of the "technology treadmill" has long been evident in agriculture.[8] When innovative farmers adopt new technologies that increase output or reduce costs, total farm production goes up as more farmers adopt the technology, causing prices to fall, which, in turn, forces more farmers to adopt the technology, even as the added benefits of adoption are eliminated. Thus, although there is *economic* incentive for farmers to be early adopters of new technology, there may also be considerable *social* pressure against setting the technology treadmill in motion. A farmer who lost his farm expresses this dilemma well:

With the technology we have today, you can go out and buy a four-wheel-drive tractor and you can go over so many hundred acres of land a day, and being those things are available, people are going to buy them. It's a natural progression, *but it's unnatural at the same time*. We have the technology to farm really large farms, and now they're concentrating—well, they've been doing it with poultry for years—now we're seeing it in hogs and in cattle feeding and all these other areas. There really is no way that you can stop it.

This farmer sees technological innovation as a "natural progression," yet "unnatural at the same time." This suggests that community sanctions against competitive consumption do operate, especially when the risks of non-adoption are difficult to calculate. Farmers in Star Prairie are skeptical of, and deeply worried by, new trends in agriculture and the pressure they feel to increase production. As one crusty farmer remarked:

There's a lot of advisors out there who say, get big, use chemicals, spend too much money, and we'll get rich because you'll pay us before you take anything for your own living. But the young people who start out now, the bankers and the people who are in charge [of approving farm loans] give them everything right away. But that's society that has told us that [we need these things]. Keep up with the Jones's and the Jones's don't know where they're going.

Farmers eye the innovations of their neighbors with a mixture of apprehension and cynicism. Do other people know something they don't? Should they be upgrading and expanding too? Or is this newfangled setup simply a case of wanton materialism and flashy display? Being able to judge the wisdom of other farmers' actions is only possible within the framework of a local community culture that specifies what count as honorable goals and what options a person has to achieve them. Debt, as I have indicated before, is not rejected out of hand as means toward certain ends, provided those ends fall within the purview of what the community has judged to be morally worthy. Yet debt, and its attendant risks, opens up an ethical gray area. For putting your fate in the hands of a loan officer is always a devil's bargain: are you using the banker, or is the banker using you? Some farmers, generally those who had positive experiences with their lenders, spoke of the need to establish "trust" and a "working partnership" with loan officers. Others, usually those who ran into trouble with their loans, spoke of the need to protect themselves from the gangster-like predations of that class of folk they called "Mister Bankster." Rather than signaling a cultural divide between "yeoman" and "entrepreneurial" farmers, these divergent attitudes toward debt suggest incipient *class divisions* not ethnic differences per se—recognizing that ethnicity, and *white ethnicity* in particular, can be deployed in the service of class distinctions (see, e.g., diLeonardo 1984; Rieder 1985).

As sociologist Patrick Mooney has persuasively argued, the farm crisis highlighted an overall process of dispossession in American agriculture, as capital, in the form of debt, has relentlessly appropriated farmers' property, wealth, and autonomy in the labor process (Mooney 1986). From this perspective, the farm crisis was essentially a crisis in the credit form of production. As a rising number of farmers defaulted on their loans, banks and other lending agencies accumulated considerable land and property, which they eventually rented back to farmers in the form of restructured loan packages:

The traditional alternative to the credit form of production is tenancy. The advocacy of tenancy as a solution to the problem of credit (often referred to with the misnomer "debt restructuring") is, of course, merely a transformation of production based on the appropriation of interest to a form of production based on the appropriation of rent. In either case, the labor of the family farmer suffers both exploitation by capital and loss of autonomy in the managerial component of the labor process. (Mooney 1986:453)

In a culture based on an entrepreneurial conception of the self, growing reliance on credit-based production and absentee ownership constitutes a powerful threat to farmers' sense of identity and moral order. In Star Prairie, I believe, the farm crisis served to dramatize an underlying tension between farmers who have sufficient capital to manage their operations with minimal amounts of debt, and those who, for whatever reason, must largely rely on the use of credit. Yet this tension remains incipient for the very reason that even those who must borrow to finance their operations are firm believers in—and consider themselves beneficiaries of—systems of production based on the appropriation of interest and rent. They are, in short, deeply committed to the cultural logic of capitalism, even as they remain alert to the danger that they may themselves become a casualty of that system.

This is why, I believe, the rhetoric of "risk" and "risk-taking" is so compelling to farmers who seek to explain why some people survived the farm crisis and others did not. The rhetoric of risk reframes the danger of dispossession and capital penetration as an individual moral dilemma. Rather than dwelling on the question of who benefits from high interest rates, farmers wonder when debt is a legitimate management tool and when it signifies a weakness of character. The retired farmer I quoted earlier speaks for most in Star Prairie when he evaluates the moral culpability of those who lost their farms during the credit crisis:

The biggest wave of foreclosures came from hot-dogs. These are the guys that had the four-wheel-drive tractors ahead of time and just bought equipment worth much more than their whole herds and so on. They had a bran' new four-wheel-drive pickup and they went to Texas in the wintertime. They lived on credit cards. And I didn't have too much compassion for them when they went broke. That's, in my estimation, mismanagement. The next group of people are the people I felt very sorry for, cuz I knew a lot of 'em. These were people who had worked hard, had their farms paid for, and had sons coming along, and Dad said, "I'll help you. I'll mortgage my farm and I will get you both started," and all three lost everything. Those were the people I had compassion for.

By seizing upon one of the greatest disasters that can befall members of a rural community—the loss of the family farm—the rhetoric of risk identifies certain ways of acting or thinking that the community as a whole *already* disapproves of. Thus, it is "hot-doggy behavior," the blatant expression of competitive individualism, not the use of credit per se, that incurs collective disapprobation. To emphasize the rhetorical aspects of risk assessment is not to say that the community's perception of the risks involved in financial leveraging has no purchase on reality. On the contrary, the dangers are quite real, and this is what gives the rhetoric of risk its bite. Chances are, if a farmer is up to his eyeballs in debt after expanding his operation, things will not go too well for him in any case, and certainly not if the economy plunges into a deep recession. It is not an ironclad law, however, that going into debt will automatically lead to foreclosure, nor that buying a new tractor is always asking for trouble. In short, the local discourse of risk and blame functions to absolve some people of responsibility for misfortune while holding others morally accountable for the same fate.

Very few farm lenders, for example, feel they bear any responsibility for the staggering number of "non-performing loans," as they call them, that piled up on their desks during the 1980s. "I've never made a bad loan," one bank vice president assured me, despite the fact that his bank initiated numerous foreclosures at the height of the farm crisis. "Every loan looks like a good loan at the time you make it," he explained with a smile, "It's kind of a joke around here, but it's true." The language of neutrality and objectivity in risk assessment enables lenders to point the finger of blame at farmers who took on more debt than, as it happened, they were able to handle. That rural banks were also failing during this period only compounded the perceived consequences of farmers' "risky behavior": not only had they gambled away their own inheritance, they put other people's life savings at risk as well.

Ultimately, however, the rhetoric of risk serves to limit, or deflect, the degree to which the community is able conceptualize the social consequences of macroeconomic forces that are beyond the control of individuals. Local residents may look at the farm failures of their neighbors and chalk it up to miscalculation or mismanagement, but they do not blame these individuals for any of the arguably related phenomena which undermine the well-being of the community as a whole. Bankrupt farmers are not blamed for the closure and consolidation of rural schools, the boarded-up shops and decline of sociability on Main Street, the shrinking congregations of rural churches, the fiscal crises of hospitals and other municipal services, nor for the growing proportion of elderly whose primary source of income is the taxpayer's dollars. In short, the rhetoric of risk is able to hold individuals accountable for their own losses, but it is not very effective at holding anyone responsible for losses that affect the whole community. In fact, within this discourse, the state is seen, not as a bulwark against the hazards that individuals face in an open market system, but as the principle source of those dangers. To the extent that the state actively sponsors the penetration of capital in agriculture, this perception is not altogether unfounded.

The Fragile Community

Even the most successful farmers in Star Prairie acknowledge that the restructuring of agriculture has taken its toll on the community. The single-room schools of their youth have long since vanished, and there are no longer enough children in the county to support more than one high school. Ministers ride a circuit of rural churches that have become too small to call a pastor of their own, while those who preside over the larger churches in town worry about the dwindling size of their flocks. A doctor from the Twin Cities who decides to set up practice in the county is feted like visiting royalty, even as potluck dinners are regularly held to raise money for the hospital emergency room, always in danger of closing for lack of funds. It wasn't always like this, old timers say. Time was, you couldn't find a parking place in town on a Saturday night, there was so much going on and so many people to see. The movie theaters and variety stores left some years back, and most of the cafes are gone. The dance pavilion down by the park, it's still there, but it's not like it was—the young people go to the big cities for their fun and entertainment. Now there is talk of selling the county fair grounds to the developer of a discount drug store, and some say it's the final straw.

There have been a lot of final straws in this community that clings to the edge of the prairie. And yet it is still here. The challenge for an anthropology of economic disorder is to ascertain in what form, and with what cultural consequences, rural communities survive economic restructuring. People in Star Prairie say that things are not like they were during the depression, a time when everyone was in the same boat and you tried to help each other out in whatever way you could. Nowadays, the same people who would harvest your crops for you if you are ill or laid up in any way, treat you like a criminal if you can't pay your bills. During the farm crisis, the same church ladies who brought pies to your house when there was a death in the family avoided you in the grocery store after notice of your foreclosure appeared in the local paper. For every farmer who lost his land, there were several others in line to buy it. For every family forced to stand by in anguish as their farm equipment was auctioned off to the highest bidder, there were neighbors who acquired top of the line machinery at fire sale prices. "What's bad for some farmers is always good for others," one such bargain hunter explained, "and *this* is the whole concept behind farming. If you want to survive, there's two ways of praying: you can say, 'God, let it rain,' or you can say, 'God, *don't* let it rain over there.' " Or, as another farmer quipped, "Basic economics is to find somebody dumber than you are and give him the business: you have to take advantage of somebody."

Community, in this cultural context, bears little resemblance to the storybook variety where neighbors come to your aid, no matter what. Nor is this the kind of community that gives birth to the social solidarity required to sustain broad-based political struggles against entrenched economic interests. Why, we may ask, are social bonds in rural American so fragile? What makes solidarity so hard to come by? Part of the problem lies in the increasing specialization of agricultural production, which puts farmers at cross purposes from the outset: grain farmers who want higher prices for their crops are in competition with livestock farmers who want lower prices for their feed. But part of the problem also lies with the premium placed on economic independence and self-sufficiency. Members of this community are characteristically suspicious of any scheme that purports to solve their problems by turning to the government or outside agencies for help. This leads to the aggravating appearance of complacency that often frustrated local political activists:

We could go into the elevator right now and make conversation with farmers, and the dumb shits will start arguing. 'God, we need $5 corn,' I'd say. And they'll say, 'God, no, we don't need $5. If I had $3, I'd be just fine.' But in order to be on par with everything else in our economy, we need $5. Milk needs to be $22 a hundred [weight] instead of $10. Sheep, hogs, everything—it's half of what it ought'a be. But you can talk to farmers that'll argue like hell with you that that would be too much money. Our theory in the Ag Movement is that if you can raise prices now, and keep the family farms here, we won't have corporations that will raise the price the consumer pays by twice that amount. But we couldn't convince 'em, so it's over. I don't think there will ever be another movement that will be so close as we were to making this happen. So the farm crisis of the 80s, it was the farmers' fault—for not organizing to set his own price. The blame goes back to the farmer.

Although most farmers agree that their troubles can be traced to low commodity prices, the protest movement of the 1980s failed to garner widespread support for its agenda. I believe collective action failed because protesters developed a rhetoric of blame that was anathema to Star Prairie's farmers. If your cultural identity depends on being in control of your own destiny, of relying on no one but yourself—and certainly not the government—to meet your basic needs, then you will be inclined to take the prices you are given and make the best of your situation. Independence and self-reliance are, after all, the hallmark of the entrepreneurial self. Higher prices— especially if they are designed to support farmers who have been deemed "bad managers"—would, in an important respect, take the challenge and the meaning out of farming. Guaranteed prices would be like guaranteed weather or an employee's wages, and under such conditions, *anyone* could make a living at farming. But Star Prairie's farmers believe that farming is not for everyone. It takes a special kind of person, they say, to deal with the crises that arise in farming every single day. From this perspective, the farm crisis was nothing new: farmers are *always* in crisis, and those who survive are highly re- spected for it. Commodity prices are not thought of as wages, or as payments one bargains for collectively—for if prices were wages, then a farmer wouldn't be his own boss.

The drama taking place in rural America is best characterized, I think, by the image of a fragile community. Despite their valorization of the entrepreneurial spirit, farmers do not for the most part fancy themselves as rugged individualists at loose in the wilderness. Indeed, it is the ability to tame nature and turn its bounty toward social ends that gives their cultural system its moral center. Farmers think of themselves as feeding the world, and doing so selflessly. These are not hard-hearted businessmen who turn a buck for the sheer pleasure of watching it multiply. They are, in Star Prairie at least, hard-working Americans whose average household income, after taxes and farm- related expenses, is often below what is considered middle class—and in many instances, barely above the national poverty line. They are survivors in a community that is changing in ways they never dreamed of, yet they survive in the stoic, no frills way they have always survived. It is no exaggeration to say that most feel haunted by forces beyond their control, and that they are not optimistic about their fu- ture. Long-term residents run a gauntlet of ghosts whenever they drive down familiar county roads. Every few miles or so, at every wind break or cluster of trees where a farm house has vanished or fallen to ruin, there is the memory of a neighbor who is no longer there. And as the distance opens up in the space between one farm site and the next, an anxious foreboding settles in, as each farmer wonders who will be the next to go. Although we rarely think of the economic disorder stalking the American countryside as a form of terror, there are profound parallels in the traumatic social isolation that attends the state-sanctioned loss of community.[9]

Farmers in Star Prairie do not feel that the nation has turned its back on them completely. However painful their personal losses, their system of morality does not, by and large, permit them to blame others for their misfortune. Yet the social upheaval they have experienced during the farm crisis and in its aftermath has led them to suspect that America no longer values the hard work they do and the sacrifices they make. An invisible hand has been rearranging the pieces on their real-life Monopoly board, and family farmers know they are the most vulnerable players. Thus, although they do not experience the loss of a farm collectively, they nevertheless have a sense that what binds them together as members of a community is in danger of being lost. What binds them, I believe, is their abiding faith in the virtues of an entrepreneurial self: a conception of self which offers a distinctive cultural identity based on family continuity and the proven ability to manage the risks of making a living on the land. In this sense, Star Prairie reveals what is most paradoxical about the culture of modern capitalism: we desire the freedom it promises, but we long for the security it destroys.

Chapter 11
Considerably More Than Vegetables, a Lot Less Than Community
The Dilemma of Community Supported Agriculture

Laura B. DeLind

Over the last thirty years, the many hidden, or externalized, costs of an industrially modeled and corporately controlled agri-food system have grown increasingly apparent (Krebs 1992; Kneen 1993; Goering, Norberg-Hodge, and Page 1993). Environmentally, "factories in the field" dependent on petrochemical inputs and large-scale, capital intensive technologies have depleted soils, compromised air and water resources, and undermined ecological processes and balances (Carson 1994; Pimental and Lehman 1993; Orr 1992; Odum 1989). Socially and economically, family-scale farmers, farm families, rural communities, and the lifeways they supported have disappeared, unable to compete with vertical integration and the corporate concentration of wealth and power nationally and internationally (Jackson, Berry, and Colman 1984; Thu and Durrenberger 1998; Lyson and Raymer 2000; Heffernan 1999a; Bonnano et al. 1994; Friedmann 1993a). Democratically and culturally, the standardization and commodification of labor and landscapes have overridden local, even national, authority and diversity in the pursuit of capital efficiencies and increased profit taking (Grey 2000; Mander and Goldsmith 1996; Fowler and Mooney 1990; Shand 1997; Allen 1994; Shiva 1997; Berry 1977).[1]

In terms of food itself, public concerns and scientific controversies challenge the industry's claim that it delivers a cheap, safe and ubiquitous food supply (Consumers Union 1999; Montague 1990–2000). Bacterial contamination is endemic to many foods, poultry being a case in point (Consumers Union 1998). Pesticide residues in both domestic and imported produce put large portions of the population at risk, while the long-term effects of genetically modified foods are simply unknown (U.S. Congress SCANF 1993; Lappé and Bailey 1998; see also Reisner chapter 13). Likewise, the nutritional quality of mass-produced and heavily processed foods has been seriously questioned and related to contemporary disease complexes (Kramer 1991; Fallon 1999; Cummings 1999; Gussow and Clancy 1986). It has been observed that consumers are now feeding on symbols rather than substance and buying food for what isn't in it—fewer calories, less salt, no saturated fats. By contrast, some 30 million Americans (half of them children) are chronically undernourished, finding food of any sort, but especially fresh, unprocessed foods, neither cheap nor readily accessible (Poppendieck 1998). And as urban race riots, oil embargoes, and power failures attest, the existing food system is quite vulnerable, dependent on long-distance trade and transportation. Few of the nation's fifty states produce more than 10 to 15 percent of their own food (UME 2000).

As the contradictions and limitations of the existing food system become more obvious, mainstream Americans become more anxious. In an attempt to protect themselves and their families on both a long and short-term basis, people have sought out and created alternative institutions to resist the established agri-food system. This resistance takes many forms. Stevenson (1998) speaks of "warrior work" and "builder work." For him, warrior work is overtly political in nature, designed to influence political processes and shape public opinion by exposing and attacking the concentration of wealth and power within the global food sector. Builder work, by contrast, is more consumer and lifestyle oriented, seeking economic and political change through alternative market behavior and patterns of personal consumption. These orientations and the changes they engender, however, are themselves seldom internally consistent or fully transformative (Grey 2000). Requiring increased government inspections or expanded labeling, for example, may offer consumer assurance, but may effectively override biodiversity, local agriculture, and democratic process (DeLind 2000). Expanding organic markets does not, of itself, address labor exploitation or universal access to good food (Allen and Kovach 2000). It is important, then, to critically assess the purpose and the practice of alternative strategies—what they profess to do, what they do do, what they don't do, and for whom. In the arena of social and political activism, success is not simply a matter of speed or of bureaucratic acceptance. The latter can often signal the appropriation and recasting of energy and influence consistent with prevailing hegemony (see Tokar 1997; Hall chapter 12). But, if resistance is to have a life of its own beyond single or simple solutions, then it must also feed and be fed by the exercise of citizenship. Reinvigorating civil society, in turn, will require securing real spaces, physical as well as social, within which "average" people can continuously come together to debate issues, engage in work, rethink power, and redistribute resources in ways that are just and sustainable.

This chapter discusses one increasingly popular "builder-type" alternative to the existing agri-food system, community supported (or shared) agriculture (CSA). It presents CSA as a hybrid institution, one which (a) serves as a market instrument for small diversified farmers and conscientious consumers, and (b) provides a place, a set of activities, and affective or embedded relationships upon which a shared sense of purpose and community can emerge (Cone and Kakaliouras 1995, 1998; Hinrichs and Kramer 1998; Hinrichs 2000; DeLind 1999; DeLind and Ferguson 1999). It argues that CSA has more nearly realized the first of its two "selves." While farmer-member relationships may be characterized by familiarity and trust, the "community" in community supported agriculture exists more as metaphor than as fact. Indeed, this may contribute to its market appeal, and constitute a unique selling point. Finally, the discussion reflects on the degree to which this internal accommodation is problematic for catalyzing further resistance to and transformation of the prevailing agri-food system. It relies on survey results from Michigan, Ohio and Indiana (MOFFA 1999), discussions on the national CSA listserve, the work of other researchers, and the author's own five-year involvement with community farming in Michigan.

Community Supported Agriculture

As a concept, community supported agriculture is a fairly radical departure from industrial agriculture. It is a model that advocates a direct, face-to-face relationship between those who grow food and those who eat it. It is designed to reduce the physical, social, and mental distance that now characterizes the global food system. Within this model, farmers and consumers form "a relationship of mutual support and commitment" (Van En 1998;115; Henderson 1999:3). Ideally, each is aware of, and attends to, the needs of the other, creating in the process a bond of trust and responsibility. Adjectives like "partnership," "collaborative," "mutual," and "shared" are used repeatedly to describe the CSA relationship (ATTRA 2000; AFSIC 2000; CIAS 2000; UME 2000).

In CSA, small, diversified farmers are central, visible, and accountable. They raise food, not commodities. They feed people—people they know—not distant markets. This is possible because local consumers variously referred to as farm members and shareholders are willing to support them in their efforts. At the beginning of each growing season, members buy shares ranging from about $200 to $600 in the farm operation. This up-front investment provides a farmer with a modest income, operating capital, and a predictable and appreciative market. Shareholders may also provide farm labor and organizational assistance as individuals or members of core groups.

In return for this support, members receive a weekly supply of fresh, chemical-free (typically organic) vegetables, herbs, and flowers throughout the growing season, which can be anywhere from 16 to 52 weeks depending on the region. In addition to vegetables, some CSAs also offer their members such things as honey, eggs, and poultry; some provide value-added products like breads, soaps, beer, and salsas. The produce received is said to have "the farmer's face on it."

In this manner, CSA farmers and members come to share the risks and rewards of food production. Both recognize that when working with natural systems there can be no guarantees—hailstorms and droughts, like compost, happen. Both CSA farmers and members are willing to absorb these humbling shocks and, in the process, establish an obligation to the land, to each other, to local food security, and to a wider community rooted in place. Early promoters took great pains to explain that CSA was "not just about vegetables."

This distinction is essential to CSA and highlights its dual or hybrid personality. On the one hand, CSA is a marketing arrangement or "technique" (ATTRA 2000)—a means for individual farmers and individual consumers to resist and disengage from the global food system. Producers and consumers come together to broaden and personalize their classically defined roles. By cooperating with one another across the market divide, they reclaim choice and the opportunity to eat and grow closer to home—to unhook from the corporate food system. Their continued interaction, it is said, makes both producers and consumers more fully aware of the relations of production that underlie the food that they eat. Ultimately, it makes it possible for them to ask questions like "What is a just wage?" "What is a just price?" and "How do I live in a community?" (Wiens 1994).

On the other hand, CSA is something quite different—a means, with farming at its center, for reestablishing the connections and responsibilities that extend beyond self-interest and define community and create commonwealth. In this sense, CSA is not a market instrument at all, but part of a whole way of life, a whole way of thinking and being. It frames a social as well as an ecological landscape within which an "associative economy" reestablishes and reaffirms livelihoods and wisdoms fitted to place (Lamb 1996). Through collective effort and engagement, CSA makes possible a belonging that may well embrace the spiritual, as distinct from the impersonality of commodity production and consumption (McFadden 1999). As Kittredge has put it,

To the extent that alternative institutions recenter our lives in small, local groups of people with whom we have mutual obligations, they can rebuild human community. CSAs, in particular, can satisfy the most fundamental human need and do so in a way that provides us with delicious enjoyment, bonds us in useful work together, and humbles us with continual consciousness of our place in the wonder of nature. (1996:260)

CSA, then, "implies both a critique and a solution directed at perceived problems in the larger food and agricultural system" (Ostrom 1997:48). People are being drawn to it for both philosophical and pragmatic reasons, and the conjunction of food, farm, and community is felt by many to constitute the real genius of CSA. The numbers seem to support this. In the mid-1980s only a handful of CSAs existed. Today, an estimated 1,000 such farming enterprises engage the loyalty of 50,000 to 100,000 households nationwide. In response to heightened public inquiry, the Robyn Van En CSA Center together with the USDA Sustainable Agriculture Network maintains a national data base on CSAs organized by state (AFSIC 2000). There are now coalitions of regional CSAs and annual national conferences. As one advocate has written, "Each new CSA is another little piece of liberated territory and a step towards the sustainable world which is our only possible future" (Henderson 1996:29).

But rhetoric has a way of masking reality, or said a bit differently, reality has a way of doing what it will despite the enfolding rhetoric. This, it appears, is the case with CSA. As CSAs grow more popular and therefore larger and more numerous, the dislocation between their two internal directives grows more apparent. Behavior does not conform to an ideal social philosophy but assumes a more material or instrumental nature. Hinrichs (2000) speaks of this opposition as the "tension between embeddedness and marketness." While an agrarian-type notion of community still remains strong, CSA, in the great majority of cases, represents little more than an excellent source of locally raised, organic produce, a source that provides at least partial employment for the small farmer and a niche market for the active green consumer. As welcome as this may be, it also reveals the slippage between ideal and real expressions of community within the context of CSA. The reality suggests that there is little need to attend to the internal dynamics that challenge this hybrid institution and calls into question the claim that it strengthens citizenship and promotes activism and deeper social and political reform.

Shared Commitment

The operational hallmark—the glue—of CSA is the symbiotic relationship that is felt to exist between farmers and members. At a minimum, one wants to grow good food and the other wants it grown. Ideally, this relationship is sufficient to explain their mutual or shared commitment to the farm and to one another. As Groh and McFadden have expressed it in their now classic work on CSA, "We have no choice about whether to farm or not, as we have a choice about whether to produce T.V. sets or not. So we have to either farm or to support farmers, everyone of us, at any cost. We cannot give it up because it is inconvenient or unprofitable" (1997:xv). This perspective assumes that the commitment between farmers and consumers is mutually necessary and compelling. It defies capital efficiencies and/or market instrumentality; it does not trade in commodities or in individual self-interest. This claim, however, does not play out nearly so clearly on the ground.

While some CSAs are begun by consumers searching for a farmer to grow for them, most (79 percent) are begun by a farmer who has made or would like to make a long-term economic and lifestyle commitment to farming (Henderson 1999). In the majority of these cases, the farmer owns the land and views the farm as a private enterprise. However dedicated she or he may be to ecological practices and social responsibility, making a comfortable and dependable living is an equally critical concern. CSA farmers, then, as small business owners must resolve in their own minds, bodies, and farming operations the disjuncture between community-interest and self-interest.

It is hardly surprising that farmers will often adopt CSA as one of several economic strategies to diversify their overall income. In this way they hedge their bets and share only part of their production and farming effort. This management has led to some paradoxical behavior. One farmer, for instance, put his CSA up for sale. While it is certainly possible to sell a business, can an individual own a community and can a community in any traditional sense of the term ever be sold?[2] Similarly, discussions and articles in trade magazines advise farmers on how to "price community" (Community Farm 1999). Members, they argue, are buying a set of relationships and amenities which add value to the vegetables. These non-edible attributes should be reflected in the price of a share. In this manner, market economics are being superimposed upon what are claimed to be deeply cooperative relationships. Conversely, affective ties are not free of financial consideration.

For farm members, their commitment to CSA is more diverse and less complex. Surveys indicate that members join CSAs for three major reasons: to obtain fresh vegetables; to protect the environment; and to support a farmer (Cone and Kakaliouras 1995, 1998; Kane 1996; DeLind and Fackler 1999; Henderson 1999). There is, curiously, little interest on the part of most members to use the farm or local food production as a venue or catalyst to build community. As one member of a Michigan CSA candidly explained, "When I want community I can go to my dance community, or my church community, or my teacher colleagues, or I can email my high school buddies. I don't need [the CSA]."

Whatever the assortment of reasons that lead to CSA membership, a shareholder's commitment, unlike the farmer's, exists only on a season to season basis. There is no necessity or guarantee that a member will extend or invest his time, money, or talents beyond this finite six to twelve month period. With the dominant food system comfortably and conveniently in place, and with organic produce now in many food coops and supermarkets, members can attend to their three big concerns as independent and contented consumers. Likewise, surveys indicate that members are far more willing to be "engaged," "forgiving," and "financially expansive" before their first seasonal experience than afterwards (Kane 1996; Kane and Lohr 1998; Goland 2000). Reality has a way of bursting well-intentioned, Disney-like bubbles. Or as one member reminded both herself and her daughter after an hour spent weeding lettuce, "See how much work this is? Now you'll appreciate being able to buy your food at Felpausch."

Unlike farmers, members can and do maintain a casual and highly discretionary relationship to "their" local farmer and farming enterprise. Vacations, soccer camps, employment schedules, travel time to and from the farm all pull against any additional commitment. Only a small proportion of CSAs currently make on-farm work a membership requirement. Of thirty-five CSAs surveyed in Michigan, Ohio, and Indiana, twenty-five had no working members (MOFFA 1999). The numbers appear comparable nationwide (Henderson 1999). In some cases, farmer-owners feel that working members get in the way of personal and business efficiencies, of their control of the operation. One skilled CSA farmer, for example, explained that she doesn't like to deal with the disruption of children or the often costly mistakes of adults; she even found the time spent training interns to be an imposition. Nonetheless, she seals her letters with a sticker that reads, "Sow Community."

In far more cases, however, farmers have had little success coaxing members to get their hands dirty. They have become "mom and pop shops" by default. Most farmers now accept the fact that "their" members are "very busy people." They no longer seem to critically wonder, as did one early CSA organizer, "What is the matter with people's lives that they can't find fourteen hours in a summer to come out to work at the farm?"

Shared Responsibility

With member turnover rates as high as 40 to 50 percent a year, it is the CSA farmer, not the shareholder, who must work harder to create the loyalty sufficient to insure the operation's survival. Mastering the labor intensive demands of raising organic produce is not sufficient. CSA farmers also spend enormous amounts of energy recruiting and retaining members. How-to manuals, trade journals, newsletters, and listserves all discuss retention strategies as often as they advise on irrigation systems, bean varieties, and/or techniques for pest management.

Contrary to the notion of shared risk, most farmers now purchase local, off-farm produce to make up for a shortfall, rather than acknowledging and redistributing it. They are also very careful not to push surpluses by requiring members to take more than they want. They prewash and prebag produce. They bake cookies and serve herbal tea on distribution days. They offer such things as honey, cider, garlic braids, and dried and edible flowers to add value and charm to weekly distributions. They provide drop-off sites in town, at work, or, for a fee, at a member's front door. They write weekly newsletters and provide recipes on how to use fresh produce. They cater to individual choice rather than one-size-fits-all shares. They design vacation shares, weekend shares, salad shares, city shares. They offer payment options and some even accept payment by credit card, allowing major financial institutions to further regulate and benefit from what are personal, face to face relationships. CSAs may join together to supply members with expanded food options such as meat, eggs, and berries. Many grow for 200, 500, 800, and occasionally 1,000 households.

This is commerce, not community; it is niche marketing and in most cases good short-term management. Understandably, it is what any small merchant must do to survive and what most did some fifty years ago before losing out to superstores and "one stop shopping" (Parenti 1996). As an overall strategy, it works to minimize individual risk rather than to share it; it trades on personal service and courtesy as a way to secure a place within a local or regional economy. Core groups, when they exist, attend to a portion of these additional administrative, public relations, and educational responsibilities.[3] They do represent a commitment to the farm and farmer and a pooling of individual skills and resources to benefit the collective enterprise. Most often, however, it is the CSA farmer who absorbs the workload and subsidizes the operation with her health, her family, and her off-farm income, a situation that encourages burnout and labor exploitation.[4] Catering to the convenience of members also permits them the luxury of overlooking and underappreciating what it took to produce their food in the first place. It is hardly surprising that those who spend the least time at the farm with their hands in the soil, those who are the least physically engaged, are the most critical of insects, dirt on their vegetables, and anything other than picture perfect produce (DeLind 1999).

There is, then, contrary to classical CSA rhetoric, little sharing of risk with the farmer. Indeed, according to a recent discussion on the CSA listserve, many farmers have eliminated using the words "shared risk" altogether on their membership agreement forms. With the contract thus simplified to exchanging dollars for vegetables, the familiar questions, "Am I getting my money's worth," and "Am I giving members their money's worth?" assert themselves and frame a discussion quite different from that which motivated many founders of the movement: "What is a just wage?" "What is a just price?" and "How do I live in a community?" (Wiens 1994). A share in a CSA equates more closely to the price one pays for vegetables than it does to an investment of conscience in a farm, a landscape, a way of living and consuming, or a deliberate campaign to reform the food system.

For all its emphasis on mutual obligation, CSA farmers still must compete in a marketplace that too often externalizes the energy, labor, and environmental costs of food production and that rewards economic privilege. As a result, those farmers who do not take vows of simplicity, or otherwise radically alter *their* lifestyles to accommodate economic reality—in short, those who seek a middle-class income from their farm—often find themselves in conflict with their own deeply held values. It is the CSA farmer, after all, not the CSA member, who most frequently goes without medical insurance.[5] Nor is this disparity likely to disappear. Cone and Myhre (2000:19) found that those CSAs with the lowest member participation had the highest member income and that 33 percent of this group had incomes greater than $100,000. By contrast the income of a highly successful, full-time CSA farmer was reported as "$30,000 in a good year" (Hu 2000). Most CSA farmers earn less than half this amount (Henderson 1999:92).

The Community Myth

This does not mean that members are disinterested. In fact, as a population they tend to be politically and environmentally concerned if not organizationally active. Rather, they are interested on their own, highly fragmented time schedules and for their own private, not collective, purposes. As any CSA survey can attest, these purposes vary widely. One indignant (ex)member harangued a grower who had instituted an on-farm work requirement that she had absolutely no interest in volunteering on the farm; she was never going to come out and pull weeds. What she wanted was to support a farm and a farmer who would grow food for her (and she had a very fine-grained notion of what good food should look like). Others view the CSA farm as a theme park of sorts, a lovely place to come, bring the kids, have a picnic or potluck, and "pet the corn."

Cone and Kakaliouras have reflected on this level of involvement. "What is puzzling to us," they write,

is the low priority given to community and the relative lack of talk about it. . . . CSA members . . . express a desire to visit their farm and to participate in its events. Some give accounts of wonderful moments at harvest festivals. But in shareholder interest, an opportunity to attend festivals and events ranked next to last. . . . From our conversations we conclude that in reality "community" . . . refers more to community of interest rather than to community built on mutual relationships of rights and obligations, on reciprocity. (1998:29)

But is this really so puzzling? CSA sits squarely on, and trades in, a myth, the myth of community as a dense and enduring set of interpersonal relationships, fitted to time and place, that represents the collective will and serves and protects the collective needs of its members. Scholars have been questioning and deconstructing this ideal notion of community for some time (Adams 1962; Kusnetzky et al. 1994; Guijt and Shah 1998; Smith 1966). They contend that however pleasing a notion, this centripetal, homogeneous, and selfless form of social organization simply does not exist nor has it ever existed. To be sure, as Kittredge explains, the "[b]arn building, quilting, joint harvesting, church repair," the collective work associated with the traditional American community, did occur, and it did "contribut[e] to the sense of having earned the right to 'belong' " (1996:260). But such behavior was far more the product of ecological and political circumstance than of willful enlightenment. *— Community, — geographic, common interest*

Daniel Kemmis (1996) makes this point very clearly when he reflects on the barn raising that took place in the agrarian community of his childhood. These, he recalls, were not people who chose to associate with one another or to work with one another. Simply put, they had to do so if they were to keep on farming and eating. It was a matter of survival. Nor, it must be pointed out, did the ensuing sense of belonging necessarily signal a set of democratic, equitable, or sustainable relationships. Self-interest, it would seem, resigns itself to collective or community interest awkwardly at best and then only when the individual does not have the wherewithal to go it alone. The accommodation is not an easy one. However ironic, bowling alone appears to be the liberated condition.

CSA, by contrast, is a voluntary association or voluntary community of people dedicated to expanding personal choice, not constraining individual freedom or mobility. Share members choose not only their vegetables, but whether or not to participate in this alternative institution in the first place. Their immediate survival does not depend on it. Furthermore, CSA offers few barriers to entry or exit; members can join or depart at will. Members are free to seek out more comfortable relationships and escape to more rewarding environments when confronted with disappointment or displeased by real or imagined inefficiencies. No matter how nice it may be to have food with the farmer's face on it, there simply is no corresponding need for members to make a personal sacrifice or spend time negotiating a less than perfect, but workable solution.

Within CSA, such things as clean food, local food, and a healthy environment are highly valued, but so are personal autonomy and convenience. And, for those members most frequently attracted to the institution (i.e., well-educated, white, middle- and upper-middle-class professionals), the former has not yet placed limits on the latter. The "pinch" to live in balance, to live with the right measure of freedom and constraint is seldom actually felt (Etzioni 1996). The very fact that CSAs keep growing larger, expanding in membership and territory covered, rather than maintaining smaller, more locally focused and inclusive associations, suggests the absence of immediate physical and political pressures, mutual commitment, and reciprocal obligation. It comes as little surprise that few, if any, CSAs have memberships that reflect the wider regional population, economically, educationally, or ethnically (Hinrichs and Kramer 1998; Cone and Myhre 2000; Hinrichs 2000). As a social movement, CSA is more about managing personal lifestyle than it is about challenging existing economic and political institutions, mobilizing resources to reform labor relations, and/or overcome structural inequity (Ostrom 1997; DeLind and Ferguson 1999).

Beyond Vegetables

Romantic notions aside, CSA has much in common with other direct marketing arrangements (e.g., farmer's markets, u-picks, subscription operations). The farmer and the shareholder assume a loosely cooperative relationship in the business sense of that term. The formal contract between them may be minimal, but so are the characteristics that come to define a community of place. Add to this the fact that members, who may live ten or twenty or sixty-plus miles from the farm, are under no obligation to physically engage with this place or with the people who labor there, and community becomes a concept that is socially and experientially quite hollow, despite its market appeal.

This in no way suggests that CSA is without merit, that it has no value or that there are no exceptions to personal self-interest. It is a creative marketing instrument that goes a long way toward humanizing the economy and toward reclaiming our ability to feed ourselves. What is being suggested, however, is that CSA as preached and practiced tends to confuse or conflate local (or regional) with community. Even at its most attenuated, CSA trades in clean, organically raised food and can track the journey from production through distribution and consumption. But, to call the relationships that underlie this journey a community because they have an ecologically responsible and/or caring nature does not just miss the point, it gets in the way of securing these efforts and using them to build a more decentralized and democratic food system.

To insist or expect that CSA is "about community" can create disappointment and exhaustion on the part of both farmers and members (DeLind 1999). Over the last fifteen years, countless CSAs have failed and thousands, perhaps tens of thousands, of members have dropped out, all people who were, or thought they were, ready to do something to reform the food system. On the flip side and of equal concern is the sense that a pat on the back, a potluck, and/or an occasional passing of the hat is enough collective effort to produce real social and economic change. This comfortable myopia reinforces the sense that social and political activism need only be personally satisfying to be effective. The latter is the theme song of the "green consumer" and one which does little to challenge the expression of individual accommodation as the way of managing within a globally oriented and commodity-driven world.

Herein lies a dilemma. Stripped of its community mystique CSA is a small business arrangement in which farmers and members negotiate their respective positions across a more personable market divide. Are the acts of buying and selling local food, of themselves, sufficient to bring about ecological accountability and a deep social and economic challenge to the food system? Probably not. When citizenship is defined by way of consumerism, there is little need for an "inner shift" out of the market paradigm. There is not much transformational leverage. "Our judgments as citizens," Sclove explains, need to consider but also transcend our narrower interests as consumers. When it comes to public policy and the common good, our citizen-selves ought to be sovereign over our consumer-selves. . . . Democracy, after all, is not just another, ordinary consumer good (like corn chips or underarm deodorant) and it is not an arbitrary lifestyle option. Democracy is a first-order social value—a necessary condition for being able to decide fairly what other considerations, besides democracy itself, to take into account in determining public policy. (2000)

But it is perhaps because CSA has an internal dilemma that it, upon occasion, responds to this challenge in ways that set it apart from other forms of direct marketing. It is this still malleable inconsistency and not its more familiar and self-conscious community-building rhetoric that casts CSA in a unique light and offers the potential to create a place within which citizenship—not farmership or consumership—may flourish. The CSA model, for example, is being adopted by nonprofit institutions: churches, faith-based organizations, peace and education centers, environmental trusts, and hunger programs. Within this sheltering environment, CSA is one of a synergistic set of programs. Here it can operate less as a commercial, profit-making endeavor and more as a public demonstration or working site designed to use natural resources and reframe consumption in ways consistent with the organization's primary mission. Local food and farming—land, labor, and food itself—are tucked into and become a component part of a wider set of social concerns, frequently those of social justice and food security.

Conversely, a few CSAs are themselves adding nonprofit programs to their existing food and farming activities as a way of addressing issues of social conscience. These projects need not be farmer-driven and they may operate independently from the vegetable business. Nevertheless, they are a deliberate attempt to move private property and enterprise into public service. The assumption is that the social value generated by such things as educational lectures on soil health, farmland preservation, and alternative energy, by self-provisioning workshops, gardening programs for children, or production earmarked for hunger relief will focus local attention on existing structural problems within the current food and farming system.

Similarly, a small number of older CSAs operated by charismatic farmers and an active core membership are placing privately owned resources, primarily land, into collective or group ownership. In several cases, the threatened loss of farmland has caused the CSA to work with local or national land trusts to stabilize its tenure and place development restrictions on the farmland (Hu 2000; Byczynski 1998). In other cases, private farmer-owned property is being dedicated to collective ownership and a commonly agreed upon agricultural use. In cases such as these, group interest, expressed through physically embodied as well as material commitment, and long-term public benefit begin to hold their own against the individualizing demands of the marketplace. It signals a movement on the part of citizens toward securing local resources and local futures.

Experiential learning grounded in a real place together with the possibility of taking collective or public ownership of that place has the power to shift self-interest into civic responsibility. Brian Donahue's story of suburban Weston, Massachusetts, serves as a case in point (1999). There, the development of a working agricultural (CSA) and forest commons, in addition to providing beauty, history, food, lumber, and fuel, physically taught residents, generally by way of their children, how to value and utilize their own natural resources. As Donahue explains, this commons has become a working venue for strengthening a land ethic and a social consciousness which, when needed, inform citizen action. Scott Sanders provides additional insight into the connection between place-bound awareness and citizenship:

To become intimate with your home region, to know the territory as well as you can, to understand your life as woven into the local life does not prevent you from recognizing and honoring the diversity of other places, cultures, ways. On the contrary, how can you value other places if you do not have one of your own? If you are not yourself *placed*, then you wander the world like a sightseer, a collector of sensations, with no gauge for measuring what you see. Local knowledge is the grounding for global knowledge. Those who care about nothing beyond the confines of their parish are in truth parochial, and are at least mildly dangerous to their parish; on the other hand, those who *have* no parish, those who navigate ceaselessly among postal zones and area codes, those for whom the world is only a smear of highways and bank accounts and stores, are a danger not just to their parish but to the planet. (1993:114)

But, there is more here than knowing your place. It is combining this knowledge with real work, work which does not separate people from nature or dissociate personal identity and professional practice from the demands of everyday life. Boyte and Kari (1996) recognize the instrumental nature of work and common space in the production of citizenship. For them "work is not beside the point. It is at the center of citizenship" while public work, in turn, is at the center of democracy. But public work, they explain, requires the presence of public spaces, "places for accountable productive work with people whom one might well not like or agree with on many issues. Public space is a distinctive vital arena in its own right, where citizens exchange ideas and power, achieve visibility, engage in conflict and collaboration" (146).

barriers to realizing csa vision?

Herein, then, may lie the largely unrealized promise of CSA, the fact that it allows in a way other direct marketing strategies do not the conjoining of public work and public space. Quite apart from marketing superior vegetables, CSA can, when loosened from this primary directive, serve as a forum for citizenship. It can become a place from which to encounter and engage with the realities, rights, and responsibilities of living, not because people like or chose to associate with one another (though they may), but because their work in place, together with the engagement and sacrifice that this requires, generates a sense of ownership in something larger than themselves. Or as Kemmis states, "public life can only be reclaimed by *understanding and then practicing* its connection to real, identifiable places" (1990:6, emphasis added).

CSA can reinforce the essential nature of work and of the non-virtual. It can contribute to, if not host, grounded debate that when entered into by a shifting pool of area residents may come to alter natural resource use, redirect market decisions, and expose the conditions that undermine small farmers, farm labor, and rural landscapes locally and non-locally. This is not community building in the classical and mythical sense of the term. But it is work that supports an alternative commerce, informed decision making, and regional integrity. It closes the distance between people and their food supply and establishes many centers of active problem solving. "No one," Boyte and Kari warn, "is innocent in the erosion of democracy. Yet public work provides a medium for everyone of us, in every environment to participate in the great American experiment. Indeed, the fate of our democracy and our commonwealth rests on our effort" (1996:200).

Part IV
The Politics of the Environment

Chapter 12
Canadian Agricultural Policy
Liberal, Global, and Sustainable

Alan Hall

Since the early 1990s, the concept of sustainable agriculture has become a prominent feature of agricultural state policy and discourse in
Canada and elsewhere (Agriculture and Food Sectoral Task Force
1991; Agriculture and Agri-food Canada and OMAF 1992a; OMAF
1991). Some analysts see the official adoption of the term as the successful outcome of the alternative agriculture movement's political
and deconstructive efforts to shift agriculture away from productivist
conventional agriculture (Buttel 1992; Kloppenburg 1991). Pointing
to an array of developments in state policy and farm practices such as
the growth of integrated pest management, conservation tillage, LISA
(Low Input Sustainable Agriculture)[1] in the U.S., and organic farming
methods, some have gone further to argue that we may be seeing the
beginnings of a paradigmatic shift in agricultural theory and practices
(Dunlap and Van Liere 1984; Beus and Dunlap 1990). While some
analysts are optimistic that significant changes towards sustainability
are occurring, others have cautioned that there is an ongoing struggle
over the meaning of sustainability. This struggle involves agribusiness
and larger farmer interests, making the outcome in terms of concrete
changes in agricultural practices less than certain (Macrae, Henning,
and Hill 1993; National Research Council 1989a). As Buttel (1992)
points out, even chemical companies have had little difficulty making
claims that chemical agriculture is sustainable since these chemicals
are integral to the financial success of most farm operations.

Despite these concerns, relatively little research has been done looking at the social and political construction of sustainable agriculture
and its manifestations in government policy and discourse. Rural sociologists have generally focussed their research attention on the practices and beliefs of individual farmers, researchers, and policy makers

operating within these different paradigms, with the aim of identifying the factors contributing to or constraining the development of sustainable agriculture (Lockeretz and Wernick 1980; Dalecki and Bealer 1984; Beus and Dunlap 1994). Few researchers have followed up on the argument of Buttel (1992) and others that the concept of sustainable agriculture is vulnerable to appropriation and use by the agricultural establishment as a means to resist more substantial changes in agricultural methods and to support the accumulation interests of agribusiness (Allen et al. 1991; Buttel 1992; Buttel and Gillespie 1988; Hall 1998a, 1998b; Kloppenburg 1991; Macrae, Henning, and Hill 1993; see also Goodman and Redclift 1991 for a discussion of the broader concept of sustainable development).

This article applies this appropriation argument to the Canadian context. I argue that state environmental policy in agriculture has been integrated and subsumed within an overall shift in agricultural policy. This shift is aimed primarily at sustaining economic growth through a neoliberal model of agriculture which emphasizes global markets, intensive cost-efficient management, flexible specialization, and reduced government supports (Marsden 1992; Ward 1993). The official discourse on sustainable agriculture claims that agriculture as a whole is moving to a sustainable status *within* the context of these broader efforts of agribusiness and the state to modernize and globalize agricultural production (Macrae, Henning, and Hill 1993). The environmental objectives of sustainable agriculture have been reconstructed and integrated within an overall neoliberal discourse on agricultural development and restructuring.

In making this argument, I am also building on the work of Adkin (1992, 1994) and others who suggest that the concept of sustainable development has been constructed in ways which allow capital and the state to manage the contradictions of environmental degradation and accumulation by conveying the principal message that capitalist economic development and the environment are compatible, self-regulating goals (Lipietz 1992). As Adkin (1992) has argued, this discourse made it appear *as if* corporations were suddenly motivated by profit and efficiency interests to conserve and protect the environment, denying the history of corporate pollution or explaining it away as a misunderstanding. This critique understands the official discourse on environmental sustainability as reproducing hegemony, in the Gramscian sense, by presenting a model of capitalist accumulation that appears to meet environmentalist and public demands for environmental protection at the same time that it meets the goals of economic growth and capital accumulation (Gramsci 1971).

It is acknowledged that the appropriated version of "sustainability" may yield some positive environmental outcomes. For example, there is evidence that practices such as integrated pest management and conservation tillage have produced benefits in terms of pesticide use, water contamination and soil conservation, as well as economic benefits in terms of cost savings (Langdale, Leonard, and Thomas 1985; Milham 1994; Priddle 1993). However, this does not mean that we are achieving long-term sustainability and the evidence of a consistent positive impact has itself been subject to question (e.g., Alberts and Spomer 1985; Hallberg 1988; Hinkle 1983). "Sustainable" methods like conservation tillage retain a heavy emphasis on pesticides and chemical fertilizers, while integrated pest management also assumes a continued need for chemical inputs (Hinkle 1983). More broadly, the problem of sustainability is reduced to technical issues as if the intensifying emphasis on competitiveness and productivity were irrelevant to farm practices that impact on the environment. Thus, the question which motivates this chapter is whether the contradictions of an enhanced emphasis on productivist agriculture are being hidden by claims of modest benefits through various technical innovations, while other more sustainable methods and production orientations with more far reaching implications for social relations are being excluded. As Gramsci (1971) argued, hegemonic discourses are effective in part by offering some concrete evidence of change; the trick is that the changes do not alter or challenge the underlying structures of dominance and subordination.

This chapter focuses specifically on the development of a state discourse on sustainable agriculture largely through an examination of federal and Ontario policy documents.[2] The analysis begins by showing that within the context of the 1980s farm crisis, state agricultural policy intensified its focus on productivity and efficiency and adopted marketing models for operating within a more deregulated global context. It is then demonstrated that while the ideas underlying sustainable agriculture emerged initially as a challenge to the government's approach to the crisis, the meaning of sustainability was transformed within an official state and corporate discourse to reflect and support the neoliberal state policy on economic growth, deregulation, and restructuring.

The Farm Crisis and State Policy

Following World War II, Canadian grain production became increasingly capital intensive with larger, more mechanized, and more specialized farms entirely dependent on expensive chemical and hybrid seed inputs (Basran and Hay 1988; Winson 1992; Knuttila chapter 3).

At the same time, with the increased production and the increased concentration of food processors and retailers in Canada and internationally, the prices paid to grain farmers for their production declined in real terms. This meant a falling rate of income/profit for farmers (Winson 1992). However, state intervention in commodity markets and farm support programs effectively institutionalized continued growth in productivity and output through increased chemical inputs, mechanization, and intensive exploitation of soils. During the 1970s, the economic contradictions of this system were partly relieved by expanding export markets and export oriented state policies and programs. Farmers were encouraged by rising food prices, low interest rates, inflated land values, and state export policy to invest heavily in land purchases and new equipment. While this was a relatively good period for some farmers, their debt load increased significantly (Gertler 1992; Gertler and Murphy1987).

As in most other industrialized nations, Canadian agriculture entered a period of serious crisis in the 1980s (Basran and Hay 1988; Barnett chapter 9). The combination of the Third World debt crisis and the worldwide recession brought the long-standing problem of overproduction and price instability into clear focus as export markets declined and prices dropped. Farm land prices declined while interest rates increased dramatically. Net farm incomes as a share of gross farm receipts declined from 36.3 percent in 1961 to 21.5 percent in 1981 and then dove to 14.5 percent in 1983 (Gertler and Murphy 1987:246). This was particularly traumatic for farmers who had been encouraged during the 1970s to expand through land, equipment, and other purchases. Debt ratios in Canada increased from 3:7 in 1971 to 5:4 in 1982 (Gertler and Murphy 1987:247). Within this context, the major drop in commodity and land prices, coupled with high interest rates, was catastrophic for farmers, many of whom lost their farms or were forced to seek off-farm employment to survive (Lind 1995).

This farm crisis also created significant fiscal and political problems for the state, agribusiness capital, and the existing farm leadership in the form of increased political militance among farmers (Pugh 1992). A survivalist movement emerged to defend farmers in trouble and membership grew in the more militant National Farmers Union (NFU) (National Farmers Union 1991, 1992). From all quarters of the farm community, including the more conservative Ontario Federation of Agriculture (OFA), there were increased demands for government financial assistance programs (Ontario Federation of Agriculture 1994; National Farmers Union 1990, 1991, 1992; Gertler 1992; Gertler and Murphy 1987). The crisis also challenged the federal government's agricultural policy emphasis on increased production and the expansion of export markets to offset price declines. In response, the federal and provincial governments, in conjunction with similar moves internationally (such as Uruguay Round of GATT negotiations on farm trade), began to move to restructure and reorient agricultural production policies in key areas.

The ministry of agriculture identified a number of major causes of the crisis which came to define the significant shifts in agricultural policy and discourse. While external forces such as increased global competition and continued subsidy wars were seen as critical, analysts also identified weaknesses within the farming community. As stated in a key federal agriculture policy statement in 1989:

There are compelling reasons to develop a new vision. The issues facing the industry are increasingly complex and often linked to each other. The vision which the federal government has for the future of agriculture rests on four pillars—more market responsiveness, greater self-reliance in the agri-food sector, a national policy which recognizes regional diversity, and increased environmental sustainability. (Agriculture Canada 1989:34)

Particularly critical to this analysis is the way in which this statement constructs environmental sustainability to conform to the objectives of market responsiveness and self-reliance.

(Re)Solving the Economic Crisis

The first two pillars in the government's 1989 policy statement, market reliance and self-reliance, were particularly crucial in defining the major shifts in production and marketing policies. The first, market responsiveness, spoke to the need for more flexibility in production—the capacity to rapidly adapt to changes in the marketplace. As stated in the government policy paper: "More market responsiveness means moving quickly in adapting our production and marketing systems to respond to new market opportunities" (Agriculture Canada 1989:35). More concretely, this meant first that farmers must become more flexible producers, capable of shifting their production from year to year and of moving into new (usually global) markets as they develop. There is also a quality component to the strategy which emphasizes expanding into certain smaller but high value crop markets: for example, speciality kinds of soybeans for the Japanese market.

Second, it meant finding new ways of lowering costs on the farm and in processing. A key component of this effort was a shift in focus from high yield production to a leaner and more cost-efficient production model. Within this strategy, the central solution to the farm crisis was one in which farmers and the agricultural industry would survive and compete by producing more cheaply and efficiently.

> In Canada, the dominant pattern has been for production to exceed demand, and Canadian agriculture has been beset by the high cost of production relative to farm income. . . . Greater production efficiency together with the development and production of products to meet specific consumer demands will be essential. (Agriculture Canada 1987:2)

Beginning in the mid-1980s, agricultural research, education, and extension services were increasingly oriented towards remaking farm production into "lean and flexible" farm production (e.g., Agriculture Canada 1985; Agriculture and Agri-food Canada 1992, 1994a, 1994b; SWEEP 1992).[3] Smart farming was redefined in the process as farming with less; that is, the central objective was to get the farmer to maximize cost-efficiency rather than just crop yields. The measure of success was no longer the amount of yield but rather the profitability of that yield. This meant a more intensive management of the farm. Specific cost-saving strategies were promoted in the areas of fertilizer management, pest management, human resources management, and so on. These were also emphasized as distinct areas for careful planning and analysis using a more explicit cost-efficiency and cost-benefit logic.

The third key means of increasing market responsiveness was the "removal of barriers," such as the wide range of interprovincial and international trade barriers which were seen as preventing Canadians from being "as competitive as they can be" (Agriculture Canada 1989). This focus on trade barriers introduces a central concern with deregulation, but the concern with deregulation is developed much more substantially within the discourse on the "second pillar" of Canadian policy, greater self-reliance. Deregulation as developed within the concept of self-reliance is not just about eliminating traditional trade barriers such as tariffs but also the elimination of government farm support programs which were presented as discouraging farmers from being cost competitive and from seeking out new markets.

> Farmers expect to depend on the marketplace to earn their long-run return. Effective support programs can cushion farmers against sudden changes in the markets or the weather. But continuing subsidies, with little expectation of improved market prospects, should signal the need to work out a plan for a transition to a more self-reliant basis of operation. (Agriculture Canada 1989:10)

Consistent with the long-standing state emphasis on agricultural exports, maintaining competitiveness in the international marketplace is the central rationale for the need to reduce government interference in the marketplace, as well as the promotion of ever greater levels of efficiencies through improvements in farm management and production practices.

The importance of our export markets to the strength of our industry, and a continuation of strong global competitiveness means that we will have to ensure that market signals are transmitted to individual entrepreneurs. Programs, policies, and traditional industry practices cannot distort these signals which are critical if the industry is to respond aggressively. We also need to work at ensuring that Canadian farmers have the highest level of management skills . . . to allow them to be as efficient and competitive as possible. (Agriculture Canada 1989:27)

Reflecting this emphasis, in 1993 the federal and provincial governments set a goal of increasing agri-food exports by 50 percent by the year 2000 which, it was argued, could only be achieved through a major effort "to enhance our competitive performance" (Goodale 1993:13). Relative to the impact of neoliberalism in other industries, the move to deregulate agriculture in Canada has been modest in practice in that subsidies have remained an integral part of the system. Yet, it was also clear within the context of Canada's negotiation of the North American Free Trade Agreement and its participation in the 1990–92 GATT negotiations that the Canadian government was moving to a much stronger position on free trade in agriculture by the early 1990s (Cohn 1990:165). As the federal minister of Agriculture Ralph Goodale put it: "I think we have to become an innovative and flexible sector of the Canadian Economy. . . . Farmers don't want subsidy programs. They just want a fair return out of the marketplace. GATT helps more than any other trade deal in history to achieve that objective" (Hornberger 1994:E1).

The Challenge of Sustainable Agriculture

As growing emphasis on the need for increased producer efficiency, flexibility, and competitive self-reliance was developing as state policy, a competing vision of agriculture had also emerged during the 1980s which, initially at least, appeared to challenge many of the productivist assumptions underlying conventional agriculture (Batie 1990; Buttel 1992; Manning 1986). Rather than the conventional emphasis on capital intensive, large-scale, highly mechanized, high chemical input farms, proponents of sustainable or alternative agriculture advocated the reduced use of synthetic farm chemicals, smaller farm units, environmentally appropriate technology, the conservation of finite resources, greater farm and regional self-sufficiency with more direct sales to consumers, and minimally processed foodstuffs (Beus and Dunlap 1990). Although there were important variations in the definitions of sustainable agriculture from the outset (Advisory Panel on Food Security 1987), many of the initial formulations were widely understood and presented as substantial challenges to the current conventional production regime in agriculture (Buttel 1992; Manning 1986; Merrill 1983). As Buttel (1992) points out, the concept of sustainable agriculture emerged around the same time as the broader concept of sustainable development but unlike sustainable development, which appeared largely as a construction of international environmental and development organizations, and which was much more "science" and "technology-based" from the outset, the concept of sustainable agriculture developed more broadly and diffusely from within agriculture itself (see also Beus and Dunlap 1990). While this included agricultural scientists and agro-ecologists, there was also a substantial grassroots farmer and community/consumer basis to the early social constructions of sustainable agriculture. For example, in Canada, the Ecological Farmers Association of Ontario (EFAO) and the Canadian Organic Growers (COG) were both grower and consumer-based organizations which emerged in the 1980s with a primary emphasis on organic gardening and farming. The development of an urban-based environmental movement and the increasingly politicized recognition of the health and ecological effects of pesticide and fertilizer use were also central forces in pushing the development of alternative ideas within agriculture (Standing Committee on Agriculture 1992:xv). This included an increasing awareness of the economic effects of nitrogen- and phosphorus-based fertilizer run off in the Great Lakes (SWEEP 1989). Soil erosion and conservation also became significant political issues in the early 1980s (Science Council of Canada 1986). In 1984, for example, the Senate's Standing Committee on Agriculture, Fisheries, and Forestry produced a report that concluded that Canada risks the permanent loss of a significant proportion of its agricultural capacity if a major commitment is not directed towards soil conservation (Standing Committee on Agriculture 1984:11). Morever, while concerns about the environmental effects of agriculture were central to sustainable agriculture from the outset, there were social justice components as well (Tovey 1997). This linked sustainable agriculture, and more specifically organic farming, to the maintenance of the family farm and rural communities, and cast sustainable agriculture as a challenge to corporate industrial agriculture and to the globalization of agricultural markets (Buttel 1992:22; see also Tovey 1997).

Within the Canadian context, a good example of this challenge is provided by a 1990 policy document on sustainable agriculture which came out of a conference sponsored by the National Farmers Union (NFU) and the Catholic Rural Life Conference (National Farmers Union 1990). Two sets of sustainable objectives were established in the document; one was "environmental," while the other was the protection of the "family farm and economic security." To achieve these objectives, the document called for a number of major changes in the agricultural production and marketing system. To meet its environmental objectives, the policy first attacked the existing system's emphasis on productivity and efficiency:

Over the past 40 years, North American agriculture has been a model of efficiency and productivity [but] this level of intensity and productivity is not sustainable. . . . Moderation is not enough. . . . The goal must be the operation of agricultural land at *optimum* not maximum productivity, with virtually no soil loss. We believe that this goal can be reached by farms of moderate size— typically family size. . . . Large-scale corporate agriculture driven by the maximisation of profits have not proven to be good stewards. (National Farmers Union 1990:2, emphasis added)

To meet its environmental objectives, the document then called for an end to the farmers' dependency on chemical-based production, endorsing a major state and research investment in organic and low-input farming methods.

In terms of the family farm and economic security objectives, the NFU policy document confronted some of the central elements of Canadian agricultural policy by calling for an end to the cheap food policy and the export dependency policy, and an expansion of supply management systems and price controls on all commodities.

Economic security of the family farm must be ensured since it is only through the family farm that the land and its people can be maintained. There can be no greater indictment of our system than the loss of many thousands of farm families who were demonstrably the most efficient producers. While this has shown the failure of the "free market" system, it has also exposed the economic system as being void of any social dimension. . . . Supply management must become more prominent. (National Farmers Union 1990:3)

As Beus, Dunlap, and others have argued, when constructed in this way, sustainable agriculture can be understood as a competing paradigm with an ideological framework, fundamentally distinct from conventional agriculture, which calls for basic changes in the organization of agricultural production (Beus 1995; Beus and Dunlap 1990; Freudenberger 1986; Tovey 1997). Put in Gramscian terms, sustainable agriculture had potential as a counter-hegemonic discourse which was emerging in response to the negative economic and environmental impacts of conventional capitalist agriculture (Adkin 1992). By counter-hegemonic, I mean that the discourse is critical of the central assumptions of conventional capitalist agriculture and provides an alternative requiring radical changes in thinking and social relations. Certainly, among its early advocates, sustainable agriculture was explicitly constructed as both an alternative response to the crisis and an attack on the government's solution to the crisis. As the National Farmers Union put it, it was the "continuing economic crisis" which demanded the radical changes they were proposing (National Farmers Union 1990:3).

Further evidence that sustainable agriculture emerged as a call for radical changes is offered in the work of Beus and Dunlap (1990, 1994) which attempts to determine whether the alternative advocates of sustainable agriculture were introducing a fundamental shift in paradigms. While many analysts have attempted to provide their own definitions of sustainable agriculture, Beus and Dunlap (1990:398–99) have sought to distinguish empirically the paradigmatic roots of the perspective by analyzing the writings and interviews of farmers, policy makers, agribusiness representatives, and agricultural scientists identified as advocates of alternative vs. conventional agriculture. From this research, they argue that although there are wide variations within the different camps, there are a number of distinct assumptions associated with sustainable agriculture that suggest a paradigm shift. According to their findings, conventional and alternative agriculturists differ along six main dimensions. The first is centralization vs. decentralization. While the conventional supporters emphasized national/global production, processing, and marketing systems, and more concentrated control of land, resources, and capital, the sustainable advocates stressed local/regional production, processing, and marketing; dispersed populations with more farmers; and dispersed control of land and other resources. The second dimension was dependence vs. independence. In this case, the conventional emphasis was on large, capital intensive production units and technology; heavy reliance on external sources of energy, inputs, and credits; consumerism and market dependence; and on science and experts. The sustainable emphasis was on smaller, low capital production units and technology; reduced reliance on external sources of energy, inputs, and credit; more personal and community self-sufficiency; and personal knowledge, skills, and wisdom. The third dimension is competition vs. community in itself. For conventional advocates, farming was a business like any other; competitive self-interest was the prevailing ethic; no value was placed on cooperative farm traditions, rural cultures or communities; and profit, speed, and quantity were viewed as measures of success in farming. For sustainable respondents, the farm was viewed as a way of life as well as a business; cooperation and farm traditions were valued; physical farm work was seen as rewarding and meaningful; and farm success was measured in terms of quality, permanence, and beauty. The fourth dimension is defined as the domination of nature vs. harmony with nature. The conventionalists viewed humans as separate and dominant over nature; the environment was viewed as resources, production was seen as being maintained by chemicals, and food was understood as improved through processing. Those with the harmony with nature perspective saw farming as part of and subject to nature; nature was valued for its own sake; and production was maintained by developing healthy soil with minimal processing of food. The fifth dimension refers to an emphasis on specialization vs. diversity. Rather than standardized production systems, crop specialization, and monoculture, separation of crops and livestock, and highly specialized science and technology, the sustainable agriculturists stressed a broad genetic base, more plants grown in polycultures, multiple crops in complementary rotations, integration of crops and livestock, locally adapted production systems, and interdisciplinary, systems-oriented science. The final dimension is exploitation vs. restraint. In the former model, external costs were ignored and emphasis was placed on short-term benefits: it encouraged heavy use of nonrenewable resources, high consumption, and economic growth, and valued materalism and financial success. Advocates of the sustainable agriculture paradigm, on the other hand, emphasized the need to consider all external costs; short-term and long-term outcomes were viewed as equally important based on renewable resources, conservation of non-renewable resources, and restraints on consumption to benefit future generations; and personal success was valued as self-discovery, simple lifestyles, and non-materialism.

Although the six dimensions are understood by Beus and Dunlap (1990) as representing an ideal model around which some variation exists among the sustainable advocates, the model provides a framework for contrasting and identifying some of the contradictions in the official government discourse on sustainable agriculture. Certainly, the alternative version of sustainable agriculture as defined by these findings appears as a direct attack on Canada's federal agricultural policy and its overall orientation on export driven economic growth, along with many of its major initiatives for restructuring farm production and management methods along lean and flexible production lines. For example, while the advocates of alternative agriculture were encouraging more labor intensive small-scale mixed farming operations serving local and regional needs, the state's emphasis was on flexible specialization, export markets, and leaner production based on more intensive management and larger-scale capital intensive tech-nology based operations (Dahlberg 1986). Since the state's approach also translated into continued dependency on synthetic chemicals and enhanced emphasis on bioengineered and genetically manipulated seeds, there was also a basic conflict with the sustainable movement's call for a radical reduction in chemical and technological dependence. By advocating a greater emphasis on developing agriculture to meet local and regional markets, the advocates of sustainable agriculture were also advocating a move away from the neoliberal state's emphasis on economic growth, intensive global competition, and a more deregu-lated global marketplace. They promoted instead an environmental ethic as a political and economic imperative (Buttel 1993; Gertler 1992). This opposing alternative position was clearly evident in the National Farmers Union policy statement:

The Canadian economy must be a protected economy or be aligned with a trading bloc with the same aspirations. The Canada-U.S. Free Trade Agree-ment promoted liberalized access . . . which is in conflict with our policy objec-tives of agricultural self-reliance and domestic priority. (National Farmers Union 1990:2)

Within this same document, supply management is also recommended as an important policy approach along with other legislative initiatives on land use and concentration, to ensure that small family farms can be maintained (National Farmers Union 1990:3). This focus directly conflicts with developments in Canadian agricultural policy which ac-cepted the dismantling of these programs as a necessary feature of globalization.

    This suggests that in its alternative form, the discourse on sustain-able agriculture presented the state with a substantial political prob-lem: how to continue to promote free trade and neoliberal agricultural policies as the solution to the crisis without reinforcing the emerging development of a counter-hegemonic movement for increased domes-tically oriented environmental and economic regulations. I argue that one of the solutions to the problem came in the form of the appropria-tion of the concept of sustainable agriculture and the development of an official hegemonic discourse which constructed its meaning in ways consistent with neoliberal agricultural policy and agribusiness inter-ests. In so constructing sustainable agriculture, the state and agribusi-ness recast and reintegrated the solutions to the environmental and economic problems of agriculture so that sustainability appeared to embrace the objectives and means of economic growth (e.g market re-sponsiveness, cost efficiency, self-reliance) as the *means* of achieving environmental sustainability.

(Re)Constructing Sustainable Agriculture

The Canadian and Ontario governments began to use the term "sustainable agriculture" in the mid-1980s. Its integration within the official discourse was relatively complete by the early 1990s and it began to appear as a phrase constantly attached to the end of any government vision statement on agriculture. As Ralph Goodale, federal Minister of Agriculture, stated in a major 1994 policy speech:

My vision for Canada's agriculture and agri-food industry is for a growing, competitive, market-oriented industry that is profitable, responds to the changing food and nonfood needs of the domestic and international customers, is less dependent on government support, and contributes to the well-being of all Canadians and the quality of rural life in rural communities, while achieving farm financial security, *environmental sustainability*, and a safe high quality food supply. (Goodale 1994:6, emphasis added)

There were a series of government documents, publications, and policy statements developed in early 1990s at the provincial and federal levels which also adopted the term, including the federal government publication, "The Health of Our Soils: Toward Sustainable Agriculture" (Agriculture and Agri-food Canada 1995), the Canada/Ontario Agriculture Green Plan (Agriculture and Agri-food Canada and OMAF 1992a), and the Senate Standing Committee Report on Agriculture, "The Path to Sustainable Agriculture" (Standing Committee on Agriculture 1992). It should also be stressed that this perspective was promoted through various corporate, farm media, and farm organization channels as well (e.g., AGCare 1992). Within these various different sources, however, there were a number of common elements which were critical in reconstructing the project of sustainability.

From the outset, it was emphasized within the government's discourse that the means and goals of sustainable agriculture were consistent and compatible with the interests of farmers, agribusiness, and the general public. Indeed, one of the key claims was that good environmental practices were essential to maintaining export markets. As Goodale (1994:17) put it, "our environmental image will provide benefits and achieve premiums in our international marketing efforts." Protecting the environment was suddenly good for business, while potential for conflicts was largely denied, downplayed, or ignored.

A central message in this emerging state discourse was the idea that agriculture was changing to meet the "environmental challenges" of long-term sustainability: "In the surprisingly short period of two decades, the members of Ontario's Agricultural and Food systems have not only developed a strong environmental awareness, but have shifted their daily practices and their institutional framework to meet this environmental challenge" (Agriculture and Food Sectoral Task Force 1991:3).

What is also often critical to this discourse is the dual claim that farmers have always been conscious of and receptive to environmental issues, but are now moving largely on their own accord, informed by emerging scientific knowledge, new technologies, and some government assistance, to practice more sustainable agriculture.

Ontario farmers have always sought and developed new and better ways to farm. Understanding the irreplaceable value of productive agricultural land and water resources, more and more they have been turning their attention to growing crops and raising livestock in ways that protect and enhance the environment: the practice of sustainable agriculture. (Agriculture and Agri-Food Canada and OMAF 1992a)

In presenting the official view of sustainable agriculture, most policy documents avoid any clear definition of what sustainable agriculture means in practice.

The development of more sustainable agricultural methods since 1970 has taken place so rapidly, utilized such a wide variety of techniques, and come from such a broad range of sources, that it has proven impossible to tightly define. Nor should we want to restrict the development . . . within the bounds of any narrow definition. . . . While there may be disagreement about the exact definition of "sustainable agriculture," a remarkable consensus has formed that Agriculture and Food in Ontario can and is becoming more sustainable. (Agriculture and Food Sectoral Task Force 1991:3)

When definitions were offered, they tended to be both general and all-encompassing without reference to specific principles for achieving the general goals of environmental protection and enhancement:

The practice of sustainable agriculture is the growing of crops and the raising of livestock in ways that protect and enhance the environment. Sustainable agriculture also encompasses issues of protecting wildlife habitat, managing waste, protecting genetic resources, adapting to climate changes, and developing energy efficiency. (Agriculture and Agri-Food Canada 1992)

As Buttel (1992) predicted, given this refusal to define sustainable agriculture in terms of concrete practices, a wide range of practices and beliefs were now being included in what the government considered "sustainable farming." A "sustainable farmer" ranged from someone who had purchased a more efficient field sprayer to someone who had planted a wind break to someone who was using organic farming methods. This then made it much easier to claim a widespread consensus on the "fact" that Canadian agriculture was becoming more sustainable (Agriculture and Food Sectoral Task Force 1991:3).

While the image being conveyed here was that sustainable agriculture was taking a wide range of forms at the farm level, certain kinds of changes in farming practices were being emphasized over others in the government, corporate, and farm literature, and through government and corporate supported funding, extension, and research programs (Dakers 1995:12; Agriculture and Agri-Food Canada 1995; OMAF 1991). These efforts emphasized soil conservation and the management of water run-off (Agriculture and Agri-food Canada and OMAF 1994a, 1994b). For example, a major $30 million federal-Ontario project to reduce phosphorus in the Great Lakes and soil and water degradation, the Soil and Water Environmental Enhancement Program (SWEEP), placed much of its emphasis on the promotion of fertilizer management programs and conservation tillage (SWEEP 1989, 1992, 1993). Virtually no resources were provided for research on or the adoption of organic farming.[4] Similar developments were evident in the other major government programs including Ontario Land Stewardship Program and the Ontario Tillage 2000 project (Standing Committee on Agriculture 1992:31–32). Programs were also supported by corporate funding such as the E-Plus "Farming for Economic Efficiency and Environmental Excellence" program sponsored by the chemical transnational company CIBA-Geigy, which promoted the adoption of certain kinds of soil conservation techniques such as no-till (Innovative Farmers of Ontario 1994).

Moreover, neither the specific changes being promoted in farming practices nor the rationales behind them challenged in any way the basic assumptions of government policy on the restructuring of farm production and marketing. Conservation tillage, for example, did not represent a major shift away from the conventional productivist orientation (Goodman and Redclift 1991). Indeed, conservation tillage, especially a particular approach called no-till farming, was principally promoted and adopted by the government on productivity and efficiency grounds (Hall 1998b). As one major federal report stated:

No till makes "CENTS." With reduced labor requirements, less fuel usage and fewer trips over the field, farmers come out money ahead. . . . With a no-till system, fewer hours are needed to farm the same number of acres. This cut in labor requirements allows farmers to farm more acres with the same number of people. (SWEEP 1993:2)

As Lighthall (1995) has also pointed out, these kinds of sustainable methods have been strongly supported by agribusiness and the larger heavily capitalized farm operators because they sustain a reliance on chemical inputs and new technologies to achieve ever greater economies of scale. Other widely promoted "sustainable" approaches such as the promotion of integrated pest management for fruit farmers, although potentially beneficial in encouraging a reduction of pesticides, were also presented in efficiency terms (Agriculture and Agri-food Canada and OMAF 1992b:51–52).

What is also striking about the official discourse on sustainability is its lack of attention to the family farm issue. Instead, productivity and efficiency are central components of sustainability, both environmental and economic. Within the new discourse, it is the capacity of farmers using new, more environmentally friendly technologies to achieve higher levels of productivity and efficiency that defines sustainable farming. The fact that this requires higher levels of capitalization and retains the emphasis on competitiveness and export markets is not recognized as problematic for "family farmers."

In broader ideological terms, the discourse conceals the conflict which sustainable advocates had identified between the need for economic growth and environmental protection. Instead, governments were able to announce programs which appeared to perform the simultaneous functions of promoting *both* economic growth and a healthy environment. For example, when the federal and Ontario governments introduced their Soil and Water Environmental Enhancement Program in 1986 to address the fertilizer pollution problem, they cited two key objectives: the first was to reduce phosphorus loadings, while the second was "to improve the productivity of South West Ontario Agriculture by reducing or arresting soil erosion" (SWEEP 1992). In its report, "The Path to Sustainable Agriculture," the Senate Standing Committee on Agriculture then cited the combination of these two objectives within SWEEP as the defining feature of sustainable agriculture: "This dual objective, to rationalize production and improve the environment, is of particular interest to the Committee since this is what sustainable agriculture is all about" (Standing Committee on Agriculture 1992:30).

It was in the context of these kinds of changes in farming practices that politicians and policy makers were then able to report the "discovery" that environmental sustainability was "good for business":

Many farmers, retailers, processors, and researchers have found that making an operation more environmentally sustainable can also serve to increase its economic viability. The goal of sustainable development has always been shared by members of our agricultural community, down through the generations. However, the central insight which flows from it has come as a bit of a surprise to many: that our daily activities can become both more environmentally sensitive and more economically viable. That is, the economy and the environment are not eternal enemies, but in fact, natural allies. (Agriculture and Food Sectoral Task Force 1991:3)

What becomes clear in this discourse is that the government's commitment to sustainable agriculture translates into a simultaneous commitment to high levels of economic growth. Indeed, it is interesting to note that the integration of the two discourses on sustainable agriculture and economic development reaches a new level as politicians and policy makers begin to use the term "sustainable" to refer to both economic growth and environmental goals. Again, as the Minister of Agriculture, Ralph Goodale, stated in his 1994 policy speech:

My vision for the future of the agrifood sector builds on the . . . themes of growth and security. . . . In the area of growth, our objectives are to achieve *sustainable* agriculture and agrifood growth. In the area of security, our goals are to attain resource and environmental *sustainability*. (Goodale 1994:8, emphasis added)

In describing these sustainable objectives as "inextricably interrelated," the Minister fails to recognize any potential conflicts between these two goals. He only cautions that the major policy constraint is "fiscal reality," which then becomes the central rationale for the limitations on state investment in farm research, extension, and support programs (Goodale 1994:8). What he doesn't explain is why all the investment is directed towards expensive biotechnologies supported by agribusiness, while virtually nothing is devoted to organic farming research.

Within the government and, indeed, within the establishment farm media and agribusiness corporate discourse, the meaning of "sustainable agriculture" was transformed to convey the idea that environmental interests have been integrated with economic growth *without* the need for radical changes in agricultural production or in the agrifood system (see AGCare 1992). Moreover, the discourse repeatedly conveys the idea that agriculture is changing *within* the context of economic restructuring and globalization to become environmentally sustainable. As quoted above, the economy and the environment can now be seen as "natural allies," and the need to develop "sustainable farming practices" as simple "common sense" (Agriculture and Food Sectoral Task Force Report 1991:3).

In the surprisingly short period of two decades, the members of Ontario's Agricultural and Food systems have not only developed a strong environmental awareness, but have shifted their daily practices and their institutional framework to meet this environmental challenge. (Agriculture and Food Sectoral Task Force 1991:3)

Again, what is also often central to this discourse is the dual claim that farmers have always been conscious of and receptive to environmental issues, but are now moving largely on their own accord, informed by emerging scientific knowledge, new technologies, and some government assistance, to practice more sustainable agriculture.

Concretely, for the state, farmers, and agribusiness, this then provided the justification for policies and programs which have emphasized voluntary compliance, education, and research over a more tightly regulated regime (Hall 1998a). A good example of this was the Ontario government's announcement of *Food Systems 2002* in 1988 (OMAF 1989; Surgeoner and Roberts 1993). This was set up by the Liberal Ontario government to "assist growers in cutting their use of pesticides by 50 percent over a 15 year period" (OMAF 1989). This program was firmly grounded in the idea that farmers will make the changes voluntarily since there were no formal regulations requiring or specifying how the target was to be met. It consisted entirely of funding for increased extension services, research, and education programs.

Government funding of this sort also supported various other joint initiatives involving farmer groups and chemical companies which were directed at the user. For example, a program in Ontario called the Environmental Farm Plan (EFP) is administered and delivered by a conglomerate of conventional farmer organizations called AGCare (Agricultural Groups Concerned About Resources and the Environment). It is essentially an environmental audit which farmers use to assess whether their farm operations are meeting certain standards of practice and conditions, with a major emphasis on chemical storage, equipment, and use practices. The program is entirely voluntary and until the government offered a $500 grant for participants, very few farmers enrolled in the program. Within this context, changes in government regulations governing agricultural pesticide use have been minimal, the major exception being a new registration requirement for farmers which involves taking and passing a one day pesticide safety course (OMAF, AGCare, and OME 1993). The central message here was very consistent with the neoliberal emphasis on deregulation. We are assured that the "market," left largely to its own devices, is shifting farmers to become environmentally sound.

Interestingly enough, the state and corporate discourse on sustainable agriculture has not only provided a rationale for limited changes in regulations in areas such as pesticide use, it is also being used as a rationale for the deregulation of agriculture more broadly:

> Environmental sustainability means ensuring that farmers respect the need to preserve the carrying capacity of the natural resource base and that government policies and programs do not contribute to the degradation of the environment. In some cases, this may mean reducing or eliminating production, marketing, or regulatory barriers which inhibit progress toward an economically viable and more environmentally sound agriculture. (Agriculture Canada 1989:36)

While there is no doubt that some government regulations and programs do support environmentally unsound practices (Johnson 1991), the problem is that the "barriers" being identified by the government were understood as jointly inhibiting economic growth and environmental sustainability as if they were the same objective. In other words, a barrier to environmental sustainability was only identified as such if it also interfered with economic growth. Thus, not only is the concept of environmental sustainability no longer a threat to the state's deregulation and restructuring objectives, sustainability has become part of the rationale and language for deregulation and restructuring.

Conclusion

This chapter argues that the meaning of sustainable agriculture has been constructed within the context of Canadian agricultural policy to fit the state's production and marketing policies on deregulation and restructuring. As has been shown, this not only concealed the conflicts between the goals of environmental sustainability and economic growth, it allowed the government to promote the virtues of restructuring and deregulation within its promotion of sustainable agriculture.

Although competing visions of sustainability persist, particularly in the form of organic farming (Hall and Mogyorody 2001), the construction of an official version on sustainability has helped to undermine the capacity of farm and environmental activists and organizations to build on the early progress of sustainability as a counter-hegemonic discourse. Certainly, within the Canadian context, organic farming remains marginal as a political and economic force, both in the rural and the urban contexts (Hall and Mogyorody 2001). While the weaknesses in the Canadian organic movement are not a simple product of the state's appropriation of the sustainability discourse, it may well have played a critical role in allaying public concerns about pesticide and food safety, and convincing conventional farmers to stay with the state's program. As Adkin (1992) has argued, this kind of official or corporate construction of environmentalism emphasizes the capacity of the marketplace and market forces to respond to societal changes and indeed to profit from them, Within the contexts of neoliberalism and globalization, this emphasis on the power of the market to resolve social problems reflects and reinforces the central ideas of neoliberalism, that is, state deregulation and the positive power of the deregulated market. As such, the appropriation of a counter-hegemonic movement, and the construction of a productivist discourse on sustainable agriculture has helped to reproduce farmer and public consent to the deregulation and restructuring of agriculture.

Chapter 13
Constructing Genetic Engineering in the Food and Fiber System as a Problem

Urban Social Movement Organizations as Players in Agricultural Discourse

Ann Reisner

Even using the three previous centuries of agricultural industrialization as a standard, genetic engineering (GE) in agriculture could potentially increase the penetration of capital into food production to an unprecedented degree (e.g., Jacobson, Lefferts, and Garland 1991; Kneen 1999; Lappé and Bailey 1998; Nottingham 1998; Teitel and Wilson 1990). The degree of control that GE technology offers to industry giants, and the friendliness of government to this industrial control, could dramatically change both the structure of the agricultural industry and the individual consumer's relationship to food as a "natural" product. Furthermore, both the new agricultural technologies and the scale of agricultural enterprises they enable stimulate new actors to enter the political arena that was once largely controlled by production agriculture and associated corporations. These new actors, a coalition of "green," health, and other advocates, are increasingly able to define issues and establish political agendas in ways that many farmers perceive as antithetical to farmers' interests. Nowhere is this more apparent than in the debates concerning agriculture and genetic engineering.

Techniques to transfer genetic information from one species to another were developed during the 1980s (Wright 1994). Virtually instantly, industry became aware of the possibilities for large profits this new development enabled. The first project to apply genetic engineering commercially, developing bacterial production of human insulin to treat diabetes, was started in 1982; agricultural companies started field testing genetically engineered plant resistance to insects, viruses and bacteria as early as 1985 (Krimsky and Wrubel 1996).

Genetic engineering involves taking a gene segment from one living organism (plant, animal, or bacterial) and transferring it to another organism. Two principal methods are used for the transfer. In the first, the shotgun approach, scientists coat selected genes onto gold pellets which they then fire into a layer of cells from the target organism. In the second, the secret agent approach, laboratory scientists smuggle a piece of genetic material into the target organism's genetic material via a virus. In comparison to the technologically unsophisticated methods of genetic selection through selecting and saving or hybridizing seed, genetic engineering is highly manipulative, expensive, and takes considerable training, skill, and equipment. Genetic engineering also has the capacity for more radical changes than traditional methods of genetic improvement in that scientists using this technique can and do introduce genes from other species, even from other kingdoms.

Until the Food and Drug Administration's hearings in 1999, prompted in part by widespread protest at the World Trade Organization meeting in Seattle, GE products largely were introduced into fields and grocery shelves without widespread public comment or debate. The protests of social movement activists in Seattle and elsewhere brought the issue of genetic engineering in food to public attention in the United States. In so doing, social movement organizations (SMOs) added a distinct voice to the public discourse on the use of genetic engineering in agriculture.[1] The purpose of this chapter is to examine the social movement discourse on genetic engineering and how closely it resembles the discourse(s) of other major players in the public arena.

Social Movement Theory

Individuals alone generally have little power over systems that are cruel, indifferent, or otherwise do not responds to their needs, wants, goals, or values. Social movements are one of the few ways that groups that are otherwise blocked, including farmers, can initiate change.[2] In organizing and joining social movements, individual actors are able both to pool resources—money and time—in getting their messages to others, and to speak with the more powerful voice of the group. Being able to mobilize large numbers is one of the more potent weapons of mass movements. The second power of movements is definitional, being able to formulate and articulate a vision that fundamentally challenges the dominant worldview. Often, the challenge involves drawing attention to social relations of power that are not seen, or that are viewed as unchangeable or dismissed as unimportant. Typically, social movements offer an alternative definition of these relations as noticeable, changeable, and important.

Social movement research, however, has been a back-and-forth swing between content and process since the early days of theorizing on the subject. Much of the early work was content based and focused on the triggers leading to social movement emergence. This research was slowly abandoned when researchers found no consistent relationship between grievances and movement emergence (McAdam, McCarthy, and Zald 1996).

The next wave of theorizing started from the assumption that if grievances were, as the previous decades of work had shown, reasonably independent of movement emergence, then it must necessarily be true that movements developed because some organizations were able to more effectively capture and utilize resources and capitalize on strains or tensions within the social system. Two closely related traditions, resource mobilization theory and political process theory, dominated much of the 1970s and 1980s. Both were centrally concerned with how movements organize and capitalize on political opportunities rather than with what those movements believed. By the end of the 1980s and the early 1990s, however, scholars within these traditions began discussing the lack of theorizing about movement goals, that is, about how the aims of movements matter to participants and to movement development (e.g., Gamson 1992).

Frame theory developed from this concern (see Snow and Benford 1988, 1992). Snow et al. (1986), among the earliest theorists in this area, argued that three dominant frames are common to all movements: (1) a diagnostic frame that points to a flaw in society, (2) a prognostic frame that outlines, often in very general terms, what should be done to correct the problem, and (3) a moral claim that sets the basis for the rightness of opposing the established power structure. For example, mainstream environmentalists' diagnostic frame posits that the earth is an interconnected system and that excessive human intervention (e.g., pollution, overpopulation) seriously compromises the earth's ability to repair itself. To correct this problem (the prognostic frame), human activity must be modulated in order to reduce the level of human interference with natural systems to a tolerable level. Not surprisingly, given this frame's emphasis on systems, the approach most mainstream environmentalists take is also systemic: passing laws, developing regulations, or establishing incentives designed to reduce industrial pollution. The moral claim for action is essentially self-interest: the environmental system is necessary for human survival.

Frame theorists' approach, while content directed, is still relatively content free. In contrast, discourse analysis, particularly the critical discourse analysis (CDA) perspective of such scholars as Fairclough (1989), van Dijk (1988a, 1988b), and Wodak (1996, 1997), offers a method by which to reintroduce content factors into movement analysis. "CDA focuses on the ways discourse structures enact, confirm, legitimate, reproduce, or challenge relations of power and dominance in society" (van Dijk 2001).

According to the critical discourse analysis perspective, power can be exercised either coercively or by manipulating consent. The most successful use of power is when its use is unseen, taken for granted as "inevitable" or "unquestionable." Discourse analysis, then, as a tool for looking at a text, tries to rip apart "unquestioned" assumptions and look at the power relations underlying those assumptions. In the words of linguist Norman Fairclough, one of the more influential theorists of discourse analysis:

> My approach will put particular emphasis upon "common sense" assumptions which are implicit in the conventions according to which people interact linguistically, and of which people are generally not consciously aware. . . . Such assumptions are *ideologies*. Ideologies are closely linked to power, because the nature of the ideological assumptions embedded in particular conventions, and so the nature of those conventions themselves, depends on the power relations which underlie the conventions; and because they are a means of legitimizing existing social relations and difference of power, simply through the recurrence of ordinary, familiar ways of behaving which take these relations and power differences for granted. (1989:2)

Discourse analysis includes analyzing the process of producing a text, describing the text itself, and interpreting how the text will be read. Discourse analysis assumes that the social conditions of production set constraints on producing written, verbal, and visual texts. Individuals are constrained in much the same way for interpretation. These constraints are relatively serious, if generally unseen. These texts collectively structure, articulate, and constitute how society and social relations are formed. In exposing these relations, critical discourse analysis (and the analyst) are doing political work.

Fairclough distinguishes three stages of discourse analysis (Fairclough 1989:26): *description*, an analysis of the formal properties of text; *interpretation*, an analysis of producing and interpreting the text; and *explanation*, an analysis of how the social relations of power set the context in which the text is both produced and interpreted. In so doing, discourse analysis explicitly criticizes unstated relations of power, pointing out where the interests of powerful groups are being glazed over or disguised through language. Close attention to how power and social relations are hidden by assumptions that obscure which groups benefit from social control is common to all critical discourse analysis. As Fairclough states,

> Institutional practices which people draw upon without thinking often embody assumptions which directly or indirectly legitimize existing power rela-

tions. Practices which appear to be universal and commonsensical can often be shown to originate in the dominant class or the dominant bloc, and to have become naturalized. (1989:33)

In sum, discourse analysis starts by assuming that we (people who act in the world) cannot do whatever we want, whenever we want to do it. We, in fact, act in fairly organized routine ways. The forces that reinforce structural stability usually do so by manipulating our consent, though some, such as the police, rely on force or the threat of force. Discourse analysis looks at one method of organizing and manipulating consent: the construction of meaning through the production of language.

Methods and Selection of Players and of Transcripts

As a perspective, discourse analysis does not have a rigorously defined theoretical or methodological structure. Scholars working within this tradition tend to borrow rather eclectically from a wide variety of leading scholars, including theorists who are epistemologically opposed on key issues. For example, articles within the critical discourse tradition may borrow from Habermas for a discussion of legitimization and from Foucault when dealing with domination and discipline, even though the two scholars take diametrically differing stances on rationality. Methodologically, discourse analysis can be equally diverse. In his book, *Language and Power*, Fairclough (1989) analyzes conversations, job interviews, teenage magazines, advertisements, news stories, political epics (e.g., Thatcherism), and construction of societal "features" (e.g., building the consumer). What is common to all the analyses is the three categories mentioned above: (1) a description of the text, often a literal reproduction of it, (2) an interpretation of the text, especially those features which would obscure an alternative reading, and (3) an explanation of the social relations which the text obscures.

My methods of data selection and analysis are more clearly described than much of the critical discourse analysis done in media or cultural studies. Critical discourse analysis tends to gloss over the methodological descriptions of data collection required for statistical analysis (see Fairclough 1989; van Dijk 1988a, 1988b, 1991; Wodak 1996, 1997; Wodak, ed. 1989 for examples of discourse analysis case studies.) The following paragraphs explain how and why the texts which served as the data base for this essay were chosen and analyzed.

Four different sectors have been intimately involved in the production and application of food biotechnology. Businesses, such as Monsanto, are the driving force, seeing immense potential for profit and control in the new technologies. Universities conducted the basic research that developed the technology of genetic engineering, and are continuing to do applied work on crop and livestock development. Government agencies have been heavily involved in funding research programs and also regulate and monitor the safety of genetically engineered crops. Finally, farmers plant and harvest the altered crops. These four sectors have been increasingly opposed by a loose coalition of popular groups, here termed social movement organizations. These SMOs represent diverse groups of environmental, organic and sustainable farmers, consumers, and health advocates.

To examine the major players active in constructing the public discourse on biotechnology, I selected segments from biotechnology websites and publicity pieces on biotechnology from three land grant universities in the midwest corn and soybean belt, Illinois, Iowa, and Wisconsin. For multinational companies, I chose Monsanto, which has invested heavily in agricultural biotechnology, and Cargill, a major grain dealer; for government, the two most important regulatory agencies, the U.S. Department of Agriculture and the Food and Drug Administration; and, for farmers, the American Farm Bureau, which generally represents the interests of the largest, most corporate farmers. For social movements, I examined the websites of all organizations involved in Turning Point, a national coalition of social movement organizations opposing genetic engineering in agriculture (see Table 13.1). I used my knowledge of the field initially to select the players but also used the selected texts to check whether there were additional active groups. The only additional "player" mentioned in the texts was the American public en masse: "consumers," "citizens," "the people," "popular opinion." In essence, however, "the people" were the battleground for the different discourses offered, with all of the players speaking for and to the "best interests" of this group. Such a rhetorical position effectively puts the consumer in the position of object, rather than an actor-subject.

To show how the process of discourse analysis works when it is closely grounded to a particular text, I examined multiple organizations for what, presumably, would be the least controversial aspect of biotechnology, its definition. The transcripts and a detailed analysis are reported for each group of players. Exemplary selections from the transcripts of the findings are followed by a description of that group's overall discourse on genetic engineering. The final section specifically looks at the text for power relations: which groups disguise those relations and how they do so. My analytic categories, such as "naturalize, minimize and universalize" were developed out of a close reading of the text, rather than being theoretically determined prior to the data analysis.

TABLE 13.1. Member Groups of the Turning Point Project

Organizational Type	Organizations	Membership or Supporters
Progressive scientist groups	International Center for Technology Assessment, The Council for Responsible Genetics, The Campaign for Responsible Transplantation	General
Food and agriculture	Food First, Institute for Agriculture and Trade Policy, The Center for Food Safety, International Forum on Food and Agriculture, Organic Consumers Association, Pesticide Action Network, Foundation on Economic Trends	General
Environmental	Sierra Club, Friends of the Earth, Earth Island Institute, Greenpeace U.S.A., Mothers and Others for a Livable Planet, International Society for Ecology and Culture, Rainforest Action Network, The Edmonds Institute, Center for Ethics and Toxics, Native Forest Council, Native Forest Network, Religious Campaign for Forest Conservation	General
Consumer	Consumer Choice Council, U.S. Public Interest Research Group	General
Progressive	Mothers for Natural Law of the Natural Law Party	General
Animal rights	Humane Society U.S.A.	General
Left labor	International Forum on Globalization	General

Sources: Campaign for Responsible Transplantation 1999; Center for Ethics and Toxics 1999; Center for Food Safety 1999; Consumer's Choice Council 2000; Council for Responsible Genetics 1999; Earth Island Institute 1999; Edmonds Institute 1999; Food First/Institute for Food & Development Policy 1999; Foundation on Economic Trends 1999; Friends of the Earth 1999; Greenpeace 1999; Humane Society U.S.A. 1999; Institute for Agriculture and Trade Policy 1999; International Center for Technology Assessment 1999; International Forum on Food and Agriculture 1999; International Forum on Globalization 1999; International Society for Ecology and Culture 1999; Mothers and Others for a Livable Planet 1999; Mothers for Natural Law 1999a, 199b; Native Forest Network Campaign 1999; Organic Consumers Association 1999; Pesticide Action Network of North America 2000; Religious Campaign for Forest Conservation 2000; Sierra Club 1999; U.S. Public Interest Research Group 1999.

Findings

Agribusinesses

Monsanto: The Basics of Plant Biotechnology

For centuries, humankind has made improvements to crop plants through selective breeding and hybridization—the controlled pollination of plants.

Plant biotechnology is an extension of this traditional plant breeding with one very important difference—plant biotechnology allows for the transfer of a greater variety of genetic information in a more precise controlled manner.

Traditional plant breeding involved the crossing of hundreds or thousands of genes, whereas plant biotechnology allows for the transfer of only one or a few desirable genes. This more precise science allows plant breeders to develop crops with specific beneficial traits and without undesirable traits.

Many of these beneficial traits in new plant varieties fight plant pests—insects, weeds, and diseases—that can be devastating to crops. Others provide quality improvements, such as tastier fruits and vegetables; processing advantages, such as tomatoes with higher solids content; and nutrition enhancements, such as oil seeds that produce oils with lower saturated fat content.

Crop improvements like these can help provide an abundant, healthful food supply and protect our environment for future generations. (Monsanto 2000)

Cargill: What Is Food Biotechnology?

Under its broadest definition, food biotechnology started thousands of years ago when primitive man advanced from hunting and gathering food to farming. For thousands of centuries, plant breeders selected, sowed, and harvested seeds to produce enough food to sustain life and to develop desirable traits in their crops such as better taste, richer color and hardier plants.

At the beginning of this century, farmers carefully selected plants with beneficial traits. . . . Though they did not understanding the underlying scientific principles involved, early farmers have been harnessing biotechnology for centuries to make or modify plants and food productions.

Scientists now understand many biological processes and this has allowed the development of new techniques to alter or copy some of these natural processes. Techniques of modern biotechnology allow scientists to create crops and foods that are equivalent to or even improved over those made using traditional methods. However, the new methods are faster, cheaper, and more reliable. In some cases, modern biotechnology makes available products that were non-existent before. (Cargill 2000)

Monsanto and Cargill naturalize, minimize, universalize, and diffuse the discourse on biotechnology; equally as significant, they make no mention of any profit motive associated with their development of genetically modified organisms (GMOs). Both Monsanto and Cargill emphasize, in the earliest possible placement of their explanation of biotechnology, that plant biotechnology is "centuries" (Monsanto 2000) or "thousands" (Cargill 2000) of years old, that is, it is a "natural" technique. Both companies tie the definition of biotechnology to a long history of crop development: "mak[ing] improvements to crop plants through selective breeding and hybridization" which is characterized as "traditional plant breeding" (Monsanto 2000) or as having "started thousands of years ago when primitive man advanced from hunting and gathering of food to farming" (Cargill 2000). Given no counter to these assumptions, the reader would be left to assume that, since humans have used biotechnology from the beginning of farming, there must be very little dangerous about it.

Minimizing the differences between other forms of biotechnology and genetic engineering goes hand in hand with naturalizing the technique. According to Monsanto's definition, "plant biotechnology" is (simply) "more precise," "controlled," and "allows for the transfer of a greater variety of genetic information" (Monsanto 2000). Cargill described the new method as "faster, cheaper, and more reliable" (Cargill 2000). The discourse, then, provides reasons for adopting the new technology (precision, control, speed, reliability, and economy) that are, on the face of it, rational without being alarming. That is, given the assumption that farming is primarily an economic enterprise, it makes sense, without needing further explanation, that a person or a company would adopt a technique that is faster and cheaper, while the converse is not true.

The social relations involved—a limited number of multinational companies motivated by profit making fundamental decisions on what is necessary or desirable in food—and the inherent possibility of contradictions between corporate and consumer interests are heavily obscured in the choice of actors and of benefits. The actors in biotechnology are "humankind," "primitive man," "mankind," "plant breeders," "farmers," and "scientists" (Cargill only). Not once are corporate presidents, accountants, lawyers, boards of directors, or other executives associated with decision making in multinational companies, nor are profits, market share, and stock dividends mentioned as driving forces in decision making. Instead the benefits are universalized: "fighting plant pests," "quality improvement," "abundant, healthful food," and "protecting our environment." In their public statements, Monsanto and Cargill obscure the actual social relations of production—the relationship between capital and their investments in biotechnology—effectively masking the huge potential for power and profit they anticipate from their investments.

In this sense, the complete text differs little from the short segments containing Cargill's and Monsanto's definitions of biotechnology. Each company text emphasizes the benefits of biotechnology, stopping just short of declaring that biotechnology is the silver bullet sent to slay all the world's problems. Biotechnology will help "meet the challenge of feeding an additional three million human beings" (Monsanto 2000) by providing the increases in agricultural productivity needed to feed the world. Biotechnology will increase food quality, food safety, food nutrition, and crop yields, and eliminate allergens in food. It will, or already has, produced "tomatoes with a fresher flavor," "strawberries that retain their natural sweetness," and potatoes that "absorb less oil when fried" (Monsanto 2000).

Biotechnology can help preserve biodiversity and otherwise protect "our environment for future generations" (Monsanto 2000). Among their claims, they assert that biotechnology can develop organisms that will produce material now made from nonrenewable resources, and crops that will allow farmers to preserve more soil. Products from genetic engineering can help save the rain forest and reduce greenhouse gas emissions (Monsanto 2000). Furthermore, Monsanto claims, biotechnology products are safe. They claim that those organisms and food products that are released into the environment or the marketplace are carefully reviewed by the appropriate government agencies—the U.S. Department of Agriculture, the Food and Drug Administration, and the Environmental Protection Agency. The only drawback to biotechnology, according to the Monsanto text, is consumer "hysteria," particularly in Europe, where consumers do not trust government regulator's ability to protect the food supply (Monsanto 2000).

Government, Universities, and Farmers

U.S. Department of Agriculture

What is biotechnology? Agricultural biotechnology is a collection of scientific techniques, including genetic engineering, that are used to create, improve, or modify plants, animals, and microorganisms. Using conventional techniques, such as selective breeding, scientists have been working to improve plants and animals for human benefit for hundreds of years. Modern techniques now enable scientists to move genes (and therefore desirable traits) in ways they could not before—and with greater ease and precision. (USDA 2000a)

U.S. Food and Drug Administration

When most people talk about bioengineered foods, they are referring to crops produced by utilizing the modern techniques of biotechnology. But really, if you think about it, all crops have been genetically modified through traditional plant breeding for more than a hundred years. Since Mendel, plant breeders have modified the genetic material of crops by selecting plants that arise through natural or, sometimes, induced changes. Gardeners and farmers and, at times, industrial plant breeders have crossbred plants with the intention of creating a prettier flower, or hardier or more productive crops. These conventional techniques are often imprecise because they shuffle thousands of genes in the offspring, causing them to have some of the characteristics of each parent plant. Gardeners or breeders then look for the plants with the most desirable new trait. With the tools developed from biotechnology, a gene can be inserted into a plant to give it a specific new characteristic instead of mixing all of the genes from two plants and seeing what comes out. Once in the plant, the new gene does what all genes do: It directs the production of a specific protein that makes the plant uniquely different. This technology provides much more control over, and precision to, what characteristic breeders give to a new plant. It also allows the changes to be made much faster than ever before. (Interview with Commissioner Jane E. Henney [U.S. FDA 2000b])

Iowa State University

Although the university's new Plant Sciences Institute will make use of and contribute to the newest technology of genetic modification, Iowa State scientists have been modifying crops for years. In fact, consumers have eaten food and otherwise benefited from crops that have been genetically modified for 500 years. Many foods have been modified by traditional methods of breeding, which bring two plants together by transferring pollen from one variety to another and selecting for desirable traits. Newer methods include biotechnology in which scientists isolate and transfer specific stretches of DNA using specialized enzymes. An evolving technology now allows scientists to splice genes and, with great precision, move genes between unrelated species. (Crosbie 2000)

American Farm Bureau Federation

Biotechnology enhances natural mechanisms to give rise to new products. The process is nothing new. Mankind has been altering natural organisms since early times to obtain benefits. Examples include selectively breeding plants and animals to enhance desirable traits, fermenting grain to produce alcohol, and tanning hides with tannin to produce leather. Such advances took considerable time. Biotechnological research is speeding up the process in breath-taking fashion. (American Farm Bureau 2000)

Government agencies (USDA 2000a, 2000b; U.S. FDA 2000a, 2000b) and universities (University of Illinois 2000a, 2000b, 2000c; University of Wisconsin 2000), both of which have interests in promoting genetically engineered crops, and the Farm Bureau (American Farm Bureau 2000), which generally aligns itself with agribusiness, all use similar techniques to define biotechnology and all produce a discourse which closely resembles that of agribusiness. As do agribusiness companies, the USDA naturalizes genetic engineering by linking this technique to selective breeding. The advantages of genetic engineering, as defined, are not that it is highly different or unusual, but that it allows for greater precision and control in use.[3] Biotechnology is again associated only with desirable outcomes, such as "improv[ing] plants and animals," and the advantages are generalized to humanity as a whole. In the case of the FDA, the commissioner (U.S. FDA 2000b) links genetic modification to the most common and "everyday" actors— gardeners and farmers—while university and the USDA transcripts use the generic "scientist" as actor (e.g., University of Wisconsin 2000; USDA 2000a, 2000b). The government's, the universities', and the Farm Bureau's complete text are all similar to Monsanto's, including that consumer fears, particularly in Europe, have encouraged resistance to bioengineered food products.[4] "Many believe that fears in Europe," an Iowa publication (Crosbie 2000) states, "have grown from diminished trust in government and industry to protect and inform the public, particularly following the mad cow disease disaster."[5] Government agencies, universities, and the Farm Bureau support the adequacy of government regulations, thus, at least implicitly, accepting the principle that GEOs are substantively equivalent to naturally occurring organisms. The FDA assumes that genetically engineered food has a known safety profile.[6]

Social Movement Organizations

National Family Farm Coalition

Genetic engineering defined: Genetic engineering involves taking a gene from one species and splicing it into another to transfer a desired trait. This could not occur in nature where the transfer of genetic traits is limited by the natural barriers that exist between different species and in this way genetic engineering is completely new and incomparable to traditional animal and plant breeding techniques. Genetic engineering is also called biotechnology. Another name for genetically engineered crops is genetically modified organisms (GMOs). (National Family Farm Coalition 2000)

Greenpeace

In traditional forms of breeding, variety has been achieved by selecting from the multitude of genetic traits that already exist within a species' gene pool. In nature, genetic diversity is created within certain limits. A rose can cross with a different kind of rose, but a rose will never cross with a mouse. Even when species that may seem to be closely related do succeed in breeding the offspring are usually infertile. For example, a horse can mate with an ass, but the offspring, a mule, is sterile. These boundaries are essential to the integrity of any species.

In contrast to traditional breeding, genetic engineering involves taking genes from one species and inserting them into another in an attempt to transfer a desired trait or character. For example, selecting a gene which leads to the production of a chemical with antifreeze properties from an arctic fish (such as the flounder) and splicing it into a tomato or strawberry to make it frost-resistant. It is now possible for scientists to introduce genes taken from bacteria, viruses, insects, animals or even humans, into plants.

It has been suggested that, because we have been modifying the genes of plants and animals for thousands of years, genetic engineering is simply an extension of traditional breeding practices. While it is true that the food crops we are eating today bear little resemblance to the wild plants from which they originated, it is clear that through this new technology organisms are being manipulated in a fundamentally different way. (Greenpeace 1999)

Consumers Choice Council

Genetically modified organisms are organisms whose genetic makeup has been directly altered by humans. . . . Genetic engineering does not represent our first effort to influence the characteristics of living organisms. For thousands of years, humans have taken advantage of naturally occurring genetic variation within species to selectively breed organisms with desirable traits. Many of the characteristics of domestic animals and agricultural crops have been developed through such selective breeding.

What is so revolutionary about genetic engineering is that it involves the transfer of genetic material between organisms that would never be able to breed in any natural or laboratory setting. Vast evolutionary boundaries can be crossed, such as those separating different phyla, or even different kingdoms.

Human beings have the ability to mix the genetic composition of organisms that have been on separate, distinct evolutionary paths for thousands or millions of years. For example, we have placed genetic information from humans into mice, and scorpion genes into corn. . . . While these techniques promise many advances in agriculture and medicine, they also pose great ethical and biological dangers, risks, and uncertainties, as discussed in the next section. (Consumer's Choice Council 2000)

Campaign for Food Safety

The technology of genetic engineering (GE), wielded by transnational "life science" corporations such as Monsanto and Novartis, is the practice of altering or disrupting the genetic blueprints of living organisms—plants, animals, humans, microorganisms—patenting them, and then selling the resulting genes—foods, seeds, or other products for profit. . . . GE is a revolutionary new technology still in its early experimental stages of development. This technology has the power to break down fundamental genetic barriers—not only between species—but between humans, animals, and plants. By randomly inserting together the genes of non-related species—utilizing viruses, antibiotic-resistant genes, and bacteria as vectors, markers, and promoters—and permanently altering their genetic codes, gene-altered organisms are created that pass these genetic changes onto their offspring through heredity. Gene engineers all over the world are now snipping, inserting, recombining, rearranging, editing, and programming genetic material. . . . For the first time in history transnational biotechnology corporations are becoming the architects and "owners" of life. (Campaign for Food Safety 1999)

Both those supporting and those opposing biotechnology agree on the most fundamental aspects of genetic engineering: the technique involves genetic manipulation and the major actors involved are farmers, corporations, government, scientists, and consumers. After those very basic points, GE supporters and SMOs differ on virtually every detail. Social movement discourses are, above all, critical. First, social movement discourse highlights genetic engineering's "radical" (Greenpeace 1999; Sierra Club 1999) discontinuity from traditional genetic manipulation methods. Genetic engineering is "completely new and incomparable to traditional animal and plant breeding techniques" (National Family Farm Coalition 2000). It is a method that manipulates organisms in a "fundamentally different way" (Greenpeace 1999). Second, genetic engineering "could not occur in nature" because nature has "natural barriers" (National Family Farm Coalition 2000) that do not allow species boundaries to be crossed (Greenpeace 1999; Organic Consumers Association 1999). Again and again, SMOs point out that genetic engineering is an artificial (constructed) method: GE can put genetic bits of fish in tomatoes, humans in mice, scorpion genes in corn and so on (Cummins 1999). Third, SMOs closely link the definition of technology to negatives. Genetic engineering poses "great ethical and biological dangers, risks, and uncertainties" (Consumer's Choice Council 2000) and it "disrupt[s] the genetic blueprints of living organisms" (Center for Food Safety 1999).

The SMOs emphasize that the technical capacity to manipulate genetic material outruns the scientific understanding of the implications of these manipulations. While agribusiness descriptions of GE stress precision in selecting what genetic material is introduced, the SMO descriptions stress the lack of precision in placement. According to all accounts (both GE supporters and detractors), the placement of genetic material in the recipient organism is relatively imprecise. Neither method, using "guns" to "fire" genetic material at the host DNA or using plasmids to "smuggle" genetic material into the host organism, allows scientists to control where the genetic snippet is placed. SMOs argue that since a genome's expression could potentially be affected by its near neighbors on the genetic strand, inserting DNA could destabilize the way that the host DNA works (Greenpeace 1999; Organic Consumers Association 1999). They also assert that even if scientists could specify the target position in which to insert the gene, current understanding of how genes regulate themselves is too limited to know which location would be safe (Consumer's Choice Council 2000; Greenpeace 1999).

Environment.   SMOs' concern for the environment and for human health stems directly from their claim that no one fully understands the downstream effects of releasing GE organisms (Institute for Agriculture and Trade Policy 1999; Native Forest Network 1999; Consumer's Choice Council 2000), not the scientists who develop the organisms, the governments that "regulate" them, or the companies that stand to profit. The counter discourse to Monsanto's presentation of GEs as more predictable than traditional crop or breed selection goes as follows. SMOs start with the assertion that natural ecosystems are highly complex and interlinked (Consumer's Choice Council 2000). Since inserting the desired genetic fragments into host organisms is so inherently imprecise, there will inevitably be "unanticipated outcomes" (Center for Ethics and Toxics 1999; Organic Consumers Association 1999).[7] These "outcomes" will reverberate along and through the network of associations in the ecosystem. Collective human wisdom available at this point cannot predict either short-term or long-term consequences of releasing GE organisms (Consumer's Choice Council 2000), nor—unlike cars—do we collectively have the capacity to locate and recall these organisms should something go wrong (Organic Consumers Association 1999).

Genetic engineering, say some, is a "molecular Auschwitch," a "greater threat . . . than nuclear war," which could cause "irreversible, devastating damage to the ecology" (Organic Consumers Association 1999) and/or "overwhelm the ability of ecosystems to adapt" to rapid change (Center for Ethics and Toxics 1999). Certain of the more foreseeable problems include insect and virus resistance that has been incorporated deliberately into desirable plants "finding their way into weeds and wild relative(s)" (Native Forest Council 1999), and/or GE crops lowering soil fertility or producing toxins harmful to birds or other animals, including beneficial insects (Organic Consumers Association 1999).

SMOs specifically point out GMOs' potential to threaten biodiversity. By engineering plants with genetic traits not found in the wild, scientists could be developing superior competitors or competitors that are outside the range of checks and balances developed by nature. Like exotic species, these GE developed varieties could become superweeds or superpests capable of overwhelming native species.

Health.   As with the environment, SMOs argue, GMOs could have unplanned and unanticipated effects on the delicate and intricately interconnected system that is the human body. The potential for these effects should be "cause for alarm," rather than complacency (Center for Ethics and Toxics 1999; Native Forest Network 1999; Sierra Club 1999). Small changes as a result of genetic manipulation could increase, or switch on, the genes that start the production of toxic substances (Center for Food Safety 1999; Consumer's Choice Council 2000; Mothers and Others for a Livable Planet 1999; National Forest Council 1999; Organic Consumers Association 1999). Consumers with food allergies could be exposed to potentially severe, even fatal, doses of allergens in foods that bear no physical resemblance to the types of food that consumers associate with the allergen, or consumers could develop new allergic reactions to new substances in the altered food.[8] The quality of food and its nutritional value could be lowered (Center for Food Safety 1999; Consumer's Choice Council 2000; Greenpeace 1999; Native Forest Council 1999; Organic Consumers Association 1999) and the use of antibiotic-resistant marker genes could increase the level of antibiotic-resistant bacteria (Native Forest Council 1999; Native Forest Network 1999; Organic Consumers Association 1999). Over the long term, even subtle alterations in food could increase the risk of cancer (Native Forest Network 1999; Organic Consumer's Association 1999). SMOs point to specific cases, instances where an allergen was inadvertently introduced using genetic material from Brazil nuts (Cummins 1999), beneficial phytoestrogens were lowered in GE soybeans thus reducing the nutritional value of the food (Cummins 1999), and cancer risks were, at least potentially, increased.[9]

Threat to Sustainable Farming.   SMOs' concern for the effects of GE crops on sustainable farming cuts across both physical and social/economic lines. According to the SMOs, GMOs pose a danger of toxic trespass, genetic drift from GE crops contaminating organic farmers' crops (Native Forest Council 1999). Furthermore, if farmers misuse and overplant GE crops that appropriate natural pesticides that organic farmers use, as in the case of BT corn, organic farmers will lose important weapons for fighting crop losses from pests.

In addition to the physical dangers, the new crops could reduce genetic diversity for social/economic reasons, SMOs say. Biotechnology promotes reliance on a few crop cultures and encourages farmers to stop growing the local varieties that have been adapted to local needs and cultural traditions over generations (Pesticide Action Network of North America 2000; Green Guide 1999). According to the SMOs, the loss of locally adapted varieties of seed is, in itself, a negative. Both environmental groups (such as Sierra Club 1999) and sustainable agriculture groups (including the Organic Consumers Association 1999) value local or indigenous control over global: local farmers should be able to choose what they grow and save under local conditions. This, they argue, is the real threat to food security, the loss of agricultural biodiversity that would come as small farmers who saved their own seeds are transformed by capital intensive agriculture into "bioserfs," growers who are dependent on buying the genetically more limited varieties of company seed (Organic Consumers Association 1999; Sierra Club 1999). Additionally, since adopting GE corn will tie farmers more closely to capital intensive agriculture and its accompanying restrictions, GE agriculture also threatens cultural systems, disrupting patterns of interaction developed over generations (Sierra Club 1999).

Democratic Process.   Not only is GE risky, but the process by which GE products have been introduced is flawed. Consumers, SMOs assert, have a right to know and to have access to information about the food that they are eating (Center for Food Safety 1999; Council for Responsible Genetics 1999; Consumer's Choice Council 2000; Food First 1999; Friends of the Earth 1999; Pesticide Action Network of North America 2000). Furthermore, the public has a right to be able to participate in democratic processes to see that food produced from altered organisms is adequately regulated (Consumer's Choice Council 2000; Council for Responsible Genetics 1999; Sierra Club 1999). Up to this point, they assert, there has been virtually no, or at the least very limited, public debate (Institute for Agriculture and Trade Policy 1999).

SMOs reject the FDA's criterion of "substantive equivalence," which assumes genetically engineered foods are similar enough to non-engineered foods not to warrant the more stringent regulations given to new food additives. SMOs call for long-term testing and labeling (Center for Food Safety 1999; Consumer's Choice Council 2000; Food First 1999; Center for Food Safety 1999; Friends of the Earth 1999; Greenpeace 1999; Institute for Agriculture and Trade Policy 1999; Mothers for Natural Law 1999b; Pesticide Action Network of North America 2000; Organic Consumers Association 1999). Labeling is necessary because it will allow consumers the option to "exercise free choice" and the ability to boycott GE products (Greenpeace 1999).[10]

According to the SMOs, the driving forces propelling GE technology are the classic forces of capital: profits, control of markets, and increasing monopolization and specialization in food production. SMOs point out that a handful of companies, including Monsanto, Novartis, Zeneca, Aventis, and Dupont, dominate the market in genetic engineering in food (Greenpeace 1999). Their motive is to control GE in agriculture. GE in this context is described as a "money machine" that will get "quick profits for a few huge corporations" (Pesticide Action Network of North America 2000). Furthermore, other SMOs point out, GE technology, and the patent rights that have been granted to companies, will allow a few corporations to dominate global markets for food, fiber, and seed (Organic Consumers Association 1999; Pesticide Action Network of North America 2000; Sierra Club 1999). Greenpeace quotes Robert T. Fraley, co-president of Monsanto's agricultural sector, as saying, "This is not just a consolidation of seed companies, it's really a consolidation of the entire food chain" (Greenpeace 1999). Or as the Organic Consumers Association wrote, "for the first time in history, transnational biotechnology corporations are becoming the architects and 'owners' of life" (Cummins 1999).

The alternative discourse offered by the SMOs as a group forcefully challenges the very foundation of the corporate discourse, which rests on universalized benefits. The SMOs' discourse states that multinational corporations are first and foremost interested in profits and this motive will dominate any interaction. SMOs also argue that the U.S. government, specifically the FDA's policy of substantive equivalence, is far too lax. Multinationals, SMOs say, already are forcing consumers to accept an unfair risk, in essence forcing consumers to act as "guinea pigs" for fundamentally new and, hence, potentially dangerous food products (Institute for Agriculture and Trade Policy 1999; Mothers for Natural Law 1999b). As the Organic Consumers Association (1999) points out: "These are some of the same companies that once promised a carefree life through pesticides and plastics. Would you trust them with the blueprints of life?"

Second, the SMO discourse stresses that multinational corporations will not use biotechnology to feed a "hungry world" (Pesticide Action Network of North America 2000); rather, the argument that biotechnology is needed to feed the world population is "one of the industry's favorite self-justifications" (Green Guide 1999). In fact, SMOs argue, the greater danger presented by biotechnology firms is their potential to consolidate control over the small farmer (Green Guide 1999; Greenpeace 1999; Sierra Club 1999). SMOs point out that Monsanto, Novartis, and other multinationals have successfully pushed for patent laws that will essentially give them exclusive patent rights over their germ plasm. The effect of these patent laws is to make saving company seed illegal, which not only violates a centuries-old tradition of saving and trading seed, but also increases the total control that corporations have over farmers.[11] Some SMOS argue that this is tantamount to biopiracy and should not be condoned as a moral, as well as ecological, issue (Cummins 1999).

SMOs are clear on the socioeconomic implications of the penetration of capital into international agriculture. As with the green revolution which requires farmers to generate capital to purchase inputs, the premiums on genetically engineered seeds will make farming with GE seeds too expensive for the smaller peripheral farmer. If the genetically engineered crops gain dominance, smaller and organic farmers will be forced out because of the proliferation of pests resistant to natural pesticides or because of market restrictions.

The SMOs also imply that the quest for profit will override any altruistic corporate tendency to produce food for the poor. First, they argue, current biotech crops do not, contrary to the pro-biotechnology claims, improve crop yields (Green Guide 1999). Second, bioengineered crops are, by and large, not the crops that are the food staples for the poor in peripheral countries (Green Guide 1999). Third, while biotech companies say that bioengineered crops will decrease the use of pesticides, many of the GMOs have been developed for resistance to herbicides produced by the biotech corporation (Organic Consumers Association 1999).

Noting that corporations are primarily motivated by capital accumulation and hence unlikely to monitor the safety of food products, the SMOs also question the ability of government agencies to adequately check for food quality. As indicated in the analysis of their discourses, universities, government, and corporations all represent government agencies as safeguarding food. SMOs, in contrast, present U.S. government policy as complicit with multinational corporations' move to control the food supply (Greenpeace 1999; Mothers and Others for a Livable Planet 1999). In particular, SMOs criticize the United States government as allowing a "revolving door . . . between the White House and the genetic engineering industry" (Greenpeace 1999; see also Green Guide 1999; Sierra Club 1999). International consumer activists have accused the American biotechnology industry and U.S. government of "bio-colonialism, . . . imposing [biotechnology] and its consequences on many billions of peoples" (Guardian 1999). The U.S. has fostered this accumulation by pressuring the World Trade Organization to give priority to free trade, allowing corporations to patent new genetically engineered varieties, and permitting a series of acquisitions and mergers among related companies in the biotechnology industry (Greenpeace 1999).

Conclusion

Businesses such as Monsanto who have bet their financial future on the success of biotechnology are less exposed to conflicting pressures and roles than are governments and universities who deal with a variety of constituents with multiple agendas. Hence Monsanto, and other companies that are promoting biotechnological produce, can stand as a pure type of those interested in manipulating the discourse on biotechnology for private gain.

Monsanto's construction of biotechnology positions genetic engineering in agriculture as a benevolent development for all of humanity (in fact, all of the natural world). It does so by closely linking genetic engineering to other, centuries-old, traditions of genetic manipulation through such mechanisms as selective breeding or seed selection, thus establishing genetic engineering's safety through association. The reasons for adopting the technique are essentially those of convenience (more precise, faster, cheaper), while the benefits are widely shared (better, tastier, more nutritious food; better for the environment). The discourse also closes off biotechnology from public questioning, by placing the authority and the responsibility for safeguarding the public from questionable products directly on government agencies, in particular the Food and Drug Administration. Their claims that the benefits are both universal and substantive and that the public is rigorously safeguarded, leaves no opening for a rational reason to oppose GE in agriculture. So it is fairly predictable that company discourse characterizes negative reaction as "hysterical," and localizes that hysteria in a group of people that, at least in the United States, can be safely considered as "other" (Europeans).

Government agencies, universities, and the Farm Bureau share the basic discourse of agribusiness. All closely link genetic engineering to traditional forms of genetic selection and provide benign reasons, such as convenience, for adopting the technology. They describe U.S. government agencies as adequately safeguarding the public interest; they stress universalized benefits from genetically engineered produce; and they are silent in regard to the potential for private profit and corporate control of the food supply. Differences among these actors center on assessment of the risks associated with genetic engineering and revolve around the following points: (1) the procedure allows manipulations that are not possible in nature; (2) government agencies may not have the knowledge to regulate safely; and (3) reasonable people could regard genetically engineered organisms as potentially not beneficial. Those institutions with historically close relations to agribusiness, the Farm Bureau and the USDA, have the greatest degree of similarity to the corporate discourse, including describing government agencies' regulation procedures as stringent and negative consumer reaction as "hysterical." Universities allow for the greatest degree of unknowns connected to the use of genetic engineering. But by calling for additional research to investigate these risks, universities again close off the need for public action: scientists, not the public, should be the active agents in investigating and reducing risk.

The public and private actors associated with researching, regulating, growing, and selling food all provide voices that negate any reason to question biotechnology; SMOs unwrap the discourse on genetic engineering by highlighting the need for public debate and action. SMOs' descriptions of genetic engineering draw attention to the unique, unproven, and unnatural combinations of genetic material possible with this method and to the potential environmental and health risks involved. The SMO discourse, taken as a whole, lists a wide range of possible risks, but few benefits, for consumers and small and organic farmers. SMOs also deny that many of the proposed benefits discussed in the conventional discourse will in fact materialize. Where advocates talk of removing allergens from food, SMOs mention incidents where allergens were introduced. Where advocates talk about feeding the poor, SMOs point out that the crops being engineered are not the staple foods the poor eat. Where advocates promise increased nutrition with GE products, SMOs point to foods that have lost nutritional value. SMOs systematically discount virtually all of the beneficial claims that biotechnology advocates make for GE food by pointing to exceptions, cases in which GE products have or would be more likely to produce negatives than positives.

In addition to being oppositional, the SMOs are also critical. That is, SMOs offer an *explanation,* an analysis of the underlying social relations of power. They uncover what was obscured, the control and profit motives of agribusiness. The SMOs take as a basic claim that the global agribusiness companies are profit-driven enterprises and that whatever developments these companies sponsor will be primarily motivated by the need to maximize profits. While the advocates point out the universalized benefits of genetic engineering, the SMOs point out that these multinational corporations have shown little or no willingness to engage in GE manipulations that would lower their profits, for example, by developing products that reduce the use of the herbicide they sell. While advocates talk of the universalized benefits from GMOs, SMOs point out that multinational corporations will gain enormous control over a product that is essential for life—food—and that this power would allow these multinational corporations to exert overwhelming pressure over people and nations.

The second half of the critical stance that SMOs take is uncovering the powerful ties between government and industry. Multinational corporations, SMOs assert, already have an unhealthy degree of influence on government policies, both regulatory and executive. The U.S. government has been and is now pushing for trade policies and patent laws that would increase the force that multinational corporations could exert. In addition, the "revolving door" between corporate jobs to government employment makes industry far too close to the agencies that regulate GE products. Industry interests for profit already are considered more than consumers' rights to safe products, SMOs argue, which is demonstrated by both the FDA's policy of substantive equivalence and by its refusal to require labeling on products from GMOs.

Finally, the social movement organizations involved in the discourse are, in large part, not rural or farmer-based organizations. Collectively, the Turning Point coalition represents an unusually wide range of movements, which have coalesced on a single issue (Turning Point Project 1999; Reisner 2001). Groups that are associated with the natural food and environment movements form the largest segments of the Turning Point coalition, but animal rights, consumer, and labor movement groups have also signed on. The largest number are environmental groups that traditionally have drawn their membership from middle-class urban residents, and generally have focused on issues of conservation and industrial pollution. However, these groups are now actively protesting industrial or corporate agriculture. In fact, as agriculture is more fully dominated by capital, the same protest groups that have criticized industry for environmental pollution and dangerous consumer products are turning their attention to commercial agriculture. Hence, the industrialization of agriculture has added a new dimension to agricultural protest, the urban protester. These urban, middle-class protesters, particularly those associated with the environment, have had considerable experience with mobilizing on the national level, specifically in lobbying for national legislation. They bring this considerable expertise and experience to agricultural issues at a point in the nation's history when the majority of the population has no direct ties to farming. The near passage of strong environmental policy in the 2001 farm bill demonstrated that these social movement groups have become active players in agricultural discourse, opening up the public discourse to new, and potentially powerful, publics that have little to no direct experience with farm life.

Agricultural movements of the past and the urban-based movements of today differ profoundly on multiple dimensions: within vs. without, market vs. non-market, short run vs. long run, private good vs. public good, self-interest vs. indirect interest. Agricultural movement activists have been familiar with consumer issues—most farmers are consumers themselves—but agricultural movements, like the agricultural sector as a whole, are fundamentally concerned with agriculture as generating private goods. The overwhelming pressures of economic survival force farmers into a self-interested stance that is necessarily short-run—from planting season to planting season. Agricultural farm activists, as a part of this sector, are as familiar with these issues of survival as are farmers; many times these activists are themselves farmers.

Urban-based environmental organizations on the national level tend to be non-market, oriented to the long run, and fundamentally concerned with the environment as a public good. They also tend, in public discourse at least, to view agriculture as a public good, showing far less concern about farmers' financial stability than do organizations representing farmers, including agricultural SMOs like the American Agricultural Movement and the Family Farm Coalition. Although some agricultural SMOs are represented within the Turning Point coalition, the coalition's dominance by urban environmental and consumer groups marginalizes these farmers' concerns with financial sustainability. The dominant discourses of all the actors in the debate over the creation and commercialization of genetically modified agricultural products is carried out largely in the rhetoric of a greater public good. While corporations and scientists gesture toward farmers' utilitarian interests, they focus on the large, capital intensive farmer who will buy their products. Except obliquely, when claiming that the new GE technologies will alleviate world hunger, they make no effort to address the concerns of the struggling mid-sized farmer and ignore organic and sustainable farmers. The SMOs, by their focus on public goods and moral economies, also leave little room for the day-to-day concerns of these farmers. Both construct a universe of discourse in which alternative forms of agricultural production are rendered largely invisible. By rendering "the people" as the object rather than the subject of discourse, the people who actually produce our food and fiber are removed from the stage of political action.

Extreme splits between environmental activists and conventional agriculture are also likely to exaggerate any tendencies of "them" versus "us" antagonisms between conventional agriculture and outside groups proposing change, which would very likely increase large-scale farm organizations' opposition to change advocated from a "public good" perspective. But recurring farm opposition to actions that are widely perceived as for the public good would also, in the long run, be likely to erode public support for this particular type of farming and for its current categorization as a morally good occupation.

Chapter 14
Eating in the Gardens of Gaia
Envisioning Polycultural Communities

Harriet Friedmann

Three principles are at the heart of a food system that can support human communities within the earth community:

1. Grow what is good for the earth.
2. Eat what is good to grow.
3. Live in relationships that make the first two possible.

Like most principles, they are easy to state but difficult to achieve. They are radically different from the principles that organize industrial monocultures and mass-produced edible commodities. They reflect a conclusion opposite to that of an influential book which ten years ago brilliantly described the relationship between political economy and nature: Goodman, Sorj, and Wilkinson (1989:188–89) concluded that with microelectronics and biotechnology, "the agrofood system . . . joins the broader long-run tendency in industry to trivialize primary commodity inputs, or nature," ending "the pre-history of the food industry" and marking its "incorporation within the broader dynamics of the industrial system and post-industrial society."

I see in the "trivialization of nature" a transformative potential. Indeed natural processes cannot be trivialized, but the biotic and material cycles that are disrupted by the linear workings of the industrial food system can create crises for human foodgetting. This is one way to interpret the pollution of water, air, and soil, the change of water and air cycles controlling climate, and the loss of species, leading to what Leakey and Lewin (1995) call the sixth extinction since life began some four billion years ago. New sciences of symbiotic evolution, ecosystem dynamics, and biosphere regulation of the conditions supporting life suggest that human activity in the food web will either lead to unknown catastrophes—check your newspapers for famines, plagues, and wars—or human foodgetting will enter a new phase of learning from and working with earthly cycles. This new phase of life on earth is called "neotechnic" by design visionary John Tillman Lyle (1994) and more broadly, "the ecozoic era" by Brian Swimme and Thomas Berry (1992).

A new approach that goes under several names suggests a new way for humans to work with the rest of nature. Bill Mollison (e.g., 1988), who calls his approach "permaculture," has demonstrated in a variety of agro-ecosystems and social contexts that working with natural cycles creates more abundance with less work than the dominant industrial approach, which forces a small number of species to grow in conditions rendered as homogeneous as possible. Vandana Shiva (1993) has shown that standard measures of productivity ignore most of the polycultural species of traditional agriculture. When measures take into account the great diversity of cultivated and wild plants, each harvested from and returned to one of many interwoven cycles, polycultures yield more food and renew conditions for further harvests. Productivity of human labor, calculated as a ratio of monetary inputs and outputs, is misleading, especially when production entails burning fossil fuels. If one wishes to analyze the long-term sustainability of a production system, it is more accurate to calculate the ratio of energy inputs and outputs. Bayliss-Smith's (1982) calculations show swidden cultivation to be far more productive than industrial agriculture; so was preindustrial English farming, which used scientific observations to further enhance harvests from natural cycles. Permaculture and related ways of working with natural and material cycles promise to increase rather than diminish fertility and to enhance human harvests from natural cycles.

The social organization appropriate to polycultural foodgetting is the subject of this chapter. History can be stylized as monoculture in tandem with hierarchy, with both contained within the limits of local ecosystems; both disasters and successes demonstrate the point. History, exactly as old as writing, coincides with what we call civilization, and began with specialist roles of scribes, priests, and aristocrats, as well as the newly specialized roles of artisans and farmers (Kautsky 1982). In what is probably the oldest civilization, Mesopotamia, division of humans into dominating and dominated classes coincided with the dominance claimed over plants and animals (Diamond 1997:265–92). Plants and animals of Mesopotamia, notably wheat, barley, and cattle, were already organized through monocultures, and the civilization that grew out of that particular complex of hierarchies eventually birthed European modernity with its industry, communications media, and other extensions and deepenings of homogeneity.[1] As Western civilization engulfs, contests, and transforms other societies, both civilized and preliterate, human society may be reaching the social and ecological limits of monoculture. In that sense, permaculture may be post-civilizational as well as postmodern (Eisenberg 1998). My view is that the evolution of humanity now makes possible, in imagination, knowledge, and practice, a far more democratic and just world than humans have ever seen, with far less work and far more play, or rather, less division between the two. It has the potential to be composed of polycultural communities based on polycultural foodgetting.

Paradoxically, the necessity and the possibility for such a world has been created by all the stages of integration of regions and cultures that began with European colonial conquest. Human foodgetting became a truly global activity through Europe's creation of colonial empires. European empires were of two distinct types, which created distinct trajectories within the transcontinental markets that connected metropoles and colonies. In colonies of rule, peasants continued to grow crops, some familiar and some introduced from distant ecosystems, in familiar places if in new relationships. In European settler regions, whole complexes of humans, plants, animals, and ways of growing and eating were transplanted and indigenous complexes displaced (Cronon 1983; Crosby 1986). As a result, the challenges facing each type of postcolonial region differ regarding the destruction of wild places and villages that have supported human life for ten thousand years. Each region has the potential for a distinct response to the necessity and the possibility for a new phase of human activity in our earthly home.

Growing What Is Good for the Earth: Gaia's Garden

Our present system of agriculture mimics industry. It is a linear process that imports external substances and exports wastes (Dahlberg 1993). We treat all natural substances and forces as "resources" and "raw materials" when we source them, and as final products or wastes when they leave production sites or consumption sites. This design is degenerative of water, energy, and matter contained in our useful objects. It treats our manufactured life support systems as the quickest route from source to sink (Lyle 1994). This "source to sink" way of treating our economic processes is rapidly destroying all the wild, that is self-organizing, aspects of the world (what we can carefully call "nature," especially if we remember to include ourselves as natural beings). So far nature has absorbed or contained the disruptions wrought by human activity since learning to use fire and since several prehistoric extinctions of large mammals (Diamond 1992). When sources become depleted and sinks full, we have to look around and see how much of the self-renewing cycles of the earth and living beings remain. And we have to learn to work with degenerated places—and a disrupted (from human perspective) biosphere.[2]

The alternative model for the whole of society is to garden. Any gardener knows that not anything grows anywhere. Any gardener also knows that quite a lot of alteration of ecosystem processes is possible. It is increasingly clear from environmental history that any possible "nature" unaffected by humans is not knowable, if indeed it ever existed since humans came into being. The idea of wilderness, and its complementary idea of empty land, was a colonial fiction applied by Europeans to the strange new ecosystems of the Americas, Australia, and New Zealand. It is now becoming clear that what Europeans called New England, for instance, was intensely tended by Indians, particularly through fire, but also through a variety of other means that enhanced the presence of desired plants and animals. Colonists who delighted in the abundance of deer, for instance, considered them part of the natural wilderness, not realizing that Indians were managing open areas and forests in ways to encourage browsing. Not surprisingly, the deer disappeared when colonists appropriated the land (Cronon 1983).

A sustainable future for gardening lies somewhere in the space between the necessary human management of ecosystem processes, and the possible changes allowed by those processes. Unlike the treadmill of searching for external sources of used-up nutrients and external sinks for wastes, it points to a future of learning how to direct and play with natural cycles, how to mimic natural cycles, how to improvise as cycles change spontaneously and in response to human actions, how to live reciprocally, to return what we take. These are lessons for human community, I shall argue, as well as for human foodgetting, and they can be learned now because of new understandings available to humans about our nature, ecosystems, and evolution.

The time for gardening, for working with ecosystem cycles, and globally with biospheric flows, is upon us. In the frail international agreements on climate change and biodiversity, it is beginning. The most urgent question is: When will we commit to regenerative practices, to creating what Lyle (1994) calls Gaia's Garden? How much of the great biotic creativity of the past 65 million years will remain to us? Let us look at how pioneers/bioneers have begun.

Two broadly different strategies arise from distinct problems facing Old and New World agro-ecosystems. The distinctions arose largely through a relationship that began with European colonial rule and has unfolded through the distinct periods of the world system (Friedmann 1991; McMichael 2000). From an agro-ecosystem perspective, colonial empires introduced new species into the gardens and fields of both Old and New Worlds. Crosby (1972, 1986) calls it the Columbian exchange, emphasizing its unifying quality. He calls it ecological imperialism to emphasize the inequality of effects that underlay the irregular movement from gardens to industrial monocultures. In the Old World exotic plants were both introduced as export monocultures—with often drastic ecological damage (Davis 1999)—and incorporated into the gardens and cuisines of village plots. In the New World, whole families of Old World species displaced native families. This created the possibility for industrial agriculture to lay a steel grid across a landscape, grow exotic plants and animals with techniques imported from a different ecosystem, and replace the complexity of ecosystem processes with complicated social inventions from trains to futures markets (Naess 1994:122). It also created, after a hundred years of soil and water mining, the necessity to consider permaculture in a completely reconstructed context: an agro-ecology dominated by introduced species—humans, plants, and livestock. Amazingly and almost invisibly, it also provided the context, particularly strong in some areas, for inventing the most extraordinary syncretic, hybrid, or Creole gardens.

Each context requires a distinct strategy. In the South (and possibly in other continuously cultivated regions over many centuries, even millennia), the strategy promoted by advocates for biodiversity is legal protection for remaining peasant farmers. Shiva et al. (1997) argue that the crops grown and gathered by long-standing communities are the joint product of nature and of the ancestors of present farmers. They cannot be appropriated as private property and must be protected through "community intellectual rights" protected by national and international agreements (for which they identify instruments). Something like this (or some other form of protecting traditional farmers) is a guarantee for all of humanity of the continuing evolution under human guidance of the landraces that feed humans, as well as the basis for further evolution through democratic incorporation of scientific knowledge. One approach to democratic combinations of Western science with traditional knowledge is what Norberg-Hodge (1992) calls "counter-development," in which communities learn to understand and value both what they already have (and risk losing) and how Western technologies can enhance rather than undermine what they value, in agriculture as in other aspects of life. Another approach seeks the revival and protection of "lost crops"—those not valued by European colonists and eventually by indigenous cultivators as well—through more conventional means. The U.S. National Research Council has sponsored work to document and restore food crops and the ways of growing them appropriate to local ecosystems in the Andes and elsewhere. Here the intention is to discover crops that might be transplanted, much as potatoes once were, to augment food production in distant regions (National Research Council 1989).

In settler regions—the United States, Canada, Argentina and neighboring regions, Australia and New Zealand, parts of Southern Africa—now considered the breadbaskets of the world, the challenge is to invent alternative agronomic systems which do not rely on fossil fuels—the dead bodies of our billion year old ancestors—and "chemicals with which our cells have had no evolutionary experience," but which can renew fertility as they yield harvests to humans. These must rely on biology and ecology as well as knowledge of plants from near and far, areas of study still far apart. They aim to replicate the conditions of the original prairies and still yield harvests edible by humans (Jackson 1997). Of course, the connection between Old and New Worlds, now most telling in the displacement of peasant villages by corporate monocultures, at once requires and makes possible the mutual support of Old and New World strategies.

Old World

The neolithic village has for 10,000 years been the framework for most agricultural human livelihoods and the support for urban centers. Only in the twentieth century has the village become the context for a minority of humans throughout the world. It is fully destroyed at great risk to the life support systems of humans and our allied creatures, such as wheat, rice, maize, soya, cattle, chickens, which (along with the allies we don't like such as pigeons and dandelions) help us colonize self-organizing ecosystems and provide our food, as we provide theirs (Eisenberg 1998). Villages long depended on wild forests, seas, and deserts that bordered fields and gardens and surrounded irrigated plains and terraced mountains. Village (agri)cultures either renewed the material and biotic cycles in fields, forests, and seas, or were forced to alter their ways by saline or eroded soils, by the deserts created by overharvesting, overgrazing, or altering flows of water, or otherwise failing to give back what was taken. So we have much to learn from indigenous and peasant practices that have endured. Traditional farming worked with plants and ecosystems to create all the landraces on which humans depend. Most of these allied settlements of humans, plants, and animals remain only in what we now call the South (Kloppenburg 1988:46).

Vandana Shiva and her colleagues at the Research Foundation for Science, Technology and Ecology in Delhi (1997) have drawn on the philosophy and politics of Gandhi to argue for legal systems that institute collective rights for inheritors of landscapes long altered by farming, or "agro-ecosystems." The inheritance includes cultivation, harvesting, and preparation techniques, plus knowledge of plants, animals, and interrelations with changing waters, soils, forests, and all the rest which humans have developed in conjunction with the creativity of living organisms and ecosystems. These practices and knowledge of foods, fodder, medicines, pest-resistant plants, and other uses of plants, coevolved with the mix of crops in their fields and gardens over hundreds, even thousands, of years, and continue to evolve.

Shiva and her colleagues argue that the appropriation of plants and knowledge of their uses by agrifood (and pharmaceutical) corporations amounts to an enclosure of the biological and intellectual commons, both parallel to and deepening the land enclosures that began the displacement of villages centuries ago. Land enclosures continue to expel villagers in remaining areas of polyculture, now assisted by the appropriation and patenting of vernacular knowledge and cultivars. The group specifies an alternative legal system called Community Intellectual Rights. It aims to institute in law a recovery of the biological and intellectual commons and in this way to create the basis for communities to continue coevolving with their fellow domestics. Based on the specific provisions of the International Convention on Biodiversity, the group advocates a specific set of practical laws to prevent "bioprospecting" by transnational corporations. It frames intellectual property within a larger legal context that recognizes traditional knowledge and innovation and allows communities to protect the conditions for sustaining them.

Innovation in Indian villages, as in other Old World agro-ecosystems, include introduced plants. Maize, potatoes, and capsicum are among the benefits brought by the Columbian exchange to enrich Indian gardens and cuisines. Innovation has included altering traditional practices in ways that complement polycultural gardens and allow cuisines to change, even to transform (see further in the next section). This is important in illustrating Shiva's point that the power relationships embedded in emerging intellectual property regimes deny innovation or value to farmers (and healers, and others called "traditional") and justify appropriation by corporations. Many patents actually result from natural creativity in conjunction with many generations of cultivators who are at once skilled in agronomy and attentive to continuous changes in local conditions of soil and climate. This could, in patent terms, be called prior knowledge. But Shiva recognizes that privatization of plants and knowledge is also an enclosure of the intellectual commons against scientists, farmers, gardeners, healers, and others throughout the world.

Three things are important to note. First, protection of common intellectual rights is protection of polycultural agro-ecosystems. Privatization of plants and knowledge is part of a project to replace polycultures with industrial monocultures. In part it is an extension of the green revolution, which Shiva criticized in earlier work (1993). It is also a new phase in the standardization of ecosystems. For instance, soya is now being introduced to India in a variety of forms from cultivars to cooking oils. It is originally an Asian crop, but it is introduced as part of a complicated industrial agrifood system centered on livestock production that emerged in the United States and spread to other New World regions in the second half of the twentieth century. It is not adopted and adapted from farm to farm, village to village, biome to biome, culture to culture, as were wheat or rice or sugar which migrated over millenia from east and west.[3] Soya comes to India not as variants of tofu from neighboring cultures, but as part of a standard global set of interlinked monocultures (Shiva 1997).

This is the second point: the links between agro-ecosystems have changed. Colonial links introduced both export monocultures and Creole innovations in polycultural gardens. Descendants of African women with seeds braided into their hair and Indian indentured workers who carried mango on their voyages created polycultural gardens from the plants of the world in Jamaica. Maize and manioc are introduced staples of many African village polycultures. Creole polycultures have evolved and continue to evolve in each agro-ecosystem. They are important to protect as well as the ancient polycultures of India, Mexico, and other ancient agricultures. But Creole gardens are now under threat by industrial monocultures. The new links do more standardizing than mixing.

The third point is that linking is cumulative. The wild areas that surround each agro-ecosystem absorb many of the depleting and polluting effects of cultivation. The wild, self-organizing areas of the earth are vanishing. With global atmospheric and hydrospheric changes, it is safe to say that no such areas exist in a stable way, even though all life in varying degrees depends on their continuance. In another way of speaking, the rest of nature is being colonized without attention to the free services it has provided. Yet new science, new awareness of risks, and new bonds with the remaining natural world, are calling out more vocally. The threat is also the opportunity. We have a word for the biosphere, an emerging consciousness that the earth is a unified, evolving, self-regulating habitat for all organisms, including humans, and an incipient awareness that human life depends on wise adaptation and management of ourselves and our habitats.

New World

The monocultural farming of exotic species in the New Worlds was a far more radical displacement and suppression of entire biomes than was the introduction of colonial monocultures into traditional peasant regions of Africa or Asia (Cronon 1991). It presents a far more formidable challenge to intellect and practice. What was displaced in the grasslands of North America (and elsewhere) was an entire ecosystem. The ecosystem included humans the Europeans encountered, who cultivated valleys and hunted large grazing buffalo; the buffalo, and the perennial grasses adapted to their trampling, their grazing; and the dramatic changes of the climate, from extremes of temperature to dry periods to fires. What replaced all this was a grid imposed upon the land, organized not around rivers but around steel rails that cut their own path. The land was plowed by steel, the only material strong enough to penetrate the tough perennial grasses, and fenced by barbed wire. Inside the fences were colonists from the Old World—humans, cattle, and wheat. They were joined by maize from Central America used not in the ancient combination with squash and beans cultivated in the river valleys of North America by native Americans, but in monocultures destined to feed pigs and cattle. Finally, Asian soya was introduced to make the simplest possible rotation with maize, and to partner maize to feed the livestock to feed the humans. (To complete the picture, sugar, the largest single monocrop in the world, is mostly grown in exotic habitats.)

Elements of Old World polycultures lost their intimate connection with the plants and human practices that had shaped their evolution as landraces. They were planted in monocultural fields renewed by industrial chemicals, subsumed in a world of steel. Within a few decades the stored fertility of soils that had not been deeply disturbed for thousands of years since the passing of the glaciers washed away.[4] It continues to wash away. The human focus on what is near and soon prevents us from emotionally taking in the scale of the abundance and the loss.

In this context, industrialists replaced naturalists as designers of cultivated fields (Jackson 1996:27–60). Building on the new science of chemistry and the new technologies of internal combustion engines, agronomists singled out specific plants, nutrients, poisons, and machines for experiment. For instance, marquis wheat, a variety that matured more quickly than earlier varieties, allowed European settlers to colonize the Canadian prairies with its short growing season. Farmers depended on agronomists to learn how to maximize yields of specific plants using industrial substances and techniques. It worked well for several decades. But the substances and techniques have cumulative costs: loss of biological diversity, loss of complex soils, pollution and depletion of waters, resistance of insect and plant competitors to toxins. The race to shore up each element of the system threatens eventually to succumb to cumulative depletion and pollution.

Wes Jackson, pioneer scientist-farmer, is in the tradition of the High Farmers of England in his scientific attention to natural ecosystem processes. He has the advantage of twentieth-century sciences of population biology and understanding of ecosystems. He has the further advantage of democratic sensibility and cooperation.

Jackson and his students at the Land Institute at Salina, Kansas, have the challenge of discovering or inventing a mix of native and exotic species that can mimic ecosystem cycles and succession in a context of drastic displacement of the native species. His project is to create a "domestic prairie" that will allow humans to both harvest sufficient quantities of edible food and allow the system to evolve. Polycultures work with multiple crops and can mimic ecological succession by altering the mix of crops as conditions change: one perennial grows taller and shades the area where grasses once thrived. This is what happens in a meadow, as perennials push aside annuals and eventually grow taller. It is why grasses grow at the edges of forests and why forests eventually take over prairies unless prevented by forces like fire and trampling buffalo herds.

The aim is rarely to cultivate the soil. Jackson likes to tell a story: A Sioux Indian who saw the upturned soil when it was plowed for the first time by a pioneer farmer, said "wrong side up" (Eisenberg 1998:59). The joke is supposed to be on the Indian. Jackson knows that the joke, if it was one, was on the farmer. The ancestors of the Sioux had burned back the forests encroaching on the prairie, had thus encouraged the buffalo to grow in numbers to both trample the perennial grasses to toughen them along with fire, and to provide the needs of the humans. Native Americans cultivated river valleys with digging sticks, and their polycultural gardens worked to enhance soil and water as well as harvests. The killing of the buffalo by Europeans devastated prairie peoples by destroying their animal allies. Breaking the grasses and fencing the land destroyed their plant allies. Like Europeans who cannot live without wheat and cattle, native Americans could not live without the buffalo and the grasses, which they tended in a vast garden.

Jackson and fellow North American agricultural ecologists find themselves in an exceptional situation. Unlike Indonesian or Indian communities that have increased both food harvests and ecosystem fertility over many generations, mixing fish and plants, animals, trees, grains, and vegetables (Todd 1984; Bayliss-Smith 1982), in the prairies, humans, cattle, and wheat together colonized an alien ecosystem with the force of steel, chemicals, and eventually fossil fuels. Industrial agriculture applied chemicals and fossil fuels to take its distance from natural cycles and relationships to an extreme. The North American prairies spawned the elaborate commercial and monetary devices, such as futures markets, to substitute for reduced ecosystem complexity (Cronon 1991), as well as the agrochemical corporations that attempt to compensate for loss of soil fertility and competition by insects and disease organisms for the monocultural crops planted by humans. Industrial fertilizers and pesticides, based on non-renewable fossil fuels and hard to control toxins, have locked monocultural farmers into an addictive treadmill, in which ever more industrial products are needed to make up for ever lower fertility and ever greater losses of crops to resistant insects and weeds. The present industrial technology to increase the effectiveness of these compensatory (and profitable) products is based in agricultural biotechnologies. Now corporations devoted to monocultural crops join government aid programs to export the type of agriculture created in a short time—less than two centuries—which has degraded the natural processes of temperate grassland and forest ecosystems in America and elsewhere. The vicious circle closes when landraces are endangered by monocultural plantings of industrially produced (and patented) seeds, using industrial inputs, in regions where human food crops were continuing to evolve through the guidance of peasant farmers.

In agro-ecosystems devoted to monocultural production of annual exotic crops, economic categories replace biological and landscape categories. Jackson and Bender (1984:xiv) bemoan thinking of land only as a "resource," an approach destined to destroy its resourcefulness in time: "Economic considerations, taken exclusively, appeal to those unable to tolerate . . . ambiguities . . . —they satisfy the narrowly analytical mind, the mind given to the sort of thing simple enough to be accommodated by equations and graphs." Jackson is no postmodern critic, of course, but a plant geneticist and a practical agronomist. His partner Dana Jackson (1984:106) points out that "industrial gardening has evolved right along with industrial agriculture." It is a context in which ecological processes have been displaced and can no longer be observed or worked with unless a conscious effort is made. This effort is the work, paradoxically, of science, understood as a self-reflective, sceptical, and experimental approach to interpretation of sensory experience.

The solution is to deepen and make reflexive the awareness of ecosystem processes practiced by traditional farmers, with varying success. For example, many regions face depleted water supplies. Rather than building pipelines to irrigate crops, it is necessary to consider how natural cycles and interactions preserve water, a marker of healthy soil. Knowledge moves from the practical—how to keep the plants watered in this place—to the general—what are the conditions that foster water retention in soils; and then, how they can work in this place. This is the sort of awareness that links theory and practice, the general and the particular, the scientist and the gardener. To follow this example, water is conserved by the same features that renew soil and stabilize pests: a mix of species that complement one another, one using the waste of another, one complex succeeding another as the conditions of light, nutrients, water, and other features evolve. It is polyculture with a difference. It is polyculture that has to be created from degraded agro-ecosystems, using creative mixes of native and introduced plants and animals. New World agro-ecologists can learn from horticultural and peasant colleagues, but they need all the soil, hydrological, mineral, plant, animal, and ecosystem knowledge that the practical and experimental world can provide. They have to experiment more widely and watch just as closely. Their improvisation draws on the experiences and organisms of the world. We need farmer-scientists and scientist-farmers.

Eating in a Polycultural Society: Commensality

The human capacity to experiment has always been part of the survival of humans in new and changing conditions. Humans are omnivores. The human capacity to feel disgust at taboo foods has also contributed to survival. Both capacities now provide the bodily and emotional basis for human choices to eat what is good to grow.

Max Weber taught us that commensality, or eating together, marks the boundaries of social groups and refusal to share food marks distance and hierarchy. Lin Yutang, a Chinese writer, called patriotism "the memory of foods eaten in childhood" (Allport 2000:11). Just as the gardens of immigrants adapt traditional crops and practices to local conditions; just as immigrant and native-born gardeners teach and learn from one another about what to grow; so neighbors from many regions of the earth teach one another about new foods, new preparations, new culinary tastes and techniques. Commensal institutions, such as the varieties of community kitchens in Latin America, can be adapted to foster sharing among many cultures sharing the same settlement. Community gardens and community forms of distribution, such as Good Food Boxes and Community Share Agriculture, allow neighbors to explain and experiment with plants, cooking techniques, and recipes from around the world. These are all experiences I am familiar with in Toronto. I have had glimpses of similar polycuisines in other cities, even in small towns and villages.

Horticultural (i.e., polycultural) societies eat an astonishing variety of plants and animals, both cultivated and collected from forests, meadows, waterways, and oceans. The distinction between domestic and wild is better understood as a continuum within landscapes managed with different intensities. These societies experiment with increasing the supply of what they like to eat, but eat what they can harvest. Our ancestors spread across the world from Africa, bringing along some allies, such as dogs, and finding new companion species with which to settle into domestic households or with which to move in seasonal migrations. Civilizations and all the ways of thinking, relating, and acting we call cultures, grew up on the foundation of the allied domestic species that settled with humans, to be fed and nurtured, and to give their substance to humans as food. Rice, maize, and wheat became central to the meaning systems, the emotions, and the institutions of distinct cultures, and other plants and animals acquired and gave meaning to daily and cyclical meals and dishes.

Colonial integration created a range of syncretic culinary cultures which I am calling "creole," both Jambalaya in Louisiana and tomato sauces in Europe. Consider the cuisine of Jamaica. Salt fish, rice, and ackee are the national dish. Salt cod must be imported, as it was in the days of colonial rule and slavery. Merchants created a thriving trade by buying cod from North Atlantic fishers to sell to slave owners who gave it to their slaves to eat. (In return fishers bought rum made from Caribbean sugar, which entered into the cultural cuisine of the North Atlantic.) Colonial Jamaica in its dominant commercial face was monocultural and exotic—European masters, having killed off indigenous peoples, had no interest in local plants and animals. They bought everything from abroad: African slaves, Asian sugar cane, and salt cod as slave food. Still, Africans, like most people still in touch with food-getting, carried seeds when they could, sometimes woven into their hair. Okra, watermelon, and yams (some African, others from mainland South America) eventually became parts of the cuisines of Jamaicans. When Indian indentured workers were brought in to replace slaves after abolition, they brought plants, spices, and cooking techniques different from both European and African ones. Rice, curries, and mangoes from Asia join with local fish and Eurasian goats, chickens, and pigs to make unique, creole cuisines.

Just as it is difficult to imagine many Indian or Northern European dishes without potatoes (Andean), or southeast Asian dishes without peanuts (African) or chiles (Central American), so it is difficult to imagine many Mexican or Argentinian landscapes and dishes without cattle or chickens or pigs. Creole cuisines are different from both the indigenous traditions that preceded them, and the standard industrial meals now threatening to displace them. While food industries scan the cultural horizons for "ethnic" dishes to standardize and market widely, while Taco Bell opens in Mexico, while the blending of cuisines in the blades of the corporate processor proceeds apace, another multiple, evolving set of innovations is bubbling up all over.

Creole innovations and commensality provide a basis for polycultural communities. Not the blandness and predictability of "pizza" and "egg rolls" in the freezer of the supermarket, but the surprise of invention. Commensality in a polycultural context requires attention to others and interest in their ingredients and recipes and techniques. It requires valuing one's own knowledge and cultures, something still new for traditional women's work such as cooking. It offers community as a frame for individuals and families, allowing for experimentation and evolution of combinations of domestic and public life, of emotional and task relationships.

Commensality and gardening complement each other. Both return food to the center, where it belongs. Industrial agriculture and mass-produced edible commodities have gained a foothold by banishing most humans from cultivation and cooking. In the end many of us do not even share meals. To return to food is to return to our habitats and our bodies, to explore our senses and our desires in work and play, to create together the places where we and our descendants can live in evolving relationships with each other and with the larger earth community.

Polycultural Society and Politics: Community of Communities of Communities

To grow what is good for the earth and to eat what is good to grow implies that we live in communities with foodgetting and foodsharing at the center. It implies that humans develop an attentive and respectful relationship to one another, to the other species who share the habitat or could be attracted to it (those we like and those we don't like), and to the flows of water, wind, and sunlight. Like the ecosystems and biomes in the biosphere, humans and other creatures are more closely or distantly connected, but interdependence is global. Humans who understand that we will thrive by growing what is good for the earth and eating what is good to grow will have a sense of responsibility. They will respect the integrity of ecosystems and the necessity for humans to work with biotic and material cycles and flows. To do this is to improvise, to play, to dance between the poles of wildness and domesticity in each human and each community and each place. Eisenberg (1998) calls this Earth Jazz.

What are some practical features of polycultural society? An emerging perspective on sustainable habitats replaces management with design. It introduces subtlety. Design evolves as life does. Instead of a track or a road, which fixes the route and the destination, design is more like sailing. The destination is in mind but tacking with the wind and waves creates the indirect and zigzag path unique to this journey; and large boats yield to small ones. Brian Milani (2001:91–95) summarizes the principles of eco-design:

- Intrinsic value is primary. Matter serves a goal and can be conserved. Money is a means to facilitate regenerative exchanges. Gardens and meals frame many activities.
- Natural flows of water, wind, vegetation, and food webs frame material life, leading over time to social boundaries corresponding to ecosystem boundaries. Community share agriculture prefigures this: farmers can adjust to what their customers want to eat, but customers/partners learn what is possible and desirable for the land and how it changes. They often work with the farmers.
- No waste. Everything is an input for something else. This encourages efficiency in materials and organization and prevents use of toxic materials. Jackson and others show how design of polycultures conserves water, renews soils, and contains pests. It replaces matter and forbids pollutants and poisons. It requires recycling of human wastes and animal wastes; gardens can do this, for instance the Todds' living machines (Todd 1984).
- Elegance and multifunctionality. This implies webs for all processes constructed in analogy with food webs. Food at the center is a model as well as a life support.
- Appropriate scales and linked scales; integration across multiple scales; gardens relate to watersheds which relate through many scales to the hydrological cycles of the planet.

- Diversity, or what I call polycultures, for human communities and all relations to matter, flows, and organisms.
- Self-reliance, self-organization, self-design, based on hierarchies that recognize the defining importance of the base or foundation; this fosters flexible interdependence. Every living thing eats and is eaten. Living flows are the base upon which all activities and relationships depend.
- Participation and direct democracy: polycultural communities are in constant self-formation and renewal; attention to ecological processes matches attention to human relationships; on larger scales, computers facilitate this in principle. International (eventually inter-bioregional) institutions to monitor and design ecosystem processes, including cultivation and pastures, in mutually enhancing ways. These are prefigured by recognition of the biosphere and common responsibility in several treaties, such as biodiversity and climate change.
- Human creativity and development; humans deeply engaged with natural cycles and each other have multiple skills and activities, and develop capacities for both responsibility and play. Natural interdependence presents consistent surprises. To welcome rather than fear surprises is to enter into creative lifeways. This is a lesson from gardening—organisms and ecosystems are resilient and generous.
- Strategic role of spatial design, both of the built environment and the landscape, which are more closely integrated. Permaculture emphasizes the efficiencies and complementarities gained by spatial rearrangement. Rooftop gardens conserve energy in buildings, reduce climate change from heat reflected from bare roofs, provide beauty and food and gathering places and opportunities to garden. Gardens, fields, and pastures provide places in the continuum between the domestic and the wild, places where individuals can explore and work with different balances between the two.

The challenges of even beginning to reverse the priorities towards intentional design of diversity and flows are, needless to say, immense. From the historical perspective suggested above, the challenges are distinct for continuously cultivated regions and regions requiring radical renewal of ecosystems. These do not correspond perfectly to the Old and New World divide.

Traditional communities often contain oppressions of women, children, castes, and minorities. Slavery appears to be growing in many parts of the world. Even aspects of traditional communities that are respectful of others and of their habitats face pressures to change as global integration impinges on local ecosystems. Their challenge is to incorporate scientific knowledge and techniques into sustainable and restorative practices, and to be open to democratic participation and development of all individuals: to value what has been developed over generations by the ancestors in conjunction with the living habitat while opening to what is useful from outside. Norberg-Hodge (1991) calls this counter-development and gives inspiring examples from Ladakh.

New World challenges are even greater. In contrast to indigenous or peasant societies, which offer remnants of existing polycultures to observe, Americans and others in similar societies have to undo the very monocultures that emerged as part of the creation of settler states. It is difficult even to see the problem, which is as pervasive as the money that has risen to the top of our hierarchy of needs. Monocultural farming and homogenized foods (and other commodities) have marginalized humans through unemployment. Worse, they have employed humans (and animals and plants) in activities destructive of the bases of life (making goods and providing services that undermine ecological stability and diversity). Living in societies dominated by economies dependent on credit and ever-increasing consumption, individuals are constrained to buy goods not only to reduce labor (increasingly dubious in centers experiencing time famines) or to increase pleasure (increasingly dubious as foods and building materials and transportation may be toxic), but even to compensate for degraded natural gifts (i.e., bottled water or travel to places where air is unpolluted).

Economies in so-called advanced societies have for a little over a century been, as Karl Polanyi (1957) put it, disembedded from the human and natural substance of society. Unable to value natural gifts of soil, water, minerals, and living beings, these societies are full of disembedded humans. Of course we cannot dispense with these natural gifts, but the illusion that we can is powerful and disempowering. The same illusion fosters another: that we can live as individuals relatively free from the fates of other humans and of other members of the earth community. Where traditional societies need more individual freedom and more science to add to their farmers, monocultural societies need more gardening, more cooking, and more attention to interdependence, to add to their science.

In every place I have examined, individuals, neighborhoods, organizations, even (often marginal) branches of government, are engaged in activities that prefigure one of the many dimensions of practice and relationship leading to a way of life based on ecological design. Food projects are consistently energizing and inspiring when they empower people in relation to each other and their habitat. Gardening is having a widespread revival, and seedsavers and seedsharers are paradigmatic of new social relations. Commensality and gardening connect individuals to bodily, social, and ecological realities and can be fun. On this foundation can be built the experiences and institutions for democracy and self-reliance.

A social world guided by permaculture principles reshapes work. Foodgetting, as it must, occupies a higher proportion of social labor, but in a society living within ecological limits, there is less labor and more of that labor is playful, that is, both skilful and creative. In a permaculture society, knowledge about the material and biotic cycles of the earth is as important as literacy and numeracy. Labor has more to do with skilful attention than routine or physically strenuous activities. These ways of working contain larger elements of play than most industrial, bureaucratic, or service jobs, and offer a basis for life that combines the most desirable elements of scientific and creative work.

New perspectives on evolution, particularly the role of symbiosis explored by Lynn Margulis (1993), open the possibilities for new understanding of human nature and human societies. Each organism has evolved through a process of shaping or sculpting by eons of experiences. "Natural selection is life's power to sculpt diversity in a creative fashion" (Swimme and Berry 1992:126). We humans are organisms deeply shaped by our heritage as eaters and eaten, as respirators, as companions of dogs, grasses, cattle, and birds, as mammals and primates, as social beings. All of these features enter in the very shapes of our faces and limbs, into our reactions to predators, to time, to our fellows, and to our young. Differentiation of humans reflects deep communion with the living processes in each region of the earth (Diamond 1997). Polycultural communities linked into a more densely interconnected human society throughout the biosphere is the emergent reality. Over time it will reshape every human. Collectively we shall choose the balance of forces doing the reshaping, whether through conflict and domination or through intentional community.

Civilization gave us many cultures, many human groups coevolving with maize or rice or yams or wheat. Each evolved in its place, shaped by the forces of the earth and the other beings in that place. That occurred over thousands of years. Civilizations have been mixed and matched in many ecosystems for several hundred years. Now two paths open. In one, the transplanted civilization of Europe, consisting of humans, plows, wheat, and cattle, spawns a weedy world of a small number of adaptable creatures spread evenly across homogenized landscapes (Quammen 1998). In the other, cultures bump against each other and allow themselves to be reshaped, to be sculpted by and into shape-shifting polycultures.

Individuals choose whether to embrace the bumping and sculpting. Many philosophical and theoretical traditions play with the ways that humans find changing balances between uniqueness and shared cultures, between individuality and interconnection. In our time and places the challenge is to rediscover how to rebuild communities not only of humans, but of all beings sharing our world. A new way of thinking appreciates the micro-organisms that create our soil and digest our food in our guts, the insects that pollinate the flowering plants, the predators that control rodents as well as share our livestock. It cultivates the capacity to bond which is our mammalian and primate inheritance. It leaves behind the wars of tribal peoples with their neighbors and expands compassion to encompass other communities linked into larger communities, and into the earth community.

The perilous state of life on earth makes possible the imagination of restored wildness, and the longing for conscious participation in the self-organizing life of earth. At some time a critical mass of humans may take in the idea that we may not live to finish burning the fossils of our ancestors or to complete the plunder of the last 65 million years of biotic creativity since the last great extinction of species. What will we find? When we begin to restore water, air, and soil and protect life forms faster than we degrade ecosystems, when we realize in our bones that the diversity and flow of life reverses entropy and decide to work with it, we will either find ourselves reduced in numbers, living in a weedy and desolate world, or we will recover the intimate bonds of our ancestors to the earth community. To do that in a densely populated and degraded biosphere, we will use all the science we have to shift from degenerative to regenerative ways of getting what humans need from the earth. It will be a shift, according to John Tillman Lyle (1994), from engineering to gardening, from power to subtlety, from displacing ecosystem processes to guiding them to give us beauty and function. It will be Eisenberg's "earth jazz"—improvisation based in skill, attention, and interconnectedness between humans and the rest of nature.

Concluding Thoughts

At this moment in the human adventure it is beginning to be possible to imagine a *conscious* arrangement of human relationships and practices to enhance our habitats, and a *responsible* management of the whole earth community. Our pre-civilizational ancestors perforce inhabited and managed their habitats in locally sustainable ways, and when they exhausted them, moved on. Now there are no places to move, and the few remaining contemporary "indigenous" societies are squeezed into marginal lands. The revival of indigenous cultures, however altered, and their international political alliances, are one hope for all humans to preserve memories of the specific biotic communities of ecosystems, however simplified and degraded. The vast majority of human experience lies in the foraging, hunting, and horticultural knowledge of our human ancestors who have lived the longest in each place. The management of ecosystems, both unconscious (in the sense of overhunting, overgrazing, overburning) and conscious, is as old as human foodgetting using stone and fire.

In his perspective-shifting analysis of a horticultural society in the Amazon, the Achuar, Philippe Descola (1994:5–6, 73, 161–64, 324) reveals both the practices and the conceptual categories of foodgetting in relation to the whole of life. Descola interprets Achuar lifeways as both socializing and adapting to nature, a play of practices which make possible the reproduction of energy exchanges between humans and the ecosystem. Gardening allows for more reliable harvesting than foraging alone, and both are done. He counted 175 domestic species in Achuar gardens, used for food, medicines, narcotics, dyes, pottery glazes, and the like, and 41 forest species either spared during clearing or acclimated in gardens as tolerated weeds. The Achuar do not make this distinction between domestic and wild. Their term "aramu" describes all plants in the garden other than weeds and distinguishes plants which are subject to human manipulation from others. The same term describes plants found in the forest, which we would call wild, when they can be managed in place (e.g., protected) or when they can thrive also in gardens. The Achuar forage, hunt, and fish as well as garden and manage some forest plants. They organize their annual cycle in relation to ten species, contained within the broad division between wet and dry seasons, some harvests being cultivated and some wild: e.g., turtle egg season, frog season, chonta palm season, and late fruit season. They have little hierarchy, though wife abuse sometimes occurs and war with neighboring ethnic groups is endemic. The Achuar see themselves at the pinnacle of a hierarchy of beings, but other human groups, including those with whom they marry, are more alien in some ways, and further down the ladder than Tsunki (water spirits), several types of game and cultivated plants, which are seen to follow mating rules more like the Achuar. One way of understanding these horticulturalists is as living in the continuum between what we call the domestic and the wild. Their capacity to communicate with other beings, to work with the subtle and changing flows and cycles of their habitat, to delight in the activities we call work and play, is something we might wish to emulate. Their rejection of the common humanity of their neighbors and conceptual limits defined by their place, is something happily superseded.

The challenge of creating polycultural futures is to meld the wisdom of premodern experimentation with the rigorous and sceptical approach of modern science, the enforced conformity of premodern societies with the conscious cooperation of free individuals. The key to the shift, I have argued, is a renewed appreciation of our relationship with the rest of nature, most especially the soils and waters that provide our food. Aldo Leopold (1999:161–75), great American conservationist, argued as early as 1939 that settler regions need to completely redesign agriculture for "land health." Half a century before Vandana Shiva (1993) criticized imported green revolution agronomy as monocultures of both earth and minds, Leopold already saw that "our self-imposed doctrine of ruthless utilitarianism" had led to a "regimentation of the mind" in judging land use by a single measure, such as the yield of a single crop. Settler regions imported techniques and families of beings from their relatively stable agro-ecological settings in northwest Europe. By leaving behind their stable and diverse contexts, the necessarily simplified European families of species occupied a different, grassland ecosystem, and simplified it far more than had their ancestors in Europe, or the indigenous families of species they displaced. In this simplified agro-ecosystem, early successes with single crops deepened the hubris and encouraged the shortened time horizons of a world centered on money rather than the health of the land and all its flows and beings. A mere four generations after settlement, Leopold was able to observe the degradation and depletion of soil, water, and biota in both farmlands and grasslands.

Leopold's plea for governments and societies to support farmers to be ecologists expressed a *conscious* approach to land management, based on science and individual freedom, that recovers the ancient wisdom, possibly pre-civilizational and almost certainly premodern, that humans are natural beings whose individual and collective fates are inseparable from the health of ecosystems. Beginning in the 1970s, with the concept *biosphere*, humans have available, should we choose to embrace it, the understanding that all our habitats are woven into one earth habitat, that our habitat is degraded, and that we need all our science, guided by all our wisdom, to recover. The unity of humanity envisioned and promised by the Enlightenment surely is realizable only by embrace of the unity of the earth community.

What is unique to the period since 1492 is not only that ecological simplification has been accelerated by ecological imperialism, but also that cultural diversity has become the norm almost everywhere. Over millennia languages and technologies encompassed and destroyed many distinct early civilizations and prehistoric cultures, and civilizations formed through hierarchical castes and empires imposed by one culture group on others (Diamond 1997:295–375). Colonial rule extended and deepened both the simplification of absorbed and displaced peoples and the mixing of peoples in societies that combined individual citizenship with different degrees of democracy. After five hundred years of colonial and postcolonial politics, only a handful of languages dominate the world, and among these English seems at this moment hegemonic—just as only a dozen monocultural crops predominate in all large agro-ecosystems. At the same time colonial rule brought together the cultural repertoires and inventiveness of humans, and companion animals and plants, from many parts of the world. In their kitchens and gardens, Africans, Asians, and Europeans (all composite categories combining many cultures), and indigenous peoples, those creating the gardens and cuisines for themselves and their masters, experimented and shared recipes and plants and techniques of living. Just as all the Creole languages of the world express the specific ingredients of the peoples brought haphazardly together, so the cuisines and gardens in each place represent the continuing human experiment in being at once distinct and interconnected, adapting to each place with all the relationships at hand.

To make the less conspicuous reality of polycultures the consciously chosen path of human society within the earth community is an enormous challenge. Recovering awareness of humans as foodgetters and society as centered on foodgetting is a way to begin. Can polycultural futures be built garden by garden and kitchen by kitchen? That path has not so far sufficed to allow the polycultural possibilities to emerge strongly from the heart of the monocultural juggernaut, both social and agronomic. To bring awareness of humans as foodgetters into politics at all levels, from communities to global institutions, is to search for governing principles very different from those promoting monocultures. In my view, a vision of polycultural futures has great potential to ground and unite efforts to renew, extend, and deepen democracy.

Notes

Chapter 1. Introduction

1. This process has been widely documented in the scholarly and popular media. See, e.g., Browne 2001; Danbom 1995; Dudley 2000; Duncan 1999; Fitchen 1991; Salamon in press; Davidson 1990.

2. The critique of development has been broad, ranging from practical demonstrations of the failure of many development policies, to a thorough-going critique of the paradigm of "development" and "modernization." See, in addition to Ferguson 1990, Long and Long 1992; Escobar 1995; Scott 1998.

3. The study of agriculture and of rural life has been, to a great extent, marginalized within the central disciplines of the social sciences and humanities and placed within specialized areas of colleges of agriculture within the land grant universities where researchers' roles are largely instrumental and policy oriented (Hurt 1996; Marcus and Lowitt 1999).

4. Finegold and Skocpol (1995), in their analysis of the agricultural New Deal, provide an excellent summary of theories of the relationship between state and society, including what they term pluralist, elite, Marxist, and rational choice theories, as well as their own institutional theory. See also Stock and Johnston 2001.

5. Bingen and Busch, eds. (in press).

6. An important debate on the class status of "petty commodity producers" appeared in the pages of the *Journal of Peasant Studies* in the late 1970s. See especially Friedmann 1978, 1980; Mann and Dickinson 1978, 1980; see also Buttel and Newby 1980. These analyses tended to view economic relations as determinative of other historical processes. James Scott (1998:196–201) argues that early twentieth century modernizers, both capitalist and socialist, sought to transform agriculture from individual to industrial systems of production, but that ideology more than specific interest drove their efforts. See also Fitzgerald 2002.

7. Objects created through capitalist relations of production enter the universe of circulation not only as "commodities," existing as pure exchange values, but also as useful things, that enter the universe of human meaning-making. The relationship between exchange values and use values remains a complex problem in social analysis (see Appadurai 1988).

8. After World War II the government, through the Agricultural and Home Extension Service and through providing support for agricultural production primarily to men, promoted the role of consumer to farm women (Adams 1993, 1994a; Fink 1986; Jellison 1993).

9. The U.S. and Canadian governments had always used the lands wrested through military and other means from Indian peoples (but not from French or Mexican inhabitants of acquired territory) as important federal powers. Federal implementation of land reclamation and irrigation works coincides with the distribution of virtually all arable land to private hands.

10. Dudley (2000 and chapter 10) explicitly argues with those who pose distinct "ideal types"—farmers adhering to an entrepreneurial (Salamon 1992) or industrial (Barlett 1993) ethos contrasted with those adhering to a "yeoman" ethos.

11. The success of these two religious groups in expanding their numbers as agricultural producers indicates that alternatives exist to conventional farming effected through individual entrepreneurship. They expose the contingent nature of what are often experienced as inevitable, "natural" social forms.

12. Erving Goffman (1974) has been the most influential sociologist to develop the concept of "frame" to describe the set of meanings that are condensed into a "shorthand" that can then be deployed, putatively unambiguously, in public debate. He also uses a dramaturgical analogy to interpret social action. See also Snow and Benford 1988.

Chapter 2. The Social Economy of Development

1. All periodizations are more than heuristics; they represent outcomes of theoretical and political boundary practices. Different approaches to periodization derive from the different commitments to qualitative (see Skocpol 1979:33–40) or quantitative (see Isaac and Griffin 1989) research. Other methodologists such as Charles Ragin (personal communication) treat periods as cases—at times within cases—to be constructed in the process of research. For a discussion of cases, and what they are across methods, see Ragin and Becker 1992. The periods delineated here initially emerged as part of an exercise exploring changing relations between nature, labor, and community as they relate to agricultural capital in the region. While somewhat accidental, it is interesting that each period from 1850 to 1993 is ten years shorter than the last.

2. The depressed center of the desert results from ductal thinning of the earth's crust derived from the meeting of the East Pacific and Mid-Atlantic Ridges (Elders et al. 1970).

3. For historical interpretations behind this position, see LaFeber 1963; Williams 1969.

4. The other side of this coin, i.e., the geographic response at a national level to the expansive internationalization of agricultural markets, is associated with the intensification of irrigation development. By the turn of the century, with the "closing of the frontier," the extensive intensification of agricultural production had more or less reached its limits within the continental U.S. This meant that the remaining options for developing the agricultural potential throughout the whole of the nation were the intensive extension of agriculture into deserts through irrigation and the adoption of more productive forms of cultivation, which farmers were slow to adopt. See Shulman chapter 6.

5. Opening in 1911, the Meloland Experimental Farm and Cooperative Ex-

tension Office is the University of California's oldest, continuously open county Agricultural Station (Tout 1931).

6. The federal government clearly represented a constraint on the CDC's development, as the Reclamation Bureau sought jurisdiction over irrigation works in the region when local citizens complained about poor water delivery and water quality. See Tout (1931:97–98) for a good account of these issues. It should be noted that the low level of the banks in Mexican territory would not have supported a headgate had the company wished, or been able to afford, to install one.

7. Mann (1990) argues that agriculture's relationship to natural processes inhibit the development of fully capitalist agriculture. However, in the Imperial Valley, the situation is far more complex in that the disjuncture between labor time and production time they theorize is moderated by the diversity of crops grown, the 365 day a year growing season, and more or less abundant seasonal labor supplies have been generally at hand. Further, natural obstacles, such as the flood, enabled the establishment of the groundwork for capitalist agriculture as much as they constrained its development. See Rudy (1994b) for a theoretical position on these issues.

8. The people of the valley voted that the county seat be El Centro. There was tremendous competition over the location of the county seat between Imperial, constructed by the CDC, and El Centro, built by a populist entrepreneur/banker by the name of Holt, and the founder of Holtville. El Centro won in large part because Holt purchased all of the newspapers in the valley a few months prior to the election. This is in Tout 1931. A fictionalized account of the settlement of the valley, the flood, and the role played by Holt was published by Harold Bell Wright (1911), a popular author of the day. This book was made into an epic silent film, with Cary Grant in his first bit role, as well.

9. The issue of whether or not a private individual or company can stake a legitimate claim on interstate waters traditionally regulated by the federal government has largely gone unasked in the context of not only the stake having preexisted the Bureau of Reclamation but the irrigation works having been put in place prior to federal intervention.

10. See Taylor 1928; Fisher 1953; Pisani 1984; Fuller 1991; Daniel 1982, among others. Most simply put, the successional patterns of labor importation go from Chinese, Japanese, "Hindu," Filipino, through to Mexican and limited numbers of African American and midwestern workers during the depression.

11. The involvement of the consulate is tied to the beginnings of such "union" struggles in conservative Mexican Mutual Aid Societies often as concerned with cultural practices as they were economic justice.

12. The best evidence of this comes from the extensive research included in the LaFollette Commission (Senate Education and Labor Committee 1940) reports and the frustrations of General Glassford, the federal mediator during the 1934 strike, and the relative ease by which growers were able to obtain the bracero agreement. The best accounts of this are in Fisher 1953 and Wolf 1964.

13. Agricultural and domestic labor were the two categories of work excluded from the federal labor laws which legitimated industrial union organizing in the mid- to late 1930s.

14. Tout (1931) claims that the early depression largely skipped the Imperial Valley. This information is largely confirmed by data from the office of the

Agricultural Commissioner of Imperial County for that period. Gross income continued to rise throughout the 1930s, despite the ecological, labor, and political problems which exploded during that time. The suspension of loans and constraints on productivity are referred to in Tout and also in internal materials of the IID, in the administrative promotional materials generated by the county, and in the auditor's reports on the bankruptcy of the IID.

15. This figure is derived from IID Crop Acreage fact sheets, California Agricultural Commissioner Crop and Livestock Reports on the value and acreage of commodities generated in the valley. This increase is well above the rate of inflation: what could be purchased for $100 in 1942 required $256.44 in 1972 (U.S. Bureau of Labor Statistics 2002).

16. A fascinating juxtaposition, here, is that the bracero program ended in 1965 and, despite dire predictions from growers, vegetable income increased dramatically.

17. This strategy, while better for marketing, contributed to pest problems reviewed in the next section.

18. The IID maintains the unique status of simultaneously being a state irrigation district and a federal drainage district. Soil Conservation Service payments are included in many Agricultural Commissioner Reports from the 1930s until the middle of the 1950s. These payments have continued, though the amounts have yet to be discovered.

19. See Industrial Planning Associates 1957; Imperial County Community Economic Development Department 1993.

20. These dire predictions had been the basis for extending the bracero program long beyond its initial legislation in the face of a "labor shortage" during the early stages of World War II. Galarza argues that some of this "shortage" was produced by the unwillingness of agricultural producers to pay viable wages to American citizens and permanent residents. Ernesto Galarza's organizing and academic work during the 1950s and 1960s showed that the bracero program not only abused the migratory Mexican workers but also disabled U.S. agricultural workers' ability to organize in the name of better working conditions and a livable wage. See Galarza 1956, 1974, 1977. With no domestic work force, when the bracero program was terminated, informally recruited, often "illegal" Mexican workers were "necessary" for agricultural production.

21. One of Sen. Tunney's key advisors was Warren Christopher. Another of the O'Melveny and Myers attorneys, Allyn Kreps, also worked for the valley's exemption. Kreps later worked on Alan Cranston's Senate campaign in 1968 and became an aide to Cranston after his election (Barnett 1978:68).

22. It also turns out that Nixon purchased his San Clemente property from the estate of Stephen Elmore, the father of the president of Imperial Resources Associates (Franklin 1981:286).

23. These data are from IID Acreage Reports from the years cited.

24. The suits initiated in 1967 by the Bureau of Reclamation and in 1969 by Ben Yellen had been decided in contradictory fashion; each had been reversed on appeal—after being combined under the aegis of the Federal Appellate Court—and then sent on to the Supreme Court for final adjudication (Fradkin 1981).

25. The IID has been able to draw more water than formally allocated under the Compact because of the relative underdevelopment of water infrastructures elsewhere along the lower Colorado.

26. At no point during the conference was it suggested that agricultural practices be adjusted, or that the form of agriculture and industrial development become more democratic or more inclusive. Surprisingly, despite being invited, no representatives of the major environmental groups in California attended the conference. Less surprisingly, it appeared that no representatives of labor or minority groups in Imperial County were invited.

27. All of the plans proposed in 1994 were variations on a theme by plans initially developed, shelved, and temporally displaced, in the late 1960s.

28. This observation is based on interviews with three employees of the Meloland Cooperative Extension Office.

Chapter 3. From the National Policy to Continentalism and Globalization

The arguments presented in this chapter have been under development for some time. Portions of the thesis have appeared previously in a paper presented to the Rural Sociological Society, Toronto, August 14, 1997, in papers delivered at the CSAA and at the Communities at the Crossroads: Resistance and Renewal Conference at the University of Regina, and at a seminar for the Department of Sociology at the University at Saskatchewan. I am indebted to Bob Stirling and Wendee Kubik for their feedback and critical insights.

Chapter 4. The Contested Terrain of Swine Production

The authors would like to acknowledge grant support for this research from the College of Agriculture, Food, and Natural Resources at the University of Missouri–Columbia.

1. Animal Unit is a measure used to classify animal feeding operations based on the species and number of animals in each operation. For swine, one animal unit is equal to 2.5 swine weighing over fifty-five pounds.

2. A family farm is defined as a farming operation where the majority of the capital, labor, and management are provided by the members of the family.

3. The law requires divestiture of any land owned for farming within two years by a corporation that earns the majority of its income from non-farm sources (Stout 1996).

Chapter 5. The Contingent Creation of Rural Interest Groups

1. For example, Charles Tilly (1978) and Craig Jenkins (1985).

2. This study was generously funded by the Ford Foundation, the Sociology and Anthropology Programs of the National Science Foundation, and the Agricultural Experiment Station of the University of California, Davis. Conducted between 1976 and 1989, this ethnographic exploration of the regional commodity system involved documentary research, participant observation, and interviews with individuals involved in all facets of production, support, and marketing. These included growers, wage workers, labor supervisors, and sharecroppers, as well as farm advisors, agricultural commissioners, employment and immigration officials, union staff, labor lawyers,

university researchers, and the representatives of grower and processor organizations. In 1986–87 in-depth interviews of three to five hours in length were conducted with 28 percent of the growers in the two-county region, followed up by ranch visits of one to two hours. Interviews of comparable length were conducted with 70 labor suppliers, both wage laborers and sharecroppers.

3. With few exceptions the designated sharecroppers were men, though women contributed as unpaid family or hired workers.

4. This information parallels the findings of the 1986–87 interviews, in which 50 percent of the sharecroppers interviewed cited the possibility of higher household income as the major advantage of sharecropping, but a substantial 40 percent cited the possibility of greater independence and control. Ninety percent cited the greater risk of income variation as the major disadvantage.

5. The deposition of Driscoll supervisor Kazumasa Mukai provides detailed information as to the character of sharecropper supervision (*Real v. Driscoll* 1976).

Chapter 6. The Origin of the Federal Farm Loan Act

1. The debate over the lingering influences of Populism during this period continues to be unresolved. Hofstadter's argument (1955) suggests Populism constituted a wellspring for the later design of rural credit reform. An alternate argument (Caine 1974) is that the aftereffects of the agrarian uprising necessitated Progressive Era state intervention not to institutionalize Populist ideals, but rather to prevent radical ideas from becoming law. On Hofstadter's problematic contribution, see Ostler 1995.

2. The surveys identified approximately 600 articles relevant to the reform of agriculture policy in the farm, farm-organization, and urban agrarian press. The farm press consisted of regional and some national trade papers. The farm organization press consists of official organs of the three major farm organizations of the period. Urban agrarian papers targeted an industrialist readership with a keen sense of the importance of agriculture in the U.S. economy. A system of coding by issue focus was developed to organize the press data gathered through the surveys. The survey method in the study was straightforward. The publications were scanned visually for headlines linking an article either to the rural credit debate or to related agrarian issues. All relevant articles were photocopied and analyzed for content. Immersion in this large stream of primary historical data revealed a set of interrelated problems. Emerging from this coding were the most salient issues and opinions that framed the debate in the press about rural credit. The summaries of the articles were then arranged chronologically in their assigned issue-code categories. Each stream of primary historical data was further analyzed in this manner, suggesting unique yet mutually reinforcing chronologies of causality leading up to the passage of the FFLA.

3. Herrick's unimpeachable Republican credentials apparently did not interfere with the strong ideological and policy alliance he developed with the new Democratic President, Woodrow Wilson, in 1913, nor with his Secretary of Agriculture, the equally partisan Democrat David F. Houston. The triumvirate of Herrick, Houston, and Wilson represented a powerful, yet not impreg-

nable, line of defense against the idea that the federal government should underwrite a new rural credit system.

Chapter 7. Low Modernism and the Agrarian New Deal

1. An earlier version of this chapter was presented at the annual meeting of the Social Science History Association, New Orleans, La., October 1996. Financial support for this research came from the Wisconsin Agricultural Experiment Station, College of Agricultural and Life Sciences, University of Wisconsin—Madison. Thanks to Spencer D. Wood for his assistance and to Jane Adams, David Hamilton, Elizabeth Sanders, and Mary Summers for their useful suggestions.

2. See also Fitzgerald (1996), who does not deploy the rhetoric of high modernism here but treats M. L. Wilson similarly. Elsewhere, based on a collective biography of the social and intellectual background of Wallace, Wilson, and four like-minded social scientists, I dissent from Scott's and Fitzgerald's claim that they were high modernists (Gilbert 2001). In contrast, this chapter focuses on the agrarians' ideological and programmatic efforts during the New Deal itself. Another leading New Dealer in the Department of Agriculture, Rexford G. Tugwell, better fits the high-modernist mold. After helping frame the early farm legislation of 1933 and founding the Resettlement Administration in 1935, Tugwell's influence waned. He left the government the following year so was not around for the later New Deal. For a comparison of Tugwell and other so-called "urban liberals" with Wallace and the other agrarians, see Gilbert 2000a. I try to evaluate Tugwell's high modernism in Gilbert 2000b. I appreciate the helpful comments of Jane Adams, Deborah Fitzgerald, Jim Scott, and Mary Summers on these matters.

3. I don't recall hearing the term "low modernism" before. However, Scott Lash (1994:212) uses "low modernity" in a book on reflexive modernization, and DiBattista and McDiarmid (1996) employ "low moderns" in their literary study. Thanks to Cliff Westfall for the Lash reference.

4. As part of the reconstituted BAE, the division went by "Farm Population and Rural Welfare" from 1939 until 1947, when it reverted to its original name of "Farm Population and Rural Life." On the division generally, see Bureau 1941a; Larson and Zimmerman (forthcoming); Larson, Moe, and Zimmerman 1992; Christie 1996.

Chapter 8. The New Deal Farm Programs

1. Research for this article has been funded in part by grants from the Agrarian Studies Program, a University Dissertation fellowship, a Robert M. Leylan Fellowship from Yale University, and a fellowship in the History of Home Economics and Nutrition from the New York State College of Human Ecology and Mann Library at Cornell University. Many thanks to U. T. Miller Summers, Olaf Larson, Jess Gilbert, Robert Johnston, Glenda Gilmore, Nancy Cott, Rogers Smith, Stephen Skowronek, Richard Kirkendall, and panelists and audiences at meetings of the Agricultural History Association, the Organization of American Historians, the Yale Political Science Department, and the

University of Pennsylvania History Department for their thoughtful readings, comments, assistance, and inspiration.

2. For studies of the philosophy and goals of these USDA programs in agriculture, see Gilbert 1996 and Kirkendall 1982:195–240.

3. For the conflicts surrounding "government chickens," see Raper 1943: 282–84.

4. The Rapers' memoirs note that most of the comments from readers that the *Herald-Journal* received were favorable (Raper and Raper 1977:67–68).

5. For Alexander's role in developing critiques of the cotton programs and the rationale and coalitions behind the later New Deal's efforts to deal with rural poverty in the South, see Baldwin 1968:6–7, 78–83, 95–96, 127–32, 145, 149–50, 154, 161, 162, 181–82, 190, 237–72.

6. For one example of how critics like Norman Thomas and scholars have treated the USDA's "purge of the urban liberals," see Daniel 1985:104–5; Kirkendall 1982; Gilbert 2000a[2]; Baldwin 1968.

7. Jess Gilbert and I argue that an investigation of the later careers and thought of these New Deal liberals could shed important light on the goals and conflicts that shaped development programs as well as the New Deal Department of Agriculture.

8. Brinkley (1995) seems to blame the liberals for the consequences of their lost battles.

9. One exception is suggested by a brief reference to a speech by John Kenneth Galbraith to the National Governors' Association in the summer of 1987 (Allen and Elliott 1988:23).

Chapter 9. The U.S. Farm Financial Crisis of the 1980s

This chapter was first published in *Agricultural History* 74 (2):366–80 and is based on a paper presented at the 80th Anniversary Symposium of the Agricultural History Society, Mississippi State University, June 18, 1999.

1. For a discussion of family and community impacts, see Friedberger 1993.

2. All data on inflation, unemployment, and interest rates are taken from various editions of the U.S. Bureau of the Census, *Statistical Abstract of the United States*. Inflation is measured as the annual percentage change in the Consumer Price Index.

3. Dollar amounts expressed in real terms have been adjusted for inflation to constant 1982 dollars using the implicit GNP deflator.

4. Due to inflation, these figures actually underestimate the real drop in land value, and the real drop in equity is underestimated.

Chapter 10. The Entrepreneurial Self

This chapter was originally presented as an invited paper at the Colloquium Series of the Program in Agrarian Studies at Yale University in March 1996. Sections have been previously published as "The Problem of Community in Rural America" in *Culture & Agriculture* 18 (2) 1996: 47–57.

1. As Barnett shows in chapter 9, those forced out of business during the farm crisis were the younger, well-educated operators of larger, technically efficient farms. The exodus of this generation, combined with a decline in new

entrants to farming, has left vast regions of the Great Plains with an aging population and a shrinking economic base. See also Bultena, Lasley, and Geller 1986; Jolly et al. 1986; and Murdock and Leistritz 1988.

2. In an earlier study, I examined the cultural mediation of economic dislocation in an industrial community. See Dudley 1994.

3. For a trenchant analysis of this paradox, see Walzer 1990.

4. Star Prairie is a fictitious name used to protect the identity and privacy of my informants. The complete account of this research appears in my book, *Debt and Dispossession: Farm Loss in America's Heartland* (2000).

5. An influential statement of this view is Bender 1978. Bender's work builds on the concept of community developed by anthropologists Robert Redfield and Oscar Lewis. See Redfield 1930, 1955; Lewis 1951, 1953.

6. Chibnick (1987) provides a good overview of the kinds of questions anthropologists are asking about changing ways of life in contemporary rural America. See especially Barlett 1987; Salamon 1987.

7. This formulation of dichotomy is drawn from Salamon and Davis-Brown (1986), where the authors find a difference between "yeoman" (German) and "entrepreneurial" (Yankee) ethnic identities, but the general features of their distinction are present in all of the ethnographic studies cited below.

8. The term "agricultural technology treadmill" was coined by Willard Cochrane (1958).

9. Two important studies of social trauma have influenced my thinking: Erikson 1976; Gordon 1977.

Chapter 11. Considerably More Than Vegetables, a Lot Less Than Community

1. A clear illustration of cultural harmonization can be found in the following quote attributed to the president of Nabisco, a company now owned by Philip Morris, the largest food conglomerate in the United States. "One world of homogeneous consumption . . . [I am] looking forward to the day when Arabs and Americans, Latins and Scandinavians will be munching Ritz Crackers as enthusiastically as they already drink Coke or brush their teeth with Colgate" (Mander 1991:136).

2. By contrast, there are cases in which a CSA membership has followed "their" farmer to a new location having been instrumental in securing the resources to make the move or to purchase conservation easements.

3. The "core group" is considered the heart of CSA as a member-worker co-operative (Henderson 1996). Nevertheless, only seven of thirty-five CSAs surveyed in Michigan, Ohio, and Indiana had an internal decision-making body resembling a core group (MOFFA 1999).

4. Some CSA farmers have sought additional labor by hiring migrant laborers, offering internships, attracting marginal populations (e.g., handicapped adults), or hosting AmeriCorps teams. However, each solution to excessive workload requires additional training and organizational coordination.

5. In an effort to address this inequity, regional CSA alliances have emerged and serve as resource and information clearinghouses. Their principal aim is to reduce individual farm exposure and economic vulnerability by increasing the consumption of local food and the generation of farm income. Yet, CSAs themselves constitute a market for computer programs, how-to manuals,

newsletters, recipes, building plans, etc., frequently marketed by small growers turned commercial "expert."

Chapter 12. Canadian Agricultural Policy

1. SARE (Sustainable Agricultural Research and Education) replaced LISA in 1988.

2. The arguments in this chapter are also based on a study of grain and oilseed farmers in a southwestern Ontario county. The study involved case studies of organic, no-till, and conventional farmers, interviews with a wide range of mainly local farm leaders, agribusiness representatives, and government officials, and observations of local farm organizations.

3. It should be recognized that this shift in orientation was not constructed within the government programs alone. There was also an emphasis within the farm media on the promotion of lean and value-added production ideas (e.g., Carter 1992; Hough 1994).

4. This has only begun to change very recently. In July 2001, for example, the federal government announced the creation of the first meaningful federal research program on organic farming (Agriculture and Agri-Food Canada 2001). This may suggest the beginning of a shift in policy towards an acknowledgement of organic farming (see Hall and Mogyorody 2001). Still, the federal government and most provincial governments continue to emphasize and fund an approach to sustainable agriculture which largely excludes organic farming (Agriculture and Agri-Food Canada 2000; Agriculture and Agri-Food Canada and OMAF 2000).

Chapter 13. Constructing Genetic Engineering in the Food and Fiber System as a Problem

This chapter is partially supported by the University of Illinois College of Agriculture, Consumer, and Environmental Sciences Office of Research.

1. Agriculture has previously been relatively "immune" to non-farm social protest activists, possibly because it has been protected by public acceptance of the validity of the agrarian ideal (Marx 1964). Rachel Carson's *Silent Spring* (1994 [1962]) during the 1960s spurred the first organized public opposition to pesticide use and stimulated the nascent environmental movement. Nevertheless, the primary focus of environmental organizations was on wildlife preservation, rather than organized resistance to conventional agriculture.

The natural/organic/health food movement, which grew concurrently with the alternative lifestyle or hippie movement of the 1960s and 1970s, advocated eating lower on the food chain for health and other ethical reasons (Belasco 1989; Cox 1994; Jacobson, Lefferts, and Garland 1991; Robbins 1987). Less processing, including fewer or no pesticides, went hand in hand with the preference for a simple lifestyle (Cox 1994). Hence, while the natural foods movement was implicitly a critique of conventional agriculture, proponents generally advocated alternative means of growing or marketing crops rather than opposing conventional agriculture on the national or legislative level (see DeLind chapter 11; Reisner 2001).

2. Farmers, in fact, have a rich history of resistance and rebellion (see Danbom 1995; Mooney and Majka 1995; Stock 1995).

3. Only the University of Iowa transcript hinted at something truly new, that with genetic engineering scientists can move genes across species. The USDA and Iowa State University, also clearly advocates for biotechnology, concentrate on benefits, pointing out many of the same advantages that Monsanto mentions: biotechnology can help the environment, alleviate world hunger and boost nutritional values of food. Both also mention risks with biotechnology, but point out that these risks are limited or are carefully monitored. The FDA and the University of Illinois text are the most neutral. The FDA tends to concentrate on the safety of food rather than other aspects of biotechnology. The University of Illinois (2002) points out both potential benefits and risks, although the overall impression is favorable, given reasonable caution.

4. Of all groups, the Farm Bureau is the most strident advocate of biotechnology. Not only does the Farm Bureau list the widest variety of benefits, but it is the harshest critic of opponents of biotechnology, claiming that "vocal activists" have started a "campaign of misinformation, aimed at killing agricultural biotechnology before it has a chance to fully mature and bring with it a wide range of benefits."

5. The benefits of biotechnology that the Farm Bureau statement includes are: better-tasting foods (sweeter and firmer bell peppers, sweeter peas), more nutritious foods (vegetable oils lower in saturated fats, peanuts with improved protein balance, fruits and vegetables with more vitamin C and E, food with lower levels of allergens), improved food handling for both consumers and processors (seedless melons that can be used for single servings, bananas with delayed ripening, frost-resistant strawberries), environmental advantages (reduced pesticide residues, conserved fuel), and advantages for farmers (guaranteed yields, increased yields, increased productivity, improved harvest quality, value-added potential for products, decreased use of pesticides, improved risk management, management time savings, lower equipment costs with no-tillage systems, and increased land-use efficiencies with narrower rows).

6. Foodstuffs with known profiles are exempt from the intense review required for new food additives. The Commissioner of the Food and Drug Administration, Jane E. Henney, said, "In the case of bioengineered foods, we are talking about adding some DNA to the plant that directs the production of a specific protein. DNA already is present in all foods and is presumed to be GRAS [generally recognized as safe]. . . . DNA is present in all foods and its ingestion is not associated with human illness. . . . If the plant looks normal and grows normally, if the food tastes right and has the expected levels of nutrients and toxins, and if the new protein put into food has been shown to be safe, then there are no safety issues" (U.S. FDA 2000).

7. Furthermore, because these organisms "can reproduce, migrate and mutate," they are inherently more unpredictable than either inorganic or organic chemicals (Organic Consumers Association 1999).

8. Those who list allergic reactions as a concern include: The Center for Food Safety 1999; Consumers Choice Council 2000; Greenpeace 1999; Mothers and Others for a Livable Planet 1999; Native Forest Council 1999; Organic Consumers Association 1999; Sierra Club 1999.

9. There are some indications that an increased risk of cancer is associated with increased levels of Insulin Growth Factor-1 in GE-developed Bovine Growth Hormone (BGH) produced milk. Ironically, company publications also use BGH milk as an example to point out the safety of GE products.

10. The Sierra Club's position calls for significant government oversight in terms of testing the potential for both short- and long-term damage to human and environmental health, as well as any effects on indigenous peoples and sustainable farmers (Sierra Club 1999).

11. A sample of this type of charge is: "The patenting of genetically engineered foods and widespread biotech food production threatens to eliminate farming as it has been practiced for 12,000 years. GE patents such as the Terminator Technology will render seeds infertile and force hundreds of millions of farmers who now save and share their seeds to purchase ever more expensive GE seeds and chemical inputs from a handful of global biotech seed monopolies. If the trend is not stopped, the patenting of transgenic plants and food-producing animals will soon lead to universal "bioserfdom" in which farmers will lease their plants and animals from biotech conglomerates such as Monsanto and pay royalties on seeds and offspring" (Cummins 1999).

Chapter 14. Eating in the Gardens of Gaia

1. While Western civilization derives from Mesopotamian roots, it also draws directly from the other early civilizations in Egypt and, less directly, the Indus Valley and the Hwang Ho or Yellow River Valley in China, all of which developed more or less extensive, irrigation-fed, grain-based monocultures.

2. James Lovelock (1991), with Lynn Margulis creator of the "Gaia" hypothesis, points out that humans are not necessary to life on earth. Other biologists, such as E. O. Wilson (1992), point out that worms and his personal favourite, ants, are far more important to sustaining earthly cycles. According to the Gaia view, named after the Roman goddess of the earth, the metabolism of living organisms sustains the continuous disequilibrium of gases in the atmosphere which support life; in other words, the hydrological, atmospheric, and mineral cycles are sustained by living organisms, through photosynthesis, respiration, decay, etc., just as water, air, and minerals sustain life.

3. A biome is a large ecosystem, such as a rainforest rather than a pond, or a desert rather than a mountainside.

4. Most of the peoples who inhabited North America before the Europeans arrived cultivated crops using shifting cultivation technologies that disturbed only the surface soils and that left most of the ground covered. It was the combination of continuous cropping and deep plowing of the land, and the opening of previously uncultivated prairies with steel plows and, where boggy, drainage, that degraded the soil.

Bibliography

About National Legislation. 1912. *National Grange Monthly* 9 (June): 3.

Adams, Jane. 1993. Resistance to "Modernity": Southern Illinois Farm Women and the Cult of Domesticity. *American Ethnologist* 20 (1): 89–113.

———. 1994a. Government Policies and the Changing Structure of Farm Women's Livelihood: A Case from Southern Illinois. In *The Economic Anthropology of the State*, ed. Elizabeth M. Brumfiel, 65–92. Monographs of the Society for Economic Anthropology. Lanham, Md.: University Press of America.

———. 1994b. *The Transformation of Rural Life: Southern Illinois, 1890–1990*. Chapel Hill: University of North Carolina Press.

———. 1997. Quiescence Despite Privation: Explaining the Absence of a Farm Laborers' Movement in Southern Illinois. *Comparative Studies in Society and History* 39 (3): 550–71.

Adams, Richard N. 1962. The Community in Latin America: A Changing Myth. *The Centennial Review* (Summer): 409–34.

Adkin, L. E. 1992. Counter-Hegemony and Environmental Politics in Canada. In *Organizing Dissent: Contemporary Social Movements in Theory and Practice*, ed. W. K. Carroll, 247–63. Toronto: Garamond Press.

———. 1994. Environmental Politics, Political Economy, and Social Democracy in Canada. *Studies in Political Economy* 45 (3): 13–169.

Advisory Panel on Food Security. 1987. *Food 2000: Global Policies for Sustainable Agriculture*. World Commission on Environment and Development. London: Zed Books.

AFSIC (Alternative Farming Systems Information Center). 2000. Website. http://www.nal.usda.gov.afsic/csa/csadef.html.

AGCare (Agricultural Groups Concerned About Resources and the Environment). 1992. *Our Farm Environmental Agenda*. Guelph, Ont.

Aglietta, Michel. 1979. *A Theory of Capitalist Regulation*. London: Verso.

Agriculture and Agri-Food Canada. 1992. *Today's Way to Grow: Canada-Ontario Agriculture Green Plan*. Pamphlet. Guelph, Ont.

———. 1995. *The Health of Our Soils: Toward Sustainable Agriculture in Canada*. Ottawa: Supply and Services Canada.

———. 2000. Vanclief Announces $10 Million to Farm Environmental Program. News Release, June 9. Leamington, Ont.

———. 2001. Centre Set to Bolster Canada's Organic Expertise. News Release, July 12. Baddeck, N.S.

Agriculture and Agri-food Canada and OMAF (Ontario Ministry of Agriculture and Food). 1992a. Canada-Ontario Agriculture Green Plan. Ottawa.

————. 1992b. *Horticultural Crops.* Best Management Practices Series, Environmental Sustainability Initiative. Ottawa.

————. 1994a. *Water Management.* Best Management Practices Series, Environmental Sustainability Initiative. Ottawa.

————. 1994b. *A First Look: Practical Solutions for Soil and Water Problems.* Best Management Practices Series, Environmental Sustainability Initiative. Ottawa.

————. 2000. *Contributing to Canada's Sustainable Development Strategy: 1992–97 Canada-Ontario Green Plan.* Ottawa: Supply and Services Canada.

Agriculture and Food Sectoral Task Force. 1991. *Ontario Food Sector Task Force Draft Report.* Ontario Roundtable on the Environment and Economy. Toronto.

Agriculture Canada. 1985. *Saving Energy and Dollars on the Farm.* Ottawa: Supply and Services Canada.

————. 1987. Canadian Agricultural Research and Technology Transfer: Future Directions. Working Paper.

————. 1989. *Growing Together: A Vision for Canada's Agri-food Industry.* Ottawa: Supply and Services Canada.

Alberts, E. and R. Spomer 1985. Dissolved Nitrogen and Phosphorus Runoff from Watersheds in Conservation and Conventional Tillage. *Journal of Soil and Water Conservation* 40 (January–February): 153–57.

Allen, John, Rebecca Filkins, Sam Cordes, and Eric J. Jarecki. 1998. Nebraska's Changing Agriculture: Perceptions About the Swine Industry. Working Paper 98–5. Lincoln: University of Nebraska Center for Rural Community Revitalization and Development.

Allen, Kristen and Barbara J. Elliott. 1988. The Current Debate and Economic Rationale for U.S. Agricultural Policy. In *U.S. Agriculture in a Global Setting,* ed. M. Ann Tutwiler, 9–33. Washington, D.C.: National Center for Food and Agriculture Policy.

Allen, P., D. Van Dusen, L. Lundy, and S. Gliessman. 1991. Integrating Social, Environmental and Economic Issues in Sustainable Agriculture. *American Journal of Alternative Agriculture* 6: 34–39.

Allen, Patricia. 1994. The Human Face of Sustainable Agriculture: Adding People to the Environmental Agenda. Issue Paper No.4. Center for Agroecology and Sustainable Food Systems. Santa Cruz: University of California.

Allen, Patricia and Martin Kovach. 2000. The Capitalist Composition of Organic: The Potential of Markets in Fulfilling the Promise of Organic Agriculture. *Agriculture and Human Values* 17 (3): 221–32.

Allison, Roger. 1995. What's the Stink. Missouri Rural Crisis Center. Retrieved May 22, 1998 from: http://www.inmotionmagazine/com/hog2.html.

Allport, Susan. 2000. *The Primal Feast: Food, Sex, Foraging, and Love.* New York: Harmony Books.

American Farm Bureau. 2000. BIOtechnology. Last revised May 23. Retrieved June 12 from: http://www.fb/org/issues/biotech/biotech_farmers.html.

Amplia Huelga la Union de Trabajadores Agricolas Unidos. 1979. *El Sol* 6 (September): 1.

Appadurai, Arjun, ed. 1988. *The Social Life of Things: Commodities in Cultural Perspective.* Cambridge: Cambridge University Press.

Arce, Alberto. 1997. Globalization and Food Objects. *International Journal of Sociology of Agriculture and Food* 6: 77–108.

Arce, Alberto and Eleanor Fisher. 1997. Commodities, Exchanges, and Personhood in a Global Context: Bolivian Coca, Tanzanian Honey, and Chilean

Apples. Paper presented at Research Committee 40 of the International Sociological Association conference, Toronto.

Arce, Alberto and Norman Long. 2000. *Anthropology, Development, and Modernities: Exploring Discourses, Counter-Tendencies, and Violence*. New York: Routledge.

Arnot, Charlie. 1996. Representative of Premium Standard Farms. Personal
communication. November 8.

ATTRA. 2000. Website. http://www.attra.org/attra-pub/csa.html.

Badger, Anthony J. 1989. *The New Deal*. New York: Noonday Press.

Bailey, Liberty Hyde, Henry Wallace, Kenyon L. Butterfield, Walter H. Page,
Gifford Pinchot, C. S. Barrett, and W. A. Beard. 1909. *Report of the Country
Life Commission*. 60th Congress, 2d sess. Senate Doc. 705. Washington, D.C.:
Government Printing Office.

Baldwin, Sidney. 1968. *Poverty and Politics: The Rise and Decline of the Farm Security Administration*. Chapel Hill: University of North Carolina Press.

Baran, Paul and Paul Sweezy. 1966. *Monopoly Capital*. New York: Monthly Review Press.

Barlett, Peggy. 1987. The Crisis in Family Farming: Who Will Survive? In
Farm Work and Fieldwork: American Agriculture in Anthropological Perspective,
ed. Michael Chibnick, 29–57. Ithaca, N.Y.: Cornell University Press.

———. 1993. *American Dreams, Rural Realities: Family Farms in Crisis*. Chapel
Hill: University of North Carolina Press.

Barnett, Paul G. 1978. *Imperial Valley: The Land of Sun and Subsidies*. Davis:
California Institute for Urban Studies.

Barone, Michael and Grant Ujifusa. 1987. *The Almanac of American Politics
1988*. Washington, D.C.: National Journal.

Barrett, Charles S. 1909. *The Mission, History, and Times of the Farmers Union*.
Nashville, Tenn.: Marshall and Bruce.

———. 1916. Something Must Be Done to Help the Tenant Farmers. *Pacific
Farmers Union* 8 (July): 2–3.

Barrette, Michael. 1996. Hog-Tied by Feedlots. *Zoning News*: 1–4.

Basran, G. S. and David Hay. 1988. *The Political Economy of Agriculture in Western Canada*. Toronto: Garamond Press.

Batie, S. 1990. Agricultural Policy and Environmental Goals: Conflict or Com-
patibility. *Journal of Economic Issues* 24 (2): 565–73.

Baumgartner, F. R. and B. D. Jones. 1993. *Agendas and Instability in American
Politics*. Chicago: University of Chicago Press.

Bayliss-Smith, Tim. 1982. *The Ecology of Agricultural Systems*. Cambridge: Cambridge University Press.

Beard, Charles A. 1939. Government and the Humane Spirit. *Land Policy Review* 2 (September–October): 1–6 .

Belasco, Warren J. 1989. *Appetite for Change: How the Counterculture Took on the
Food Industry*. Ithaca, N.Y.: Cornell University Press.

Bell, Bill, Jr. 1998. Judge Upholds a Health Ordinance That Targets Large,
Smelly Hog Farms. *St. Louis Post-Dispatch* October 30: B2.

———. 1999a. EPA Asks to Join Lawsuit Against Giant Hog Producer in Missouri. *St. Louis Post-Dispatch* July 24: 18.

———. 1999b. Judge Approves Settlement in State's Suite over Hog Farm
Waste. *St. Louis Post-Dispatch* August 4: B4.

———. 1999c. Nixon Agrees on Settlement in Suit over Hog-Waste Spill. *St.
Louis Post-Dispatch* July 30: B4.

———. 2000a. EPA Steps Up Pressure on Large Hog Operations. *St. Louis Post-Dispatch* April 29: 6.

———. 2000b. Milan, MO., Has Welcomed a Meatpacking Plant and with It Come Daunting Problems. *St. Louis Post-Dispatch* April 2: A8.

Bellah, Robert, Richard Madsen, William Sullivan, Ann Swidler, and Steven Tipton. 1996 [1985]. *Habits of the Heart: Individualism and Commitment in American Life.* Berkeley: University of California Press.

Bender, Thomas. 1978. *Community and Social Change in America.* Baltimore: Johns Hopkins University Press.

Berch, Bettina. 1985. The Resurrection of Out-Work. *Monthly Review* 37 (6): 37–46.

Berk, G. 1994. *Alternative Tracks: The Constitution of the American Industrial Order, 1865–1917.* Baltimore: Johns Hopkins University Press.

Berlan, J. P. 1989. Capital Accumulation, Transformation of Agriculture, and the Agricultural Crisis: A Long Term Perspective. In *Instability and Change in the World Economy,* ed. A. MacEwan and W. K. Tabb, 205–24. New York: Monthly Review Press.

Berry, Wendell. 1977. *The Unsettling of America: Culture and Agriculture.* San Francisco: Sierra Club Books.

Better Banking System Demanded by Farmers. 1911. *Wisconsin Equity News* 4 (December 10): 4.

Beus, C. 1995. Competing Paradigms: An Overview and Analysis of the Alternative Conventional Agriculture Debate. *Research in Rural Sociology and Development* 6: 23–50.

Beus, C. and R. Dunlap. 1990. Conventional vs. Alternative Agriculture: The Paradigmatic Roots of the Debate. *Rural Sociology* 55 (4): 590–616.

———. 1994. Agricultural Paradigms and the Practice of Agriculture. *Rural Sociology* 59(4): 620–35.

Binder, David. 1995. Jamie Whitten, Who Served 53 Years in House, Dies at 85. *New York Times* September 11: D13.

Bingen, Jim and Lawrence Busch, eds. In press. *Standards and the Shape of Our Global Food and Fiber System.* Kluwer Academic Publishers.

Blanke, David. 2000. *Sowing the American Dream: How Consumer Culture Took Root in the Middle West.* Columbus: Ohio University Press.

Bliss, J. M., ed. 1966. *Canadian History in Documents, 1763–1966.* Toronto: Ryerson Press.

Bodenheimer, Edgar, John B. Oakley, and Jean C. Love. 1980. *An Introduction to the Anglo-American Legal System.* St. Paul, Minn.: West Publishing.

Bogue, A. G. 1976. Land Credit for Northern Farmers. *Agricultural History* 50: 68–100.

Bonanno, Alessandro. 1991. The Globalization of the Agricultural and Food System and Theories of the State. *International Journal of Sociology of Agriculture and Food* 1: 15–30.

———. 1992. Globalization of the Agricultural and Food Sector: The Crisis of Contradictory Convergence. In *The Agricultural and Food Sector in the New Global Era,* ed. Alessandro Bonanno, 25–50. London: Concept Publishing.

———. 1993. The Agro-Food Sector and the Transnational State: The Case of the EC. *Political Geography* 12(4): 341–60.

———. 1994. The Locus of Polity Action in a Global Setting. In *From Columbus to ConAgra: The Globalization of Agriculture and Food,* ed. A. Bonanno, L. Busch,

W. H. Friedland, L. Gouviea, and E. Mingione, 251–64. Lawrence: University Press of Kansas.

Bonanno, Alessandro, Lawrence Busch, William H. Friedland, Lourdes Gouviea, and Enzo Mingione, eds. 1994. *From Columbus to ConAgra: The Globalization of Agriculture and Food*. Lawrence: University Press of Kansas.

Bonanno, Alessandro and Douglas H. Constance. 1996. *Caught in the Net: The Global Tuna Industry, Environmentalism, and the State*. Lawrence: University Press of Kansas.

————. 1998a. Global Agri-Food Sector and the Case of the Tuna Industry: Global Regulation and Perspectives for Development. *Journal of Developing Societies* 14 (1): 100–126.

————. 1998b. The Global Economy and Democracy: The Tuna-Dolphin Controversy Revisited. *International Journal of the Sociology of Agriculture and Food* 7: 67–112.

————. 2000. Mega Hog Farms in the Texas Panhandle Region: Corporate Actions and Local Resistance. *Research in Social Movements, Conflicts, and Change* 22: 83–110.

Bonanno, Alessandro, Douglas H. Constance, and Heather Lorenz. 2000. Powers and Limits of Transnational Corporations: The Case of ADM. *Rural Sociology* 65 (3): 440–60.

Bonnen, James T. and William P. Browne. 1989. Why Is Agricultural Policy So Difficult to Reform? In *The Political Economy of U.S. Agriculture: Challenges for the 1990s*, ed. Carol S. Kramer. Washington, D.C.: National Center for Food and Agricultural Policy.

Bourdieu, Pierre. 1977. *Outline of a Theory of Practice*. Cambridge: Cambridge University Press.

Boyte, Harry and Nancy N. Kari. 1996. *Building America: The Democratic Promise of Public Work*. Philadelphia: Temple University Press.

Brinkley, Alan. 1995. *The End of Reform: New Deal Liberalism in Recession and War*. New York: Alfred A. Knopf.

Brooks, T. J. 1912. Rural Cooperative Credit. *The Progressive Farmer* 27 (May 4): 20.

Brown, Lester R. 1974. *By Bread Alone*. New York: Praeger Publishers.

Brown, William Paul. 2001. *The Failure of National Rural Policy: Institutions and Interests*. Washington, D.C.: Georgetown University Press.

Bryant, Tim. 1999. Company Hog Farm Owes Neighbors $5.2 Million, Jury Rules. *St. Louis Post-Dispatch* May 1: A1.

Brym, Robert. 1993. The Canadian Capitalist Class. In *Social Inequality in Canada*, ed. James Curtis, Edward Grabb, and Neil Guppy, 31–48. Scarborough, Ont.: Prentice Hall.

Bultena, Gordon, Paul Lasley, and Jack Geller. 1986. The Farm Crisis: Patterns and Impacts of Financial Distress Among Iowa Farm Families. *Rural Sociology* 51 (4): 436–48.

Bureau of Agricultural Economics. 1940a. Operating Report Covering the Cooperative Land-Use Planning Program for the Year Ended June 30, 1940. Division of State and Local Planning. Washington, D.C.: National Archives, Record Group 83, Entry 215, Box 1.

————. 1940b. Service and Research in Community Organization. Division of Farm Population and Rural Welfare. Washington, D.C.: National Archives, Record Group 83, Entry A1, Box 2.

————. 1941a. Division of Farm Population and Rural Welfare Annual Report. *Farm Population and Rural Life Activities* 15 (October): 3–38.

————. 1941b. Operating Report of the Division of State and Local Planning Covering the Cooperative Agricultural Planning Program for the Year Ending June 30, 1941. Washington, D.C.: National Archives, Record Group 83, Entry 215, Box 1.

Burridge, Kenhelm. 1969. *New Heaven, New Earth: A Study of Millenarian Activities*. New York: Basil Blackwell.

Busch, Lawrence and Keiko Tanaka. 1996. Rites of Passage: Constructing Quality in a Commodity Subsector. *Science Technology & Human Values* 21: 3–27.

Buttel, Frederick H. 1989. The U.S. Farm Crisis and the Restructuring of Agriculture: Domestic and International Dimensions. In *The International Farm Crisis*, ed. M. Redclift and D. Goodman, 46–74. New York: St. Martin's Press.

————. 1992. Environmentalization: Origins, Processes, and Implications for Rural Social Change. *Rural Sociology* 57 (1): 1–27.

————. 1993. Socioeconomic Impacts and Social Implications of Reducing Pesticide and Agricultural Chemical Use in the United States. In *The Pesticide Question: Environment, Economics and Ethics*, ed. D. Pimenthal and H. Lehman, 153–81. New York: Chapman and Hall.

Buttel, Frederick H. and G. Gillespie. 1988. *Agricultural Research and Development and the Appropriation of Progressive Symbols: Some Observations on the Politics of Ecological Agriculture*. Bulletin No. 151, Department of Rural Sociology. Ithaca, N.Y.: Cornell University.

Buttel, Frederick H. and Howard Newby, eds. 1980. *The Rural Sociology of the Advanced Societies: Critical Perspectives*. London: Allanheld, Osmun.

Byczynski, Lynn. 1998. CSA Membership to Buy Development Rights. *Growing for Market* 7 (2): 9.

Caine, Stanley P. 1974. The Origins of Progressivism. In *The Progressive Era*, ed. Louis Gould, 11–34. Syracuse, N.Y.: Syracuse University Press.

California Division of Pest Management Environmental Protection and Worker Safety. 1978. Report on Environmental Assessment of Pesticide Programs: Draft. Sacramento: California Department of Food and Agriculture.

California Employment Development Department. 1992a. *Annual Planning Information: Imperial County*. Los Angeles: EDD Southern Area Labor Market Information Group.

————. 1992b. *Farm Labor Contractors in California*. California Agricultural Studies No. 92–2. Sacramento: EDD Labor Market Information Division.

Callaghan, Polly and Heidi Hartmann. 1992. *Contingent Work: A Chart Book on Part-Time and Temporary Employment*. Washington, D.C.: Economic Policy Institute.

Callicotte, W. R. 1911. Report of the National Legislative Committee on National Legislation. *Pacific Farmers Union* 3 (March 3): 1.

Campaign for Food Safety. 1999. News and Analysis in Genetic Engineering. Retrieved from: www.organicconsumers.org/ge/cfs20cfm.

Campaign for Responsible Transplantation. 1999. CRT Campaign for Responsible Transplantation. Retrieved November 20 from: http://www.crt-online.org/.

Careless, J. M. S. 1986. *Canada: A Story of Challenge*. Toronto: Macmillan.

Cargill. 2000. Biotechnology: Just the Facts. Last revised 1999. Retrieved April 3 from: http://www.cargill.com/aghorizons/news.

Carroll, William. 1985. Dependency, Imperialism, and the Capitalist Class in

Canada. In *The Structure of the Canadian Capitalist Class*, ed. Robert Brym. Toronto: Garamond Press.

Carson, Rachel. 1994 [1962]. *Silent Spring*. New York: Houghton Mifflin Co.

Carter, C. 1992. Look to Technology and Innovation for Economic Prosperity. *Voice of the Essex Farmer* March 31: 4.

Castro, Janice. 1993. Disposable Workers. *Time* 29 (March): 43–47.

Cecelski, David and Mary Lee Kerr. 1992. Hog Wild. *Southern Exposure* 20 (32): 9–15.

Center for Ethics and Toxics. 1999. Website. http://www.cetos.org/. Retrieved November 20.

Center for Food Safety. 1999. Website. http://www.centerforfoodsafety.org/. Retrieved November 20.

Centers for Disease Control and Prevention. 2000. Food Borne Infections. Retrieved from: http://www.cdc.gov/ncidod/dbmd/diseaseinfo/foodborne infections_t.htm.

Chapman, J. 1912. Report of Committee on Agricultural and Financial Development and Education. In *The Commercial and Financial Chronicle: Proceedings of the Convention of the American Bankers' Association,* held in Detroit, Michigan, September 10–13, 1912, 144. New York: William B. Dana.

Chibnick, Michael, ed. 1987. *Farm Work and Fieldwork: American Agriculture in Anthropological Perspective*. Ithaca, N.Y.: Cornell University Press.

Christie, Margaret M. 1996. Carl C. Taylor, "Organic Intellectual" in the New Deal Department of Agriculture. M.S. thesis, University of Wisconsin, Madison.

CIAS (Center for Integrated Agricultural Systems). 2000. Community Supported Agriculture: Growing Food . . . and Community. Research Brief 21. Retrieved from: www.wisc.edu/cias/pubs/rebrief/021.html.

Clemens, Elisabeth S. 1997. *The People's Lobby: Organizational Innovation and the Rise of Interest Group Politics in the United States, 1890–1925*. Chicago: University of Chicago Press.

Clough, S. B. and C. W. Cole. 1967. *Economic History of Europe*. Boston: D. C. Heath.

Cochrane, Willard. 1958. *Farm Prices: Myth and Reality*. Minneapolis: University of Minnesota Press.

———. 1993. *The Development of American Agriculture: A Historical Analysis*. 2nd ed. Minneapolis: University of Minnesota Press.

Cohn, T. 1990. *The International Politics of Agricultural Trade: Canadian-American Relations in a Global Agricultural Context*. Vancouver: University of British Columbia Press.

Columbia Daily Tribune. 1999. Counties' Right to Restrict Hog Farms Upheld. November 24: B1, B6.

Coming to His Own. 1912. *National Grange Monthly* 9 (April): 10.

Community Farm, The. 1999. *Pricing Community* 7 (Autumn): 1, 3.

Conant, Charles A. 1912. Land and Agricultural Credit. In *The Commercial and Financial Chronicle: Proceedings of the Convention of the American Bankers' Association,* held in Detroit, Michigan, September 10–13, 1912, 120. New York: William B. Dana.

Cone, Cynthia Abbott and Ann Kakaliouras. 1995. Community Supported Agriculture: Building Moral Community or an Alternative Consumer Choice. *Culture and Agriculture* 17: 28–31

———. 1998. The Quest for Purity, Stewardship of the Land, and Nostalgia for Sociability: Resocializing Commodities Through Community Supported Agriculture. In *CSA Farm Network Vol. II*, ed. Steve Gilman, 26–29. Stillwater, N.Y.: Northeast Organic Farming Association.

Cone, Cynthia Abbott and Andrea Myhre. 2000. Community-Supported Agriculture: A Sustainable Alternative to Industrial Agriculture? *Human Organization* 59 (2): 187–97.

Connor, Fred. 1996. Gentry Co. (Mo.) Extension Service. Personal communication. May 30.

Constance, Douglas H. and Alessandro Bonanno. 1999a. CAFO Controversy in the Texas Panhandle Region: The Environmental Crisis of Hog Production. *Culture and Agriculture* 21 (1): 14–26.

———. 1999b. The Contested Terrain of the Global Fisheries: "Dolphin-safe" Tuna, the Panama Declaration, and the Marine Stewardship Council. *Rural Sociology* 64 (4): 597–623.

———. 2000. Eco-Regulation of the Global Fisheries: Unilever, the World Wildlife Fund and the Marine Stewardship Council. *Agriculture and Human Values* 17 (2): 125–39.

Constance, Douglas H., Alessandro Bonanno, and William D. Heffernan. 1995. Global Contested Terrain: The Case of the Tuna-Dolphin Controversy. *Agriculture and Human Values* 12 (3): 19–33.

Constance, Douglas H. and William D. Heffernan. 1991. The Global Poultry Agro/Food Complex. *International Journal of Sociology of Agriculture and Food* 1: 26–42.

Consumer's Choice Council. 2000. Website. http://www.consumerscouncil.org/. Retrieved January 12.

Consumers Union. 1998. Consumer Reports Find 71 Percent of Store-Bought Chicken Contains Harmful Bacteria. Press release, February 23. Retrieved from: http://www.consumersunion.org/food/pestny899.htm.

———. 1999. Do You Know What You're Eating? An Analysis of U.S. Government Data on Pesticide Residues in Foods. February. Public Service Projects Department. Yonkers, N.Y.: Consumers Union.

ContiGroup. 1998a. Continental Grain Company CEO Discusses New Strategic Focus. ContiGroup.Com. Press release, November 11. Retrieved January 15, 1999, from: http://www.contigroup.cgcpr.html.

———. 1998b. ContAgriIndustries ContiGroup.com Business Units. Retrieved January 15, 1999, from: http://www.contingroup.com/contiagri.html.

Conway, John. 1994. *The West: The History of a Region in Confederation*. Toronto: Lorimer.

Conway, John and R. Stirling. 1988. Fractions Among Prairie Farmers. In *The Political Economy of Agriculture in Western Canada*, ed. G. S. Basran and David Hay. Toronto: Garamond Press.

Cooperative Banks and American Farmers. 1912. *American Review of Reviews* 45 (April): 615–17.

Cory, Harry T. and William P. Blake. 1915. *The Imperial Valley and the Salton Sink*. San Francisco: J. J. Newbegin.

Council for Responsible Genetics. 1999. Website. http://www.gene-watch.org/. Last revised: August 30. Retrieved November 20.

Cox, Craig. 1994. *Storefront Revolution: Food Co-ops and the Counterculture*. New Brunswick, N.J.: Rutgers University Press.

Creighton, Donald. 1955. *John A. Macdonald: The Old Chieftain*. Toronto: Macmillian.

Cronin, Mary M. 1997. Fighting for the Farmers: The Pacific Northwest's Nonpartisan League Newspapers. *Journalism History* 23 (Autumn): 126–36.

Cronon, William. 1983. *Changes in the Land: Indians, Colonists, and the Ecology of New England.* New York: Hill and Wang.

————. 1991. *Nature's Metropolis: Chicago and the Great West.* New York: W. W. Norton.

Crosbie, Karol. 2000. Evolution of an Idea: ISU Experts in Many Fields Seek to Understand and Communicate the Risks and Benefits of Genetically Modified Crops. *Visions* 13 (1): 36–40.

Crosby, Alfred. 1972. *The Columbian Exchange: Biological and Cultural Consequences of 1492.* Westport, Conn.: Greenwood Press.

————. 1986. *Ecological Imperialism: The Biological Expansion of Europe 900–1900.* Cambridge: Cambridge University Press.

Crosby, Stanley W. 1930. The Imperial Valley of California: An Example of Geographic Instability. Ph.D. diss., University of Chicago.

Cruel Facts as to Farm Usury. 1915. *The Orange Judd Weekly Farmer* November 6: 11.

CSA listserve. Moderated list, csa-l@prairie.net.org. Subscription to CSA list on: http://www.prairienet.org/discussion/listoflists.phtml.

Cummings, Claire Hope. 1999. Entertainment Foods. *The Ecologist* 29 (1): 16–19.

Cummins, Ronnie. 1999. Hazards of Genetically Engineered Foods and Crops: Why We Need a Global Moratorium. Retrieved November 20 from: http://www.organicconsumers.org/.

Dahlberg, Kenneth, ed. 1986. *New Directions for Agriculture and Agricultural Research.* Totowa, N.J.: Rowman and Allanheld.

————. 1993. Regenerative Food Systems. In *Food for the Future*, ed. Patricia Allen, 75–102. New York: Wiley.

Dakers, S. 1995. *Agricultural Soil Conservation: Federal Policy.* Current Issue Review. Ottawa: Research Branch, Library of Parliament.

Dalecki, M. and B. Bealer. 1984. Who Is the "Organic" Farmer? *The Rural Sociologist* 4 (1): 11–18.

Danbom, David B. 1979. *The Resisted Revolution: Urban America and the Industrialization of Agriculture, 1900–1930.* Ames: Iowa State University Press.

————. 1995. *Born in the Country: A History of Rural America.* Baltimore: Johns Hopkins University Press.

Daniel, Cletus E. 1982. *Bitter Harvest: A History of California Farmworkers, 1870–1941.* Berkeley: University of California Press.

Daniel, Pete. 1985. *Breaking the Land.* Urbana: University of Illinois Press.

Darling, Howard. 1980. *The Politics of Freight Rates.* Toronto: McClelland and Stewart.

Davidson, Osha Gray. 1990. *Broken Heartland: The Rise of America's Rural Ghetto.* New York: Free Press.

Davis, Mike. 1999. A World's End: Drought, Famine, and Imperialism, 1896–1902. *Capitalism, Nature, Socialism* 10 (2): 3–46.

Dearing, J. W. and E. M. Rogers. 1996. *Agenda-Setting.* Thousand Oaks, Calif.: Sage.

DeLind, Laura B. 1995. The State, Hog Hotels, and the "Right to Farm": A Curious Relationship. *Agriculture and Human Values* 12: 34–44.

————. 1999. Close Encounters with a CSA: The Reflections of A Bruised and Somewhat Wiser Anthropologist. *Agriculture and Human Values* 16: 3–9.

————. 2000. Transforming Organic Agriculture into Industrial Organic Products: Reconsidering National Organic Standards. *Human Organization* 59 (2): 198–208.

DeLind, Laura B. and Holly Harman Fackler. 1999. CSA: Patterns, Problems, and Possibilities. In *The Many Faces of Community Supported Agriculture (CSA): A Guide to Community Supported Agriculture in Indiana, Michigan, and Ohio*. Hartland: Michigan Organic Food and Farm Alliance.

DeLind, Laura B. and Anne E. Ferguson. 1999. Is This a Women's Movement? The Relationship of Gender to Community Supported Agriculture in Michigan. *Human Organization* 58 (2): 190–200.

Descola, Philippe. 1994. *In the Society of Nature*. Cambridge: Cambridge University Press.

Diamond, Jared. 1992. *The Third Chimpanzee: The Evolution and Future of the Human Animal*. New York: HarperCollins.

————. 1997. *Guns, Germs, and Steel: The Fates of Human Societies*. New York: W. W. Norton.

Diaz, P. and P. Gingrich. 1992. Crisis and Community in Rural Saskatchewan. In *Rural Sociology in Canada*, ed. David Hay and G. S. Basran. Toronto: Oxford.

DiBattista, Maria and Lucy McDiarmid, eds. 1996. *High and Low Moderns: Literature and Culture, 1889–1939*. New York: Oxford University Press.

diLeonardo, Micaela. 1984. *Varieties of Ethnic Experience*. Ithaca, N.Y.: Cornell University Press.

————. 1985. Deindustrialization as a Folk Model. *Urban Anthropology* 14 (1–3): 237–58.

DiPietre, Dennis and Carl Watson. 1994. *The Economic Effect of Premium Standard Farms on Missouri*. CA 144. University Extension, Commercial Agriculture Program, University of Missouri.

Domhoff, William. 1990. *The Power Elite and the State*. New York: de Gruyter.

Donahue, Brian. 1999. *Reclaiming the Commons: Community Farms and Forests in a New England Town*. New Haven, Conn.: Yale University Press.

Douglas, Mary. 1992. The Person in the Enterprise Culture. In *Understanding the Enterprise Culture: Themes in the Work of Mary Douglas*, ed. Shaun Hargreaves Heap and Angus Ross, 41–62. Edinburgh: Edinburgh University Press.

Dowd, Munson J. 1956. *History of Imperial Irrigation District and the Development of Imperial Valley*. Brawley, Calif.: Imperial Irrigation District.

Du Bois, W. E. B. 1992 [1935]. *Black Reconstruction in America*. New York: Atheneum.

Dudley, Kathryn Marie. 1994. *The End of the Line: Lost Jobs, New Lives in Post-industrial America*. Chicago: University of Chicago Press.

————. 2000. *Debt and Dispossession: Farm Loss in America's Heartland*. Chicago: University of Chicago Press.

Dummermuth, Matt. M. 1997. A Summary and Analysis of Laws Regulating the Production of Pork in Iowa and Other Major Pork Producing States. *Drake Journal of Agricultural Law* 2 (2): 477–527.

Duncan, Cynthia M. 1999. *Worlds Apart: Why Poverty Persists in Rural America*. New Haven, Conn.: Yale University Press.

Dunlap, R. and K. Van Liere. 1984. Commitment to the Dominant Paradigm and Support for Environmental Quality. *Social Science Quarterly* 65: 1013–28.

Durrenberger, E. Paul and Kendall M. Thu. 1996. The Expansion of Large

Scale Hog Farming in Iowa: The Applicability of Goldschmidt's Findings Fifty Years Later. *Human Organization* 55: 409–15.

Earth Island Institute. 1999. Earth Island Institute: Innovative Action for the Environment. Retrieved November 20 from: http://www.earthisland.org/.

Easterbrook, W. A. and H. Aitken. 1956. *Canadian Economic History.* Toronto: Macmillian.

Edmonds Institute. 1999. Website. http://www.edmonds-institute.org/. Retrieved November 20.

Eisenberg, Evan. 1998. *The Ecology of Eden.* Toronto: Random House.

Elders, Wilfred A., Robert W. Rex, Tsvi Meidav, and Paul T. Robinson. 1970. *Crustal Spreading in Southern California: The Imperial Valley of California Is a Product of Oceanic Spreading Centers Acting on a Continental Plate.* Riverside: The Institute of Geophysics and Planetary Physics, University of California, Riverside.

Ensminger, Douglas. 1940. The Community in County Planning. *Land Policy Review* 3 (March–April): 44–51.

Erikson, Kai. 1976. *Everything in Its Path: The Destruction of Community in the Buffalo Creek Flood.* New York: Simon and Schuster.

Escobar, Arturo. 1995. *Encountering Development: The Making and Unmaking of the Third World.* Princeton, N.J.: Princeton University Press.

Etzioni, Amitai. 1996. The Responsive Community: A Communitarian Perspective. *American Sociological Review* 16 (February): 1–11.

Faircloth, Anne. 1996. First: Those Pigs at Morgan Stanley Investment Banking. *Fortune* October 14: 36.

Fairclough, Norman. 1989. *Language and Power.* New York: Longman.

Fallon, Sally. 1999. Nasty, Brutish and Short? *The Ecologist* 29 (1): 20–26.

Farm Credit Bill. 1916. *Wallace's Farmer* 41 (May 19): 4.

Farmers' Problems. 1914. *Farm Journal* 38 (August): 15.

Farmers' Problems. 1916. *Farm Journal* 40 (March): 38.

Farmers' Victory in Loan Law. 1916. *The Orange Judd Weekly Farmer* 8 (July): 4.

Farm Mortgage Reform Is Here. 1916. *The Orange Judd Weekly Farmer* 3 (June): 5.

Federal-State Market News Service. 1972. *Marketing California Strawberries, 1967–71.* San Francisco: U.S. and California Departments of Agriculture.

Ferguson, James. 1990. *The Anti-Politics Machine: Development, Depoliticization, and Bureaucratic Power in Lesotho.* Cambridge: Cambridge University Press.

Finegold, Kenneth and Theda Skocpol. 1995. *State and Party in America's New Deal.* Madison: University of Wisconsin Press.

Fisher, Lloyd H. 1953. *The Harvest Labor Market in California.* Cambridge, Mass.: Harvard University Press.

Fitchen, Janet. 1991. *Endangered Spaces, Enduring Places: Change, Identity, and Survival in Rural America.* Boulder, Colo.: Westview Press.

Fitzgerald, Deborah. 1996. Blinded by Technology: American Agriculture in the Soviet Union, 1928–1932. *Agricultural History* 70 (3): 459–86.

———. 2001. Accounting for Change: Modernity and Agriculture. In *The Countryside in the Age of the Modern State: Political Histories of Rural America*, ed. Catherine McNicol Stock and Robert Johnston, 189–212. Ithaca, N.Y.: Cornell University Press.

———. 2002. *Yeoman No More: The Industrialization of American Agriculture.* New Haven, Conn.: Yale University Press.

Flamming, Douglas. 1992. *Creating the Modern South: Millhands and Managers in Dalton, Georgia 1884–1984*. Chapel Hill: University of North Carolina Press.

Flora, Jan L. and John M. Stitz. 1985. Ethnicity, Persistence, and Capitalization of Agriculture in the Great Plains During the Settlement Period: Wheat Production and Risk Avoidance. *Rural Sociology* 50 (3): 341–60.

Foner, Eric. 1988. *Reconstruction: America's Unfinished Revolution*. New York: Harper and Row.

Food First/Institute for Food & Development Policy. 1999. Website. http://www.foodfirst.org. Last revised: October 18. Retrieved November 20.

Forbes. 1998. Murphy Family Farms. Forbes 1997 Top 500 Private Companies. Retrieved January 15, 1999, from: http://forbes.com/tool/toolbox/private500/1997/5383.htm.

Foundation on Economic Trends. 1999. Biotechcentury.org: A Project of the Foundation on Economic Trends. Retrieved November 20 from: http://www.biotechcentury.org/.

Fowke, Vernon Clifford. 1946. *Canadian Agricultural Policy : The Historical Pattern*. Toronto: University of Toronto Press.

———. 1957. *The National Policy and the Wheat Economy*. Toronto: University of Toronto Press.

Fowler, Cary and Pat Mooney. 1990. *Shattering: Food, Politics, and the Loss of Genetic Diversity*. Tucson: University of Arizona Press.

Fradkin, Philip L. 1981. *A River No More: The Colorado River and the West*. New York: Alfred A. Knopf.

Freese, Betsy. 1994. Fed Up with the Big Boys. *Successful Farming* 18–20.

French, A. L. 1913. Is the Farmer Entitled to Easier Money? *The Progressive Farmer* 28 (January 11): 35.

Freudenberger, C. 1986. Value and Ethical Dimensions of Alternative Agricultural Approaches. In *New Directions for Agriculture and Agricultural Research*, ed. K. Dahlberg, 348–64. Totowa, N.J.: Rowman and Allanheld.

Friedberger, Mark. 1993. Women Advocates in the Iowa Farm Crisis of the 1980s. *Agricultural History* 67 (Spring): 224–34.

Friedland, William H. 1984. Commodity Systems Analysis: An Approach to the Sociology of Agriculture. In *Research in Rural Sociology and Development: A Research Annual*, ed. Harry K. Schwarzweller, 221–35. Greenwich, Conn.: JAI Press.

———. 1991a. Introduction. In *Towards a New Political Economy of Agriculture*, ed. William H. Friedland, Lawrence Busch, Frederick H. Buttel, and Alan P. Rudy, 1–34. Boulder, Colo.: Westview Press.

———. 1991b. The Transnationalization of Agricultural Production: Palimpsest of the Transnational State. *International Journal of Sociology of Agriculture and Food* 1: 48–58.

———. 1994a. Fordism, Post-Fordism, Mass Production, and Flexible Specialization: Whatever Is Going On in the World. Paper presented at the seminar Restructuring the Food System: Global Processes and National Responses, May 15–18, Center for Rural Research, University of Trondheim, Norway.

———. 1994b. The New Globalization: The Case of Fresh Produce. In *From Columbus to ConAgra: The Globalization of Agriculture and Food*, ed. A. Bonanno, L. Busch, W. H. Friedland, L. Gouveia, and E. Mingione, 210–31. Lawrence: University Press of Kansas.

———. 1995. Globalization, Fordism-Postfordism, Agricultural Exceptionalism: The Need for Conceptual Clarity. Paper presented at the workshop

The Political Economy of the Agro-Food System in Advanced Industrial Countries, University of California, Berkeley.

Friedland, William H., Lawrence Busch, Frederick H. Buttel, and Alan P. Rudy, eds. 1991. *Toward a New Political Economy of Agriculture*. Boulder, Colo.: Westview Press.

Friedmann, Harriet. 1978. Simple Commodity Production and Wage Labour in the American Plains. *Journal of Peasant Studies* 6: 70–100.

———. 1980. Household Production and the National Economy: Concepts for the Analysis of Agrarian Formations. *Journal of Peasant Studies* 7 (2): 158–84.

———. 1986. Patriarchy and Property: A Reply to Goodman and Redclift. *Sociologia Ruralis* 26(2): 186–93.

———. 1991. New Wines, New Bottles: The Regulation of Capital on a World Scale. *Studies in Political Economy* 36: 19–42.

———. 1992. Distance and Durability: Shaky Foundations of the World Food Economy. *Third World Quarterly* 13: 371–83.

———. 1993a. After Midas's Feast: Alternative Food Regimes for the Future. In *Food for the Future: Conditions and Contradictions of Sustainability*, ed. Patricia Allen, 213–33. New York: Wiley.

———. 1993b. The Political Economy of Food: A Global Crisis. *New Left Review* issue 197: 29–57.

———. 1999. Circles of Growing and Eating. In *Food in Global History*, ed. Raymond Grew, 33–57. Boulder Colo.: Westview Press.

Friedmann, Harriet and Philip McMichael. 1989. Agriculture and the State System. *Sociologia Ruralis* 29 (2): 93–117.

Friends of the Earth. 1999. Friends of the Earth: Environmental Advocates since 1969. Retrieved November 20 from: http://www.foe.org/.

Fuller, Varden. 1991. *Hired Hands in California's Farm Fields: Collected Essays on California's Farm Labor History and Policy*. Berkeley: University of California, Agriculture and Natural Resources Publications.

Galarza, Ernesto. 1956. *Strangers in Our Fields*. Washington, D.C.: U.S. Section Joint United States–Mexico Trade Union Committee.

———. 1964. *Merchants of Labor: The Mexican Bracero Story: An Account of the Managed Migration of Mexican Farm Workers in California, 1942–1960*. Santa Barbara, Calif.: McNally and Loftin West.

———. 1977. *Farm Workers and Agri-business in California, 1947–1960*. Notre Dame, Ind.: University of Notre Dame Press.

Galbraith, John Kenneth. 1987. *Economics in Perspective*. Boston: Houghton Mifflin.

Gallagher, John. 1983. *To Kill the Crow*. Moose Jaw, Sask.: Challenge Publishers.

Galston, William A. 1985. *A Tough Row to Hoe: The 1985 Farm Bill and Beyond*. Washington, D.C.: Hamilton Press.

Gamson, William A. 1992. *Talking Politics*. New York: Cambridge University Press.

Ganey, Terry. 1994. Corporate Farm Got Special Help from Legislature. *St. Louis Post Dispatch* February 6: 4.

Germany's Success with Cooperative Banks. 1912. *The Prairie Farmer* 84 (January 1): 7.

Gertler, M. 1992. The Social Economy of Agricultural Sustainability. In *Rural Sociology in Canada*, ed. David A. Hay and G. S. Basran, 173–88. Toronto: Oxford University Press.

Gertler, M. and T. Murphy. 1987. The Social Economy of Canadian Agriculture: Family Farming and Alternative Futures. In *Family Farming in Europe and America*. ed. B. Galeski and E. Wilkening, 239–70. Boulder, Colo.: Westview Press.

Ghorayshi, Parvin. 1986. The Identification of Capitalist Farms. *Sociologia Ruralis* 26 (2): 46–159.

Giddens, Anthony. 1979. *Central Problems in Social Theory*. London: Macmillan.

———. 1987. *Social Theory and Modern Sociology*. Palo Alto, Calif.: Stanford University Press.

———. 1994. *Beyond Left and Right: The Future of Radical Politics*. Palo Alto, Calif.: Stanford University Press.

Gilbert, Jess. 1996. Democratic Planning in Agricultural Policy: The Federal-County Land-Use Planning Program, 1938–1942. *Agricultural History* 70 (2): 233–50.

———. 1997. A Usable Past: New Dealers Henry A. Wallace and M. L. Wilson Reclaim the American Agrarian Tradition. In *Rationality and the Liberal Spirit: A Festschrift Honoring Lee Morgan*, ed. Department of English at Centenary College, 134–42. Shreveport, La.: Centenary College.

———. 2000a. Eastern Urban Liberals and Midwestern Agrarian Intellectuals: Two Group Portraits of Progressives in the New Deal Department of Agriculture. *Agricultural History* 74 (2): 162–80.

———. 2000b. New Dealer Rexford G. Tugwell's Radical Planning Vision: "High-Modernist"—and Democratic? Paper presented at the annual meeting of the Rural Sociological Society, Washington, D.C.

———. 2001. Agrarian Intellectuals in a Democratizing State: A Collective Biography of USDA Leaders in the Intended New Deal. In *The Countryside in the Age of the Modern State: Political Histories of Rural America*, ed. Catherine McNicol Stock and Robert Johnston, 213–39. Ithaca, N.Y.: Cornell University Press.

Gilbert, Jess and Carolyn Howe. 1991. Beyond "State vs. Society": Theories of the State and New Deal Agricultural Policies. *American Sociological Review* 56 (April): 204–20.

Give It a Chance. 1916. *National Grange Monthly* 13 (September): 14.

Gjerde, Jon. 1997. *The Minds of the West: Ethnocultural Evolution in the Rural Middle West, 1830–1910*. Chapel Hill: University of North Carolina Press.

Goering, Peter, Helena Norberg-Hodge, and John Page. 1993. *From the Ground Up: Rethinking Industrial Agriculture*. London: Zed Books.

Goffman, Erving. 1974. *Frame Analysis: An Essay on the Organization of Experience*. Cambridge, Mass.: Harvard University Press.

Goland, Carol. 2000. Local Food Systems, Community Supported Agriculture, and Diet. Paper presented at the conference The Role of Culture in the Agriculture of the Twenty-first Century sponsored by the Culture and Agriculture section of the American Anthropological Association, February 25–26, Antonio, Tex.

Goldschmidt, Walter. 1978 [1947]. *As You Sow: Three Studies in the Social Consequences of Agribusiness*. Montclair, N.J.: Allanheld, Osmun.

Goodale, Ralph. 1993. Report on Agricultural Ministers Conference, July 5–7. Charlottetown, P.E.I.

———. 1994. Future Direction for Canadian Agriculture and Agri-food. Speech to the House and Senate Standing Committee on Agriculture, Ottawa, September 29.

Goodman, David and M. Redclift. 1991. *Refashioning Nature: Food, Ecology and Culture.* New York: Routledge.

Goodman, David, Bernardo Sorj, and John Wilkinson. 1987. *From Farming to Biotechnology.* Oxford: Blackwell.

Goodman, David and Michael J. Watts. 1994. Reconfiguring the Rural or Fording the Divide? Capitalist Restructuring and the Global Agro-food System. *The Journal of Peasant Studies* 22 (1): 1–49.

Goodman, David and Michael. J. Watts, eds. 1997. *Globalizing Food: Agrarian Questions and Global Restructuring.* London: Routledge.

Goodwyn, Lawrence. 1978. *The Populist Movement: A Short History of the Agrarian Revolt in America.* New York: Oxford University Press.

Gordon, Avery. 1997. *Ghostly Matters: Haunting and the Sociological Imagination.* Minneapolis: University of Minnesota Press.

Gottlieb, Robert and Margaret FitzSimmons. 1991. *Thirst for Growth: Water Agencies as Hidden Government in California.* Tucson: University of Arizona Press.

Gouveia, Lourdes. 1994. Global Strategies and Local Linkages: The Case of the U.S. Meatpacking Industry. In *From Columbus to ConAgra: The Globalization of Agriculture and Food,* ed. A. Bonanno, L. Busch, W. H. Friedland, L. Gouveia, and E. Mingione, 125–48. Lawrence: University Press of Kansas.

Graham, Otis L., Jr. 1985. The New Deal. In *Franklin D. Roosevelt: His Life and Times,* ed. O. L. Graham and Meghan Robinson Wander, 285–91. Boston: Da Capo Press.

Gramsci, Antonio. 1971. *Selections from the Prison Notebooks.* New York: International Publishers.

Grant, George. 1965. *Lament a Nation.* Toronto: McClelland & Stewart.

Gray, James. 1977. *The American Civil Liberties Union of Southern California and Imperial Valley Agricultural Labor Disturbances: 1930, 1934.* San Francisco: R&E Research Associates.

Green Guide. 1999. Take These Simple Actions Today! Green Guide 68 (June). Retrieved from: http://www.mothers.org/action/index.html.

Greenpeace. 1999. Genetically Engineered Food: Who Is in Control? Retrieved November 22 from: http://www.greenpeace.org/.

Greider, William. 1987. *Secrets of the Temple.* New York: Simon & Schuster.

Grey, Mark A., ed. 2000. Food Power: Case Studies in Industrial Agricultural and Its Alternatives in the United States. *Human Organization* 59 (2): 143–208.

Groh, Trauger and Steven McFadden. 1997. *Farms of Tomorrow Revisited: Community Supported Farms—Farm Supported Communities.* Kimberton, Pa.: Bio-Dynamic Farming and Gardening Association.

Grossfield, Stan. 1998. Animal Waste Emerging as U.S. Problem. *The Boston Globe* September 21: A1.

Guijt, Irene and Meera Kaul Shah. 1998. *The Myth of Community: Gender Issues in Participatory Development.* London: Intermediate Technology Publications.

Guardian. 1999. Biotech Industry Attacked. October 13. Retrieved May 25, 2002, from: http://www.guardian.co.uk/Archive/Article/0,4273,3911770,00 .html

Gussow, Joan Dye and Katherine L. Clancy. 1986. Dietary Guidelines for Sustainability. *Journal of Nutrition Education* 18 (1): 1–5.

Habermas, Jurgen. 1975. *Legitimation Crisis.* Boston: Beacon Press.

Hall, Alan. 1998a. Pesticide Reforms and Globalization: Making the Farmers Responsible. *Canadian Journal of Law and Society* 13 (1): 187–213.

————. 1998b. Sustainable Agriculture and Conservation Tillage: Managing the Contradictions. *Canadian Review of Sociology and Anthropology* 35 (2): 221–52.

Hall, Alan and V. Mogyorody. 2001. Organic Farmers in Ontario: An Examination of the Conventionalization Argument. *Sociologia Ruralis* 41 (4): 399–422.

Hallberg, G. 1988. Agricultural Chemicals in Ground Water: Extent and Implications. *American Journal of Alternative Agriculture* 2 (1): 3–15.

Hansen, P. and A. Muszynski. 1990. Crisis in Rural Life and Crisis in Thinking Directions for Critical Research. *Canadian Review of Sociology and Anthropology* 27 (1): 1–22.

Hardin, Charles M. 1946. The Bureau of Agricultural Economics Under Fire: A Study in Valuation Conflicts. *Journal of Farm Economics* 28 (August): 635–68.

Harl, Neil E. 1990. *The Farm Debt Crisis of the 1980s.* Ames: Iowa State University Press.

Harrison, Bennett. 1994. *Lean and Mean: The Changing Landscape of Corporate Power in the Age of Flexibility.* New York: Basic Books.

Hartsock, Nancy C. M. 1987. The Feminist Standpoint: Developing the Ground for a Specifically Feminist Historical Materialism. In *Feminism and Methodology,* ed. Sandra Harding, 157–80. Bloomington: Indiana University Press.

Harvey, David. 1989. *The Condition of Post-Modernity.* Cambridge, Mass.: Basil Blackwell.

Hedley, M. 1985. Mutual Aid Between Farm Households: New Zealand and Canada. *Sociologia Ruralis* 25 (1): 26–39.

Heffernan, William. 1999a. Consolidation in the Food and Agriculture System: A Report to the National Farmers Union. Retrieved February 5 from: http://www.nfu.org/whstudy.html.

————. 1999b. Societal Concerns Raised by CAFOs. Retrieved from: http://ctic.purdue.edu/Core4/ManureMgmt/Paper85/html.

————. 2000. Concentration of Ownership and Control in Agriculture. In *Hungry for Profit: The Agribusiness Threat to Farmers, Food, and the Environment,* ed. F. Magdoff, J. B. Foster, and F. H. Buttel, 61–75. New York: Monthly Review Press.

Heffernan, William D. and Douglas H. Constance. 1994. Transnational Corporations and the Global Food System. In *From Columbus to ConAgra: The Globalization of Agriculture and Food,* ed. A. Bonanno, L. Busch, W. H. Friedland, L. Gouveia, and E. Mingioine, 29–51. Lawrence: University Press of Kansas.

Heilbroner, Robert. 1968. *The Making of Economic Society.* Englewood Cliffs, N.J.: Prentice Hall.

————. 1992. *Twenty-First Century Capitalism.* Concord, Ont.: Anansi.

Henderson, Elizabeth. 1996. Nurturing a Core Group. In *CSA Farm Network,* ed. Steve Gilman, 27–29. Stillwater, N.Y.: Northeast Organic Farming Association.

Henderson, Elizabeth with Robyn Van En. 1999. *Sharing the Harvest: A Guide to Community Supported Agriculture.* White River Junction, Vt.: Chelsea Green.

Hendrickson, Mary and Kenneth Pigg. 1998. The Limits to Neighborliness: CAFO Controversy in Missouri. Paper presented at the annual meeting of the Rural Sociological Society, Portland, Ore.

Herrick, Myron T. 1912. Banks for the Farmer. *Moody's Magazine* 14 (September): 185–89.

————. 1913. The Farmer and Finance. *Atlantic Monthly* 111 (February): 170–78.

————. 1916. Some Objections to the Federal Farm Loan Act. *North American Review* 204 (December): 837.

High Interest Rates. 1915. *The Prairie Farmer* 87 (October 23): 10.

Hinkle, M. 1983. Problems with Conservation Tillage. *Journal of Soil and Water Conservation* 38 (May–June): 201–6.

Hinrichs, Clare G. 2000. Embeddedness and Local Food Systems: Notes on Two Types of Direct Agricultural Market. *Journal of Rural Studies* 16(3): 295–303.

Hinrichs, Clare and Kathy Kramer. 1998. The Challenge of Class for Community Supported Agriculture: Insights from Iowa. Unpublished paper, Department of Sociology, Iowa State University, Ames.

Hoag, G. W. 1976. *The Farm Credit System: A History of Financial Self-Help.* Danville, Ill.: Interstate Printers.

Hobson, A. 1931. *The International Institute of Agriculture: An Historical and Critical Analysis of Its Organization, Activities, and Policies of Administration.* Berkeley: University of California Press.

Hofstadter, Richard. 1955. *The Age of Reform: From Bryan to F.D.R.* New York: Alfred A. Knopf.

Holley, Donald. 1975. *Uncle Sam's Farmers: The New Deal Communities in the Lower Mississippi Valley.* Urbana: University of Illinois Press.

Hollis, Henry F. 1916. *Rural Credits: Report of the Joint Committee on Rural Credits.* 64th Congress, 1st sess. H.R. 494. Washington, D.C.: Government Printing Office.

Holtcamp, Janice, David O'Gorman, and Daniel Otto. 1994. Community Perceptions of Water Quality Impacts from Large-Scale Hog Confinements. Staff Paper No. 261. Iowa State University.

Hornberger, R. 1994. Facing Up to the Future: Diversification and Management Skills Will Help Family Farms Survive Well into the Future. *Windsor Star* February 26: E1.

Hough, K. 1994. Premium Value Corn Markets. *Ontario Corn Producer, Special Issue.* 9(9): 4–6.

House of Commons. Debates. 1880. Parliament of Canada. July 15.

————. Debates. 1886. Parliament of Canada. April 30.

————. Debates. 1939. Parliament of Canada. January 12.

Hu, Winnie. 2000. Paying to Keep Farmers Down on the Farm. *New York Times* July 21: A15.

Humane Society U.S.A. 1999. Website. http://www.hsus.org/. Retrieved November 20.

Hundley, Norris. 1975. *Water and the West: The Colorado River Compact and the Politics of Water in the American West.* Berkeley: University of California Press.

Hunt, E. K. 1990. *Property and Prophets.* Grand Rapids, Mich.: Harper and Row.

Hurt, R. Douglas, ed. 1996. Special Issue on Twentieth-Century Farm Policies. *Agricultural History* 70 (2).

Ikerd, John. 1998. Sustainable Agriculture: An Alternative Model for Future Pork Producers. In *The Industrialization of Agriculture: Vertical Coordination in the U.S. Food System,* ed. Jeffrey S. Royer and Richard T. Rogers, 265–94. Brookfield, Vt.: Ashgate.

Imperial County Community Economic Development Department. 1993.

Overall Economic Development Program. El Centro, Calif.: Imperial County Community Economic Development Commission.

Industrial Planning Associates. 1957. *Industrial Potentials of Imperial County: A Survey Prepared for the Board of Trade of Imperial County, California.* San Francisco: Industrial Planning Associates.

Innis, Harold A. 1930. *The Fur Trade in Canada: An Introduction to Canadian Economic History.* Toronto: University of Toronto Press.

———. 1940. *The Cod Fisheries: The History of an International Economy.* Toronto: University of Toronto Press.

———. 1950. *Empire and Communications.* Oxford: Clarendon Press.

Innovative Farmers of Ontario. 1994. Everything You Need to Know About E Plus: Farming for Economic Efficiency and Environmental Excellence. Pamphlet.

Institute for Agriculture and Trade Policy. 1999. Website. http://www.iatp.org/. Retrieved November 20.

Interest Bug and the Farmer, The. 1914. *Progressive Farmer* 29 (August 29): 11.

International Center for Technology Assessment. 1999. Website. http://www.icta.org. Retrieved November 20.

International Forum on Food and Agriculture. 1999. Website. http://www.iffa.org/. Retrieved November 20.

International Forum on Globalization. 1999. Website. http://www.ifg.org/. Retrieved November 20.

International Society for Ecology and Culture. 1999. Working on Three Continents to Promote Ecological Regeneration, Community Renewal, and Economic Localisation. Retrieved December 1 from: http://www.isec.org.uk/ISEC/core.html.

Isaac, Larry W. and Larry J. Griffin. 1989. Ahistoricism in Time-Series Analyses of Historical Process: Critique, Redirection, and Illustrations from U.S. Labor History. *American Sociological Review* 54 (6): 873–90.

Jackson, Dana. 1984. The Sustainable Garden, In *Meeting the Expectations of the Land,* ed. W. Jackson, W. Berry, and B. Colman, 106–14. San Francisco: North Point Press.

Jackson, Wes. 1996. *Becoming Native to This Place.* Washington, D.C.: Counterpoint.

———. 1997. Call for a Revolution in Agriculture. In *People, Land, and Community,* ed. Hildegarde Hannum, 250–64. New Haven, Conn.: Yale University Press.

Jackson, Wes and Marty Bender. 1984. Investigations into Perennial Polyculture. In *Meeting the Expectations of the Land,* ed. W. Jackson, W. Berry, and B. Colman, 183–94. San Francisco: North Point Press.

Jackson, Wes, Wendell Berry, and Bruce Colman. 1984. *Meeting the Expectations of the Land.* San Francisco: North Point Press.

Jacobson, Michael, Lisa Y. Lefferts, and Anne Witte Garland. 1991. *Safe Food: Eating Wisely in a Risky World.* Los Angeles: Living Planet Press.

James, S. C. 1995. Fall Building a Democratic Majority: The Progressive Party Vote and the Federal Trade Commission. *Studies in American Political Development* 9: 173–213.

Jeffrey, J. W. 1912. New Economic Movement. *California Cultivator* September 12: 250.

Jellison, Katherine. 1993. *Entitled to Power: Farm Women and Technology, 1913–1963.* Chapel Hill: University of North Carolina Press.

Jenkins, Craig. 1985. *The Politics of Insurgency: The Farm Worker Movement in the 1960s*. New York: Columbia University Press.

Jereski, Laura and Randall Smith. 1996. Hog-Tied Wall Street Merchant Banking Firm Wallowing in Pig Farm Losses. *St. Louis Post Dispatch* May 23: C8.

Johnson, Charles S., Edwin R. Embree, and W.W. Alexander. 1935. *The Collapse of Cotton Tenancy: Summary of Field Studies and Statistical Surveys, 1933–1935*. Chapel Hill: University of North Carolina Press.

Johnson, Cheryl D. 1990. Historical Look at Farm Income. *Statistical Bulletin No. 807*, May. Washington, D.C.: USDA.

Johnson, Darra. 1997. Representative of Murphy Family Farms. Personal communication, January 9.

Johnson, G. 1991. Improving Policy Instruments for Sustainability—Rapporteur's Report. *Canadian Journal of Agricultural Economics* 39: 656–66.

Johnson, W. M. 1914. Cheaper Money—Some Things It Would and Wouldn't Do. *The National Stockman and Farmer* 37 (February 7): 5.

Jolly, Robert W., Arnold Paulsen, James D. Johnson, Kenneth Baum, and Richard Prescott. 1986. Incidence, Intensity, and Duration of Financial Stress Among Farm Firms. *American Journal of Agricultural Economics* 67 (5): 1108–15.

Jones, Arnita A. and Wayne D. Rasmussen. 1992. Wayne Rasmussen and the Development of Policy History at the United States Department of Agriculture. *The Public Historian* 14 (Winter): 19–21.

Joplin, Benjamin A. 1998. Can Townships Really Smell? Coping with the Malodorous Problems of Hog Farms in Rural Missouri. *Missouri Environmental Law and Policy Review* 5: 83–92.

Kane, Deborah J. 1996. *Maximizing Shareholder Retention in Southeastern C.S.A.s: A Step Toward Long Term Stability*. Athens: University of Georgia.

Kane, Deborah and Luanne Lohr. 1998. The Dangers of Space Turnips and Blind Dates: Bridging the Gap Between CSA Shareholder's Expectations and Reality. In *CSA Farm Network, Vol. II*, ed. Steve Gilman, 22–25. Stillwater, N.Y.: Northeast Organic Farming Association.

Karl, Barry D. 1983. *The Uneasy State: The United States from 1915 to 1945*. Chicago: University of Chicago Press.

Kautsky, John. 1982. *The Politics of Aristocratic Empires*. Chapel Hill: University of North Carolina Press.

Kemmis, Daniel. 1990. *Community and the Politics of Place*. Norman: University of Oklahoma Press.

———. 1996. Barn Raising. In *Rooted In the Land: Essays on Community and Place*, ed. W. Vitek and W. Jackson, 167–75. New Haven, Conn.: Yale University Press.

Kennan, George. 1922. *E. H. Harriman: A Biography*. Boston: Houghton Mifflin.

Kenney, M., L. M. Labao, J. Curry and W. R. Goe. 1991. Agriculture in U.S. Fordism: The Integration of the Productive Consumer. In *Towards a New Political Economy of Agriculture*, ed. W. H. Friedland, L. Busch, F. H. Buttel, and A. P. Rudy, 174–84. Boulder, Colo.: Westview Press.

Key, V. O. 1946. *Southern Politics*. New York: Alfred A. Knopf.

Kilman, Scott. 1994. Power Pork: Corporations Begin to Turn Hog Business Into an Assembly Line. *Wall Street Journal* March 28: A1, A5.

Kirkendall, Richard S. 1982 [1966]. *Social Scientists and Farm Politics in the Age of Roosevelt*. Ames: Iowa State University Press.

Kittredge, Jack. 1996. Community Supported Agriculture: Rediscovering

Community. In *Rooted in the Land: Essays on Community and Place*, ed. W. Vitek and W. Jackson, 253–60. New Haven, Conn.: Yale University Press.

Kleiner, Anna M. and Douglas H. Constance. 1998a. Circling the Wagons: The Westward Expansion of Pork Production in Support of Circle Four. Paper presented at the annual meeting of the Rural Sociological Society, Portland, Ore.

———. 1998b. Pork, Power, and Populist Response: The Environmental Issues Surrounding the Industrialization of the Pork Industry in Missouri. Paper presented at the Seventh International Symposium on Society and Resource Management, Columbia, Mo.

Kloppenburg, Jack Ralph, Jr. 1988. *First the Seed: The Political Economy of Plant Biotechnology, 1492–2000*. Cambridge: Cambridge University Press.

———. 1991. Social Theory and the De/Reconstruction of Agricultural Science: Local Knowledge for an Alternative Agriculture. *Rural Sociology* 56 (4): 519–48.

Knapp, S. A. 1910. Help for Men to Become Independent Farmers *The World's Work* 20 (May): 12888–89.

Kneen, Brewster. 1993. *From Land to Mouth: Understanding the Food System*. 2nd ed. Toronto: N. C. Press.

———. 1999. *Farmageddon: Food and the Culture of Biotechnology*. Gabriola Island, B.C.: New Society Publishers.

Knuttila, Murray and Wendee Kubik. 2001. *State Theories: Classical, Global and Feminist Perspectives*. 3rd ed. Halifax, N.S.: Fernwood Publishing.

Kramer, Carol S. 1991. Health Risks as a Cost and Driving Force in Public Food Policy Decisions. In *Understanding the True Cost of Food: Considerations for a Sustainable Food System*. Proceedings of Eighth Annual Scientific Symposium, March, 14–27. Washington, D.C.: Institute for Alternative Agriculture.

Krebs, A. V. 1992. *The Corporate Reapers: The Book of Agribusiness*. Washington, D.C.: Essential Books.

Krimsky, Sheldon and Roger Wrubel. 1996. *Agricultural Biotechnology and the Environment: Science, Policy, Social Issues*. Urbana: University of Illinois Press.

Kusnetzky, Lara, Jeffrey Longhofer, Jerry Floersch, and Kristine Latta. 1994. In Search of the Climax Community: Sustainability and the Old Order Amish. *Culture and Agriculture Bulletin* 50: 12–14.

Lachman, David. 1991. Democratic Ideology and Agricultural Policy: "Program Study and Discussion" in the U.S. Department of Agriculture, 1934–1946. M.S. thesis, University of Wisconsin, Madison.

LaFeber, Walter. 1963. *The New Empire: An Interpretation of American Expansion, 1860–1898*. Ithaca, N.Y.: Cornell University Press.

Lakoff, George and Mark Johnson. 1980. *Metaphors We Live By*. Chicago: University of Chicago Press.

Lamb, Gary. 1996. Community Supported Agriculture: Can It Be the Basis for a New Associative Economy? In *CSA Farm Network*, ed. Steve Gilman, 12–19. Stillwater, N.Y.: Northeast Organic Farming Association.

Langdale, G., R. Leonard, and A. Thomas. 1985. Conservation Practice Effects on Phosphorus Losses from Southern Piedmont Watersheds. *Journal of Soil and Water Conservation* 40 (January–February): 157–61.

Lappé, Marc and Britt Bailey. 1998. *Against the Grain: Biotechnology and the Corporate Takeover of Your Food*. Monroe, Me.: Common Courage Press.

Larson, Olaf F., Edward O. Moe, and Julie N. Zimmerman. 1992. *Sociology in Government: A Bibliography of the Work of the Division of Farm Population and*

Rural Life, U.S. Department of Agriculture, 1919–1952. Boulder, Colo.: Westview Press.

Larson, Olaf F. and Julie N. Zimmerman, with Edward O. Moe. Forthcoming. *Sociology in Government: The Galpin-Taylor Years in the U.S. Department of Agriculture, 1919–1953*. Boulder, Colo.: Westview Press.

Lash, Scott. 1994. Expert Systems or Situated Interpretation? Culture and Institutions in Disorganized Capitalism. In *Reflexive Modernization: Politics, Tradition, and Aesthetics in the Modern Social Order*, by Ulrich Beck, Anthony Giddens, and Scott Lash, 198–215. Cambridge: Polity Press.

Lash, Scott and John Urry. 1994. *Economies of Signs and Space*. London: Sage Publications.

Lawrence, Geoffrey. 1987. *Capitalism and the Countryside*. Sydney: Pluto Press.

Laycock, David. 1990. *Populism and Democratic Thought in the Canadian Prairies, 1910 to 1945*. Toronto: University of Toronto Press.

Lazarus-Black, Mindy and Susan F. Hirsch. 1994. Performance and Paradox: Exploring Law's Role in Hegemony and Resistance. In *Contested States: Law, Hegemony, and Resistance,* ed. M. Lazarus-Black and S. Hirsch, 1–31. New York: Routledge.

Leakey, Richard and Roger Lewin. 1995. *The Sixth Extinction: Patterns of Life and the Future of Humankind*. New York: Doubleday.

Leeds, Hill, Barnard, and Jewett Consulting Engineers. 1943. Survey of Conditions in Imperial Irrigation District, May 3, 1943. Los Angeles.

Leopold, Aldo. 1999. *For the Health of the Land: Previously Unpublished Essays and Other Writings,* ed. J. Baird Callicott and Eric T. Freyfogle. Washington D.C.: Island Press.

Levitt, Kari. 1970. *Silent Surrender*. Toronto: Macmillian of Canada.

Lewis, David Levering. 1992. Introduction. In W. E. B. Du Bois, *Black Reconstruction in America*. New York: Atheneum.

Lewis, John D. 1941. Democratic Planning in Agriculture, I. *American Political Science Review* 35 (2): 232–49.

Lewis, Oscar. 1951. *Life in a Mexican Village: Tepoztlan Restudied*. Urbana: University of Illinois Press.

———. 1953. Tepoztlan Restudied: A Critique of the Folk-Urban Conceptualization of Change. *Rural Sociology* 18: 121–34.

Lewis, Sanford, Marco Kaltofen, and Gregory Ormsby. 1991. *Border Trouble: Rivers in Peril: A Report on Water Pollution Due to Industrial Development in Northern Mexico*. Boston: National Toxic Campaign Fund and National Toxics Campaign.

Lighthall, D. 1995. Farm Structure and Chemical Use in the Corn Belt. *Rural Sociology* 60 (3): 505–20.

Lind, C. 1995. *Something's Wrong Somewhere: Globalization, Community, and the Moral Economy of the Farm Crisis*. Halifax, N.S.: Fernwood Publishing.

Link, A. S. 1964. *Wilson: Confusions and Crises, 1915–1916*. Princeton, N.J.: Princeton University Press.

Lins, David A. and Marvin Duncan. 1980. Inflation Effects on Financial Performance and Structure of the Farm Sector. *American Journal of Agricultural Economics* 62 (December): 1051.

Lipietz, Alain. 1987. *Mirages and Miracles*. London: New Left Books.

———. 1992a. The Globalization of the General Crisis of Fordism. In *Frontyard Backyard: The Americas in the Global Crisis,* ed. J. Holmes and Colin Leys, 23–56. Toronto: Between the Lines Press.

————. 1992b. A Regulationist Approach to the Future of Urban Ecology. *Capitalism, Nature, Socialism*, 3 (3): 101–10.

Lipset, S. M. 1971. *Agrarian Socialism*. 2nd ed. Berkeley: University of California Press.

Lockeretz, W. and S. Wernick. 1980. Commercial Organic Farming in the Corn Belt in Comparison to Conventional Practices. *Rural Sociology* 45 (4): 708–22.

Long, Norman and Ann Long, eds. 1992. *Battlefields of Knowledge: The Interlocking of Theory and Practice in Social Research and Development*. New York: Routledge.

Loomis, Charles P. and Douglas Ensminger. 1942. Governmental Administration and Informal Local Groups. *Applied Anthropology* 1 (2): 41–59.

Loomis, Charles P., Douglas Ensminger, and Jane Woolley. 1941. Neighborhoods and Communities in County Planning. *Rural Sociology* 6 (4): 339–41.

Lord, Russell. 1947. *The Wallaces of Iowa*. Boston: Houghton Mifflin Company.

Lovelock, James. 1991. *Healing Gaia: Practical Medicine for the Planet*. New York: Harmony Books.

Lowi, Theodore. 1979. *The End of Liberalism*. 2nd ed. New York: W. W. Norton.

Lyle, John Tillman.1994. *Regenerative Design for Sustainable Development*. New York: Wiley.

Lyson, Thomas A. and Annalisa Lewis Raymer. 2000. Stalking the Wily Multinational: Power and Control in the U.S. Food System. *Agriculture and Human Values* 17 (2): 199–208.

MacGibbon, Duncan A. 1952. *The Canadian Grain Trade, 1931–1951*. Toronto: University of Toronto Press.

Mackirdy, Kenneth A., John S. Moir, and Yves F. Zoltvany. 1971. *Changing Perspectives in Canadian History*. Toronto: J. M. Dent and Sons.

Macpherson, C. D. 1953. *Democracy in Alberta: Social Credit and the Party System*. Toronto: University of Toronto Press.

Macrae, R., J. Henning, and S. Hill. 1993. Strategies to Overcome Barriers to the Development of Sustainable Agriculture in Canada: The Role of Agribusiness. *Journal of Agricultural and Environmental Ethics* 6 (1): 21–51.

Magdoff, Fred, John Bellamy Foster, and Frederick H. Buttel, eds. 2000. *Hungry for Profit: The Agribusiness Threat to Farmers, Food, and the Environment*. New York: Monthly Review Press.

Majka, Linda and Theo Majka. 1982. *Farm Workers, Agribusiness, and the State*. Philadelphia: Temple University Press.

Mander, Jerry. 1991. *In the Absence of the Sacred: The Failure of Technology and the Survival of the Indian Nations*. San Francisco: Sierra Club Books.

Mander, Jerry and Edward Goldsmith. 1996. *The Case Against the Global Economy and for a Turn Toward the Local*. San Francisco: Sierra Club Books.

Mann, Susan A. 1990. *Agrarian Capitalism in Theory and Practice*. Chapel Hill: University of North Carolina Press.

Mann, Susan and James Dickenson. 1978. Obstacles to the Development of a Capitalist Agriculture. *Journal of Peasant Studies* 5 (4): 466–81.

————. 1980. State and Agriculture in Two Eras of American Capitalism. In *The Rural Sociology of the Advanced Societies: Critical Perspectives*, ed. F. H. Buttel and H. Newby, 283–325. London: Allanheld, Osmun.

Manning, E. C. 1986. Planning Canada's Resource Base for Sustainable Production. In *Canadian Agriculture in a Global Context*, ed. I. Knell and J. English. Waterloo, Ont.: University of Waterloo Press.

Marbery, Steve. 1994a. Missouri Critics Contest Continental Swine Enterprise. *Feedstuffs* 66(18): 5, 9.

———. 1994b. Pork Production 2000: Fewer Farms Doing More. *Feedstuffs* 66 (9): 1, 30.

———. 1994c. PSF to Acquire National Farms of Texas. *Feedstuffs* 66 (16): 1,3.

———. 1998. Hog Industry Insider. *Feedstuffs* 70 (11): 30.

Marcus, Alan I. and Richard Lowitt, eds. 1990. Special Symposium Issue on the United States Department of Agriculture in Historical Perspective. *Agricultural History* 64 (2).

Margulis, Lynn. 1993. *Symbiosis in Cell Evolution*. 2nd ed. San Francisco: Freeman.

Marin, Mirabel. 1989. *Agribusiness and Its Workforce in the Imperial Valley: Case Study on Agricultural Relations Along the U.S.-Mexican Border*. Berkeley: California Institute for Rural Studies.

Marsden, Terry. 1992. Exploring Rural Sociology for the Fordist Transition. *Sociologia Ruralis* 32 (2/3): 209–30.

———. 1994. Globalization, the State, and the Environment: Exploring the Limits and Options of State Activity. *International Journal of Sociology of Agriculture and Food* 4: 139–57.

Marshall, Thomas Humphrey. 1965. *Class, Citizenship, and Social Development*. New York: Anchor Books.

Martin, Philip, Sarah Vaupel, and Daniel Egan. 1988. *Unfulfilled Promise: Collective Bargaining in California Agriculture*. Boulder, Colo.: Westview Press.

Marx, Karl. 1977 [1867]. *A Critical Analysis of Capitalist Production*. Vol. 1 of *Capital*. New York: International Publishers.

Marx, Leo. 1964. *The Machine in the Garden: Technology and the Pastoral Ideal in America*. London: Oxford University Press.

MASS (Missouri Agricultural Statistics Service). 1987. *Missouri Farm Facts* 47.

———. 1998. *Missouri Farm Facts* 50: 5.

Mauss, Marcel. 2000 [1927]. *The Gift: The Form and Reason for Exchange in Archaic Societies*. trans. W. D. Halls. New York: W. W. Norton.

McAdam, Doug, John D. McCarthy, and Mayer N. Zald, eds. 1996. *Comparative Perspectives on Social Movements: Political Opportunities, Mobilizing Structures, and Cultural Framings*. Cambridge: Cambridge University Press.

McCombs, Maxwell E. and Donald L. Shaw. 1972. The Agenda-Setting Function of Mass Media. *Public Opinion Quarterly* 36 (Summer): 176–85.

———. 1977. The Agenda-Setting Function of the Press. In *The Emergence of American Political Issues: The Agenda-Setting Function of the Press*, ed. D. L Shaw and M. E. McCombs, 1–31. St. Paul, Minn.: West.

McConnell, Grant. 1963. *The Decline of Agrarian Democracy*. Berkeley: University of California Press.

———. 1968. *Private Power and American Democracy*. New York: Alfred A. Knopf.

McCormack, Ross. 1977. *Reformers, Rebels, and Revolutionaries: The Western Canadian Radical Movement, 1899–1919*. Toronto: University of Toronto Press.

McCrorie, James N. 1964. *In Union Is Strength*. Saskatoon: Centre for Community Studies.

McDean, Harry C. 1969. M. L. Wilson and Agricultural Reform in Twentieth Century America. Ph.D. diss., University of California at Los Angeles.

McFadden, Stephen. 1999. Community Farming in the Twenty-first Century: Outside the Box, But Inside the Circle. Paper for the Fourth Biennial

Meeting of the North American Chapter International Farming Systems Association, Guelph, Ont.

McMahon, Karen. 1996. Newco Picks Up the Pieces. *National Hog Farmer* August 15: 10, 14, 19.

McMahon, Karen, Joe Vansickle, and Lora Duxbury-Berg. 1998. State of the Industry. *National Hog Farmer* May 15: 16–18, 20, 22, 23, 26, 30, 31, 34.

McMichael, Philip. 1994. Global Restructuring: Some Lines of Inquiry. In *The Global Restructuring of Agro-Food Systems*, ed. P. McMichael, 277–300. Ithaca, N.Y.: Cornell University Press.

———. 1996a. *Development and Social Change: A Global Perspective*. Thousand Oaks, Calif.: Pine Forge Press.

———. 1996b. Globalization: Myths and Realities. *Rural Sociology* 61 (1): 25–55.

———. 2000. *Development and Social Change, A Global Perspective*. 2nd ed. Thousand Oaks, Calif.: Pine Forge Press.

McMichael, Philip and David Myhre. 1991. Global Regulation vs. the Nation-State: Agro-Food Systems and the New Politics of Capital. *Capital and Class* 43: 83–106.

McMillan, MaryBe and Michael Schulman. 1998. Hogs and Citizens: Community Opposition to the Corporate Hog Industry in North Carolina. Paper presented at the annual meeting of the Rural Sociological Society, Portland, Ore.

Melichar, Emanuel. 1977. Some Current Aspects of Agricultural Finance and Banking in the United States. *American Journal of Agricultural Economics* 59 (December): 967–72.

———. 1979. Capital Gains Versus Current Income in the Farming Sector. *American Journal of Agricultural Economics* 61 (December): 1091.

Merrill, M. 1983. Eco-Agriculture: A Review of Its History and Philosophy. *Biological Agriculture and Horticulture* 1 (2): 181–210.

Mihalopoulos, Dan. 1995. Farmers Fight Corporate Farming. *Missouri Digital News*. May 9. Retrieved May 22 from: http://www.mdn.org/a995/stories/hogs2.htm.

Milani, Brian. 2001. *Designing the Green Economy*. Lanham, Md.: Rowman and Littlefield.

Milham, N. 1994. An Analysis of Farmers' Incentives to Conserve or Degrade the Land. *Journal of Environmental Management* 40 (1): 51–64.

Miller, Dale. 2000. Straight Talk from Smithfield's Luter. *National Hog Farmer* May 1.

Milliken, R. C. 1914. Objects of Rural Credit: A Few Examples. *Successful Farming* 13 (October): 20.

Mills, C. Wright. 1956. *The Power Elite*. New York: Oxford University Press.

Missouri House of Representatives. 1998. H.B.1580: Changes Designation of Certain Animal Feeding Operations. April 2. Retrieved September 8, 2000, from: http://www.house.state.mo.un/bills98/HB1580.htm.

Mitchell, Broadus. 1967. *Postscripts to Economic History*. Totowa, N.J.: Littlefield, Adams.

MOFFA (Michigan Organic Food and Farm Alliance). 1999. *The Many Faces of Community Supported Agriculture: a Guide to Community Supported Agriculture in Indiana, Michigan and Ohio*. Hartland: Michigan Organic Food and Farm Alliance.

Mollison, Bill. 1988. *Permaculture—A Designer's Manual*. Tyalgum, Australia: Tagari Publications.

Monsanto. 2000. Biotech Basics: The Life Sciences Knowledge Center. Revised 1999. Retrieved April 3 from: http://www.biotechknowledge.com/primeer/primer.html.

Montague, Peter, ed. 1990–2000. *Rachel's Environment & Health Weekly*. Annapolis, Md.: Environmental Research Foundation.

Mooney, Patrick H. 1986. The Political Economy of Credit in American Agriculture. *Rural Sociology* 51 (4): 449–70.

———. 1988. *My Own Boss? Class, Rationality, and the Family Farmer*. Boulder, Colo.: Westview Press.

Mooney, Patrick H. and Theo J. Majka. 1995. *Farmers' and Farm Workers' Movements: Social Protest in American Agriculture*. New York: Twayne Publishers.

Moreno, Mylène A. 1987. La Causa in Hard Times: The United Farm Workers, 1975–1985. Honors thesis, Harvard College.

Morris, A. 1966. Agricultural Labor and National Labor Legislation. *California Law Review* 54: 1939–89.

Morton, William L. 1950. *The Progressive Party in Canada*. Toronto: University of Toronto Press.

Mothers and Others for a Livable Planet. 1999. Website. http://www.mothers.org/. Retrieved December 28.

Mothers for Natural Law. 1999a. Companies and Brand Names for Non-GE items. Revised October 31. Retrieved November 20 from: http://www.safe-food.org/.

———. 1999b. Mothers for Natural Law of the Natural Law Party. Revised October 31. Retrieved November 20 from: http://www.safe-food.org/.

Mott, T. B. 1929. *Myron T. Herrick: Friend of France*. Garden City, N.Y.: Doubleday, Doran.

Murdock, Steve H. and F. Larry Leistritz, eds. 1988. *The Farm Financial Crisis: Socioeconomic Dimensions and Implications for Producers and Rural Areas*. Boulder, Colo.: Westview Press.

Myrick, H. 1917. *The Federal Farm Loan System*. New York: Orange Judd.

Nadeau, Remi A. 1974. *The Water Seekers*. Santa Barbara, Calif.: Peregrine Smith.

Naess, Arne. 1994. Deep Ecology. In *Ecology*, ed. Carolyn Merchant, 120–24. Atlantic Highlands, N.J.: Humanities Press.

Nash, June. 1989. *From Tank Town to High Tech: The Clash of Community and Industrial Cycles*. Albany: State University of New York Press.

National Conference of State Legislatures. 1999. Confined/Concentrated Animal Feeding Operation (CAFO) 1998 Legislation. Retrieved May 18 from: http://www.nclsl.org/programs/ESNR/98cafo.html.

National Family Farm Coalition. 2000. Fact Sheet on Genetic Engineering in Agriculture. Revised November 28, 1999. Retrieved April 3 from: http://www.inmotionmagazine.com/nfrel.html.

National Farmers Union. 1990. *National Farmers Union: A Sustainable Canadian Agriculture Policy*. Proposal resulting from a conference sponsored by the Catholic Rural Life Conference and the NFU, Stratford, Ont.

———. 1991. *Farm Policy for the 90s*. Annual Convention Policy Document. Edmonton, Alb.

———. 1992. *Food and Farming in the National Economy: Who Are the Real Beneficiaries?* Pamphlet. Saskatoon, Sask.

National Field, The. 1912. *Pacific Farmers Union* 4 (May 31): 1, 4, 5.

National Hog Farmer. 1998. An Industry Swirling in Controversy. May 15: cover page.

National Project, Schools on National Agriculture Policy and Philosophical Aspects of Contemporary Civilization. N.d. Draft. Washington, D.C.: National Archives, Record Group 83, Entry 32, Box 6.

National Research Council. 1989a. *Alternative Agriculture*. Committee on the Role of Alternative Farming Methods in Modern Production. Washington, D.C.: National Academy Press.

———. 1989b. *Lost Crops of the Incas*. Washington, D.C.: National Academy Press.

———. 1992. *Water Transfers in the West: Efficiency, Equity, and the Environment*. Water Science and Technology Board, Committee on Western Water Management. Washington, D.C.: National Academy Press.

Native Forest Council. 1999. NFC Files Lawsuit Against Forest Service and BLM. Retrieved November 20 from: http://www.forestcouncil.org/.

Native Forest Network Campaign. 1999. Website. http://www.nativeforest.org/. Retrieved November 20.

Neils Conzen, Kathleen. 1985. Peasant Pioneers: Generational Succession Among German Farmers in Frontier Minnesota. In *The Countryside in the Age of Capitalist Transformation: Essays in the Social History of Rural America*, ed. Steven Hahn and Jonathan Prude, 259–92. Chapel Hill: University of North Carolina Press.

New Credit System, The. 1916. *The National Stockman and Farmer* 39 (January 29): 1.

Newman, Katherine. 1985. Urban Anthropology and the Deindustrialization Paradigm. *Urban Anthropology* 14 (1–3): 5–19.

———. 1988. *Falling from Grace: The Experience of Downward Mobility in the American Middle Class*. New York: Free Press.

———. 1995. Deindustrialization, Poverty, and Downward Mobility: Toward an Anthropology of Economic Disorder. In *Diagnosing America: Anthropology and Public Engagement*, ed. S. Forman, 121–48. Ann Arbor: University of Michigan Press.

Niosi, Jorge. 1981. *Canadian Capitalism*. Toronto: James Lorimer.

Norberg-Hodge, Helena. 1991. *Ancient Futures: Learning from Ladakh*. San Francisco, CA: Sierra Club Books.

Norrie, Kenneth and Douglas Owram. 1991. *A History of the Canadian Economy*. Toronto: Harcourt Brace Jovanovich.

Nottingham, Stephen. 1998. *Eat Your Genes: How Genetically Modified Food is Entering Our Diet*. London: Zed Books.

O'Connor, James. 1973. *Fiscal Crisis of the State*. New York: St. Martin's Press.

———. 1988. Capitalism, Nature, Socialism: A Theoretical Introduction. *Capitalism Nature Socialism* 1: 11–38.

———. 1998. *Natural Causes: Essays in Ecological Marxism*. New York: Guilford Press.

Odum, Eugene P. 1989. *Ecology and Our Endangered Life-Support Systems*. Sunderland, Mass: Sinauer Associates.

OMAF (Ontario Ministry of Agriculture and Food). 1989. *Food Systems 2002: A Program to Reduce Pesticides in Food Production*. Toronto: Queen's Printer.

———. 1991. *Common Ground Update: The Strategic Plan for the Ontario Ministry of Agriculture and Food*. Toronto: Queen's Printer.

OMAF, AGCare, and OME (Ontario Ministry of Environment). 1993. Grower Pesticide Safety Course: Manual. Ridgetown, Ont.: Ridgetown College of Agricultural Technology.

Ontario Federation of Agriculture. 1994. OFA Brief to Ontario Cabinet: February 9. Toronto.

Organ, Jerome M. and Kristin M. Perry. 1997. Controlling Externalities Associated with Concentrated Animal Feeding Operations: Evaluating the Impact of H.B. 1207 and the Continuing Viability of Zoning and the Common Law of Nuisance. *Missouri Environmental Law & Policy Review* 3 (4): 183–99.

Organic Consumers Association. 1999. Website. http://www.organicconsumers .org/. Retrieved November 20.

Orr, David. 1992. *Ecological Literacy: Education and the Transition to a Postmodern World*. Albany: State University of New York Press.

Ostler, Jeffrey. 1995. The Rhetoric of Conspiracy and Formation of Kansas Populism. *Agricultural History* 69 (1): 1–22.

Ostrom, Marcia R. 1997. *Toward a Community Supported Agriculture: A Case Study of Resistance and Change in the Modern Food System*. Ph.D. diss., Institute for Environmental Studies, University of Wisconsin–Madison.

Our Credit Facilities. 1913. *The National Stockman and Farmer* 37 (December 13): 1.

Owenby, Ted. 1999. *American Dreams in Mississippi: Consumers, Poverty, and Culture, 1830–1998*. Chapel Hill: University of North Carolina Press.

Paarlberg, Don and Robert Paarlberg. 2000. Agricultural Policy in the Twentieth Century. *Agricultural History* 74 (Spring): 136–61.

Padgitt, Steve, Paul Lasley, and Sandra Trca-Black. 1998. Social System Response to Transformation in the Swine Industry: The Wright County, Iowa Experience. Paper presented at the annual meeting of the Rural Sociological Society, Portland, Ore.

Page, B. I. 1994. Undemocratic Responsiveness? Untangling Links Between Public Opinion and Policy. *PS: Political Science and Politics* 27 (March): 25–29.

Panitch, Leo. 1993. A Different Kind of State? In *A Different Kind of State? Popular Power and Democratic Administration*, ed. Gregory Albo, David Langille, and Leo Panitch, 2–16. Toronto: Oxford University Press.

Parenti, Michael. 1996. The Blessing of Private Enterprise: The Demise of a Family Bread Business Caused by Large Commercial Bakers. *Monthly Review* 48: 12–15.

Parks, Ellen Sorge. 1947. Experiment in the Planning of Public Agricultural Activity. Ph.D. diss., University of Wisconsin–Madison.

Patrico, Jim. 1998. Can PSF Break Murphy's Law. Retrieved May 22 from: http://www.farmjournal.com/FJ/farmjournal/article.dfm/1020.htm.

Pesticide Action Network of North America. 2000. Website. http://www.panna .org/. Retrieved January 26.

Pimental, David and Hugh Lehman, eds. 1993. *The Pesticide Question: Environment, Economics and Ethics*. New York: Chapman and Hall.

Piore, Michael J. and Charles F. Sabel. 1984. *The Second Industrial Divide: Possibilities for Prosperity*. New York: Basic Books.

Pisani, Donald J. 1984. *From the Family Farm to Agribusiness: The Irrigation Crusade in California and the West, 1850–1931*. Berkeley: University of California Press.

Piven, Frances Fox and Richard Cloward. 1975. *The Politics of Turmoil*. New York: Vintage.

Plain, Ron. 1997. Changing Structure of the Hog Industry: U.S. and Abroad. Paper presented at the Professional Swine Producers Symposium, Lansing, Mich., February 6: 4

Polanyi, Karl. 1957. *The Great Transformation*. Boston: Beacon Press.

Poli, Adon. 1942. *Land Ownership and Operating Tenure in Imperial Valley, California*. Berkeley, Calif.: USDA Bureau of Agricultural Economics.

Poli, Adon and R. L. Nielsen. 1942. Nonresident Landlords of Imperial Valley, California. Berkeley, Calif.: USDA Bureau of Agricultural Economics. Draft.

Poppendieck, Janet. 1998. *Sweet Charity? Emergency Food and the End of Entitlement*. New York: Viking.

Portes, Alejandro. 1983. The Informal Sector: Definition, Controversy, and Relation to National Development. *Review* 7 (Summer): 151–74.

Priddle, A. 1993. Newfangled Farming: It's Not a Fad, No-Till Method Saves Time, Topsoil and the Environment. *Windsor Star* April 24: A12.

Princeton Post-Telegraph (Mo.). 1989a. Location of PSF in Mercer County Draws Enthusiastic Reactions from Local, State, National Representatives. April 27: 2.

———. 1989b. Premium Standard Farms Selects Mercer County for Swine Production Units. April 27: 1.

Protess, David L. and Maxwell McCombs. 1991. The Public Agenda. In *Agenda Setting: Readings on Media, Public Opinion, and Policymaking*, ed. D. Protess and M. McCombs, 1–15. Hillsdale, N.J.: Erlbaum.

Pugh, T. 1992. Free Trade and the Farm Crisis. *Union Farmer* November: 8–9.

Putnam, G. 1916. The Land Credit Problem. *Bulletin of the University of Kansas Humanistic Studies* 2: 1–107.

Quammen, David. 1998. Planet of the Weeds: Tallying the Losses of Earth's Animals and Plants. *Harper's* (October): 57–69.

Quinton, Code, and Hill. 1937. Report on Physical and Economic Condition of Imperial Irrigation District. Los Angeles. Document prepared for the Imperial Irrigation District.

Ragin, Charles C. and Howard S. Becker, eds. 1992. *What Is a Case? Exploring the Foundations of Social Inquiry*. Cambridge: Cambridge University Press.

Raper, Arthur. 1936. *Preface to Peasantry: A Tale of Two Black Belt Counties*. Chapel Hill: University of North Carolina Press.

———. 1943. *Tenants of the Almighty*. New York: Macmillan.

Raper, Arthur F. and Martha J. Raper. 1977. *Two Years to Remember and Other Writings*. Oakton, Va.: private publication.

Raynolds, Laura T. and Douglas M. Murray. 1998. Yes, We Have No Bananas: Reregulating Global and Regional Trade. *International Journal of Sociology of Agriculture and Food* 7: 7–43.

Real v. Driscoll Strawberry Associates, Inc. 1975. Complaint. C 75–661–LHB. Cal. filed April 4.

———. 1976. Deposition of Kazumasa Mukai. November 8.

Redfield, Robert. 1930. *Tepoztlan: A Mexican Village*. Chicago: University of Chicago Press.

———. 1955. *The Little Community*. Chicago: University of Chicago Press.

Reed, Michael R. and Jerry R. Skees. 1987. *Understanding Changes in Farmland Prices*. Extension Series Number 68 (July): 2, 17. Lexington: University of Kentucky, Department of Agricultural Economics.

Reimund, Donn and Nora Brooks. 1990. The Structure and Status of the Farm Sector. In *The U.S. Farming Sector Entering the 1990s: Twelfth Annual Report on the Status of Family Farms*, Agriculture Information Bulletin Number 587, 9, 11–13. Washington, D.C.: USDA.

Reisner, Ann. 1996. The Moral Discourse of Pesticides: Newspaper Construction of Agriculture and the Environment. Paper presented at the Rural Sociological Society annual meeting, Des Moines, Iowa.

———. (2001). Social Movement Organizations' Reactions to Genetic Engineering in Agriculture. *American Behavioral Scientist.* 44 (8): 1389–1404.

Reisner, Marc and Sarah F. Bates. 1990. *Overtapped Oasis: Reform or Revolution for Western Water.* Washington, D.C.: Island Press.

Religious Campaign for Forest Conservation. 2000. A Religious Campaign for Forest Conservation, Building an Interfaith Forest Ethic. Retrieved January 25 from: http://www.creationethics.org/.

Revised Statutes of Missouri. Sections 350.010(2), 350.010(5), 350.010, 537.295.

Rhodes, V. James. 1995. The Industrialization of Hog Production. *Review of Agricultural Economics* 17: 107–18.

Rieder, Jonathan. 1985. *Canarsie: Jews and Italians Against Liberalism.* Cambridge, Mass.: Harvard University Press.

Robbins, John. 1987. *Diet for a New America.* Tiburon, Calif.: H. J. Kramer.

Roberts, Joseph K. 1998. *In the Shadow of Empire: Canada for Americans.* New York: Monthly Review Press.

Royal Inquiry Commission. 1938. *Report on Royal Grain Inquiry.* Ottawa: King's Printer.

Rudy, Alan P. 1994a. The Conditions of, and for, Labor: Imperial Valley, California, 1900–1942. Paper presented at Southwest Labor Historians Conference, May, University of California at Santa Cruz.

———. 1994b. On the Dialectics of Capital and Nature. *Capitalism, Nature, Socialism* 5: 95–106.

Rural Credit Legislation. 1916. *Wisconsin Equity News* 8 (March 15): 372.

Ryerson, Stanley. 1973. *Unequal Union.* Toronto: Progress Books.

Salamon, Sonya. 1985. Ethnic Communities and the Structure of Agriculture. *Rural Sociology* 50: 323–40.

———. 1987. Ethnic Determinants of Farm Community Character. In *Farm Work and Fieldwork: American Agriculture in Anthropological Perspective*, ed. Michael Chibnick, 167–88. Ithaca, N.Y.: Cornell University Press.

———. 1992. *Prairie Patrimony: Family, Farming, and Community in the Midwest.* Chapel Hill: University of North Carolina Press.

———. 2002. *Newcomers to Old Towns: Suburbanization of the Heartland.* Chicago: University of Chicago Press.

Salamon, Sonya and Karen Davis-Brown. 1986. Middle-Range Farmers Persisting Through the Agricultural Crisis. *Rural Sociology* 51 (4): 503–12.

Saloutos, Theodore. 1982. *The American Farmer and the New Deal.* Ames: Iowa State University Press.

Sanders, E. 1999. *Roots of Reform: Farmers, Workers, and the American State, 1877–1917.* Chicago: University of Chicago Press.

Sanders, Scott Russell. 1993. Settling Down. In *Staying Put: Making A Home in a Restless World,* 97–121. Boston: Beacon Press.

Sanderson, Steven. 1985. The Emergence of the "World Steer": Industrialization and Foreign Domination in Latin American Cattle Production. In *Food, the State, and International Political Economy*, ed. F. L. Tullis and W. L. Hollist, 123–48. Lincoln: University of Nebraska Press.

Schiffman, Susan. 1998. Livestock Odors: Implications for Human Health and Well-Being. *Journal of Animal Science* 76: 1343–55.

Schwartz, Charles. 1959. *The Search for Stability*. Toronto: McClelland and Stewart.

Science Council of Canada. 1986. *A Growing Concern: Soil Degradation in Canada*. Ottawa.

Sclove, Richard E. 2000. Counter the Cybernetic Wal-Mart Effect. Local Institute. Retrieved from: sclove@loka.org, loca@loca.org. Adapted and reprinted with permission from *The Christian Science Monitor* March 28, 2000, p. 11. http://www.csmonitor.com/durable/2000/03/28/fp11s1-csm.shtml.

Scott, James C. 1998. *Seeing Like a State: How Certain Schemes to Improve the Human Condition Have Failed*. New Haven, Conn.: Yale University Press.

Scott, Roy V. 1970. *The Reluctant Farmer: The Rise of Agricultural Extension to 1914*. Urbana: University of Illinois Press.

Seipel, Michael, Anna Kleiner, and J. Sanford Rikoon. 1998. Public Service Impacts of Large-Scale Hog Production in Northern Missouri Communities. Paper presented at the annual meeting of the Rural Sociological Society, Portland, Ore.

Senate Education and Labor Committee. 1940. *Violations of Free Speech and the Rights of Labor*. Washington, D.C.: Government Printing Office.

Setmire, James G., et al. 1990. *Reconnaissance Investigation of Water Quality, Bottom Sediment, and Biota Associated with Irrigation Drainage in the Salton Sea Area, California, 1986–87*. Sacramento Calif.: U.S. Department of the Interior, Geological Survey.

Shaffer, James Duncan. 1989. Selective Perceptions and the Politics of Agricultural Policy. In *The Political Economy of U.S. Agriculture: Challenges for the 1990s*, ed. Carol S. Kramer. Washington, D.C.: National Center for Food and Agriculture Policy.

Shand, Hope. 1997. *Human Nature: Agricultural Biodiversity and Farm-based Food Security*. Ottawa: RAFI.

Sharp, Paul F. 1997 [1948]. *The Agrarian Revolt in Western Canada*. Regina: Canadian Plains Research Centre.

Sherman, H. S. 1949. Myron T. Herrick: Cleveland Banker, Governor of Ohio, Ambassador to France—and the Society for Savings. Address to the Cleveland Dinner of the Newcomer Society of England.

Shiva, Vandana. 1993. *Monocultures of the Mind*. London: Zed Books.

———. 1997. *Biopiracy: The Plunder of Nature and Knowledge*. Boston: South End Press.

Shiva, Vandana, Afsar H. Jafri, Gitanjali Bedi, and Radha Holla-Bhar. 1997. *The Enclosure and Recovery of the Commons*. New Delhi: Research Foundation for Science, Technology and Ecology.

Shulman, Stuart W. 1999. The Progressive Era Farm Press: A Primer on a Neglected Source of Journalism History. *Journalism History* 25: 25–32.

Sierra Club. 1999. The Sierra Club: Protecting the Environment . . . for Our Families, for Our Future. Retrieved November 20 from: http://www.sierraclub.org/.

Skocpol, Theda. 1979. *States and Social Revolutions: A Comparative Analysis of France, Russia, and China*. Cambridge: Cambridge University Press.

———. 1985. Bringing the State Back In: Strategies of Analysis in Current Research. In *Bringing the State Back In*, ed. P. B. Evans, D. Rueschemeyer, and T. Skocpol, 5–37. New York: Cambridge University Press.

Smiley, Donald V., ed. 1964. *The Rowell/Sirois Report, Book L*. Toronto: McClelland & Stewart.

Smillie, Ben. 1991. *Beyond the Social Gospel*. Saskatoon: United Church Publishing House.

Smith, C. B. and H. K. Atwood. 1913. *The Relation of Agricultural Extension Agencies to Farm Practices*. Bureau of Plant Industry Circular No. 117. March.

Smith, Neil. 1991. *Uneven Development: Nature, Capital, and the Production of Space*. Oxford: Basil Blackwell.

Smith, Page. 1966. *As a City Upon a Hill: The Town in American History*. New York: Alfred A. Knopf.

Smith, Rod. 1998. Divisiveness of Hog Odor Issue Could Have Socio-Tragic Results. *Feedstuffs* 70 (22): 1, 22.

Smithfield Food, Inc. 2000. Website. http://www.Smithfield.com. Retrieved June 6.

Snow, David and Robert Benford. 1988. Ideology, Frame Resonance, and Participant Mobilization. In *From Structure to Action: Comparing Social Movement Research Across Cultures*, ed. Bert Klandermans, Hanspeter Kriesi, and Sidney Tarrow, 197–217. International Social Movement Research. Greenwich, Conn.: JAI Press.

———. 1992. Master Frames and Cycles of Protest. In *Frontiers in Social Movement Theory*, ed. A. Morris and C. McClurg Mueller, 133–55. New Haven, Conn.: Yale University Press.

Snow, David E., Burke Rochford, Steven Worden, and Robert Benford. 1986. Frame Alignment Processes, Mobilization, and Movement Participation. *American Sociological Review* 51: 464–81.

Sparrow, B. H. 1997. Red, White, and Blue—and Yellow: The Emergence and Decay of the Sensational Press as a Political Institution. Paper presented at the annual meeting of the American Political Science Association, Washington, D.C.

Spretnak, Charlene. 1999. *The Resurgence of the Real: Body, Nature and Place in a Hypermodern World*. New York: Routledge.

Standing Committee on Agriculture. 1984. Soil at Risk: Report of the Standing Committee on Agriculture. Canada, House of Commons. Ottawa: Supply and Services Canada.

———. 1992. *The Path to Sustainable Agriculture*. Ottawa: Supply and Services Canada.

Statistics Canada. 1941. *Census of Canada: Agriculture*. Ottawa: Dominion Bureau of Statistics.

———. 1961. *Census of Canada: Agriculture*. Ottawa: Dominion Board of Statistics.

Stevenson, G. W. 1998. Warrior Work and Builder Work: Exploring Responses to Bi-Polar Enterprise Structures in Advanced Agri-food Systems. Presentation to the joint meetings of the Agriculture, Food and Human Values Society and the Association for the Study of Food and Society, June 6, San Francisco.

Stock, Catherine McNicol. 1996. *Rural Radicals: From Bacon's Rebellion to the Oklahoma City Bombing*. New York: Penguin Books.

Stock, Catherine McNicol and Robert Johnston, eds. 2001. *The Countryside in the Age of the Modern State: Political Histories of Rural America*. Ithaca, N.Y.: Cornell University Press.

Stout, Jan. 1996. The Missouri Anti-Corporate Farming Act: Reconciling the Interests of the Independent Farmer and the Corporate Farm. *UMKC Law Review* 64: 835–60.

Strange, Marty. 1988. *Family Farming: A New Economic Vision*. Lincoln: University of Nebraska Press.

Stroud, Jerri. 1998. Hog-Producing Giant Created in Missouri: Continental Grain Plans to Buy Standard Farms: Environmentalist Slams Both. *St. Louis Post-Dispatch* January 9: C1.

Successful Farming. 1997. Pork Powerhouses 1997. *Successful Farming Online*. Retrieved May 7, 1998 from: http://www.agriculture.com/sfonline/sf/1997/october/9710porkchart.htm.

———. 1999. Pork Powerhouses 1999. *Successful Farming Online*. Retrieved June 5, 2000 from: http://www.agriculture.com/sfonline/sf/1999/october/9910porkchart.htm.

———. 2000. Pork Powerhouses 2000. *Successful Farming Online*. Retrieved October 23 from: http://www.agriculture.com/sfonline/sf/2000/october/0011powerhouses.htm.

Summary of a Year's Work. 1916. *National Grange Monthly* 13 (October): 3.

Summers, Mary. 1996. Putting Populism Back In: Rethinking Agricultural Politics and Policy. *Agricultural History* 70 (Spring): 395–414.

———. 2001. From the Heartland to Seattle: The Family Farm Movement of the 1980s and the Legacy of Agrarian State Building. In *The Countryside in the Age of the Modern State: Political Histories of Rural America*, ed. Catherine McNicol Stock and Robert Johnston. Ithaca, N.Y.: Cornell University Press.

Summers, U. T. 1986. Hot Summers in Georgia. *City: Rochester's Alternative Newsweekly*, July 5. Rochester, N.Y.

Sunbury, Ben. 1990. *The Fall of the Farm Credit Empire*. Ames: Iowa State University Press.

Surgeoner, Gordon. and W. Roberts. 1993. Reducing Pesticide Use by 50 Percent in the Province of Ontario. In *The Pesticide Question: Environment, Economics and Ethics*, ed. David Pimenthal and Hugh Lehman, 206–22. New York: Chapman and Hall.

Swanson, Louis E. 1988. *Agriculture and Community Change in the U.S.* Boulder, Colo.: Westview Press.

SWEEP (Soil and Water Environmental Enhancement Program). 1989. *Conservation Tillage Handbook*. Agriculture Canada and Ontario Ministry of Agriculture and Food. Toronto: Queen's Printer.

———. 1992. *Final Reports. Technical Evaluations of Technological Development and Subprograms of SWEEP*. Toronto: Queen's Printer.

———. 1993. *No-Till: The Basics*. Ontario Ministry of Agriculture and Food. Toronto: Queen's Printer.

Swimme, Brian and Thomas Berry. 1992. *The Universe Story*. San Francisco: HarperSanFrancisco.

Taeusch, Carl F. 1940. Schools of Philosophy for Farmers. In *Farmers in a Changing World: The Yearbook of Agriculture, 1940*, USDA, 1111–24. Washington, D.C.: Government Printing Office.

———. 1952. Freedom of Assembly. *Ethics* 63 (1): 33–43.

Task Force on Agriculture, Federal. 1970. *Canadian Agriculture in the Seventies*. Ottawa: Information Canada.

Taylor, Carl C. 1939. The Work of the Division of Farm Population and Rural Life of the Bureau of Agricultural Economics, U.S. Department of Agriculture. *Rural Sociology* 4 (2): 221–28.

Taylor, Paul S. 1928. *Mexican Labor in the United States*. Berkeley: University of California Press.

———. 1973. Water, Land, and Environment, Imperial Valley: Law Caught in the Winds of Politics. *Natural Resources Journal* 13: 1–35.

Teitel, Martin and Kimberly A. Wilson. 1990. *Genetically Engineered Food: Changing the Nature of Nature: What You Need to Know to Protect Yourself, Your Family, and Our Planet.* Rochester, Vt.: Park Street Press.

Thompson, Nancy. 1998. What's Happening? A State-by-State Summary. *Spotlight on Pork III*, 6,7. Walthill, Nebr.: Center for Rural Affairs.

Thu, Kendall M. 1996a. Piggeries and Politics: Rural Development and Iowa's Multibillion Dollar Swine Industry. *Culture and Agriculture* 53: 19–23.

Thu, Kendall M., ed. 1996b. *Understanding the Impacts of Large-Scale Swine Production.* Proceedings of an Interdisciplinary Scientific Workshop. Des Moines, Iowa: North Central Regional Center for Rural Development.

Thu, Kendall M. and E. Paul Durrenberger. 1994. North Carolina's Hog Industry: The Rest of the Story. *Culture and Agriculture* 49: 20–23.

Thu, Kendall M. and E. Paul Durrenberger, eds. 1998. *Pigs, Profits, and Rural Communities.* Albany: State University of New York Press.

Tilly, Charles. 1978. *From Mobilization to Revolution.* New York: Simon and Schuster.

Todd, John. 1984. The Practice of Stewardship. In *Meeting the Expectations of the Land,* ed. W. Jackson, W. Berry, and B. Colman, 152–59. San Francisco: North Point Press.

Tokar, Brian. 1997. *Earth for Sale: Reclaiming Ecology in the Age of Corporate Greenwash.* Boston: South End Press.

Tolley, Howard R. 1939. *Report of the Chief of the Bureau of Agricultural Economics, 1939.* Washington, D.C.: Government Printing Office.

———. 1940. *Report of the Chief of the Bureau of Agricultural Economics, 1940.* Washington, D.C.: Government Printing Office.

———. 1941. *Report of the Chief of the Bureau of Agricultural Economics, 1941.* Washington, D.C.: Government Printing Office.

———. 1943. *The Farmer-Citizen at War.* New York: Macmillan.

Tootell, R. B. 1967. The Federal Land Banks. In *Great American Cooperators,* ed. J. G. Knapp, 555–57. Washington, D.C.: American Institute of Cooperation.

Tout, Otis B. 1931. *The First Thirty Years, 1901–1931: Being an Account of the Principal Events in the History of Imperial Valley, Southern California, USA.* San Diego, Calif.: Arts and Crafts Press.

Tovey, H. 1997. Food Environmentalism and Rural Sociology: On the Organic Movement in Ireland. *Sociologia Ruralis* 37 (1): 21–37.

Turner, Victor. 1974. *Dramas, Fields, and Metaphors.* Ithaca, N.Y.: Cornell University Press.

Turning Point Project. 1999. Website. http://www.turnpoint.org. Retrieved November 20.

UME (University of Massachusetts Extension). 2000. What Is Community Supported Agriculture and How Does It Work? Retrieved from: http://www.umass.edu/umext/csa/about.html.

United States v. Silk. 1947. 331 U.S. 704.

University of Illinois at Urbana-Champaign. 2000a. The Promise of Biotechnology. Available from News and Public Affairs, Information Technology and Communication Services, 69 Mumford Hall, 1301 W. Gregory Drive, Urbana, Ill. 61801.

———. 2000b. What Are GMOs (Definition)? Retrieved April 20 from: http://web.aces.uiuc.edu/faq/faq.pdl?project_id=28&faq_id=583.

————. 2000c. GMOs Q&A. Retrieved from: http://web.aces.uiuc,edu/faq.

University of Wisconsin–Madison. 2000. Biotechnology: Food Production. Retrieved April 4 from: http://www.biotech.wisc.edu/Education/Poster/foodproductn.html.

U.S. Bureau of Labor Statistics. 2002. Consumer Price Indexes. Retrieved from: http://www.bls.gov/cpi.

U.S. Bureau of the Census. Various years. *Statistical Abstract of the United States.*

U.S. Census of Agriculture. 1945. Vol. 1. Statistics by Counties. Part 33: California. Washington, D.C.: Government Printing Office.

————. 1969a. Section 1: Summary Data. Vol. 1. Area Reports. Part 17: Missouri. Washington, D.C.: Government Printing Office.

————. 1969b.Vol. 1. Area Reports. Part 5: California. Washington, D.C.: Government Printing Office.

————. 1987. Vol. 1. Geographic Area Series. Part 25: Missouri: State and County Data. Table 1. Washington, D.C.: Government Printing Office.

————.1997a. Historical Highlights: 1997 and Earlier Census Years. Summary and State Data: Vol. 1. Geographic Area Series. Part 51. Washington, D.C.: Government Printing Office.

————. 1997b. Vol. 1. Geographic Area Series. Part 25: Missouri: State and County Data. Table 1. Washington, D.C.: Government Printing Office.

U.S. Congress. SCANF (U.S. Senate Committee on Agriculture, Nutrition and Forestry). 1993. National Academy of Sciences Report on Pesticides and Children. Hearing before the Committee on Agriculture, Nutrition and, Forestry, United States Senate, 103rd Congress, 1st sess., June 29, 1993. Washington, D.C.: Government Printing Office.

U.S. Congress. Senate. 1912. *Preliminary Report on Land and Agricultural Credit in Europe.* 62nd Congress, 3rd Sess., S. Doc. 967. Washington, D.C.: Goverment Printing Office.

————. 1913a. *Agricultural Cooperation and Rural Credit in Europe.* 63rd Congress, 1st sess. S. Doc. 214. Washington, D.C.: Government Printing Office.

————. 1913b. *Work of the American Commission Respecting Agricultural Finance, Organization, Cooperation, and the Betterment of Rural Conditions.* 63rd Congress, 1st sess. S. Doc. 177. Washington, D.C.: Government Printing Office.

————. 1914. *Agricultural Cooperation and Rural Credit in Europe.* 63d Congress, 1st sess. S. Doc. 261, pt. 1. Washington, D.C.: Government Printing Office.

USDA. 1939a. County Land Use Planning Work Outline Number 1. January. Washington, D.C.: National Archives, Record Group 83, Entry 25, Box 1.

————. 1939b. Memorandum for the Secretary Re: Procedure for Developing a Unified County (or Area) Program. February 2. Washington, D.C.: National Archives, Record Group 83, Entry 208, Box 4.

————. 1939c. Program—Third Iowa School for Extension Workers. March 13–18. Washington, D.C.: National Archives, Record Group 83, Entry 25, Box 9.

————. 1988. *Foreign Agricultural Trade of the United States Calendar Year 1987 Supplement.* June. Washington, D.C.: Economic Research Service.

————. 1990a. *Oil Crops Situation and Outlook Report.* July. Washington, D.C.: Economic Research Service.

————. 1990b. *Wheat Situation and Outlook Report.* February. Washington, D.C.: Economic Research Service.

———. 1991. *Feed Situation and Outlook Yearbook*. February. Washington, D.C.: Economic Research Service.

———. 1995. *Understanding Rural America*. Agricultural Information Bulletin No. 710. February. Washington, D.C.: Economic Research Service.

———. 2000a. Agricultural Biotechnology: Frequently Asked Questions. Retrieved April 3 from: http://www.aphis.usda.gov/biotechnology/faqs.html.

———. 2000b. Agricultural Biotechnology: U.S. Department of Agriculture. Retrieved May 1 from: http://www.aphis.usda.gov/biotechnology/faqs.html.

USDA FAS (Food and Agricultural Statistics). 1998. Swine and Pork. Retrieved January 15, 1999, from: http://www.fas.usda.gov:80/dip/circular/1998/98-10lp/pork.htm.

USDA/U.S. EPA (U.S. Environmental Protection Agency). 1999. Unified National Strategy for Animal Feeding Operations. March 9. Retrieved May 20 from: http://www.gov.epa.gov/OWM/finafost.htm.

U.S. Department of Commerce. 1982–83. *Statistical Abstract of the United States*.

———. 1990. *Statistical Abstract of the United States*.

U.S. Department of Interior, and California Resources Agency. 1974. *Salton Sea Project, California: Federal-State Feasibility Report*. Washington, D.C.: Government Printing Office.

U.S. FDA (Food and Drug Administration). 2000a. Biotechnology of Food. Revised May 18, 1994. Retrieved April 3 from: http://vm.cfsam.fda.gov/~lrd/biotechn.html.

———. 2000b. Are Bioengineered Foods Safe? Retrieved April 3 from: http://vm.cfsan.fda.gov/~dms/fdbioeng.html.

U.S. Public Interest Research Group. 1999. State PIRGS Public Interest Research Groups. Retrieved December 13 from: http://www.pirg.org/.

Van den Bosch, Robert. 1989. *The Pesticide Conspiracy*. Berkeley: University of California Press.

van Dijk, T. A. 1988a. *News as Discourse*. Hillsdale, N.J.: Erlbaum.

———. 1988b. *News Analysis: Case Studies of International and National News in the Press*. Hillsdale, N.J.: Erlbaum.

———. 1991. *Racism and the Press*. London: Routledge.

———. 2001. Critical Discourse Analysis. In *Handbook of Discourse Analysis*, ed. Deborah Schiffrin, Deborah Tannen, and Heidi Hamilton. Oxford: Blackwell Publishers.

Van En, Robyn. 1998. Community Supported Agriculture (CSA) in Perspective. In *For All Generations: Making World Agriculture More Sustainable*, ed. J. Patrick Madden and Scott G. Chaplowe, 115–21. Glendale, Calif.: OM Publishing.

Vaudagna, Maurizio. 1989. Recent Perspectives on the Late Thirties in the United States. *Storia Nordamericana* 6 (1/2): 161–90.

Vaupel, Suzanne and Philip Martin. 1986. *Activity and Regulation of Farm Labor Contractors*. Giannini Information Series, No. 86–3. Berkeley: University of California, Division of Agriculture and Natural Resources.

Veltmeyer, Henry. 1986. *Canadian Class Structure*. Toronto: Garamond Press.

Villarejo, Don and Dave Runsten. 1993. *California's Agricultural Dilemma: Higher Productivity and Lower Wages*. Davis: California Institute for Rural Studies.

Wainwright, Hillary. 1993. A New Kind of Knowledge for a New Kind of State. In *A Different Kind of State? Popular Power and Democratic Administration*, ed. Gregory Albo, David Langille, and Leo Panitch, 112–21. Toronto: Oxford University Press.

Wallace, Henry A. 1937. Thomas Jefferson: Farmer, Educator, and Democrat. *Proceedings*, Fifty-First Annual Convention, Association of Land Grant Colleges and Universities, ed. William L. Slate, 338–46. Washington, D.C.

———. 1940 [1938]. Memorandum Describing Departmental Organization. Reprinted in *Public Administration and the United States Department of Agriculture*, by John M. Gaus and Leon O. Wolcott, 466–75. Chicago: Public Administration Service.

Walsh, Tom. 1996. Waste Spills Shift Political Winds. *Columbia Daily Tribune* June 4: A10.

———. 1997. Group Serves Notice of Corporate Hog Farm Suit. *Columbia Daily Tribune* April 4: A1.

Walzer, Michael. 1990. The Communitarian Critique of Liberalism. *Political Theory* 18 (1): 6–23.

Wanta, W. and Y. W. Hu. 1994. The Effects of Credibility, Reliance, and Exposure on Media Agenda-Setting: A Path Analysis Model. *Journalism Quarterly* 17: 90–98.

Ward, N. 1993. The Agricultural Treadmill and the Rural Environment in the Post-Productivist Era. *Sociologia Ruralis* 33 (3/4): 348–64.

Wells, Miriam J. 1984. What Is a Worker? The Role of Sharecroppers in Contemporary Class Structure. *Politics and Society* 13(3): 295–320.

———. 1996. *Strawberry Fields: Politics, Class, and Work in California Agriculture*. Ithaca, N.Y.: Cornell University Press.

Wells, Miriam J. and Martha West. 1989. *Regulation of the Farm Labor Market: An Assessment of Farm Workers' Protections under the California Agricultural Labor Relations Act*. Working Group on Farm Labor and Rural Poverty. Working Paper no. 5. Davis: California Institute for Rural Studies.

Welsh, Rick. 1996. *The Industrial Reorganization of U.S. Agriculture*. Policy Studies Report No. 6. Washington, D.C.: Henry A. Wallace Institute for Alternative Agriculture.

Weymouth, G. 1916. On the New Farm Loan Bill. *Farm Life* 35 (February): 1.

Whateley, Booker T. and the editors of *The New Farm*. 1987. *How to Make $100,000 Farming 25 Acres* (alternate title: *Booker T. Whatley's Handbook on How to Make $100,000 Farming on 25 Acres*). Emmaus, Pa.: Regenerative Agriculture Association (Rodale Institute).

Whitten, Jamie L. 1966. *That We May Live*. Princeton, N.J.: D. Van Nostrand.

Wiens, Dan. 1994. Peopling the Farm. In *Our Field: A Manual for Community Supported Agriculture*, ed. Tamsin Rowley and Chris Berman. Wrozeter, Ont.: CSA Resource Centre.

Williams, Ted. 1998. Assembly Line Swine. *Audubon* March–April: 28–33.

Williams, William A. 1969. *The Roots of the Modern American Empire: A Study of the Growth and Shaping of Social Consciousness in a Marketplace Society*. New York: Random House.

Wilson, Barry, 1981. *Beyond the Harvest: Canadian Grain at the Crossroads*. Saskatoon: Prairie Books.

Wilson, C. F. 1978. *A Century of Canadian Grain*. Saskatoon: Prairie Books

———. 1979. *Canadian Grain Marketing*. Winnipeg: Canadian International Grains Institute.

Wilson, Edward O. 1992. *The Diversity of Life*. Cambridge, Mass.: Harvard University Press.

Wilson, Milburn Lincoln. 1936a. Education for Democracy. *Rural America* 14 (September): 3–6.

⸻. 1936b. The Place of the Department of Agriculture in the Evolution of Agricultural Policy. Speech, December 11. U.S. Department of Agriculture History Collection, Special Collections Section, National Agricultural Library, Beltsville, Md.

⸻. 1939a. On Using Democracy. *Land Policy Review* 2 (January–February): 1–4.

⸻. 1941. A Theory of Agricultural Democracy. Circular No. 355, USDA Extension Service.

⸻. 1973. The Reminiscences of Milburn Lincoln Wilson. Interviews conducted 1951–56. Columbia Oral History Collection, Columbia University, New York.

Wilson, Milburn Lincoln, ed. 1939b. *Democracy Has Roots*. New York: Carrick and Evans.

Wilson, O. 1912. Worthy Master's Annual Address. In *Proceedings of the National Grange of the Patrons of Husbandry: Forty-sixth Annual Session, Spokane, Washington*, ed. C. M. Freeman, 10–16. Springfield, Ohio: Springfield Publishing.

⸻. 1916. Worthy Master's Annual Address. In *Proceedings of the National Grange of the Patrons of Husbandry: Fiftieth Annual Session, Wilmington, Delaware*, ed. C. M. Freeman, 9–16. Concord, N.H.: Rumford Press.

Wilson, Woodrow. 1913. The New Freedom: Part I. *The World's Work* 25 (January): 253–64.

⸻. 1978. Inaugural Address. In *The Papers of Woodrow Wilson*, ed. A. S. Link, 27: 3–7. Princeton, N.J.: Princeton University Press.

Wing, Steve and Sussane Wolf. 1999. Intensive Livestock Operations, Health and Quality of Life Among Eastern North Carolina Residents. Report prepared for the North Carolina Department of Health and Human Services, Division of Public Health. Available at http://www.dhhs.state.nc.us/docs/ilo.pdf.

Winson, A. 1992. *The Intimate Commodity*. Toronto: Garamond Press.

Wodak, R. 1996. *Disorders of Discourse*. London: Longman.

⸻. 1997. *Gender and Discourse*. London: Sage.

Wodak, R., ed. 1989. *Language, Power, and Ideology: Studies in Political Discourse*. Amsterdam: Bejamins.

Wolf, Jerome. 1964. The Imperial Valley as an Index of Agricultural Labor Relations in California. Ph.D. diss., University of Southern California.

Wolfe, James F. 1994. Sponsor: Corporate-Farming Law's Repeal on Hold. *St. Joseph (Mo.) News-Press* March 26: 1, 5.

Wollenberg, Charles. 1973. Huelga, 1928 Style: The Imperial Valley Cantaloupe Workers Strike. In *Chicano: The Evolution of a People*, ed. R. Rosaldo, R. Rosaldo, R. A. Calvert, and G. L. Seligmann, 184–91. Minneapolis, Minn.: Winston.

Wood, Louis A. 1975 [1924]. *A History of Farmers' Movements in Canada*. Toronto: University of Toronto Press.

Woodruff, George. 1912. An American "Credit Foncier." *Moody's Magazine* 14: 127–29.

Worster, Donald. 1985. *Rivers of Empire: Water, Aridity, and the Growth of the American West*. New York: Pantheon Books.

Wright, Eric O. 1976. Class Boundaries in Advanced Capitalist Societies. *New Left Review* 98 (July-August): 3–41.

Wright, Harold Bell. 1911. *The Winning of Barbara Worth*. Chicago: Book Supply Company.
Wright, Susan. 1994. *Molecular Politics: Developing American and British Regulatory Policy for Genetic Engineering, 1972–1982*. Chicago: University of Chicago Press.
Zering, Kelly. 1998. The Changing U.S. Pork Industry: An Overview. In *The Industrialization of Agriculture: Vertical Coordination in the U.S. Food System*, ed. Jeffrey S. Royer and Richard T. Rogers, 205–16. Brookfield, Vt.: Ashgate Publishing.

Contributors

JANE ADAMS is Associate Professor of Anthropology and of History at Southern Illinois University at Carbondale. She is the author of *The Transformation of Rural Life: Southern Illinois 1890–1990* (1994), *"All Anybody Ever Wanted of Me Was to Work": The Memoirs of Edith Bradley Rendleman* (1996), and numerous articles on U.S. rural history. Her current research explores the civil rights era in Mississippi through interviews with people about the ways their racial, ethnic, religious, and gender locations shaped their experiences. She is also part of a project studying watershed planning in the Cache River Watershed in southern Illinois.

BARRY J. BARNETT is Associate Professor of Agricultural and Applied Economics at the University of Georgia. He has written extensively on U.S. agricultural policy with a particular emphasis on the Federal Crop Insurance Program. Current research interests include potential agricultural applications of emerging markets for weather derivatives. This chapter was written while Barnett was on the faculty of Mississippi State University.

DOUGLAS H. CONSTANCE is Assistant Professor of Sociology at Sam Houston State University. His primary research focus is the socio-economic impacts of the globalization of the agri-food system. He has published several book chapters, articles, and a book on this topic. He is President of the Southern Rural Sociological Association and serves on the Executive Committee of the Research Committee on Agriculture and Food of the International Sociological Association.

LAURA B. DELIND is Senior Academic Specialist in the Department of Anthropology at Michigan State University. As a scholar-activist, she writes about the contemporary agri-food system, paying particular attention to the long-term costs and social and political inequities at the local level. She is an advocate of more place-based and democratized systems of food production, distribution, and consumption. In 1996 she established Growing In Place Community Farm, a working member CSA project in Mason, Michigan.

KATHRYN MARIE DUDLEY is Professor of American Studies and Anthropology at Yale University. She is the author of *The End of the Line: Lost Jobs, New Lives in Postindustrial America* (1994) and *Debt and Dispossession: Farm Loss in America's Heartland* (2000). Her current research interests include the experience of land loss among African American farmers in the rural South and the role of the courts in adjudicating issues of racial discrimination and economic justice.

HARRIET FRIEDMANN is Professor of Sociology and a member of the faculty of the Centre for International Studies at the University of Toronto in Canada. She is the author of articles on international food regimes, farm structure (including class, gender, and age relations), agricultural regions, the political ecology of food and agriculture, and food cultures. She is former Chair of the Political Economy of the World-System Section of the American Sociological Association and former Community Co-Chair of the Toronto Food Policy Council. Her current project is to synthesize research on farm structures with international food regimes, and to link environmental history with political economy through the history of the hamburger.

JESS GILBERT is Professor of Rural Sociology at the University of Wisconsin, Madison, and also Co-Director of the Center for Minority Land and Community Security (based at Tuskegee University). He has published many articles on U.S. land tenure, African American farmers, family vs. industrial farming, and agricultural policy, and is currently finishing a book on democratic planning and agrarian intellectuals in the New Deal Department of Agriculture.

ALAN HALL is Associate Professor of Sociology at the University of Windsor. He has published a number of articles on sustainable agriculture and organic farming in Canada.

ANNA M. KLEINER is a Research Assistant and Doctoral Candidate in the Department of Rural Sociology at the University of Missouri–Columbia. Her dissertation research focuses on the economic, social, and environmental impacts of large-scale swine operations on rural communities in northern Missouri. She has extensive experience as a community and economic development practitioner in urban and rural communities within Missouri.

K. MURRAY KNUTTILA teaches in the Department of Sociology and Social Studies at the University of Regina. His books include *That Man Partridge: E. A. Partridge, His Thoughts and Times* (1994), *Introducing Sociology: A Critical Perspective* (1996), and *State Theories: Classical, Feminist and Global Perspectives* (3rd ed., with Wendee Kubik, 2001). He has written numerous papers and book chapters addressing the role of the state in Western Canadian society. He is currently researching the impact of globalization on politics in rural Canada

ANN REISNER is Associate Professor at the University of Illinois at Urbana-Champaign in the Department of Human and Community Development. She has published widely in sociology and communication journals including *American Behavioral Scientist, American Sociological Review, Journalism Quarterly*, and *Rural Sociology*.

J. SANFORD RIKOON is Professor of Rural Sociology at the University of Missouri–Columbia and Director of the Community Food Systems and Sustainable Agriculture Program. He received his M.A. and Ph.D. from Indiana University. He has published five books and more than 60 articles on environmental and rural issues in the Midwest and Eastern Europe. His latest book, coauthored with Theresa Goedeke, is *Challenging Environmentalism: The Failed Effort to Establish the Ozark Highlands Man and the Biosphere Reserve* (2000).

ALAN P. RUDY is an Assistant Professor of Sociology at Michigan State University. His work focuses on the political economy of agriculture, environmental sociology, and science and technology studies. These days he is particularly concerned with interdisciplinary regional studies and something he calls "entomological sociology"—the production of nature, in the form of insect pests, as mediated by agricultural cultivation practices. The present chapter derives from his dissertation, completed in 1995 at the University of California, Santa Cruz.

STUART W. SHULMAN is Assistant Professor of Environmental Science and Policy at Drake University. He is currently the principal investigator on two NSF-funded projects, one looking at the impact of electronic rulemaking on federal agencies, the other using service learning to develop information technology literacy and digital citizenship in the Des Moines area. His dissertation is titled "The Origin of the Federal Farm Loan Act: Agenda-Setting in the Progressive Era Print Press."

MARY SUMMERS is a Senior Fellow in the Fox Leadership Program and the Center for Research on Religion and Urban Civil Society and a lecturer in political science at the University of Pennsylvania. She has worked as a physician assistant and speechwriter and published articles on African American and agricultural politics. Her research focuses on food politics, farmers' movements, and the development of the United States Department of Agriculture.

MIRIAM J. WELLS is Professor of Anthropology in the Department of Human and Community Development at the University of California, Davis. She is author of *Strawberry Fields: Politics, Class, and Work in California Agriculture* (1996), which received the Theodore Saloutos Award from the Agricultural History Society as the best book published in that field in 1996, as well as many articles on labor and class relations, economic development and global restructuring, and the role of the state. Her current research focuses on the tensions between U.S. immigration policy and labor rights.

Index

Acknowledgments

Inspiration for this volume came from a panel, "The Ideological Matrix of Exploitation Within the American Agricultural System," organized by Laura DeLind in 1991 for the American Anthropological Association. Through its long gestation I have acquired more debts than can easily be acknowledged here. My primary thanks go to the contributors to this volume, who have been terrific collaborators. The anonymous reviewers provided careful and helpful readings. The University of Pennsylvania Press was unfailingly good to work with. In particular, Peter Agree understood the scope and significance of the project; his support and encouragement made this book possible. Erica Ginsburg shepherded the book through production and was more than generous in responding to my queries. My husband, D. Gorton, has stimulated my intellect and my imagination in the many hours spent in the Midwestern and Southern countryside, searching for photographs and for understanding. A true partner, he lifted many of the chores of our daily life from my shoulders so that I could focus fully on this project.